T. Hagger
with love
mum

BETTER COOKERY

BETTER COOKERY

by

AILEEN KING

Principal, Edinburgh College of Domestic Science

MILLS & BOON LIMITED
17–19 FOLEY STREET
LONDON W1A 1DR

First published 1957
Second edition 1958
Third edition 1960
Reprinted 1961
Reprinted 1962
Fourth (Revised) edition 1962
Reprinted 1964
Reprinted 1965
Reprinted (with colour plates) 1968
Reprinted 1971
Reprinted 1972

School Edition ISBN. 0 263. 51250. 9
Net Edition   ISBN. 0 263. 51256. 8

Printed in Great Britain by Richard Clay (The Chaucer Press), Ltd.,
Bungay, Suffolk

ACKNOWLEDGEMENTS

WHILE the responsibility for the form of the book rests with me, it was compiled in collaboration with Miss D. Pearson, Head of the Teacher Training Department, and Miss A. B. Cutting, Head of the Technical Department of Radbrook College. It is the fruit of the experience of three people who have spent many years in the practice of the craft itself and in the training of students in the understanding and attainment of good cooking.

The recipes given are those which are used in the College and have proved satisfactory over a number of years. The instructions for making and cooking the dishes are confirmed by the three members of Staff.

I am indebted to my two colleagues for the wealth of information which each in her own field has contributed and for the support they have given me in the enterprise.

I am grateful to Miss B. C. Heald for her valuable contribution of the meat diagrams and to Miss G. Conway for her unstinted help in the correcting of the proofs.

A. K.

Thanks are due to the following for kindly allowing the reproduction of colour transparencies:

	FACING PAGE
Birds Eye Foods Ltd.	32
Brown & Polson Ltd.	65
The Food Information Centre and the Nestlé Company Ltd.	128
The Food Information Centre	161
The British Egg Information Service	192
Moorhouse Products (Schweppes Ltd.)	225
McDougall's Cookery Service	320
The Food Information Centre	353

PUBLISHERS' NOTE TO REVISED EDITION

BETTER COOKERY was first published in 1957, and it will be no surprise to anyone who knows the amount of work involved in compiling and printing such a book to learn that the writing of it began in 1954 —when, though it seems almost incredible now, food rationing was still with us.

Since those days familiar foods have become more easily available, lesser-known ones such as aubergines, scampi and pimentoes have become familiar, and the enormous boom in foreign travel and the use of pre-prepared foods have perceptibly influenced the public's attitude to food and cookery. Successive editions of the book have incorporated alterations and additions to take account of these changes; and now that the main impetus of the revolution is over, and food habits show signs of settling down in a new pattern, the moment is opportune to extend and consolidate these amendments. The present edition, extensively revised and re-set, reflects a new attitude to cookery in a way that should remain valid for some time to come.

The publishers would like to express their thanks to Mrs Elizabeth Foot for valuable help in preparing the book for this edition.

CONTENTS

		PAGE
ACKNOWLEDGEMENTS	. . . . . .	v
PUBLISHERS' NOTE TO REVISED EDITION	. .	vi
INTRODUCTION	. . . . . .	ix
OVEN TEMPERATURE CHART	. . . .	x

CHAPTER

I	Choice and Care of Kitchen Utensils	. . .	11
II	Handy Weights and Measures	. . .	17
III	Shopping and Meal Planning	. . .	19
IV	Glossary of Cooking Terms	. . .	26
V	Hors d'œuvres and Savouries	. . .	33
VI	Stocks and Soups	. . . . .	44
VII	Sauces	. . . . . .	58
VIII	Fish	. . . . . .	77
IX	Meat	. . . . .	100
X	Poultry and Game	. . . .	145
XI	Vegetables and Salads	. . . .	167
XII	Frying	. . . . .	190
XIII	Steaming	. . . .	197
XIV	Egg Cookery	. . . .	199
XV	Batters	. . . . .	212
XVI	Réchauffés	. . . . .	216
XVII	Supper, Lunch or High Tea Dishes (including Cheese and Vegetarian Dishes)	226
XVIII	Puddings and Sweets	. . . .	245
XIX	Cold Sweets and Ices	. . . .	283
XX	Baking	. . . . .	319

CHAPTER   PAGE

XXI   **Cakes and Biscuits** 341

XXII   **Pastry-making** 385

XXIII   **Invalid Cookery** 404

XXIV   **Forcemeats, Stuffings and Miscellaneous Recipes** . 412

XXV   **Preservation** 424

XXVI   **Seasonings and Flavourings** 461

XXVII   **Quick-Method Foods** 467

XXVIII   **Pressure Cooking** 472

XXIX   **The Service of Wine** 478

INDEX 485

ILLUSTRATIONS

CUTS OF BEEF 101

CUTS OF MUTTON AND LAMB 102

CUTS OF PORK 103

° F—° C CONVERSION THERMOMETER . . . 483

INTRODUCTION

THE aim of this book is to present a comprehensive treatment of cookery. An attempt is made to describe and explain simply the scientific principles which underlie the various processes involved in cooking, and the wise choice of foods to give a balanced diet.

It is an important part of the aim to treat the subject rationally, and methods of cooking and manipulation are described and explained in great detail. Basic recipes are given first, followed by variations in tabulated form. The quantities given are for 4 persons unless otherwise stated. Possible reasons for failures are suggested so that the repetition of mistakes can be prevented.

The book is planned primarily for the intelligent housewife, but it is hoped that it will prove useful to students in Housecraft and Technical Colleges.

It is English Cookery that is under consideration, but ideas and recipes derived from other countries are introduced so that the housewife has a wide choice of nutritive dishes from which to produce meals with an aesthetic value.

OVEN TEMPERATURE CHART
In Degrees Fahrenheit

Our temperatures in the script	Number or letter on the thermostat	CANNON (number)	FLAVEL		GENERAL GAS	MAIN		PARKINSON	RADIATION (Regulo)
			Letters	Numbers		Letters	Numbers		
240	¼	240	—	—	240	—	240	—	240
250	½	265	—	—	265	—	265	—	265
275	1 or A	290	240	255	290	245	290	250	290
300	2 or B	315	255	270	315	270	315	280	315
325	3 or C	335	285	295	335	305	335	310	335
350	4 or D	360	315	320	365	335	365	340	360
375	5 or E	380	345	345	380	375	380	370	380
400	6 or F	400	370	370	405	410	400	400	400
425	7 or G	425	400	395	425	440	425	430	425
450	8 or H	445	430	420	445	475	445	460	445
475	9 or I	470	460	445	470	—	470	490	470
500	10 or J	490	480	470	490	—	490	—	490

If the temperatures given in the text are not the same as for your particular cooker adjust the cooker thermostat control to give the same temperature as indicated for each recipe or process; e.g. suppose a temperature is given in the text as 350° and you have a Cannon cooker on which No. 3 is 335° and No. 4 360°, turn the indicator so that it is between 3 and 4, and slightly nearer to 4.

A table to assist with conversion from ° F to ° C, if required, is given on page 483.

CHAPTER I

THE CHOICE AND CARE OF KITCHEN UTENSILS

IN cooking, as in all skilled operations, good tools are essential. It is important that equipment is chosen which is suited to the job it has to do, and good kitchen tools will last many years if used and cared for properly.

The following lists A–G give the minimum of tools required in a small household. List H comprises tools which are desirable either for additional convenience or for making more elaborate dishes.

A. Pans	Size	No.
Saucepans	1½ pt capacity	1
with lids	2½–3 pt „	1
	6–8 pt „	1
Double saucepan	2–3 pts „	1
Frying pan	7″–9″ diameter	1
Frying basket	to fit into the large pan	1
Kettle	3 pt capacity	1
Steamer to fit over the large pan or with ridged base to fit several sizes of pan		1
Milk saucepan with lip	1⅓ pt capacity	1

Pans should be heavy with a wide base; they should be made either of aluminium with a ground base, enamel of good quality to prevent chipping, stainless steel, or copper lined with tin.

Light weight pans buckle easily and, once dented, are difficult to clean. Also, if dented, they do not lie flush with the solid hotplates found on electric and solid fuel cookers, and a pan which does not lie absolutely flat on one of these cookers does not absorb heat quickly because of the spaces between the pan and the stove, and therefore heat and time are lost.

Thin pans cause food to burn or stick.

Handles must be insulated and firmly riveted to the pan.

Lids should be well fitting and so made that they can be removed without burning the hands.

Large saucepans should have a handle at both sides so that both hands can be used for lifting if necessary. Kettles for a solid fuel cooker should have a wide, thick, heavy base to ensure contact over as wide an area as possible. This speeds up boiling.

For a gas cooker a lighter weight kettle can be used, but faster boiling is obtained if the base is finned.

A special kettle with an immersion heater inside is the most economical if electricity is used.

B. Tins

		No.
Baking tin to fit the oven, allowing 2″ all round for circulation of heat		1
Baking trays, allowing 2″ all round for circulation of heat		2
Bun tins 9–12 in a set according to size of oven		1
Cake tins	5–6″	1
	7–8″	1
Plate ”	7″	1
Sandwich tins	7″	2
Yorkshire pudding tin	8″ × 12″	1

Like pans, tins should be of heavy quality to prevent the sticking and scorching of the food. The edges should be rolled so that there is no danger of cutting the hand during use.

Heavy tins keep their shape well.

Tins may be made of non-rusting tin plate or of aluminium.

C. Knives

		No.
Bread knife or saw		1
Knife sharpener		1
Pointed chopping knife	7–8″ blade	1
Palette knife	8″	1
Vegetable knife	3–4″ blade	1
Vegetable peeler		1
Round-bladed mixing knife		1

When choosing knives, buy those made by a reputable firm. The shaft should be firmly riveted into the handle and the whole knife be of a comfortable balance for use. Stainless steel knives, though convenient because they do not need cleaning, cannot be kept as sharp as the tempered steel blades.

Knives should be sharpened regularly, preferably before each time of using. A steel, a carborundum or a wheel sharpener may be used as liked, but *not* the kitchen step.   A wheel sharpener wears the knife more rapidly than does a steel.   It is worth while learning to use a steel as this produces the best results if used skilfully.

D. Spoons

		No.
Measuring spoons }	British standard	1 set
„ cups ∫		1 set
	These can be used to replace scales and weights	
Metal spoons	Table	1
	Dessert	1
	Tea	1
Wooden spoon	8″	1
„ „	10″	1

E. Additional Equipment

Cake cooling tray	18″ × 12″	1
Can opener		1
Chopping board	1″ thick	1
Colander		1
Corkscrew		1
Cutters	Plain and fancy for pastry and biscuits	1 each
Egg whisk	(Flail type)	1
Fish slice		1
Flour dredger		1
Fork		1
Grater	General purpose, 3 sizes included	1
Lemon squeezer		1
Measure	Graduated to hold 1 pint	1
Metal skewers		1 set
Pastry board	This is not necessary if the working table has an enamel or plastic top	1
Refuse bin		1
Rolling pin		1
Scales and weights		1 set
Scissors		1 pair
Sink tidy		1
Storage tins and jars		as required
Clean tins with well-fitting lids, or jars with snap tops, are suitable		
Strainer, round, wire, 6″ diameter. This can be used as a sieve		1

F. Cloths

Dish cloths or swabs	Enough to allow for frequent washing
Floor cloths	
Oven cloths	
Tea towels	

G. China, Earthenware or Glass Ovenware

Casserole with lid	1$\frac{7}{8}$ pts	1
	3 pts	1
Jelly moulds	1$\frac{1}{2}$ pts	1
	This may be tinned ware, china or aluminium	
Jugs	1$\frac{1}{2}$ pts	1
	3 pts	1
Mixing bowls	10″–12″ diameter	1
Pie dishes	1–1$\frac{1}{2}$ pts	1
	2–2$\frac{1}{2}$ pts	1
Pudding basins	$\frac{1}{2}$ pt (4″)	1
	1$\frac{1}{2}$ pts (6″)	1
	3 pts (7$\frac{1}{2}$″)	1

H. Extra Equipment

Apple corer	
Bread tins	1 lb and 2 lb size
Brushes	Greasing, pastry, vegetable
Butter patters	
Cake tins	Various shapes and sizes e.g. square, oblong, oval
Coffee percolator	
Column cutter (for preparing garnish)	
Cook's aid (rubber) for scraping bowls etc.	
Covered roaster	
Dariole moulds (tinned ware) individual	
Deep fat frying pan and basket	
Egg whisk	Round or rotary
Filleting knife	
Fish kettle	
Flan ring	Plain or fluted
Forcing bags	
Jelly border mould	1$\frac{1}{2}$ pts (tinned ware)
Mincing machine	
Mouligrater	
Omelet pan	

Parsmint cutter
Pastry cutters   Various sizes and shapes
Patty tins for tartlets
Potato masher
Pressure cooker
Serrated knife
Sieve   Wire, hair or nylon or a Moulimill
Soufflé dish
Strainers   Coffee and pointed gravy
Thermometers   Oven and sugar
Vegetable scoop   For garnish preparations
Wooden spatula

The Care of Kitchen Utensils

Equipment required   Dish cloths
                       Scrubbing brush
                       Pan scrub or steel wool

1. All cooking utensils should be washed, rinsed and dried as soon as possible after use. Dirty utensils wear out quickly and could spoil the flavour of the food. If soaked as soon as they are finished with, they are easier to clean than if the food is allowed to dry or harden. Pans or dishes used for milk, eggs or flour mixtures should be soaked in cold water to prevent sticking. This makes them easier to clean; hot water would make these foods stick.
2. If a pan has become very hot, allow it to cool slightly before putting cold water into it. The sudden change of temperature might make the pan buckle.
3. If food has been burnt in a pan, tin or pie dish, allow the utensil to soak well before attempting the cleaning of it. If necessary use a saucepan brush or steel wool to clean. Choose the type of brush and grade of wire wool which will not scratch the pan or dish.
4. If the utensil is made of enamel, soak or boil in salt water until the burnt food can be removed easily. Scourers and wire wool tend to scratch the enamel and this makes burning easier and also produces a tendency to chip. Chipped enamel dishes and pans are dangerous in use, because small bits are likely to break off and contaminate the food.
5. Aluminium pans and utensils should not be washed with soda or with washing powders which contain a strong alkali, as in course of time the surface becomes uneven because parts of the metal have been dissolved.

6. Aluminium and tin utensils should be thoroughly dried before being put away. Small patty tins and dariole moulds should be dried off in a warm place to prevent rusting.

7. Cake, bun and bread tins should not be washed after use but rubbed with a clean cloth. Any burnt bits may be rubbed off with clean dry steel wool. Tins which are washed after use allow food to burn more readily than those which are not washed.

8. Omelet pans must not be washed. To prevent food sticking to the pan, put in enough salt to cover the bottom thinly, heat it until brown, and then rub vigorously with paper. Throw away the salt and wipe with a dry cloth. Frying pans can be treated similarly if they are to be used for pancakes.

Care of New Cooking Utensils

1. Aluminium or enamel pans should be filled with cold water, brought to the boil and the water boiled for about 5 minutes. Empty out and wash in soapy water.

2. Earthenware and glass ovenware should be put in a pan of cold water, the water brought to the boil and allowed to cool with the dish in it.

3. All new tins should be baked in a moderately hot oven until they are dark in colour. Food does not brown easily in new shiny tins and it often sticks to them.

CHAPTER II

HANDY WEIGHTS AND MEASURES

IF you are to produce a dish time after time, and know that every time you will have the same successful result, you must follow a clear, accurate recipe which will include instructions for cooking as well as mixing; and the ingredients must be accurately measured. A good recipe will indicate:

1. Exact quantities—which can be given as weights or as measures such as cups or spoons. If given as measures, the recipe should state whether the measure is filled level or heaped and also the size of the measure, e.g. breakfast or tea cup, tea or tablespoon. It is not much help to a young cook if she is told to add " milk to mix ". Very often an exact volume of liquid cannot be given, but an approximate amount should be stated, together with a clear description of the consistency to be aimed at.
2. The number of portions the dish will serve, and the size of dish or tin which will be suitable for cooking.
3. Accurate cooking times and temperatures, giving, as often as possible, the best position in the oven for cooking.

Having made certain that the recipe gives all the information needed, the cook must play her part by following the instructions carefully. To weigh or measure the ingredients correctly is the first stage.

Weighing is, on the whole, more accurate than measuring, provided a reliable pair of scales and set of weights are used. Those bearing the Government stamp and weighing to ¼ oz. will serve well, but are expensive. When weighing, the food on the one pan should just balance the weights on the other; the two sides should swing level. " Good measure " is to be avoided in cooking.

Measuring is reasonably accurate if the measures are used level, that is, the top of the measure is levelled off with a knife. If the British Standards Institution measuring cups and spoons are used, consistent results can be assured. It should be remembered that ordinary household cups and spoons vary considerably in size, and many failures can be traced to this source.

All the ingredients must be either weighed or measured.

British Standards Institution Measures

Food		No. of level tablespoons giving 1 oz	Weight in ounces of 1 level standard ½ pt cup
Breadcrumbs, fresh		5	3
„ dried		3	6
Cheese, grated, fairly dry		4	4
Cornflour or custard powder		3	6
Currants		3	4
Fats	butter		
	cooking fat	2	8
	lard		
	margarine		
Flour	unsieved	3	6
Oatmeal	medium	2	6
Oats	rolled	4	4
Salt	household	2	7
Semolina		2½	7
Sugar	brown, soft or demerara	2	8
	castor	2	8
	granulated	2	8
	icing	2½	6
Sultanas or seedless raisins		2	7
Syrup or treacle		1	14

Some Comparative Measures

1 Imperial pint = 20 fluid ozs = 40 tbs

1 American pint = 16 fluid ozs = 32 tbs

1 American cup = 8 fluid ozs
                = 4½ ozs flour
                = 7 ozs sugar
                = 7 ozs butter or margarine

1 American tbs flour = ½ oz
          sugar = ¾ oz
          butter = ¾ oz

Metric measures (approximate only)
      30 grammes = 1 oz
      50 grammes = 1¾ oz
      1 Kilogramme = 2 lbs 3 ozs
      1 litre = 1¾ pts
      1 decilitre = 3½ fluid ozs

The measures given in this book are level and the recipes are for four people (as explained in the Introduction) unless otherwise stated.

CHAPTER III

SHOPPING AND MEAL PLANNING

Shopping

1. Make a list of the foods you will need to buy and note the quantities you will need. This can be done only if the menus have been planned. In making the menu, consider any food you already have in the larder, both cooked, left-over, and fresh.

2. Dry goods should be ordered once a week and it is convenient to note on a slate or pad any item which is running low so that nothing is forgotten on the weekly grocery list.

3. Perishable foods are best bought as required. Milk, green vegetables and soft fruits, fish, and offal should be used on the day of purchase. Bacon, fats and cheese will keep for a week if you have a good larder or a refrigerator. Meat will keep for 2 days if the storage place is good and the meat fresh when bought.

4. Cooked meat, pies and quick frozen foods should be used on the day of purchase.

5. Shop where there is a quick turnover of food. In this way you will get fresher food. See also that the premises and the assistants are clean and that foods which are easily contaminated by flies are covered. Fish and meat, cream cakes and cooked foods should not be purchased from open-fronted shops or stalls.

Nor should cakes be purchased if the assistant handles both the cakes and the money: coins carry germs.

6. In buying fruit and vegetables, see that they are crisp and fresh and of a good colour. To buy stale yellowish greens, flabby root vegetables and bruised fruit is wasteful because they lack quality. Stale vegetables are deficient in Vitamin C and are not worth buying.

7. Before storing away purchases of dry foods, examine them carefully and return any which are not in good condition. Quantities of dry goods are required by law to be marked on the packet. Check how much you are getting for your money.

8. It is a good plan to have a reserve shelf in the store cupboard. This can be used for preparing emergency meals and can contain extras used only for special occasions. When anything has been

removed from this shelf, it should be replaced as soon as possible. Such a shelf might contain: a selection of tinned meats and fish, canned vegetables, tins of soup, canned fruit, dried milk, vegetable extracts, small sealed tins of savoury and sweet biscuits, evaporated milk, tinned spaghetti.

Quantities of Food to Buy for Serving 2 People

Fish	Crab	1 medium
	Cutlets or steaks, e.g. cod, halibut, hake	$\frac{3}{4}$–1 lb
	Fillets	$\frac{1}{2}$–$\frac{3}{4}$ lb
	Lobster	1 medium
	Prawns, shrimps	$\frac{3}{4}$ pint
Fruit	Apples and pears	$\frac{1}{2}$ lb
	For stewing, e.g. plums, blackberries, rhubarb	$\frac{1}{2}$ lb
	To serve fresh, e.g. strawberries, raspberries	$\frac{1}{2}$ lb
Meat	Chops	2
	Cutlets	2–4
	Heart	1
	Kidney beef	$\frac{1}{2}$ lb
	„ sheep or pig	3
	Liver	6–8 oz
	Minced meat (fresh)	$\frac{1}{2}$ lb
	Sausages	$\frac{1}{2}$ lb
	Cooked meats	4–6 oz
	Steak for grilling	6–8 oz
	Stewing beef or veal with no bone	$\frac{1}{2}$ lb
	Stewing mutton (neck or breast)	$\frac{3}{4}$–1 lb

Roasting or braising or boiling. This depends very much on the joint. Nothing smaller than $2\frac{1}{2}$ lbs will roast or boil satisfactorily, as the joint shrinks during cooking and it is difficult to make a very small joint tender. An exception to this is loin of lamb or mutton, which will produce a satisfactory joint of about $1\frac{1}{2}$ lbs giving possibly 5–6 chops in the joint. A piece of meat such as topside of beef of about $1\frac{1}{2}$ lbs in weight will braise satisfactorily.

Half a shoulder of lamb will weigh about $2\frac{1}{2}$ lbs. A satisfactory piece of sirloin must be 3 lbs at least. A leg of lamb is unlikely to weigh less than 4 lbs.

Vegetables	Artichokes (Jerusalem)	$\frac{3}{4}$–1 lb
	Asparagus 6 sticks per person if served as an accompanying vegetable. 12–15 if served as a course	
	Beans, broad	1–$1\frac{1}{2}$ lb

Beans, French or runner	$\frac{1}{2}$ lb–$\frac{3}{4}$ lb
Beans, haricot or dried	2 ozs
Beetroot	$\frac{3}{4}$–1 lb
Brussels sprouts, cabbage, savoy, kale	$\frac{1}{2}$–$\frac{3}{4}$ lb
Carrots	$\frac{1}{2}$ lb
Celery	1 medium head
Leeks	$\frac{3}{4}$–1 lb
Lettuce	1 medium head
Marrow	1–1$\frac{1}{2}$ lbs
(Probably more economical to buy a larger one and use for 2 meals)	
Mushrooms	4–8 ozs
Parsnips	$\frac{3}{4}$–1 lb
Peas, garden	1 lb
Peas, dried	2 ozs before soaking
Potatoes	1 lb
Spinach	1 lb
Swedes and turnips	1 lb
Tomatoes	6 ozs
Watercress	3–4 ozs

Meal Planning

On the housewife rests the responsibility for the health of her family, and she must see that every member has the following:—

1. An abundance of fresh air and sunlight.
2. Exercise and rest.
3. A well-balanced diet including plenty of fresh water to drink.

Food is necessary to maintain life as it provides material for building and repairing the body, fuel for the production of warmth and energy, and substances which regulate the body processes and maintain health. Therefore a well-balanced diet is one which contains, in suitable proportions, foodstuffs to provide body builders (proteins and certain minerals), energy producers (mainly carbohydrates and fats) and protective foods (vitamins). There is also a category which gives little or no food value but which can make food more attractive and stimulate appetite. Such foods are pickles and sauces, clear soup, and flavouring extracts.

The foods which build and repair the body are:—

(a) Those which build flesh or muscle—meat including offal and poultry, fish, eggs, milk, cheese and certain vegetables such as peas, beans, lentils. Nuts and cereals are also sources of protein. The animal foodstuffs supply body builders which are more readily used by the body than those which come from the vegetable kingdom and are therefore to be preferred, but the other foods are used to provide variety or for economy. A certain amount of protein is obtained from potatoes and bread.

(b) Those which build bones and teeth, that is, those which supply calcium, the best sources being milk and cheese. A certain amount of calcium is also obtained from flour, green vegetables, nuts and such fish as sardines and tinned salmon.

(c) Those which make good red blood, that is, those which supply iron which is obtained from liver, kidneys, red meat, egg yolks, dark green vegetables, haricot beans, dried peas, dried fruits and black treacle.

(b) and (c) also regulate the body processes.

The foods which provide warmth and energy are:—

(a) Sugars—brown and white sugar, preserves, syrup and honey.

(b) Starchy foods—bread, cakes, cereals, potatoes and root vegetables.

(c) Fats—butter, margarine, lard, dripping, oils.

(d) Proteins—these supply energy if they are not required for body building, but they are, in the main, expensive foods and therefore most people eat less of them and obtain their energy from the less expensive sources such as carbohydrates and fats.

The sugars and starches are described as fuel foods, but in order to release energy to the body there must also be present vitamin B (thiamine). This " sparks off " the release of energy, and to use this energy the body needs oxygen. This is extracted from the air we breathe and conveyed to the muscle by the blood. Hæmoglobin, a component of the red blood cell, absorbs oxygen and carries it to every living cell. To make the hæmoglobin, iron and vitamin C are both essential. Thus to provide energy in the body, fuel food plus thiamine plus vitamin C plus iron are all necessary.

The protective foods are those which provide vitamins. There are several vitamins, which keep all parts of the body in good condition, and help to regulate the body processes, but only the four most important ones need concern the housewife as the others are present in a well-balanced normal diet.

Vitamin A is found in liver, cod-liver oil, butter, eggs, vitaminised margarine, milk, carrots and leafy green vegetables. It is necessary for growth and for healthy conditions of the eyes, the mouth and the organs of breathing. It helps resistance to infection.

Vitamin B is found in cereals, especially in flour, in yeast, eggs, meat (especially pork and bacon), milk and potatoes. Vitamin B is really a number of vitamins, and is known as "Vitamin B Complex". It is necessary for a healthy nervous system, and is important in maintaining a good appetite and good digestion. It helps the body to make use of the energy-giving foods.

Vitamin C is found in the citrus fruits such as lemons, grapefruit and oranges, in black currants, tomatoes, leafy green vegetables, and potatoes. It is a necessity for all the body cells, and an adequate supply ensures general good health and a clear skin and eyes. It is lost if fruits and vegetables are kept for a long time after harvesting (the exception is the citrus fruits) and can easily be destroyed by bad methods of cooking (see the chapter on the cooking of vegetables).

Vitamin D is found in butter, vitaminised margarine, liver and oily fish such as herrings, mackerel and pilchards and in the yolk of an egg. It is very important, as it is necessary for the fixing of calcium in the bones and teeth. That is why expectant mothers and young children are given fish liver oils. It is formed by the action of sun on the skin, and because of this is sometimes known as the Sunshine Vitamin.

A well-cooked meal or a meal which satisfies hunger or the idiosyncrasies of personal taste is not necessarily a well-balanced meal. In the day's diet the housewife should aim at including:—

Milk $\frac{1}{2}$–1 pint for adults, 1$\frac{1}{2}$–2 pints for growing children. This includes the milk used in cooking as well as in beverages and on cereals.

Eggs   3–5 per week

Meat   3 ozs uncooked—2 ozs cooked ⎫
or
Fish   5 ozs uncooked ⎬ preferably 2 of these each day
or
Cheese   3 ozs
or
Dried pulse or nuts   4 ozs ⎭

Margarine or butter   1 oz

Potatoes $\frac{1}{2}$ lb after peeling

Green vegetable ⎫ 6 ozs before cooking
or ⎬
Green salad ⎭ 1 oz

Fruit   2 servings per day, including citrus fruit, or cooked fruit or tomato

Bread, cakes and cereals as appetite demands. Whole grain cereals should be included as part of the quantity. These supply roughage, as do the green vegetables and fruits, and roughage helps the process of elimination of waste matter.

Sugar—according to appetite. (This includes jam, syrup etc.)

Water—2$\frac{1}{2}$ pints per day in all liquids taken.

A housewife has to plan the family meals in such a way that the necessary food requirements are present in roughly the right quantity for health. It is not possible to have every meal correctly balanced, but over a day or a week the balance can be maintained. Certain staple foods appear at most meals, e.g. milk, bread, margarine or butter, but otherwise it is important to have variety. An appreciation of good food, well cooked and presented, is an important factor in social relationships. Meal times, when all the family are together, are times when each other's company can be enjoyed, and provided that the preparation and cooking of the meal has been carefully thought out, the housewife can sit down and enjoy the meal.

First and foremost it should be remembered that a meal is there to be eaten and enjoyed and must therefore be attractive to look at, and to stimulate the appetite. It must taste good, and the week's food must come within the limits of the family budget. Many of us find it difficult, at first, to plan the meals so that the money lasts till the end of the week, and we have to learn how to prepare dishes which are cheap but still nourishing and appetising. While the system of rationing was in force, it was comparatively easy to plan the week's housekeeping money, but with a free market, the in-experienced housewife may find it difficult to plan her budget so that she buys the essential foodstuffs in the right proportions.

Making a meal look attractive depends partly on the dish being cooked " to a turn " and partly on its attractive colour. Foods containing vitamins A and C will be included both for their vitamin value and also for their lively and strong colouring e.g. oranges, green vegetables, salads, and tomatoes.

Another very important point in making a meal look attractive is the serving of well-prepared accompaniments; greasy, colourless or lumpy sauces and gravies can spoil any dish, and every dish is enhanced by an attractive garnish.

A meal which in its various dishes contains a variety of textures is palatable, and soft foods should be alternated with crisp food. Every meal should contain something which needs chewing, and this is particularly important for children as it helps in the growth of healthy teeth. Variety is stimulating to the appetite and this is achieved by varying the methods of cooking and the accompaniments to certain foods.

Economy is often the most important factor in budgeting. The first step towards this is buying the right quantities to avoid waste. It is always cheaper to purchase foods which are in season, and at such times foods are at their best as regards flavour and quality. It is easier to provide variety during the summer and autumn when there are plenty of home-grown fruits and vegetables, and the housewife can help her late winter and spring catering if she preserves fruit and vegetables while they are plentiful. Seasonable foods, besides being comparatively cheap, generally provide dishes which are suitable for the weather. Adapting the dishes to the time of the year is important.

Individual appetite varies considerably, and the total quantity of food taken will be largely determined by this, but all adults require approximately the same amount of body building and protective foods. People doing heavy manual work require more of the energy foods but do not need more of the others. Expectant and nursing mothers, however, need extra body building and protective foods during the whole period of pregnancy and nursing. This is largely covered if the mother drinks an extra pint of milk and the juice of an orange every day, and takes cod-liver oil. Young children, too, need these extras to help in growth, while adolescents, who generally have large appetites, should have foods containing iron and calcium, such as green vegetables, eggs and liver. Care should be taken that the appetite of the growing boy or girl is not satisfied entirely by bread, cakes and sweets, as these will not give them sufficient body building and protective foods. Cakes and bread can be taken at will after the essential foods have been eaten.

During the period of full employment and high standard of living, one of the nutritional problems has been overweight, especially in children and middle-aged women. This is often brought about by the eating of many sweets, cakes and pastries.

Surveys show that the national diet is still low in iron, calcium and vitamins A and D, indicating that there is a wrong choice of food and money is spent ill-advisedly on foods which provide fat and sugar rather than on those which will provide a nutritionally balanced diet.

In deciding on the meal, choose first the ingredient which gives the protein—that is, decide whether it is to be meat or fish or egg and cheese etc. and then decide on the vegetables and the fruit to be served and fill in the details of the course with the energy foods such as bread, pastry or pudding and fats and sugar.

At least two, and if possible three, meals in the day should have body-building foods in them, and it is better to have three smaller helpings of protein spread over the day's meals than to give all the meat or fish at one meal. This helps the digestion and assimilation, as the body makes better use of the protein if it is accompanied by vegetables or cereals.

Drinking as well as eating is important. Most adults rely on cups of tea or coffee and probably the desired 2½ pints per day will be supplied in this way. It is necessary to establish in children the habit of drinking plenty of water, which is an essential body fluid. Adequate elimination of waste matter is achieved only if plenty of liquid is taken during the day.

CHAPTER IV

GLOSSARY OF COOKING TERMS

Au Gratin

Food coated with sauce, sprinkled with brown breadcrumbs and sometimes with cheese (though not of necessity) dotted with butter or margarine and browned either in the oven or under the grill. The food is served in the dish in which it is cooked.

Bain Marie

A flat open vessel half filled with water kept at a temperature just below boiling point. Sauces, garnishes and accompaniments are kept hot without burning or reducing in quantity.

Bard, to

To cover the breast of game or poultry with slices of fat bacon to protect during cooking. The bacon should be tied securely over the bird and removed before the cooking is complete so that the breast may be browned.

Baste, to

To pour hot liquor or fat over the surface of foods to keep them moist during cooking.

Béchamel

A white sauce made by the roux method. The milk is flavoured by infusing with carrot, celery and an onion stuck with cloves before being used for making the sauce. It is the foundation of most rich white sauces such as are used in entrées of meat and fish.

Beignets

Fritters. The term may be used to apply to anything dipped in batter and fried in deep fat.

Blanch, to

To cover the food with cold water, bring to the boil, remove the food and plunge immediately into cold water. Vegetables may be

26

blanched by plunging them into boiling water for 2–3 minutes and then into cold water. The skins of tomatoes and almonds are easily removed in this way. See chapter on preservation for further uses of blanching of vegetables.

Blend, to

Generally used to mean mixing together a dry and a liquid substance. The cold liquid is added gradually to the dry ingredient and the mixture stirred continuously to prevent lumps forming. (See sauce-making.)

Also used when flour is added to heated fat as when making a roux. The term always implies careful mixing and constant stirring.

Bouquet Garni

A small bunch of herbs tied together in muslin and used to flavour soups and stews. (See Flavourings.)

Braise, to

A combination of roasting and stewing. The food is cooked in a stewpan with a tightly fitting lid so that no juices are lost. The food is placed on a bed of vegetables, or mirepoix, with just sufficient liquid to provide the gravy or sauce and keep the food moist. When the food is tender, the lid is removed from the pan and the food browned in a hot oven. Cuts of meat, game and poultry, too coarse to roast, are very successfully cooked by this method. It is also used for vegetables.

Canapés

Circles or fingers of fried bread, toast or pastry used as a base for hors d'œuvres and savouries.

Caramel

Sugar which has been heated until it colours. Gravy browning or " Black Jack " is sugar heated until it is a dark brown and then dissolved in water.

Casserole

A fireproof earthenware or glass dish with a tightly fitting lid, used for oven cooking, especially for stews. The food is served in the dish in which it is cooked. Originally it meant a copper stewpan.

Cassolette

A small case made of puff pastry or egg and breadcrumbs, and filled with a savoury filling.

Charlotte

Originally this meant a custard set in a biscuit case as in Charlotte Russe, when a flavoured mixture of cream and custard is set in a case of savoy fingers and served cold. It is also used as in Apple Charlotte to indicate a case made of fingers of bread dipped in butter filled with a purée of apples. This type of Charlotte is baked and served hot.

Chaudfroid

Fish, meat, game or poultry cooked and served cold coated with chaudfroid sauce, decorated, and glazed with aspic.

Cocottes

Small fireproof dishes, used for cooking and serving single portions.

Compôte

Fruit served in syrup or a brown stew of game, generally made from small birds.

Consommé

Clear soup (see chapter on soups).

Cream, to

To work one or more ingredients until smooth and creamy.

To combine fat and sugar so that air is incorporated. This may be done with a spoon or a beater. During the process the fat becomes pale in colour and the texture light and fluffy. The grittiness of the sugar disappears as it is worked into the fat.

Croquette

Minced meat, fish or other savoury mixture bound together and formed into cork shapes. Coated with egg and breadcrumbs and fried in deep fat.

Croûte

A thick piece of bread fried in butter or deep fat. Used for dishing game and some entrées.

Croûtons

Small dice or fancy shapes of fried bread used as a garnish. Sometimes used to describe dice of toast served with purée soups.

Dariole

Generally used to denote a small tin mould used for setting creams and jellies or for baking or steaming puddings or small soufflés. It may also mean a small cream tart or an entrée of forcemeat or mince baked or steamed in a small mould.

Devilled

Grilled meat or fish cooked with mustard, cayenne pepper or other hot condiments. A highly spiced sauce is often served as an accompaniment.

Entrée

A savoury dish served with a sauce and accompaniments. It may be either hot or cold. Originally a dish forming a complete course in itself.

Espagnole

Spanish. A rich sauce made from a brown roux and brown stock and flavoured with tomato and mushroom, ham or lean bacon and sherry. It is the foundation of most rich brown sauces. (Recipe on page 63.)

Farce or Forcemeat

A stuffing. The term farce is generally used to imply a stuffing containing meat; forcemeat implies a stuffing made of bread, suet and parsley (veal forcemeat) or sage and onions or chestnuts.

Fleurons

Crescent shapes of baked puff or flaky pastry, used as a garnish.

Fricassée

A white stew of chicken, rabbit or veal.

Galantine

White meat such as poultry or veal cooked and rolled, pressed and glazed and served cold. The meat may be stuffed or may be minced and combined with ham, tongue or other flavouring. Galantine may be coated with chaudfroid sauce and glazed with aspic.

Garnish

Decoration, generally edible, added to a dish to improve the appearance and flavour.

Gâteau

A cake, generally used to imply a rich cake elaborately filled and decorated.

Glaze, to

To brush over the tops of pies, buns, galantines etc. to improve the finished appearance. Egg and water in equal quantities may be used and should be put on before cooking. Sugar and water glaze is put on when the food is cooked. A meat glaze is clear stock reduced to a syrupy consistency.

Kedgeree

A dish of fish and rice often flavoured with curry powder, fennel, onions or spice.

Knead, to

To work a dough lightly either with the knuckles as in yeast mixtures or with the fingertips as in pastry-making. In both instances the outside of the dough is drawn into the centre.

Kromeskies

Balls or rolls of croquette mixture or farce rolled in a thin slice of bacon, dipped in batter and fried in deep fat.

Lard, to

The insertion of strips of fat bacon into the breast of poultry or game or into pieces of meat (see Braising).

The bacon is cut into strips about 2″ long and ¼″ thick and deep. By means of a " larding needle " they are threaded into the meat, leaving the ends outside.

Liaison

The binding or thickening used for soups and sauces. It may consist of flour and milk, rice flour, sago, yolk of egg or cream.

Macédoine

A mixture of vegetables cut in even sizes, generally used as a garnish. It may also be combined with mayonnaise and served as an hors d'œuvre.

The term is also used for a fruit salad or fruit set in jelly.

Marinade

A highly seasoned liquid in which meat or fish is soaked before cooking to improve the flavour and, if necessary, make tender.

The liquid is a mixture of wine, cider or vinegar flavoured with onion, garlic, herbs and spices or a selection of these. Olive oil is generally added. See also page 67.

Mirepoix

The mixture of vegetables, bacon and herbs used as a foundation on which meat and vegetables are braised (see Braising).

Mousse

A light frothy mixture, either sweet or savoury.

Panada

A very thick sauce made from fat, flour and liquid, used to bind croquette and similar mixtures.

Parboil, to

To partly cook by boiling and then complete the process by some other method, generally frying or baking.

Poach, to

To cook in seasoned liquid in an open pan at simmering point with just enough liquid to cover the food. Generally applied to eggs and certain dishes of meat, fish and game e.g. quenelles.

Purée

A smooth pulp obtained by passing certain foods through a sieve. The term is applied to certain types of vegetable soups.

Ragoût

A rich, highly-flavoured brown stew of meat or game.

Raspings

Very fine crumbs used for coating fried foods or au gratin dishes. The bread is dried slowly in the oven and when quite crisp is crushed with a rolling pin and sieved. If stored in an airtight tin the crumbs will keep for several months.

Réchauffer

To re-heat. A réchauffé is left-over food re-warmed or re-dressed.

Rissoles

Minced meat or fish similar to a croquette mixture, enclosed in thin pastry, coated in egg and breadcrumbs or crushed vermicelli and fried in deep fat.

Roux

Equal quantities of fat and flour cooked together and used as a basis for sauces or as a thickening agent. Roux may be white, fawn or brown according to the length of time of cooking.

Sauté

To toss in butter in a frying pan over a sharp heat. The term may also be used to indicate cooking in a little fat with the lid on the pan until all the fat is absorbed.

Savarin

A very light pudding made from a rich yeast mixture.

Simmer, to

To cook in liquid which is just boiling, but so slowly that the bubbles burst at the sides of the pan only.

Sippets

Crescents or triangles of fried bread used as a garnish.

Soufflé

A very light mixture, either savoury or sweet. A light baked or steamed pudding. A light cream mixture sweetened and flavoured and set with gelatine.

Tammy, to

To strain soups and sauces through a fine woollen cloth.

Tepid

Approximately blood heat obtained by adding 2 parts of cold water to one part of boiling water.

Tournedos

Fillets of beef cut $\frac{1}{2}''$ to $\frac{3}{4}''$ and cooked by searing only on both sides.

Vol-au-Vent

A round or oval case of puff pastry as light as " a puff of wind ", filled with either savoury or sweet fillings.

Zest

The outer skin of citrus fruits. This is the part of the rind which contains the essential oils and therefore the flavour. The white pith is bitter and if used spoils the flavour of the dish. The skin must be very finely grated or peeled or rubbed off with a lump of sugar.

CHAPTER V

HORS D'ŒUVRES AND SAVOURIES

Hors d'Œuvres

HORS D'ŒUVRES form the preliminary course to a meal, and generally consist of tempting morsels with a sharp flavour, taken to stimulate appetite. This course was originally used for luncheon only, but is now used extensively for dinners. The portions should be small and attractively set out and decorated, thus affording the cook an excellent opportunity to show her skill in originality of garnish and in combination of flavours. Almost any food, if not sweet, may be introduced. Hors d'œuvres are served cold and are often placed in readiness on the table, giving a colourful effect.

They may be classified as :—

1. Appetisers, which are served alone.
2. Salad varieties (hors d'œuvres variés).
3. Dressed hors d'œuvres.

APPETISERS
Avocado Pears

Peel and halve the pears, sprinkle with lemon juice and cayenne pepper or sherry and serve very cold *or* soak in French dressing for 30 mins. and serve with thinly sliced cucumber.

Cantaloupe Melon

Cut in segments, remove the seeds and chill. Serve with castor sugar and ground ginger.

Caviare

1. Leave in the jar and hand with fingers of toast or plain small biscuits. A bone spoon with a long handle should be used for serving.

2. Flavour with lemon juice and cayenne pepper and serve on croûtes of fried bread or plain biscuits.

Crayfish

Remove from the shell as directed in the chapter on fish and if possible keep the claw meat whole. Serve the claw meat arranged on a dish on a bed of watercress and coat with a good dressing.

Foie Gras

1. As a pâté. Serve in the earthenware pot (terrine) in which it is purchased. Remove the surface fat before serving. Hand with it fingers of thin dry toast.

2. As a sausage. Slice very thinly and garnish with lemon.

Grapefruit

Cut in half, and, using a sharp knife, ease the flesh inside each segment. Do not cut the membrane from the skin, as it is easier to lift out each piece of fruit from its own section if the membrane is secure. Sprinkle maraschino over the fruit, chill thoroughly and serve garnished with half a glacé cherry.

Olives

1. Wash off the brine, serve in a dish with a little iced water to keep the olives plump.

2. Peel the flesh off the olive stone in the same way that the peel is taken off an apple. Keep in one curl. Allow the flesh to spring back to shape. Fill the centre with any well-flavoured farce or filling, inserted through a forcing bag.

Oysters

Only Whitstable and Colchester oysters should be served uncooked and in the shells. They should be placed on the upper shell with a little liquor, seasoned with cayenne pepper and a few drops of lemon juice. Serve with thin slices or rolls of brown bread and butter and pieces of lemon.

Pineapple

Serve diced, garnished with sprigs of mint. Chill thoroughly.

Smoked Salmon

The flavour of this fish is produced by smoking prior to soaking in olive oil. It should be cut in very thin slices and served at once. Garnish with segments of lemon.

SALAD VARIETIES OR HORS D'ŒUVRES VARIÉS

When offered in a restaurant, this term denotes a variety of ingredients each served in a separate small dish or on a sectional platter. In the home the hors d'œuvres may be similarly served or may be arranged on individual plates.

In selecting the varieties, it is usual to allow ⅔ of the total in dressed vegetables, including the green stuff, and ⅓ as meat, fish, egg or a combination of the three.

When serving on individual plates, a leaf of lettuce may be laid on the plate and the other ingredients arranged on and around it. A garnish of watercress or fine cress may be used to provide additional greenstuff. The lettuce leaf must be crisp and unblemished in order to look attractive, and if coarse or broken leaves are used, they should be finely shredded. In this way leaves which are not perfect may be incorporated. All greenstuff should be served with French dressing. (See chapter on Salads for various dressings.)

Ingredients included in Salad Hors d'œuvres

Beetroot

Cooked and diced. Serve with French dressing or spiced vinegar garnished with chopped green herbs. Serve alone; it discolours other vegetables.

Celery

Wash and scrape for curling as for salads. Serve chilled without garnish.

Cucumber

Slice thinly. Serve with spiced or herb vinegar.

Carrots and Potatoes

Dice and serve with mayonnaise or salad dressing, use a chopped green garnish (savory, parsley, tarragon or chives) or rub the dish with a crushed clove of garlic.

Peas

Mix with mayonnaise or salad dressing.

Peas, potatoes and carrots are often mixed together and served with a green garnish.

Tomatoes

(a) Skin and slice and serve with French dressing, garnished with chopped parsley.

(b) Skin small tomatoes. Cut in half through the stalk. Place each half in a piece of butter muslin and draw it up into a ball by twisting the muslin around tightly. Glaze each tomato ball with French dressing or aspic jelly.

Egg

Hard boil and slice. Coat with mayonnaise, garnish with chopped parsley. Or use the white cut into fancy shapes as a garnish and sieve the yolk to use in the same way.

Anchovies and Sardines

Bone and tail each fish. Coat with salad oil and lemon juice.

Chicken or Game

Dice and toss in a good dressing made with an appropriate sauce as a basis.

Shell-fish

Remove from the shell, flake and toss in a cream dressing or mayonnaise.

Meat

Sausages such as Strasbourg, Lyons, Frankfurt, Salami, Bologna, Saveloy, are all served thinly sliced and garnished with parsley.

Smoked ham is served like smoked salmon, or with a slice of melon.

DRESSED HORS D'ŒUVRES

These are generally served as a separate course in place of salad varieties, and it is customary to serve one variety only. The same recipes and method of service are used when these are served as savouries at the end of a meal.

Dressed hors d'œuvres are served in small patty cases, on canapés, on pieces of cheese pastry previously baked, thinly cut toast or plain commercial biscuits. They may be small rounds the size of a half-crown, fingers or squares. The word canapé, strictly speaking, means a sofa or platform and correctly used implies a croûte of bread fried in butter, but the term is generally used to cover all varieties of base. The patty cases may be made of rough puff, flaky or puff pastry and are cut with a cutter 1⅜" across with the smaller cutter used to make the centre 1" in size. Cheese pastry cases may be made in boat-shaped patty tins.

Fillings for Patty Cases and Canapés
Patties

For the method of making patty cases see instructions for puff pastry. For a variety of fillings see chapter on meat.

Canapés

The croûtes or biscuits should first be spread with butter or a savoury spread which will hold the main ingredients in position. Variations can be made by interchanging the spreads and the fillings, or by using two or more fillings on one canapé. Garnishes should be chosen to give a smart finish and should be piquant in flavour and gay in colour.

Suggestions for Spreads

The following spreads may be piped as a garnish as well as being used as a base on the canapé.

Anchovy Butter

1 oz butter or margarine	A little coralline pepper
1–2 teasps anchovy essence	Colouring

Cream all together and flavour carefully. Colour if necessary.

Anchovy Cream

1 hard boiled egg yolk	$\frac{1}{8}$ teasp cayenne pepper
4 anchovies	1 tbs cream
1 tbs melted butter	1 teasp lemon juice

1. Pound the egg, butter and anchovies together.
2. Season and sieve.
3. Whip the cream stiffly and add the sieved mixture to this. Add the lemon juice.
4. Chill before using, especially if it is to be used for piping.

Cream Cheese or Cottage Cheese

1. Mix well with enough cream off the top of the milk to make the mixture smooth.
2. Flavour well with cayenne pepper and lemon juice.

Green Butter

$\frac{1}{2}$ oz watercress leaves	Pinch of cayenne
2 ozs butter	Colouring
$\frac{1}{2}$ teasp salt	

1. Chop the leaves of watercress and sieve, using a hair or nylon sieve to keep the colour.
2. Cream the butter, season and add the purée of leaves.
3. Colour only if necessary.

Green Pea Purée

½ lb cooked green peas, well   1 teasp salt
    drained   ⅛ teasp pepper
¼ oz butter   Colouring if necessary

1. Sieve the peas and add the butter and seasoning to the purée.
2. Add milk or sieved potato purée if necessary to make the mixture a piping consistency.

Marmite Cheese

2 ozs stale cheddar or par-   ½ oz butter
    mesan cheese   ½ teasp Marmite

1. Grate the cheese finely.
2. Mix with the butter and Marmite.

Parsley Butter

See Maître d'hôtel butter (page 65).

Shrimp or Prawn Paste

2 ozs butter   ½ teasp lemon juice
½ gill picked shrimps or prawns   Pinch of cayenne pepper

1. Chop the shrimps or prawns and pound as smooth as possible.
2. Cream the butter with the lemon juice and cayenne.
3. Add the shrimps and mix well. Use colouring if desired.

Suggestions of Fillings for Canapés	*Garnishes for Canapés*
Anchovies	Asparagus tips
Caviare	Cucumber
Crab, prawns or shrimps	Curled celery
Cheese of all types	Gherkins
Egg, hard boiled and sliced	Green garnishes, such as parsley,
Ham cut into the shape of the croûte	watercress, tarragon, chives, savory
Pâtés of all types	Olives
Sardines	Onions—small cocktail variety
Sausage meats cut in thin slices	Radishes sliced or as " roses "
Tomatoes, skinned and sliced	Walnuts shelled or pickled

Savouries

The final course of a dinner is a small tasty morsel of highly flavoured food served to stimulate the digestive juices and encourage full appreciation of the meal.   Many people prefer a savoury to a sweet and often omit the sweet course altogether, serving in its place a savoury in larger portions or of a more substantial nature.

Care should be taken in the choice of fillings so that the predominant flavour does not repeat what has already been served at the meal.

Savouries may be served hot or cold, the choice being determined by the previous course.   When a savoury replaces the sweet course it is customary to offer a choice, generally one hot and one cold, and the portions should be substantial e.g. patties $2\frac{1}{2}''$ across, croûtes $2\frac{1}{2}''$ across, slices of toast $3\frac{1}{2}'' \times 2''$.

As with hors d'œuvres, great opportunity is given to the cook to show her ingenuity and skill.   Canapés in variety may be served as savouries and a selection may be handed on a platter.   If patties with a savoury filling are served, it is usual to offer one type of filling only, and the patty case should be cut with a $2''$ cutter.

For patty fillings see chapter on meat.

Additional Recipes for Savouries
Angels on Horseback

4 oysters	butterflies of lemon
4 thin rashers of bacon	chopped parsley
4 croûtes of fried bread	

Method

1. Trim the oysters.
2. Remove the rind from the bacon and smooth each rasher with a knife to flatten it.
3. Wrap the oyster in the bacon and run a skewer through.   Two rolls on each skewer is convenient.
4. Grill slowly, turning frequently until the bacon is cooked through.
5. Serve each roll on a croûte of fried bread garnished with chopped parsley and a lemon butterfly.

Cheese Aigrettes

2 ozs flour	2 pinches of cayenne pepper
$\frac{1}{2}$ oz butter or margarine	$1\frac{1}{2}$ ozs grated cheese, preferably
1 egg + 1 yolk	parmesan
1 gill water	$\frac{1}{2}$ oz grated cheese for garnish
$\frac{1}{8}$ teasp salt	

Method

1. Put the water and butter into a pan.   Heat slowly until the fat melts and then boil until it " crackles ".

2. Remove from the heat, stir in the flour and beat to a smooth panada. Cook for 5 minutes; the mixture will leave the sides of the pan as when making choux pastry.

3. Cool slightly and add the eggs, cheese and seasonings. Beat well.

4. Heat a bath of fat, without a frying basket in it, until the fat just begins to haze, then lower the heat a little.

5. Drop the mixture into the fat in teaspoonfuls. Four or five aigrettes at a time are sufficient in a bath of fat of an ordinary size. If too many are cooked at a time, the temperature of the fat will be reduced and the aigrettes will be greasy. If they have not enough room, they will stick together.

Fry until well risen and a pale golden brown (about 5–7 mins). Keep turning with a frying spoon.

Drain on absorbent paper and toss in grated cheese just before serving.

Serve very hot.

Cheese Straws

4 ozs flour	pinch cayenne pepper
$\frac{1}{2}$ teasp salt	2 teasp cold water (approx.)
$2\frac{1}{2}$ ozs fat	$\frac{1}{2}$ egg yolk
2 ozs grated cheese, Parmesan for preference	

Method

1. Make cheese pastry (see p. 390) and roll into a rectangle. The paste should be $\frac{1}{4}''$ thick.

2. Cut the strip 3–4″ wide if the straws are to be served separately, 2–2½″ wide if they are to be served in rings.

3. Pick up the strip of pastry and pass it through a basin of flour.

4. Lay the strip of paste on the board and cut into $\frac{1}{4}$ inch strips. To do this hold the knife upright and with a straight cut slice the pastry to the required width. Cut 2 or 3 slices, allowing them to form a pile up the blade of the knife.

5. Transfer the straws on to a greased baking tray, keeping the strips quite straight on the tin. It is easier to keep them straight if several at a time are transferred from the knife to the tin.

6. If the straws are needed for a very special occasion, lay a piece of waxed or greaseproof paper on the tin. This will help to keep them even in colour.

7. Collect the scraps left after trimming the paste and roll again and cut circles with a $1\frac{1}{2}$–$1\frac{3}{4}$ inch cutter, stamping out the centres with a $1\frac{1}{4}$–$1\frac{1}{2}$ inch cutter. Bake the rings with the straws.

8. Bake in an oven preheated to 350° F, placing the straws in

the centre of the oven. Watch very carefully as they burn
readily. Time: 5–7 minutes.

To finish the Straws

1. Place a small bundle of straws through a ring and serve either
   lying flat on a dish or standing up like a sheaf of corn, *or*
2. Dip the ends in white of egg and dip one end in coralline pepper
   and the other in sieved dried parsley.

Build up the dipped straws into a geometrical design. Serve hot
or cold.

Golden Buck

3 ozs cheese, grated	½ teasp lemon juice
2 tbs beer	pinch each of salt, cayenne
½ oz butter or margarine	pepper and celery salt
2 eggs	2 slices bread toasted
½ teasp Worcester sauce	

Method

1. Melt the butter, add the beer, grated cheese and seasonings.
   Stir until creamy.
2. Add the eggs well beaten and stir until the mixture thickens.
3. Serve on fingers of hot buttered toast.

Ham Croûtes

8 circles of bread 2″ across and ⅜″ deep	2 tbs clarified butter
4 circles ham cut with the same cutter	2 ozs grated cheese
	1 teasp coralline pepper
	8 sprigs watercress

Method

1. Dip the bread in the butter and toss it in the grated cheese.
2. Place a round of ham between 2 pieces of bread.
3. Grill on both sides until brown and crisp.
4. Open the sandwich and grill the ham until tender.
5. Replace the top; sprinkle with coralline pepper.
6. Serve hot garnished with watercress.

Herring Roes on Toast

8 soft roes	2 gherkins or 1 teasp capers
4 fingers of toast	parsley
½ oz anchovy butter	2 teasp seasoned flour
1 teasp lemon juice	1 oz butter

Method

1. Toss the roes in seasoned flour and fry in the butter until the roes are lightly brown and crisp on the outside.
2. Toast the bread, spread with anchovy butter.
3. Place 2 fried roes on each finger of toast and garnish with slices of gherkin or chopped capers.

Mock Crab Toasts

2 ozs grated cheese	2 teasp made mustard
3 teasp anchovy essence	pinch of salt and cayenne pepper
2 teasp vinegar	2 slices toast

Method

1. Mix all together, rubbing with a wooden spoon until smooth.
2. Trim the toast and cut into fingers.
3. Spread these with the mixture.
4. Bake in an oven preheated to 425° F until brown, about 10 mins.
5. Serve garnished with watercress and cocktail onions.

Scotch Woodcock

2 eggs	1 oz anchovy butter
1 oz butter	4 anchovies
1 tbs milk	2 teasp capers
$\frac{1}{2}$ teasp salt	2 slices toast
pinch of pepper	

Method

1. Spread the toast with anchovy butter, cut each piece into 4 strips.
2. Cut the anchovies into strips and chop the capers.
3. Beat the eggs, add the milk, salt and pepper.
4. Melt the butter in a small pan, and when hot add the egg.
5. Stir over gentle heat until the egg thickens. Remove from the heat and continue stirring until the mixture becomes firm but not hard.
6. Pile the egg on the strips of toast.
7. Garnish with strips of anchovy and chopped capers.
8. Serve very hot.

Welsh Rarebit

3 ozs grated cheese	$\frac{1}{4}$ teasp salt
1 tbs melted butter	a dash of cayenne pepper
1 tbs milk or beer	1 slice of buttered toast
1 teasp made mustard	

Method

1. Make the toast, trim and cut into pieces of a suitable size. Butter and keep hot.
2. Melt the butter, add the grated cheese, milk or beer and seasonings.   Do not overheat.
3. Spread the mixture on the strips of toast, place in a fireproof dish and cook under the grill until brown (8–10 mins).
   If served as a savoury to replace a sweet, this amount will serve 2 persons only.

Buck Rarebit is a Welsh Rarebit with a poached egg served on the top.

CHAPTER VI

STOCKS AND SOUPS

Stocks

STOCK may be regarded as a prime essential in good cookery. It is the liquid in which meat, bones or vegetables and vegetable skins have been simmered gently for a number of hours. It may also be made from fish trimmings, skins or heads. It is a very important factor in achieving well-flavoured sauces, gravies and soups. Many recipes give " stock or water ", but the extra trouble caused by making stock is far outweighed by the added flavour of the finished dish. There is very little food value in stock, but the relatively small amounts of minerals, extractives (soluble flavouring substances) and soluble proteins which are dissolved in the water during the slow cooking process are stimulating to the appetite and add considerably to the flavour of the dish.

The best stock is made from fresh meat and bones, vegetables and fish, but this is extravagant for ordinary household use and in most homes a liquid known as Household Stock is preferred. The recipes given below for First Stock are used only in high-class dishes but are included in this book because the method is the same whatever the ingredients used. When special dishes are required, it is necessary to know how the essential good stock is produced.

An emergency stock or a stock suitable for the small household, in which the cooking equipment and space do not allow for a stock-pot, can be made by dissolving meat or vegetable extract in water (1 cube or 1 teasp extract to ½ pt boiling water or vegetable water) It is most important to buy a good extract, one which has no predominating flavour which might spoil the flavour of the finished dish. Cubes with either meat or chicken flavour are on sale.

If there is a solid fuel cooker in the home, it is a good plan to have a stock-pot standing on the cool part of the cooker so that it can cook slowly without needing any attention until all the flavour is extracted from the ingredients.

A strong, deep pan with a well-fitting lid is necessary. If it is an enamel or iron pan, the lining must not be chipped. A good-sized casserole with a lid is also efficient.

When the ingredients are cooked the liquid should be strained off and the ingredients discarded. The pan must be kept scrupulously clean and the ingredients correctly chosen.

Foods suitable for a stock-pot

1. All cooked and uncooked lean meat and bones.
2. Scraps of gristle and skin.
3. Giblets of fowl and game.
4. Bacon rinds.
5. Scraps of vegetables. If the vegetable has a very strong flavour (e.g. turnips) only a small quantity should be used. Some vegetables are unsuitable (see below).
6. Water in which vegetables have been cooked (see exceptions below).
7. Pot liquor i.e. the liquid in which fresh meat or fowl has been cooked.

Foods unsuitable for a stock-pot

1. Starchy foods e.g. potatoes, bread, barley, thickened gravies and sauces. These would make the stock sour.
2. Green vegetables and the water in which these have been cooked, as these give a bitter flavour.
3. Pot liquor from salt meat.

Glaze

Surplus stock may be boiled rapidly until it becomes the consistency of treacle. It must be skimmed frequently during the reducing process. Then it can be poured into a clean hot jar and used as required for glazing cold meats such as galantines or for finishing hot meat entrées such as fillets or cutlets. It can also be used for making emergency stock, for it is very similar in flavour to a meat extract.

Quickly Made Glaze

¼ oz gelatine
¼ pt brown stock or ¼ pt water + 1 teasp meat extract

Method

1. Put the gelatine and stock or water into a pan.
2. Heat gently, stirring all the time.
3. Add the meat extract if used.
4. Allow to cool and use when beginning to thicken.

Basic Recipe for First Brown Stock

2 lbs shin of beef	1 medium sized carrot
2 qts cold water	1 medium sized onion
½ teasp salt	1 stick celery, or
1 teasp peppercorns	½ teasp celery seeds
piece of turnip if desired	2 bay leaves

Method

1. Wipe the meat thoroughly and remove all skin and fat.
2. Cut the lean meat into small pieces; scrape the bones and remove any marrow.
3. Melt the latter or heat a small quantity of dripping or clarified fat and fry the pieces of meat and the bones quickly until all are a good brown colour, in order to improve the flavour and the colour of the stock. Strain off any surplus fat to avoid a greasy stock.
4. Add the measured quantity of cold water and leave to soak for at least half an hour to soften the meat fibres and to assist with the extraction of albumen, gelatine and minerals. Bring slowly to boiling point, add the salt and remove any grey-looking scum. Add the peppercorns and celery seeds tied in muslin; simmer for an hour or more, then add the prepared vegetables cut into large blocks; simmer the stock for four or five hours to continue withdrawing the flavouring substances from the meat.
5. Strain into an earthenware vessel and leave the stock standing overnight to allow time for any small quantity of fat to solidify.
6. Remove all traces of fat the following day.

First White Stock

Use knuckle of veal, chicken carcase, skin etc, instead of beef. Omit the frying of the meat and bones; otherwise follow the method given above.

Game Stock

Remove the breast of the birds and use for entrées. Use the carcases for stock. If a particularly good savoury stock is required it is advisable to par-roast the bird first.

Fish Stock

Fish bones and trimmings or	1 blade mace
1 cod's head	1 stick celery
1 onion	salt
6 white peppercorns	Cold water to cover

Method

1. Cleanse the cod's head well or thoroughly wash the fish trimmings.
2. Put the fish into the pan, cover with cold water, add the salt, bring slowly to boiling point; skim well. Add the peppercorns, mace, celery etc. and leave to simmer for approximately 40 minutes. Then strain and use as required for fish soups and sauces.

Note If fish stock is allowed to simmer too long a bitter flavour is produced.

Vegetable Stock

2 ozs dried beans ⎱ or 4 ozs	1 or 2 sticks celery or ¼ tea-
2 ozs peas or lentils ⎰ beans	spoon celery seeds
1 onion	blade of mace
1 carrot	few peppercorns
	2 qts cold water

Method

1. Wash the pulse vegetables thoroughly, cover with cold water and leave to soak overnight. The following day strain off the water, measure it and make up with more cold water to two quarts.
2. Put all the vegetables and the cold water into a pan. Bring to the boil.
3. Add the seasonings and herbs tied in muslin and simmer gently for 3 or 4 hours.
4. Strain and use as required for vegetable soups and vegetarian dishes.

Soups

The food value of soups is comparatively small. Those containing valuable nutrients are meat soups—such as kidney, liver and ox-tail—and soups made from pulse vegetables and from starchy vegetables. When making soups the aim is to extract from the ingredients the maximum amount of flavouring and nutrients. The chief value of soups in the diet is to stimulate the action of digestive juices and so assist with the digestion of the foods served in subsequent courses. The flavour of soups is determined by:—

(1) The quality of the stock used. The greater the amount of meat extractives and gelatine present in the stock, the better is the flavour of the soup. Many soups, particularly those with a meat stock basis, are improved in flavour by the addition of a little sherry.

(2) The correct proportion of vegetables, meat or fish to the foundation stock and the correct cooking of these.

1 pint of finished broth or soup will serve 4 portions, but it is not practical to make soup in small quantities as in these the loss by evaporation is considerable; therefore the recipes are given for 2 pints, i.e. 8 servings. Soup that is not served at the first meal may be kept in a cool place for 1–2 days and reheated to serve again.

There must be some five to six hundred known soups, yet all of them belong to one or other of the following groups:—

(1) Broths
(2) Purées
(3) Thickened or Cream Soups
(4) Clear soups or Consommés
(5) Fish Soups or Bisques

BROTHS

Broths are infusions of vegetables or meat and vegetables in seasoned liquids, e.g. Mutton Broth, Chicken, Veal, Scotch Broth or Sheep's Head Broth.

The table on page 49 shows which vegetables are suitable.

General Method for Making Broths

1. Wipe the meat with a damp cloth, remove skin, fat, gristle and marrow and cut the meat into small pieces.
2. Put the prepared meat and bones into the pan, add the salt and the measured quantity of water and washed barley if used.
3. Bring slowly to boiling point and simmer gently for approximately two hours.
4. Add the diced or grated vegetables and cook for one hour longer.

   If the broth is to be served clear, as for invalids, strain, allow to cool, remove the fat, reheat, and when boiling add garnish such as washed rice. Cook for about 15 minutes and test for seasoning, add the finely chopped parsley and serve very hot. If the meat and vegetables are to be served in the broth, proceed as above, omitting the straining process. This makes a more substantial dish.

VARIETIES OF BROTH

Name	Basic Ingredient	Liquid	Seasoning	Vegetables for Flavouring	Time of Cooking	Thickening	Special Method
Chicken	Carcase of fowl	2 pts liquid from boiling a fowl	2 teasp salt dash pepper 1 tbs chopped parsley	1 onion 1 stick celery or $\frac{1}{2}$ teasp celery salt	2–3 hrs	1 tbs rice	Break up carcase, include any skin. Strain and serve clear with rice and parsley as garnish.
Mutton	$\frac{1}{2}$ lb scrag end of neck or knuckle	2 pts stock or water	2 teasp salt 1 tbs chopped parsley $\frac{1}{8}$ teasp pepper	$\frac{1}{2}$ pt diced: leek onion carrot	2–3 hrs	1 tbs rice	Cut the meat into dice if to be served in the broth or leave whole if to be served as a joint (see meat cookery).
Rabbit	Rabbit head, ribs and scraps	2 pts	2 teasp salt dash pepper 1 tbs chopped parsley	1 onion 1 stick celery or $\frac{1}{2}$ teasp celery salt	2–3 hrs	1 tbs rice	Strain and serve clear with rice and parsley as garnish. Any pieces of meat from the bones may be served in the broth.
Scotch	$\frac{1}{2}$ lb neck of mutton or $\frac{1}{2}$ lb shin beef	2 pts	2 teasp salt $\frac{1}{8}$ teasp pepper 1 tbs chopped parsley	$\frac{1}{2}$ pt diced veg: carrot leek celery onion small amount of turnip 1 grated carrot	2–3 hrs	1 oz barley	Leave the mutton whole to serve as a separate joint. Remove after simmering for 2$\frac{1}{2}$ hrs, skim, add grated carrot and cook for 15–20 minutes, add parsley and serve at once.
Sheep's Head	1 head	3–4 pts water	3 teasp salt $\frac{1}{4}$ teasp pepper 2 tbs chopped parsley	1 pt diced or grated veg: onion carrot leek celery a little turnip	3–4 hrs	2–3 ozs barley or rice	Order the sheep's head already divided. Remove brain and keep in cold salt water until used. Clean nostrils and teeth by brushing with salt. Rinse head thoroughly. Blanch. Rinse again. Proceed as for Scotch broth.
Veal	Knuckle of veal or 2 lbs bones	2 pts	2 teasp salt dash pepper 1 tbs chopped parsley	1 onion 1 stick celery or $\frac{1}{2}$ teasp celery salt	2–3 hrs	1 tbs rice	Strain and serve clear with rice and parsley as garnish. Any pieces of meat from the bones may be served in the broth.
Vegetable	1 lb mixed vegetables, root	2 pts	bunch herbs 2 teasp salt	—	1$\frac{1}{2}$–2 hrs	1 tbs barley	Vegetables may be diced or grated. Turnip should be used very sparingly.

PURÉE SOUPS
Basic Recipe

2 pts stock	2 lbs fresh vegetables
8 ozs flavouring vegetables	or
2 teasp salt	4 ozs dried vegetables or nuts
⅛ teasp pepper	or
1 oz flour, cornflour or sago	1 lb meat or offal
¼ pt milk	
1 oz butter	

Method

1. Prepare the vegetables or nuts according to their kind, e.g. wash and soak overnight if using dried vegetables; wash and slice fresh vegetables.
2. Heat the fat and toss the vegetables in the hot fat for approximately ten minutes but do not allow them to brown.
3. Add the stock and salt. Cover with a tightly fitting lid, bring to boiling point and leave to simmer until all the vegetables are tender. During the simmering add the pepper and a bouquet garni, if liked.
4. When the vegetables are tender remove the bouquet garni and pass the soup through a sieve, remembering to remove the sieved pulp from the under-side of the sieve and to add this pulp to the liquid.
5. Blend the cornflour or flour with a little cold milk and add, with the remainder of the measured quantity of milk to the purée. Bring to boiling point and boil three or four minutes in order to cook thoroughly the starch present in the flour or cornflour. Stir well all the time. The consistency should now be that of thick cream.
6. Test for seasoning before serving.
7. Pour into a hot tureen and when serving hand separately small dice of toasted or fried bread (croûtons).

In the recipes given in the next two pages, purée soups are classified as follows :—

Pulses—bean, lentil and pea
Fresh starchy vegetables—artichoke, potato
Fresh watery vegetables—celery, marrow, tomato
Nuts—almond, chestnut
Meat—kidney, liver, ox-tail

VARIETIES OF PURÉE SOUPS

NAME	FOUNDATION INGREDIENTS	LIQUID	SEASONINGS	ADDITIONAL FLAVOURINGS INCLUDING VEGETABLES	TIME	METHOD	THICKENING
Bean or Pea or Lentil	4 ozs dried vegetables 1 oz butter or dripping	2 pts white stock ¼ pt milk	2 teasp salt ⅛ teasp pepper	onion ⎫ carrot ⎬ ½ lb celery ⎭ Each of these soups is improved if a ham bone is cooked in the soup.	2½ hrs	Follow the general method.	1 oz flour
Artichoke	2 lbs Jerusalem Artichokes 2 ozs butter	2 pts white stock ¼ pt milk 2 tbs cream	2 teasp salt ⅛ teasp pepper	1 onion ⎫ stick ⎬ ½ lb celery ⎭	approx 1 hour	Follow the general method.	1 oz flour
Potato	2 lb potatoes 1 oz butter	2 pts stock and/or veg. water ¼ pt milk	2 teasp salt ⅛ teasp pepper	onion ⎫ ½ lb celery ⎬	1½ hrs	Follow the general method.	1 oz flour, corn-flour or sago
Celery	2 lbs celery 1 oz butter	2 pts stock and/or celery water ¼ pt milk	2 teasp salt ⅛ teasp pepper	½ lb onion	1½ hrs	Follow the general method.	1 oz flour, corn-flour or sago
Marrow	2 lbs vegetable marrow 1 oz butter	2 pts white stock ¼ pt milk	2 teasp salt ⅛ teasp pepper	½ lb onion	1½ hrs	AS ABOVE	
Tomato	2 lbs fresh tomatoes 1 oz butter	2 pts stock and/or liquid from canned tomatoes	2 teasp salt ⅛ teasp pepper 2–4 teasp sugar	carrot ⎫ onion ⎬ ½ lb celery ⎭ Bouquet garni Bacon rinds	1½ hrs	AS ABOVE	
Almond	4 ozs almonds 1 oz butter	2 pts white stock ¼ pt milk	2 teasp salt ⅛ teasp pepper	1 small onion 1 or 2 sticks celery	approx 1¼ hrs	Blanch the almonds and chop finely or pass through a nut mill. Then follow the general method.	1 oz flour
Chestnut	1 lb chestnuts 1½ oz butter	2 pts white stock ¼ pt milk	2 teasp salt ⅛ teasp pepper little nutmeg little sugar	—	approx 1½ hrs	Split the chestnuts and cook in boiling water for about 10 minutes. Strain, skin and remove all brown skin etc. Then follow general method.	Because of the large quantity of starch in the nuts, no thickening is needed.

Kidney or Liver Soup

1 lb kidney or liver	onions ⎫
2 pts stock	carrot ⎬ to weigh ½ lb
2 teasp salt	celery ⎭
⅛ teasp pepper	1 oz dripping
	1 oz flour

Method

1. Cut and soak the kidney or liver in cold water for 10 mins.
2. Wash thoroughly and remove the skin and core and pipes.
3. Cut into small even sized pieces.
4. Fry the meat in the hot fat until brown. Remove from the pan.
5. Fry the onion until it is a good brown colour.
6. Pour off any surplus fat.
7. Add the remainder of the sliced vegetables, meat, seasonings and stock.
8. Bring to the boil and simmer for 1½–2 hours until the meat is tender.
9. Rub the soup through a sieve retaining some of the meat as a garnish.
10. Reheat the soup, add the blended flour and cook for 5 mins.
11. Chop the pieces of meat retained for garnish, add to the soup, and test for flavour. Serve very hot.

Ox-tail Soup

1 ox-tail	1 carrot
1 lb shin of beef	1 turnip
2 ozs butter	bunch mixed herbs
3 qts cold water	1 teasp peppercorns
1 glass cooking sherry if liked	1 tbs mushroom ketchup if
2 onions	liked
2 sticks celery	

Cooking time :
   5 to 6 hours.

Method

1. Wash the ox-tail thoroughly.
2. Cut into joints and blanch. Dry the joints well.

3. Heat half the butter and fry the joints until brown on both sides.
4. Add the shin of beef, cut up, and the water.
5. Add the salt; bring to boiling point; skim, simmer about 3 hours.
6. Heat the remaining fat and fry the onion until a good brown colour.
7. Add the remaining vegetables, the fried onion, the herbs and peppercorns tied in muslin, to the pan containing the ox-tail. Simmer for a further 2 hours.
8. Strain and if possible leave until this stock is cold.
9. Remove the meat from the bones and press the meat between two plates until it is cold.
10. Remove the layer of fat from the stock and measure 2 quarts. Bring this stock to the boil.
11. Blend the cornflour with a little cold water and add the boiling ox-tail stock, stirring well. Return to the pan and bring to boiling point, stirring all the time.
12. Shred the meat finely and add to the soup. Add a little sherry and test the soup for flavouring, adding 1 tbs mushroom ketchup if liked. Serve immediately.
13. About 4 tbs of fancy-shaped pieces of cooked carrot and turnip may be added as well as the shredded meat.

CREAM SOUPS
Basic Recipe

$\frac{3}{4}$ oz butter
$\frac{3}{4}$ oz flour
1 pt good chicken stock *or*
1 pt purée of vegetables

1 level teaspoonful salt
1 egg yolk
$\frac{1}{8}$ pt milk
2 tablespoonfuls cream or evaporated milk

Method

1. Make a roux using butter and flour (see sauce-making page 58). Do not allow the flour to become brown, as this would spoil the colour of the soup.
2. Add the stock or purée and salt and bring to boiling point, stirring all the time.
3. Add half of the measured milk to this; mix the egg yolk, cream and remaining milk and strain into the soup, stirring well.
4. Heat the soup gently until the egg yolk is cooked. Do not allow the mixture to boil, because the heat would cause the egg yolk and the cream to curdle.

Varieties of Cream Soup based on White Stock

Hollandaise Soup	Potage à la Royale	Potage à la Bonne Femme
Garnish 1 tablespoonful peas 1 ,, carrots cut into small pea-shapes or small dice 1 tablespoonful cucumber (cut as the carrot)	*Garnish* ½ oz cooked macaroni ½ oz grated cheese (preferably grated Parmesan)	*Garnish* 2 lettuce leaves A few watercress leaves small piece cucumber A few tarragon leaves
Method 1. Cook the above vegetables in a small quantity of the stock until the vegetables are tender i.e. Cook the cucumber in boiling water from 3–5 minutes. ,, peas in boiling water from 8–10 minutes. ,, carrots in boiling water from 20–30 minutes. (according to the freshness and age of the carrots). 2. Strain the stock and proceed to make the cream soup following the instructions given for the basic recipe. 3. Add the cooked vegetables to the soup after adding the egg yolk and cream. 4. Test for seasoning and serve piping hot.	*Method* 1. Follow the instructions for the basic recipe. 2. Cut the macaroni into neat pieces and add to the soup when the egg yolk and cream are added. 3. Continue to follow the instructions given in the basic recipe. 4. Serve with grated cheese.	*Method* 1. Follow the instructions for making the basic recipe. 2. Shred finely the vegetables (previously washed thoroughly). 3. Toss the prepared vegetables in approximately ½ oz heated butter until it is all absorbed by the vegetables. 4. Add these vegetables to the soup when the yolk and cream are added. Heat gently until the egg yolk is cooked but do not allow soup to boil.

Vichyssoise

2 ozs unsalted butter	4 leeks cut finely
1 onion	1½ pts chicken stock
6 ozs raw diced potato	½ pt cream
2 teasp salt	⅛ teasp pepper
2 tbs chopped chives	

Method

1. Sauté the leeks and onions in the butter until they are tender but still uncoloured.
2. Add the potatoes, stock and seasonings.
3. Simmer until quite tender. Sieve.
4. Return to pan and boil up.
5. Add the cream, heat carefully but do not boil.
6. Serve sprinkled with the chopped chives.

If it is to be served chilled, put in the refrigerator after sieving, and add the cream and chives just before serving.

CONSOMMÉS

Basic Recipe

1 qt first brown stock	1 blade mace
4 ozs lean juicy beef	6 white peppercorns
1 egg white and shell (crushed)	1 piece celery
1 small onion, scalded	1 large block carrot
2 teasp salt	

Method

1. Remove all traces of fat from the surface of the stock.
2. Shred the beef finely and soak it in ¼ pt cold water to extract the protein.
3. Put the prepared beef and all the ingredients, including unbeaten egg white and crushed shell, into a large deep pan previously rinsed with hot water to remove any traces of grease.
4. Whisk steadily over gentle heat until boiling point is almost reached. Remove the whisk and allow the stock to boil up twice or three times. Leave the covered pan in a warm place and allow the stock to infuse for about 15 minutes.
5. If a special garnish is used it should be cooked now whilst the stock is infusing. Cook the garnish in boiling water, not in the consommé as this would cause cloudiness. Consommés are named according to the garnishes served with them.
6. Strain the stock through a dry cloth twice or three times. (The egg shell and partially coagulated egg white act as a filter at this stage.)

7. Reheat the strained liquid but do not allow it to boil because the protein present would coagulate slightly and cause cloudiness.

8. Put the prepared garnish at the bottom of a hot tureen and pour on to it the consommé.

Varieties of Consommés

NAME OF CONSOMMÉ	GARNISH
à la Julienne .	Very fine shreds of carrot, turnip, celery. 1 tablespoonful of each to 1 qt consommé.
à la Royale .	Fancy shapes of savoury custard (see below).
à la Brunoise .	Carrot cut in dice ⎫ turnip „ „ ⎪ 1 tablespoonful each of these celery „ „ ⎬ leek „ „ ⎭ to 1 qt consommé.
à l'Italienne .	1 dessertspoonful cooked Italian Pasta to 1 qt.
à la Jardinière .	Very small sprigs cauliflower ⎫ Green peas ⎪ 1 tablespoon each of these Carrots cut into pea shapes ⎬ to 1 qt consommé. Turnip „ „ ⎭

Savoury Custard

1 egg yolk   pepper and salt
1 tbs milk or white stock

Have ready a small greased basin or a suitable mould. Mix together the egg yolk, liquid and seasoning; avoid beating or whisking as this would incorporate air. During cooking the air would expand, pitting the custard with small holes.

Strain the mixture into the greased basin, cover it with a greased paper and steam the custard very gently until it is firm to the touch. Turn out, drain well, cut into thin slices and from each slice, using a small aspic cutter, cut out fancy shapes. Put these into a hot tureen and pour over them the hot consommé.

WHAT WENT WRONG—AND WHY

The soup lacks flavour

(*a*) A very weak stock was used or stock was omitted.

(*b*) Vegetables were cut unevenly and the pieces used were too large. When vegetables are cut or shredded finely and evenly the maximum amount of flavour is extracted from them.

(c) The soup was cooked too quickly and for too short a time. By simmering slowly in a pan with a well-fitting lid the maximum amount of flavour is extracted from vegetables and/or meat.

(d) The maximum amount of sieved pulp was not used; frequently pulp is not removed from the under-side of the sieve, which means that it is wasted.

(e) Adequate seasonings were not incorporated.

The consistency is incorrect

(a) The soup had been allowed to cook rapidly. This had caused excessive evaporation of the liquid so the soup was too thick.

(b) Purées are sometimes too thin because ingredients have been used in the wrong proportions.

The soup is greasy

(a) A stock from which surplus fat had not been removed was used.

(b) Too much fat was used for sautéing the vegetables or the vegetables were not heated sufficiently in the fat. Adequate time should be allowed for the vegetables to absorb the fat without allowing them to become brown.

The soup is curdled

Cream soups may be spoilt in the last stage of cooking by:—

(a) Egg yolk and cream being added while the soup is too hot.

(b) The soup being overcooked after the addition of egg yolk and cream.

CHAPTER VII

SAUCES

A SAUCE is a well-flavoured liquid containing a liaison or thickening agent and used in the preparation of dishes. In continental cookery great thought and care are given to the making of all sauces: they are regarded as being of primary importance in good cooking.

When a sauce is to be made with cornflour, arrowroot or custard powder it is made without fat.

A Simple Sauce

Proportions

For a pouring sauce use 1 oz cornflour to 1 pint milk.
For a coating sauce use 1½ ozs cornflour to 1 pint milk.

Method

1. Put the cornflour into a basin. Blend to a thin cream with some of the milk using a wooden spoon.
2. Rinse a saucepan with cold water (this helps to prevent the milk sticking to the pan and burning).
3. Heat the milk to boiling point and pour over the blended cornflour, stirring all the time.
4. Rinse the pan, return the mixture and boil for 3–5 minutes for cornflour, 1 minute for arrowroot, and 3–5 minutes for custard powder.
5. Some custard powders require rather longer cooking; therefore it is advisable to follow the directions on the packet.

Sometimes a white sauce is made similarly, using flour instead of cornflour, but without fat the flavour is poor. The fat (margarine or butter) may be put into the milk and the sauce made as for a cornflour sauce. The gloss and flavour are not so good as when the sauce is made by the roux method.

Sauces with a Roux Foundation (white)

Proportions

For a Pouring Sauce   1 oz flour
                       1 oz butter
                       1 pint milk

For a Coating Sauce 2 ozs flour
                          2 ozs butter
                          1 pt liquid

For a Panada   4 ozs flour
                          4 ozs butter
                          1 pt liquid

Method

1. Melt the fat but do not allow it to become too hot.
2. Add the flour, stirring it into the fat, and cook the two together over a gentle heat without browning.
3. Draw the pan aside, and gradually add about one-third to half of the measured quantity of liquid, stirring well as the liquid is added, then return the pan to the heat and stir well. When this thickens and becomes smooth, remove and add the remaining liquid, stirring well. Return to the heat and bring to boiling point, stirring well all the time. Boil for four or five minutes to complete the cooking of the starch in the flour.

   When savoury sauces are being made, vegetables, herbs, spices etc. may be added to the sauce either before or after boiling point is reached. If vegetables have been allowed to simmer in the liquid to give the sauce additional flavour, strain the liquid through a strainer, muslin or special cloth.
4. Season, taste, re-heat and serve.

Brown Sauce

1 oz flour
1 oz dripping
1 oz chopped onion or
    shallot
1 oz chopped carrot
1 pt brown stock

1 rasher bacon diced or bacon
    rinds
1 teasp mixed chopped herbs
1 teasp tomato purée
mushroom stalks if available
salt and pepper

Method

1. Heat the dripping, fry the onion and bacon slowly until a rich golden colour.
2. Stir in the flour and cook, stirring all the time until a rich chestnut colour is obtained.
3. Draw the pan aside and add the stock, purée, herbs and pepper and salt.
4. Boil up, skim and allow to simmer for 30 mins.
5. Strain, test the flavour and reheat.

         (This sauce is also known as Demi-Glace.)

VARIATIONS OF WHITE SAUCE

Name	Recipe	Liquid(s) Most Suitable	Method	Use(s)
Anchovy	1/2 pint white sauce 2 teasps anchovy essence	Fish stock	Add essence to white sauce and serve.	With fried and baked fish; also réchauffés of fish.
Béchamel	1/2 pint white sauce 1 onion stuck with 3 cloves 1 piece blade of mace 1 piece each carrot and celery	Milk	Simmer vegetables and mace in the milk; strain; use the flavoured milk to make a white sauce.	With fish and poultry.
Brain	1/2 pint white sauce 1 set sheep's brains	1/4 pint liquor from the brains 1/4 pint milk	1. Cleanse and blanch the brains. 2. Cook about 1/2 hr. 3. Chop and serve in the sauce.	With boiled mutton or sheep's head.
Caper	1/2 pint white sauce 2 teasp capers 1 ,, caper vinegar	1/2 mutton boilings 1/2 milk	Chop capers and add to the sauce; then add the caper vinegar.	With boiled mutton.
Cardinal	3/4 pint white sauce 1/8 pint cream or evaporated milk Cayenne pepper 1/4 teasp salt 1 ,, lemon juice 3/4 oz coral butter *Coral butter* 3/4 oz butter and sufficient coral-line pepper to produce a lobster pink colour. Mix thoroughly and if necessary rub through a fine sieve before using. "coral" may be used in place of coral butter, but care must be taken that it is *absolutely* fresh.	Fish stock or a mixture of fish stock and milk	1. Make the white sauce in the usual way. 2. Add the seasoning, cream and lemon juice. 3. Then add, a little at a time, the coral butter, whisking well after each addition of butter. 4. If necessary strain through muslin. 5. Reheat the sauce, but do not boil it.	For coating fillets stuffed with lobster or for coating lobster soufflé.

Name	Ingredients	Liquid	Method	Uses
Cheese	½ pint white sauce; 2 or more ozs grated cheese	½ milk; ½ water or water from vegetables or cereals	Add cheese to sauce and melt it gently over moderate heat.	With vegetarian and egg dishes, macaroni cheese, cauliflower or onions.
Egg	½ pint white sauce; 1 hard-boiled egg	Milk	Chop egg finely; add to the sauce; reheat and serve.	With fish dishes, boiled fowl.
Fennel	½ pint white sauce; 2 tbs chopped fennel	½ milk; ½ fish stock	1. Wash fennel, remove stalks. 2. Cook till tender in boiling water. 3. Strain, chop finely and add to sauce. 4. Reheat and serve.	With fish dishes, particularly hot salmon.
Maître d'hôtel	½ pint white sauce; 2 teasps lemon juice; 2 tbs cream or evaporated milk; 1 tbs finely chopped parsley	½ fish stock and ½ milk	1. Add the parsley to the sauce; cook 1 minute. 2. Add the lemon juice, seasoning and cream or evaporated milk. 3. Reheat but do not boil.	For simple fish dishes, e.g. baked or steamed fillets of any white fish.
Mustard	½ pt white sauce; 2 teasps mustard (dry); 2 teasps vinegar	Milk	Mix the dry mustard with the vinegar. Stir into the white sauce and reheat.	With fish, particularly herrings or mackerel.
Onion	½ pint white sauce; ½ lb cooked onion	½ milk; ½ onion water	Boil onions; chop finely; add to the sauce. Reheat.	With tripe: roast and boiled mutton.
Parsley	½ pint white sauce; 1 tbs finely chopped parsley	Milk or ½ milk + meat or fish stock	Add parsley to the sauce immediately before serving.	With boiled mutton: fish dishes: hot boiled ham.
Soubise	½ pint white sauce (Béchamel); ¼ pint onion purée; 1 tbs cream or evaporated milk	½ onion water; ½ milk	Rub onion through sieve; add cream, re-heat and serve.	With cutlets.
Velouté	½ pint white sauce; 1 yolk of egg; ⅛ pint cream or evaporated milk; 2 teasps lemon juice	Well-flavoured white stock (chicken or veal stock) or rabbit stock	1. Add the lemon juice to the white sauce. 2. Strain into the sauce the mixture of egg yolk and cream. Stir well whilst adding the latter. 3. Re-heat sufficiently to cook the egg, but do not allow it to boil.	For fricassées of chicken, veal, rabbit and for quenelles and sweetbreads.

" COMPOUND " SAUCES

in which Béchamel Sauce (p. 60) is an ingredient

Name of Sauce	Amount of Béchamel	Additional Ingredients	Method of Combining Ingredients	Uses
Chaudfroid			See section on Poultry	
Hollandaise (1). See Egg Sauce for alternative method p. 68	½ pint	1 egg yolk 1 tbs cream or evaporated milk Cayenne pepper and salt 1 teasp lemon juice	1. Heat the Béchamel sauce. 2. Mix together the egg yolk and cream or evaporated milk, and stir into the sauce. 3. Heat but do not boil, stirring well. 4. Add the lemon juice and seasonings.	For coating steamed or baked fillets of fish.
Mornay	¾ pint	2 egg yolks ⅛ pint cream or evaporated milk 3 tbs chicken stock reduced to glaze (optional) 1½ ozs finely grated cheese, Parmesan if possible 1 oz butter	1. Heat the Béchamel sauce. 2. Cool slightly and blend the cream and egg yolks and add to the sauce. 3. Stand the saucepan in a vessel of boiling water and whisk into the sauce the grated cheese, butter and chicken glaze. Whisk until the sauce is smooth and creamy and use immediately.	For coating fish dishes, baked or steamed fillets of fish.
Tartare (hot)	½ pint	2 teasp finely chopped parsley 1 or 2 egg yolks 2 tbs cream or evaporated milk 2 teasp chopped gherkins 2 ,, ,, capers Cayenne pepper and salt Lemon juice	1. Make the Béchamel sauce, add the parsley and cook 1 minute to remove the raw flavour. 2. Mix together the egg yolks and cream, and strain into the sauce, stirring well; reheat, but do not boil. 3. Add the gherkins, capers, seasonings and lemon juice. 4. Test for seasoning and flavour. When a good piquant flavour is obtained, use as required.	With baked, steamed or fried fish dishes.

VARIATIONS OF BROWN SAUCE

Name	Recipe	Liquid(s) Most Suitable	Method	Use(s)
American	½ pint brown sauce 2 bay leaves 1 mushroom ¼ pint white wine	Game stock	Simmer the additional ingredients in the sauce for about 20 mins. Then strain, re-heat and serve.	For various meat dishes especially entrées.
Charcutiere	½ pt brown sauce 1 oz chopped onion 1 oz butter 1 gill white wine 2 ozs chopped gherkins French mustard 1 tbs vinegar	Brown stock	1. Sweat the onion in butter. 2. Add wine and vinegar. 3. Reduce to ½ quantity. 4. Season with the mustard. 5. Add gherkins.	Meat entrées.
Espagnole	2 ozs flour 2 ozs dripping 2 ozs raw ham or bacon 1 small carrot 1 small onion mushroom stalks (6–8) or equivalent mushrooms ½ gill sherry 2 tomatoes	Good brown stock 1 pint	1. Cook the cut-up bacon, onion, carrot and mushroom in the dripping. 2. When slightly brown, add the flour. 3. Cook gently until chestnut brown. Stir to prevent burning (½–¾ hour). 4. Add stock gradually; bring to boil, skim and simmer for ½–¾ hour. 5. Add tomato and cook 10 mins. 6. Add sherry and cook 10 mins. 7. Strain or sieve and season.	For various meat dishes especially entrées e.g. cutlets and tournedos. It is the foundation of compound sauces such as Italian, Poivrade, and Réforme.
Piquante	½ pint brown sauce 1 dessertspoon ketchup, Worcester or Harvey's sauce 1 tbs vinegar	Stock or liquor from boiling of meat (free from fat)	1. As for brown sauce, adding the vinegar and ketchup to the roux. 2. Cook for a few minutes before adding the stock.	Serve with croquettes and cutlets made from cooked meat.

"COMPOUND" SAUCES

in which Espagnole Sauce is an ingredient

Name	Amount of Espagnole	Other Ingredients	Method of Combining	Uses
Sauce Bigarade	½ pt espagnole	Juice 1 orange Juice 1 lemon ⅛ pt red wine Little castor sugar if liked Bay leaf	Heat the espagnole sauce until it boils, then add the other ingredients and boil for five minutes. Skim well and strain.	With roast duck, wild duck, widgeon and other game.
Italian	½ pint espagnole	1 oz salad oil (1 tbs) 2 shallots finely chopped 6 mushrooms finely chopped ⅛ pint white wine 1½ oz chopped ham 1 teasp tomato puree little thyme, 1 bay leaf, pepper and salt	1. Sauter or fry lightly the mushrooms and the shallots in the hot oil. Add the ham. 2. Add the wine and boil in an open pan until well reduced. 3. Add the sauce and the remaining ingredients and simmer gently about 20 mins. 4. Strain through a fine strainer, reheat and use as required.	Sweetbreads or Cutlets } à l'Italienne or Fillets of Beef Pasta dishes.
Poivrade	½ pint espagnole	¼ pint vinegar 9 peppercorns	1. Heat the vinegar in an open pan; add the crushed peppercorns and heat until the vinegar is reduced to ⅓ its volume. 2. Add the espagnole sauce, put on the lid and simmer gently about 15 mins. 3. Strain through muslin and use as required.	Game and marinated meats. Used together with espagnole sauce to make réforme (see below).
Réforme	½ pint poivrade	⅛ pint red wine 2 teasp red currant jelly	1. Make poivrade sauce as above. 2. Add the wine and the jelly, stir well and simmer for about 15 mins. 3. Strain and use as required.	Entrées of lamb, or mutton cutlets, or fillets of beef à la réforme. Venison.

BUTTER FOUNDATION SAUCES

Hard Sauce or Brandy Butter

2 ozs butter   1 tbs brandy
4 ozs castor sugar

Method

1. Cream the butter and sugar thoroughly as in cake-making.
2. When white and silky in appearance add the brandy.
3. Pipe into a small glass dish and keep in a cool place until required.
4. Serve with plum pudding.

Devilled Butter

2 ozs butter $\frac{1}{4}$ teasp dry mustard
$\frac{1}{8}$ teasp cayenne pepper   1 tbs lemon juice
2 teasp finely chopped parsley

Make as for Maître d'hôtel Butter.

Maître d'hôtel Butter

1 oz butter   little cayenne pepper
1 tbs finely chopped parsley few drops lemon juice

Method

1. Cream the butter well: then mix into it the lemon juice, parsley and pepper.
2. Form into a neat pat and leave in a cool place to solidify.
3. Serve with grilled fish or meats.

Rum Butter

$\frac{1}{4}$ lb butter   rum   } to taste
$\frac{1}{2}$ lb soft brown sugar   cinnamon

Method

1. Cream the butter and sugar together until well blended.
2. Flavour with rum, and cinnamon if liked.
3. Put into pots from which it can be served. Cover as for jam.

Melted Butter

Method

1. Put $\frac{1}{2}$ lb butter cut into small pieces into a saucepan and allow it to come to the boil.

C

2. Draw the pan aside and leave the butter to keep warm for 20 mins. Remove any froth as it rises.
3. Strain off the clear liquid into a hot sauce-boat and serve with asparagus etc.

CUMBERLAND SAUCE

4 tbs redcurrant jelly	1 lemon
$\frac{1}{4}$ pt red wine	1 teasp mustard
1 teasp finely chopped shallot	$\frac{1}{8}$ teasp cayenne pepper
1 orange	$\frac{1}{8}$ teasp ground ginger

Method

1. Peel a strip from the orange and the lemon and shred finely.
2. Scald in boiling water and drain.
3. Scald the finely chopped shallot in boiling water. Drain well.
4. Melt the jelly in a small pan, add the shallot. Infuse for 10 mins.
5. Add the wine (this traditionally is port, but a good red carafe wine is preferable to " cooking " port or " port style " wine) and the rind of lemon and orange.
6. Blend the mustard, ginger and cayenne with the juice of the orange and juice of $\frac{1}{2}$ lemon.
7. Add to the jelly and wine—allow to infuse for 5 mins.
8. Taste carefully and correct the seasoning. Serve hot unstrained or cold strained.

CURRY SAUCE

2 onions	1 tbs chutney
2 cooking apples	1 tbs moist brown sugar
2–3 ozs butter or lard	juice of 1 lemon
2 level tbs curry powder	1 oz sultanas or raisins
$\frac{1}{2}$ pt stock	$\frac{1}{2}$ teasp salt
1 tbs gooseberry jam	

Method

1. Slice the onions and heat the fat.
2. Fry the onion in the hot fat until cooked but not brown. Keep the lid on the pan (about 15 mins).
3. Add the curry powder and fry until the fat covers the powder.
4. Add the coarsely chopped peeled apple and fry until the apple is tender.
5. Add the stock and all other ingredients and simmer for 20 mins.
6. Use as it is or strain.

MARINADES

1. *For white meat or fish*

¼ pt olive oil	⅛ pt white wine or dry cider
1 teasp white wine vinegar or lemon juice	1 crushed clove garlic or 1 finely chopped shallot
1 teasp chopped parsley	⅛ teasp chopped tarragon
¼ teasp chopped thyme	¼ teasp salt. Black pepper

Mix together and baste the meat or fish, leaving it to soak for 1 hour.

2. *For dark meat and game*

Use a red wine and malt vinegar and vary the herbs, using rosemary, bay leaf, juniper berries or marjoram according to taste. Add black peppercorns. Vary by using brandy or sherry in place of the wine.

BARBECUE SAUCES

These sauces are used to baste the barbecue meat or poultry during the cooking.

The chops, steak or poussins are grilled until brown and then brushed with the sauce frequently as the cooking continues. The basting with sauce slows up the cooking process and when cooking over a barbecue pit serves instead of reducing the heat of the grill.

Simple Barbecue Sauce

½ pt tomato purée, either tinned or from sieved fresh tomatoes

⅛ pt vinegar	1 tbs Worcester sauce
2 ozs brown sugar	1 teasp chilli powder
1 teasp celery seed	1 pt water
Tabasco sauce to taste	

Simmer for 30 mins with the lid on the pan.

Meat Barbecue Sauce

3 tbs Worcester sauce	1 grated onion
3 tbs mushroom ketchup	⅛ teasp cayenne or
3 tbs A 1 sauce	Tabasco to taste
2 tbs olive oil	2 teasp brown sugar
salt to taste	1 tbs vinegar

Simmer for 15 mins with the lid on the pan.

Chicken Barbecue Sauce

½ pt dry white wine or cider	1 teasp salt
¼ pt olive oil	1 teasp paprika
1 grated onion	2 teasp chopped herbs
1 crushed clove garlic	

Simmer for 20 mins with the lid on the pan.

EGG FOUNDATION SAUCES

Hollandaise Sauce

2 egg yolks	few peppercorns
2 tbs vinegar or lemon juice	1 bay leaf
2 tbs water	2–4 ozs butter
seasoning	

Method

1. Put bay leaf, and peppercorns and liquid into a pan.
2. Heat until the liquid is reduced to half its volume; cool slightly, then strain on to the egg yolks and whisk over a pan containing hot water until the mixture is pale, thick and frothy.
3. Add the softened butter gradually, whisking after each addition.
4. Serve with fish creams and soufflés, salmon, asparagus, etc.

See page 62 for an alternative method of making.

Mayonnaise

1 raw egg yolk	½ pt to ¼ pt salad oil
1 level teasp made mustard	1 tbs vinegar or lemon juice
salt and pepper	1 to 2 tbs cream if liked
1 teasp castor sugar	

Method

1. Put the egg yolk into a large pudding basin.
2. Mix into the egg yolk all the seasonings except vinegar.
3. Add the oil drop by drop, and with the right hand stir and rub rapidly, using a wooden spoon.
4. When the egg and oil have formed a smooth ball add the oil a little more quickly, about half a teaspoonful at a time.
5. When sufficient oil has been added, gradually add the measured quantity of vinegar and then the cream if liked.

Note This sauce will keep for one or two weeks. If it has to be kept for a longer period the basin containing the mayonnaise should be heated over boiling water for approximately five minutes. Whisk well during this process. Then store in a suitable bottle.

VARIATIONS OF MAYONNAISE

Name	Recipe	Method	Uses
Aspic Mayonnaise	¼ pint mayonnaise ½ pint aspic jelly	Melt the aspic jelly and leave to become cool; then add gradually to the mayonnaise, stirring well.	Use for coating pieces of cooked fish or meat required for chaudfroids and for certain salads.
Sauce Verte	¼ pint mayonnaise 1 teasp chopped parsley 1 ,, tarragon 1 ,, capers if liked 1 or 2 anchovies or a little anchovy essence 1 hard boiled egg Little green colouring	Mix all the ingredients except the sauce. Pound well in a mortar, if available, then rub through a sieve. Add these ingredients to the sauce and a little green colouring if necessary. Serve cold.	Serve with trout, salmon, fried fish etc.
Tartare Sauce (Cold)	¼ pint mayonnaise 1 teasp chopped gherkins 1 ,, capers 1 ,, parsley	Add the chopped gherkins, capers and parsley to the mayonnaise and serve cold.	Serve with fried fish.

Mousseline Sauce

3 yolks of egg	3 tbs cream
1 tbs lemon juice	¼ teasp salt
3 ozs butter	⅛ teasp white pepper

Method

1. Put the egg yolks into a basin with the seasonings and lemon juice.
2. Stand the basin in a pan of hot but not boiling water.
3. Add a nut of butter and whisk or stir continuously until the mixture thickens.
4. Remove from the heat and whisk in the butter gradually.
5. Return to the heat, check the seasoning, but do not allow the water round the basin to boil.
6. Whip the cream and fold into the sauce.
7. Serve immediately without re-heating.
8. This sauce is served *warm*.

A double saucepan can be used instead of a basin inside a pan of water.

Custard Sauce

1 whole egg	2 teasp castor sugar
1½ gills milk	little vanilla essence

Method

1. Beat the egg to mix the white and the yolk thoroughly.
2. Heat the milk almost to boiling point.
3. Pour on to the beaten egg gradually, stirring well. Strain, if possible into a double pan, cook very gently until the custard thickens slightly, and the egg tastes cooked.
4. Remove from the heat, add the sugar and vanilla essence and serve hot or cold.

An **economical custard sauce** can be made by adding a well-beaten egg to a simple sauce. The sauce must not boil after the egg is added.

PUREE SAUCES

Apple Sauce

1 lb cooking apples	strip of lemon rind
⅛ pt water	1 tbs sugar
½ oz butter	

Method

1. Peel, core and slice the apples.
2. Stew gently in the water.
3. When tender, add the sugar; rub through a sieve; add the butter; re-heat and serve.

Bread Sauce

½ pt milk	2 ozs freshly made breadcrumbs
1 small onion	1 oz butter
1 blade mace	1 tbs cream if available (or
6 white peppercorns	evaporated milk)
¼ teasp salt	

Method

1. Simmer the onion, mace and peppercorns in the milk for approximately half an hour.
2. Strain and add the breadcrumbs and salt.
3. Simmer gently until the consistency is similar to that of very thick cream.
4. Add the butter and a little cream.
5. Re-heat and serve.

Note A double pan, e.g. a porridge pan, is very useful when making this sauce.

Tomato Sauce

1 lb fresh tomatoes or	½ oz lean bacon or a few bacon
1 lb canned tomatoes	rinds and trimmings
1 pt second stock or the	pepper and salt
liquid from canned or bot-	1–2 teasp sugar
tled tomatoes	1 oz butter
1 onion	1 oz rice flour
½ carrot (small)	1 tbs vinegar if liked or lemon
	juice

Method

1. Heat the butter, cut up the bacon trimmings and fry lightly in the butter. Then add the sliced onion and carrot and fry these lightly without browning them.
2. Wash the tomatoes, cut into quarters and add to the pan; stir well, and allow to evaporate for a few minutes.
3. Add the rice flour, stirring well, then add the stock or tomato liquor, sugar, seasonings and a little vinegar if liked.
4. Allow to simmer for about half an hour.
5. Rub through a sieve, re-heat, test for flavour and if necessary add a little more sugar. Add lemon juice.

Note The exact amount of sugar varies according to the acidity of the tomatoes.

SYRUP OR JAM SAUCES

These sauces depend for their consistency on the evaporating of sugar and water to a syrup, or they may be thickened by using cornflour or arrowroot.

Jam or Marmalade Sauce
(Recipe 1)

1 tbs jam or marmalade	¼ pt water
1 tbs sugar	little lemon juice

Method

1. Put all ingredients into the pan.
2. Stir until the sugar is dissolved.
3. Boil all until thick and syrupy.
4. If necessary add a little suitable colouring before serving.

Jam Sauce
(Recipe 2)

2 tbs jam	¼ pt water
1 oz sugar	rind and juice ½ lemon
1 teasp cornflour	little red colouring

Method

1. Put the jam, lemon rind, sugar and water into the pan and heat until the sugar is dissolved, stirring well.   Allow to infuse for a few minutes.
2. Blend the cornflour with a little cold water; strain the contents of the pan, and add to the blended cornflour.
3. Return to the pan, bring to the boil and cook three or four minutes to cook the starch in the cornflour.
4. Add a few drops of red colouring before serving.

Lemon Sauce (or Orange Sauce)

2 lemons or 2 oranges	¼ pt water
2 tbs sugar	

Method

1. Put the sugar and water into the pan and stir until the sugar is dissolved.
2. Allow to boil briskly in the open pan.
3. Wash the fruit and peel the rind very thinly—cut into very fine strips and add to the sugar-and-water syrup.
4. Continue the heating until a thick syrup is obtained.
5. If too sweet and too thick, add a little strained fruit juice to the syrup.

CHOCOLATE SAUCE

2 oz block chocolate (plain or " bitter ")
¼ pt syrup made from 2 ozs sugar and ¼ pt water
½ teasp instant coffee
1 teasp vanilla essence or 1 teasp brandy or 1 teasp rum
1–2 tbs cream if liked

Method

1. Dissolve the sugar in the water and bring to the boil.   Skim.
2. Add the coffee powder and the broken or grated chocolate.
3. When the chocolate is thoroughly melted, bring to the boil.
4. Simmer for five minutes.
5. Stir in the essence or spirits and cream if used.
6. Serve hot or cold.

BUTTERSCOTCH SAUCE

4 ozs brown sugar	2 ozs butter
3 ozs golden syrup	1½ gills evaporated milk
3 tbs water	

Method

1. Boil the sugar, water and syrup together.
2. Add the butter in small pieces.   Beat well.
3. Pour the mixture over the evaporated milk and stir till blended.
4. Stir occasionally as it cools if to be served *cold*.
5. Re-heat in a double boiler if to be served *hot*.

UNCOOKED SAUCES

Horseradish Sauce

2 tbs grated horseradish	¼ pt cream or evaporated
1 tbs vinegar	milk *or*
1 teasp sugar	⅛ pt evaporated milk and
a little mustard	⅛ pt cream

Method

1. Scrub and scrape off the peel from the horseradish, then grate it finely.
2. Half whip the cream and/or the evaporated milk.
3. Stir in the vinegar, seasonings and horseradish.
4. Serve with roast beef or fried chicken.

Mint Sauce

Fresh mint leaves well washed (sufficient to give approx $\frac{1}{4}$ pt mint)

1 tbs sugar

Vinegar and/or lemon juice as below.

Method

1. Chop thoroughly the washed mint leaves until very fine.
2. Add the sugar, vinegar and lemon juice to taste. The consistency should be thick.
3. If necessary dissolve the sugar in a little boiling water before mixing it with the mint and vinegar.

WHAT WENT WRONG—AND WHY

The sauce is lumpy

(*a*) Fat was too hot when the flour was added. Starch grains do not absorb the fat evenly. If the fat is overheated it would partially cook some of the starch grains and an uneven texture would result after the addition of the liquid.

(*b*) Failure to mix the liquid and roux smoothly. This must be done away from the heat to prevent overheating of the roux and uneven cooking.

(*c*) Failure to stir continuously while the sauce was coming up to boiling point.

(*d*) Over-evaporation during cooking after boiling up. To prevent this, cook in a double saucepan or a Bain Marie or cover with a wet paper to prevent evaporation.

(*e*) Too rapid reheating of a cold sauce or insufficient stirring while the sauce was being reheated. Such a sauce requires rapid whisking to prevent the formation of lumps.

There is a raw flavour

(*a*) The roux was insufficiently cooked. The heat should be great enough to cook the starch and so absorb the fat. If the starch is not thoroughly cooked during the making of the roux and the boiling up with the liquid, the characteristic flavour of the particular sauce is smothered by the raw taste of the flour.

(*b*) Uneven or too quick cooking of a brown roux. Burnt flour will give a raw or bitter taste to a sauce.

(*c*) The use of canned tomatoes in place of fresh. The addition of a pinch of bicarbonate of soda will counteract this acidity. Sugar also is necessary.

A white sauce lacks gloss

Insufficient cooking after the liquid had been added. The starch must cook sufficiently in order to give a gloss. Overcooking would give a burnt flavour (see next note).

A sauce becomes thin during cooking process

The sauce was cooked for too long and this caused a chemical change in the flour i.e. dextrin was formed. Dextrin is soluble and therefore the consistency thinned.

A sauce is greasy

(a) In a white sauce: Too much fat was used in the roux or the fat was not hot enough for it to be absorbed by the flour.
(b) In a brown sauce:

(i) The roux was overcooked. This caused over-dextrinisa-tion of the starch in which state the flour and fat separated.
(ii) Failure to skim during cooking. Some fat always rises to the surface during the prolonged cooking of a brown sauce.

The colour is unattractive

(a) In a white sauce: overheating of the fat and flour in the roux.
(b) In a brown sauce:

(i) Uneven cooking of the roux. Too rapid cooking causes black specks.
(ii) Stock of poor quality used for a high class sauce.

A custard curdles

Overheating the mixture of liquid and egg. When heat is applied the albumen sets and holds in it a certain amount of liquid. Over-heating, however, causes the albumen to harden and to shrink and in so doing the liquid is set free. The result is a thin watery sauce surrounding " curds " of egg albumen i.e. a curdled custard.

To check curdling

Strain the curdled custard immediately into a cool basin and whisk it well. This breaks up the albumen into minute particles before it has become solid.

A mayonnaise curdles

This is caused by adding oil too quickly to the eggs. When oil is added slowly it gradually forms a film round the egg and holds it in suspension.　If, however, the oil is added too quickly the film of oil breaks and the egg is set free, resulting in a curdled sauce.

To remedy a curdled mayonnaise

Add the curdled mayonnaise drop by drop to another yolk and whisk well—using a mechanical rotary whisk, if available.

＊　　　＊　　　＊　　　＊

For sauces to serve with pasta, see p. 234.

CHAPTER VIII

FISH

THE oceans and inland waters of all countries contain vast resources of fish in quantity and variety; edible and inedible. Some authorities forecast that with the increase of world population and the inadequacy of the supply of the meat of land animals, it will be necessary to use more food from the rivers and seas.

Fish is sold fresh, dried, smoked, salted, pickled or cured. It is usually classified as:

Fresh water fish
Salt water fish
Shell-fish (more correctly grouped as crustaceans and molluscs).

Fish is also often referred to as:

(a) fish with white flesh e.g. cod, haddock, hake, whiting, bream, Dover sole, megrim sole, plaice etc.
(b) fish with dark or oily flesh e.g. herring, mackerel, salmon.

Fish with white flesh have most of the fat stored in the liver. The fish flesh is lacking in flavour but is very easily digested; hence its use in feeding young children, invalids and old people.

Fish with dark flesh have a much fuller flavour because the fat is distributed throughout the body; such fish, however, are usually more difficult to digest than white fish and are therefore unsuitable for invalids.

Fish known as " Shell " fish are difficult to digest; oysters, frequently eaten raw, are an exception (see also page 97).

It is necessary to boil other shellfish as soon as possible after they come out of the water; hence they are usually sold cooked.

BUYING FRESH FISH

It is essential that fish should be used when absolutely *fresh* because it goes bad very quickly. When buying fish observe the following points :—

1. When fresh all fish is free from a strong smell.
2. The gills should be red.

3. The eyes should be bright.
4. The flesh should be firm and the tail stiff; a flabby tail is a sure indication that the fish is stale.
    If there is any doubt about the freshness of the fish it is advisable to plunge a skewer into the thickest part, when decay will be shown by a strong smell.
5. Fish packed in ice should be used as soon as possible after its removal from the ice, because it decays rapidly.

TO PREPARE FISH FOR COOKING

To scale fish

Lay the fish on a piece of strong paper; hold the fish by the tail; remove the scales by scraping with the back of a knife working from tail to head.   Then wash, preferably under running water, to remove any loose scales.

To clean round fish e.g. herring, trout, mackerel etc.

Using the point of a sharp knife, split the belly from the throat to about one third the length of the body of the fish, taking care to avoid cutting into the internal organs.   Using two fingers remove the internal organs; retain the roe, and burn the remainder of the organs immediately.   Wash the belly cavity with cold water.   Rub off any black skin inside the cavity.   If liked, the fish head may be removed.

To clean flat fish e.g. plaice, sole, flounder, megrim sole etc.

The belly in these is just under the head.   Remove the gills and cut a small opening in the belly; remove the gut on to a piece of paper, wash the fish well.   Burn the refuse.   If liked, the head may be removed by using the point of a sharp knife following the outline of the head.

To fillet a fish

1. Using a sharp knife, slit the fish down the backbone from head to tail.
2. Place the fish with the head away from the worker and the fillet to be removed at the left-hand side.
3. Using a sharp knife, separate the flesh from the bone by passing the knife between the two with a sharp sweep.
4. Lift the separated flesh with the left hand.
5. To remove the second fillet, turn the fish round so that the tail is now away from the worker and the fillet to be removed again at the left hand side.

6. Continue as before.
7. Turn the fish over and repeat the process until the four fillets have been removed.

To skin a fish

(A) *Before filleting*

A sole is usually skinned before filleting because the skin is thin and could not be taken cleanly from the fillets.

1. Cut a slit across the tail on the dark side of the fish.
2. Work the skin up with a knife or by using the thumb until a piece is raised large enough to hold in the fingers.
3. Dip the thumb and fingers in salt to prevent slipping and loosen the skin from the tail to the head by running the thumb between the skin and the flesh.
4. Draw the skin across to the centre of the fish on both left and right fillets.
5. Take hold of the skin at the tail end and quickly draw it towards the head.
6. Repeat this process for removing the white skin if required.

(B) *After filleting*

1. Place the fillet skin side downwards on a board with the tail end towards the worker.
2. Loosen a piece of skin at the tail end.
3. Dip the first two fingers of the left hand in salt and hold the skin of the fillet down to the board. Using a sharp knife in the right hand scrape the fillet away from the skin holding the knife at an angle of 45 degrees, sharp side to the skin.

Use fish bones and skin for making fish stock (see page 46).

To bone herrings

1. Slit, clean, and wash the herring (see page 78).
2. Turn over, placing the fish underside downwards on a board covered with paper. Press well with the thumb or a knife handle the whole way along the backbone to loosen it.
3. Turn over the fish, loosen the bone at the tail end, and using the thumb and forefinger prise up the backbone, working from tail to head. Pull the bone firmly away from the flesh; the small bones come away easily with the main bone.
4. Rinse the fish thoroughly and dry well on a clean cloth.

TO POACH FISH

This is considered a suitable method for cooking large fish which have a good natural flavour e.g. salmon. During the boiling of fish flavour is lost; therefore, it is not a good method of cooking most fish. Steaming is a more conservative method, and is therefor preferable, in order to retain nutrients.

Method

1. Clean and weigh the fish.
2. Boil sufficient water just to cover the fish (quantity varies according to the thickness of the fish in question). To improve the flavour of the fish when cooked, add the following to each quart of water:—

1 tbs vinegar or lemon juice	1 onion
3 or 4 peppercorns	a bouquet garni (see page 462)
1 carrot	salt

3. Tie the fish loosely in a piece of muslin and immerse in the boiling water. Cover the pan and immediately reduce the rate of cooking to simmering. Simmer gently for the time required.

    Simmering time

    Thick fish—Allow 10 mins for 2 lbs fish; 15 mins for 4 lbs.
    If thin fish is poached, allow only 7 mins for 2 lbs; 10 mins for 3 lbs.

4. Drain thoroughly and serve with parsley, shrimp or anchovy sauce (see chapter on sauces).

TO STEAM FISH

Method 1

1. Prepare a steamer over a pan of boiling water.
2. Sprinkle the fish with salt; wrap in foil.
3. Allow the water under the steamer to boil and the steam to circulate freely round the packet of fish.
4. Cook until the flesh leaves the bones easily. The time will depend on the thickness of the fish; therefore test it at the thickest part. If the fish is very thick and large, turn it once during cooking.

Method 2

Put a deep pie dish or casserole into the pan of boiling water, allowing the water to come nearly to the top of the dish. Lay the fish in the pie dish, cover with foil and allow the water to boil freely round the pie dish.

This is suitable for steaks and pieces of salmon.

Method 3 (especially suitable for fillets).

1. Put the prepared fillets or other small pieces of fish into a well-greased soup plate.
2. Sprinkle with salt.
3. Dot with margarine.
4. Place over a pan of boiling water or over potatoes in process of boiling.
5. Cover with aluminium foil, or with the saucepan lid. Leave from ten to fifteen minutes, i.e. until the flakes of the fish show signs of separating, and a white creamy liquid begins to run from the fish.
6. Drain thoroughly and serve with a suitable sauce.

Time for steaming varies greatly with the thickness of the fish, but it takes longer than boiling. It is usual to allow ten minutes to the pound and ten minutes over. Drain thoroughly before serving.

TO BAKE FISH

Baked fish is usually more popular than either steamed or poached fish, as very little, if any, flavour is lost during the baking. It is a suitable method of cooking the fish whole or cut in slices or filleted. The fish may be stuffed, if desired, before baking.

Baked Fish (plain)

1. Prepare and cut the fish in neat pieces.
2. Season well. Place each piece in a greased baking tin or fire-proof dish, put a small piece of margarine or butter on the top of each.
3. Cover with a greased paper and bake in the centre of a moderate oven (350° F), allowing approximately 10 minutes to each lb and 10 minutes over for whole fish, 20 minutes for steaks about 1″ thick and 10 minutes for fillets.

When sufficiently cooked drain well and serve with a suitable sauce (see chapter on sauces).

Baked Stuffed Fish

1 lb middle cut cod, hake, fresh haddock etc.
or 2 whole soles or plaice
2 ozs fresh breadcrumbs
2 teasp finely chopped parsley
¼ teasp finely grated lemon rind
¼ teasp mixed herbs or 1 oz picked shrimps
½ teasp salt
¼ teasp pepper
1 tbs melted butter
little beaten egg to bind the ingredients
1 to 2 tbs fresh dripping
1 to 2 tbs brown crumbs

Method

1. Prepare the fish according to kind. If haddock or whiting is used the fish is left whole. Scale and clean the fish and leave on its head and tail.
2. Mix the forcemeat until it sticks together when pressed with the fingertips; stuff the inside well but avoid packing the fish too tightly or it will burst, as the forcemeat swells during cooking.
3. Sew up the fish, using coarse thread, and place it in the baking tin containing the hot dripping.
4. Baste the fish with hot dripping and dredge it with brown crumbs.
5. Bake in the middle of a moderately hot oven (350° F). Allow approximately ten minutes per lb + five minutes. For a piece weighing 1 lb or less it is usually necessary to allow 20 minutes.
6. When cooked remove the thread, serve on a hot dish, garnish with lemon and parsley. Serve with a suitable sauce e.g. anchovy or tomato (see pages 60, 71).

Cuts or slices of fish may be boned, covered with stuffing and treated as above.

When soles or plaice are used prepare them as follows:—

1. Skin the sole on both sides, cut off the head, tail and fins; wash and dry the fish. Leave the skin on a plaice.
2. Cut down the centre of the white side, one inch from the head and tail. Raise the flesh from the bones but do not remove it.
3. Insert the stuffing under the fillets, previously raised from the bone, leaving the centre open and the stuffing slightly raised.
4. Brush over the fish with a little beaten egg and milk and sprinkle over this the brown crumbs.
5. Have ready the hot dripping in a shallow baking tin or a fire-proof dish and place the prepared fish in it.
6. Bake from 20 to 30 minutes in the centre of an oven set at 350° F. Drain well, serve on a hot dish, garnish with lemon and parsley.

To Bake Salmon

Choose a middle cut of salmon, preferably 2–2½ lbs in weight.

Wrap in well-buttered foil: twist the edges securely. Stand on a baking sheet and cook at 300° F, for 1 hour.

If to be served hot, slide the fish from the opened foil on to a hot dish and pour the juices round.

If to be served cold, leave in the foil until quite cold; then open carefully.

Salmon steaks can be similarly cooked. Wrap each steak separately and cook for 20 minutes.

TO FRY FISH

Fish may be fried in deep or shallow fat. See chapter on Frying.

Fried Whole Flat Fish or Steaks of Cod, Hake, Halibut etc.

2 flat fish or 4 steaks of fish	1 to 2 ozs clean white dripping
1 tbs seasoned flour	lemon and parsley for garnish
egg and breadcrumbs	

Method

1. Clean, trim, wash and dry the fish (according to the kind).
2. Draw the fish through seasoned flour.
3. Coat with egg and breadcrumbs.
4. Have ready smoking hot fat; fry the fish on both sides until a golden brown. Reduce the heat and continue cooking until the flakes begin to separate.
5. Drain thoroughly on kitchen paper.
6. Serve on a hot dish; garnish with pats of Maître d'Hôtel butter (see p. 65) or pieces of neatly cut lemon.

Fried Fish, Filleted

1 lb fish after filleting	2 tbs parsley leaves (for frying)
1 teasp flour	½ lemon
½ teasp salt; dash of pepper	egg and breadcrumbs

Method

1. Wipe and dry the fish fillets on a clean cloth.
2. Coat with seasoned flour and then with egg and breadcrumbs (see chapter on frying).
3. When the fat has a faint haze rising from it, put the fillets into the basket and lower gently into the fat. Fry until a light golden brown.
4. Drain thoroughly on soft paper; keep hot.
5. See that the fat is hot again before putting into it the remaining fillets. Fry until the same shade of golden brown as the other fillets. Drain well.
6. Serve with pieces of lemon and fried parsley (see page 85).

TO GRILL FISH

1. Heat the grill and grease the grid or the grill rack with melted butter or oil.
2. Clean and trim the fish; sprinkle with seasoning and brush all white fish with clarified butter or oil. It is unnecessary to brush over oily fish such as herring, salmon etc.
3. Place on the grill rack; grill for 2 mins on both sides with the grill on full. Then reduce the heat to about $\frac{1}{2}$ strength and continue until the flesh leaves the bones easily when tested with a skewer.
4. Have ready a suitable sauce e.g. Tartare or parsley butter, and serve with the fish immediately after grilling it.
5. Garnish with parsley or water-cress.

Small whole fish require to be cut across in deep gashes to allow the intense heat from the grill to penetrate to the interior of the fish before the outside of the fish becomes dry from the heat.

Grilled Herring or Mackerel

Allow one fish per person, follow the instructions given for grilled fish and serve with grilled tomatoes or mustard sauce or lemon juice.

Herrings Fried in Salt

Allow one fish per person. Follow the instructions for cleaning the fish, remove the head and leave whole.

Method

1. Heat enough salt in a *thick* frying pan to cover the bottom of the pan.
2. When the salt is very hot, but not brown, lay the fish on the hot salt.
3. Fry for 5 minutes on each side or until brown and crisp. Serve at once.

Soused Herrings

4 herrings	$\frac{1}{4}$ teasp salt
1 blade mace	$\frac{1}{8}$ pt water
10 peppercorns	$\frac{1}{4}$ pt vinegar

Method

1. Wash and clean the fish. Bone.
2. Roll up the fish, beginning at the tail end.

3. Pack the fish into a fireproof dish deep enough to hold the fish without its touching the lid.
4. Sprinkle with spices and pour over the vinegar and water.
5. Put the lid on the dish or cover with greased paper.
6. Bake in the centre of a moderate oven 300° F for 45 minutes.
7. Serve cold with salad.

To Fry Parsley

1. Wash the parsley and remove the stalks; dry the leaves thoroughly in a clean cloth.
2. After the food to be garnished has been fried remove the pan of fat from the source of heat and leave it to cool slightly for two or three minutes. Remove the frying basket.
3. Put the parsley into the fat for approximately two minutes i.e. until no hissing can be heard.
4. Remove the parsley with a draining spoon and drain on soft kitchen paper. Use immediately.

Fried parsley should be crisp and a good green colour. If the fat is too hot when the parsley is put into it, the parsley becomes olive green and too dark. If the fat is too cool, the parsley becomes greasy and limp instead of crisp.

Additional Fish Dishes
Sole Colbert
(sufficient for 2 persons)

1 sole	1 tbs fried parsley
½ oz Maître d'Hôtel butter (see p. 65)	egg and breadcrumbs

Method
1. Clean, trim and skin the sole.
2. Cut through the flesh on the under side from head to tail.
3. Roll back the fillets, exposing the bone.
4. Cut through the bone at the head and the tail so that it can be removed after cooking.
5. Dry the sole on a clean fish cloth.
6. Brush with egg and coat with breadcrumbs.
7. Fry whole in deep fat until a good golden brown colour, about 7–10 minutes.
8. Drain well, remove the bone carefully.
9. Fill up the hollow between the two fillets with pats of Maître d'Hôtel butter.
10. Garnish with pieces of cut lemon and fried parsley.

Fish Meunière

2 medium sized flat fish (soles, megrim soles or plaice) or 1 lb white
    fish cut into neat steaks
1 tbs seasoned flour
4 to 6 oz clarified butter or margarine
4 teasps lemon juice

Garnish

slices of finely cut lemon
2 tablespoonfuls finely chopped parsley

Method

1. Clean, trim, skin and dry the fish, if whole; or trim the steaks,
   clean, wipe and dry them.
2. Toss the prepared fish in seasoned flour.
3. Heat half the quantity of clarified butter or margarine in a
   shallow frying pan and fry the fish until it is a good golden
   brown colour on both sides and well cooked (7–10 minutes).
4. Remove the fish on to a hot dish.
5. Add the remaining clarified butter to that which is left in the
   pan after frying the fish, and heat it until a golden brown
   colour. Add the lemon juice to the hot butter and pour it
   round the fish.
6. Garnish with slices of lemon and finely chopped parsley. A
   few chopped capers may be sprinkled over the fish as an
   additional garnish.

Fish au gratin

2 medium sized flat fish or 1½ lbs cod, hake, haddock, bream, or
    halibut, cut into neat fillets of even thickness
1 teasp lemon juice   little cayenne
¼ teasp salt   2 to 3 tbs fish stock

Dressing

1 teasp finely chopped onion
2 teasp finely chopped parsley
3 teasp finely chopped mushrooms
2 tbs browned breadcrumbs
1 oz butter

Method

1. Use a gratin dish or a shallow fireproof dish just large enough
   to allow the fish to lie flat. This fish should be sent to the
   table in the dish in which it is cooked.

2. Prepare the fish according to its kind, remove the skin from the whole fish.
3. Grease the dish with half of the butter.
4. Mix together the ingredients for the dressing and sprinkle half of this mixture on the bottom of the greased dish.
5. Season the fish with salt, pepper and lemon juice and lay it on the dressing.
6. Sprinkle the remainder of the dressing over the fish and scatter brown crumbs over it. Then distribute the remainder of the butter over the surface, adding it in small pieces.
7. Pour the stock round the fish and bake in a moderately hot oven for approximately 20 to 30 minutes.

Fish Flan

3 ozs rich short crust pastry (see page 389)

Filling

¾ lb smoked haddock baked in milk
½ pt white sauce using the liquid in which the haddock is cooked
1 oz grated cheese
1 egg yolk
cayenne and a little salt

Method

1. Make a flan case and bake blind (for method see p. 266).
2. Make the white sauce; add to it the flaked fish and other ingredients; pour into the flan case.
3. Put back into the oven (375° F) and leave from ten to fifteen minutes to brown. Serve hot.

Fish Maître d'Hôtel

1 lb fillets of any white fish
1 teasp salt
¼ teasp pepper

2 teasps lemon juice
¼ pt Maître d'Hôtel sauce (see page 61)

Method

1. Skin the fillets, cut to an even thickness and wipe with a clean cloth.
2. Season each fillet with salt, pepper and lemon juice.
3. Fold each fillet in two with the skinned or cut side inside.
4. Place in a shallow tin or fireproof dish; add the fish stock and cover with a piece of greased paper.
5. Bake in the middle of an oven set at 350° F. Bake from 15 to 20 minutes, according to the thickness of the fish. When sufficiently cooked the flakes will separate.

6. Drain each fillet well; dish overlapping on a hot meat dish and coat with Maître d'Hôtel sauce.
   Use fish stock for making the sauce (see chapter on stock).

Fish Fillets with Smoked Haddock (Merluche Fumée)

1 lb fish fillets (any white fish)	⅛ pt fish stock or milk
salt, pepper, lemon juice	seasoning
1½ gills fish stock	¾ pt Hollandaise sauce (see pp.
4 ozs cooked smoked haddock	62, 68)
½ oz butter	egg and breadcrumbs
½ oz flour	

Method

1. Make a thick binding sauce (a panada) with the butter, flour and fish stock or milk (see p. 59). Add to this the finely chopped cooked smoked haddock and season the mixture well. Cool.
2. Trim the fillets; divide ⅔ of the haddock mixture into the same number of portions as there are fillets. Place one portion on each fillet and fold in two enclosing the haddock mixture.
3. Place each of these on a greased tin; add the stock; cover with greased paper and bake in the middle of a moderate oven about 15 minutes (temperature 350° F).
4. Whilst the fish is cooking form the remainder of the haddock mixture into small balls; coat with egg and breadcrumbs and fry in deep fat. Drain and keep hot.
5. When the fillets are cooked, drain well; dish them overlapping on a hot dish.
6. Coat with Hollandaise sauce and garnish with fried haddock balls.

Fish Muscat

1 lb fillets of any white fish	salt and pepper
3 tbs chutney	egg and breadcrumbs
1½ ozs muscatel raisins	2 to 3 tbs parsley leaves for fry-
½ oz chopped almonds	ing (see page 85)
2 teasp lemon juice	

Method

1. Trim and wipe the fish fillets.
2. Season each fillet with salt, pepper and lemon juice.
3. Spread a little chutney on each fillet.
4. Sprinkle over the chutney a mixture of finely chopped almonds and muscatel raisins previously stoned and chopped.

5. Roll up each fillet neatly.   Coat with egg and breadcrumbs and fry in deep fat until a good golden brown colour.   Drain thoroughly.
6. Arrange in a circle with fried parsley in the centre.
7. Serve with a suitable fish sauce.

Fish Niçoise

1 lb fillets of any white fish	1 teasp lemon juice
½ teasp salt	1½ gills fish stock
⅛ teasp pepper	

Filling

Trimmings from the fish fillets	½ beaten egg
2 tbs white sauce	seasoning, salt and cayenne pepper

Coating

¾ pt tomato sauce (see page 71)

Garnish

2 tbs strips of gherkin or pickled cucumber
1 tbs strips hard boiled egg white
1 teasp chopped truffle or cooked mushroom

Method

1. Trim the fillets neatly and season each fillet.
2. Chop the trimmings and mix with the sauce, beaten egg and seasonings.
3. Divide the above mixture into the same number of portions as there are fillets and spread a portion on each.
4. Fold neatly and put into a greased fireproof dish or shallow tin.   Add a little hot fish stock, cover with a greased paper and bake in the middle of an oven at 350° F for about 20 minutes.
5. Whilst the fish is cooking, cut the gherkins and egg white into thin strips.   Heat the strips in a little hot fish stock in a basin standing in boiling water.
6. When the fish is tender drain it well.
7. Place the fillets neatly on a hot dish; coat with tomato sauce; decorate with chopped truffle or mushroom.
8. Garnish with strips of gherkin and egg white.

Fish Portugaise

1 lb fish fillets (any white fish)	3 or 4 medium sized tomatoes
salt, pepper, lemon juice	2 tbs finely grated cheese
1 medium sized onion	2 tbs brown breadcrumbs

Method

1. Trim neatly and wipe the fillets; season each with salt, pepper and lemon juice.
2. Peel onion and cut in very thin slices; skin and slice the tomatoes.
3. Arrange the fillets neatly in a shallow fireproof dish; arrange the onion and tomatoes neatly on the fish.
4. Mix together the cheese and brown crumbs and sprinkle over the fish.
5. Bake in the middle of an oven set at 350° F for approximately 30 minutes.
    Serve in the same dish.

Fish Rouennaise (lobster filling)

Recipe as for fish fillets with smoked haddock, using fresh or canned lobster instead of smoked haddock and Cardinal sauce (see page 60) instead of Hollandaise sauce.

Fish Soufflé

1 oz butter	3 eggs
1 oz flour	$\frac{1}{8}$ pt cream or evaporated milk
$\frac{1}{4}$ pt fish stock and/or milk	$\frac{1}{2}$ teasp salt
$\frac{1}{2}$ lb raw white fish e.g. haddock,	$\frac{1}{8}$ teasp pepper
whiting or cod	$\frac{1}{2}$ teasp lemon juice

Coating

$\frac{1}{2}$ pt coating sauce (see Sauces, page 59) made with fish stock and milk.

Method

1. Have ready a steamer and a suitable mould for the soufflé.
2. Grease the mould and dust with rice flour.
3. Wipe the fish and scrape it free from the bone.
4. Make a thick sauce (panada) of the butter, flour and liquid.
5. Add the finely shredded fish to the sauce; season well; add the two whole eggs and one yolk; mix thoroughly and rub through a wire sieve. Stir in the cream.
6. Whisk the egg white very stiffly and fold into the mixture, pour into the prepared mould and cover with a greased paper.
7. Steam very gently until firm to the touch (about 40 mins.).
8. Turn out and coat with the white coating sauce.
9. Decorate with a little coralline pepper.

Fish Tartare

1 lb fillets of any white fish	1 or 2 teasp lemon juice
½ teasp salt	1½ gills fish stock
⅛ teasp pepper	¾ pt hot Tartare sauce (page 62)

Method

1. Trim, wipe and season the fillets.
2. Cook as for fish Maître d'Hôtel (page 87).
3. Drain the fillets well and coat with hot Tartare sauce.

Fish Timbale

1 lb cooked potato	1 egg
1½ oz butter or margarine	salt and pepper

Filling

½ lb any cooked fish	1 hard boiled egg
½ pt white sauce	2 tomatoes
1 teaspoonful anchovy essence, pepper and salt to taste	

Method

1. Sieve the potatoes whilst hot.
2. Add the butter, beaten egg and seasoning; heat all together, beating well. Turn on to a floured board and roll into a roll about 2 inches thick.
3. Place on a greased baking tray, join the two ends and form into a round or oval shape three or four inches high.
4. Brush with beaten egg and bake near the top of an oven set at 400° F for 20 minutes. Leave until a good golden brown.
5. Add the flaked fish to the sauce; add seasonings etc.
6. Wash the tomatoes, cut into quarters and place on a greased tin and heat in the oven for 20 minutes.
7. When the potato border is brown lift it on to a hot dish; fill with the fish filling.
8. Garnish with neatly cut hard-boiled egg and pieces of tomato.

Salmon Mayonnaise

¾ lb salmon	lettuce, cucumber, small cress
¼ gill mayonnaise	2 small tomatoes
½ gill aspic jelly (page 292)	

Method

1. Cook the salmon carefully; when cooked remove the skin and bone and press, wrapped in greaseproof paper, between plates until cold.

2. Divide into 4 portions.
3. Warm the aspic jelly until it liquefies; then mix it with the mayonnaise and strain it through muslin.
4. Stir (on ice if available) until it begins to show signs of setting. When it is thick enough to coat the back of a spoon use it to coat the pieces of salmon.
5. When set, decorate the portions with neatly cut pieces of cucumber and tomato skin and fennel or chervil leaves, and coat again with a thin coating of liquid aspic jelly.
6. When set arrange on a suitable dish and garnish with lettuce, crimped cucumber, tomatoes and cress.

Canned salmon may be used instead of fresh salmon or halibut may be used for Halibut Mayonnaise.

Simple Fish Salad

½ lb cooked white fish or any canned fish
1 lettuce
1 or 2 tomatoes
4 or 5 slices pickled beetroot

2 gherkins
2 teaspoonfuls capers
⅛ pt mayonnaise or other suitable dressing

Garnish—a few radishes and a piece of cucumber

Method

1. Wash thoroughly, rinse and dry the lettuce leaves.
2. Shred the coarse leaves; chop the gherkins and capers, dice the beetroot and tomatoes.
3. Remove skin and bone from the fish and divide into fairly large flakes; add to the above mixture.
4. Add sufficient mayonnaise to mix until the ingredients just cling together. Season the mixture well.
5. Rinse individual fish moulds or small basins with cold water and pack the mixture lightly into them.
6. Press lightly; turn out on to a suitable dish and garnish with small lettuce leaves, trimmed radishes and thinly cut crimped cucumber.

If desired a little cooked lobster, crab or a few chopped shrimps may be added to improve the flavour of the mixture.

Fish Véronique

1 lb fillets of any white fish
1½ gills fish stock
4 tbs white wine
2 teasp lemon juice

½ lb white grapes
4 very thin slices lemon
¾ pt Mornay sauce (page 62)

Method

1. Trim, wipe and season each fillet.
2. Fold neatly and place in a greased tin; add the fish stock, white wine and lemon juice.
3. Cover with a greased paper and bake in the middle of an oven set at 350° F for twenty minutes.
4. Wash, peel and remove the pips from the grapes; remove the rind and skin from the lemon slices and cut each into fine shreds.
5. Heat the prepared grapes and shreds of lemon in a small quantity of butter and keep hot.
6. Drain the fillets and keep hot.
7. Coat with Mornay sauce.
8. Garnish with the grapes and lemon shreds.

SHELL-FISH

CRABS

The best season for crabs is May to September, but they are available all the year round.   They are generally bought boiled from the fishmongers, but if taken from the sea must be killed and boiled.

Choose a crab which feels heavy and is solid when shaken; a watery sound indicates a stale crab.   The shell must be clean looking and the crab fresh smelling.   Choose the medium sized crab; avoid those which are less than 4–5 inches across the shell and those more than 7 inches across.   The small ones yield very little meat and the large ones tend to be coarse in texture.

A crab of 6 inches across the shell, weighing about 2½–3 lbs, will serve 3 people.

Dressed Crab (2–3 persons)

1 medium-sized crab, boiled	⅛ teasp pepper
2 tbs fresh white breadcrumbs	1 or 2 tbs salad oil (or cream if
1 tbs vinegar	preferred)
½ teasp salt	

Garnish

1 hard-boiled egg	Finely chopped parsley

Method

1. Rinse the crab under running water.
2. Remove the claws, crack the shells and remove the white meat. Use the point of a skewer if necessary to remove the flesh from the tips of the small claws.

3. Separate the body from the shell; remove and burn the bag near the mouth and the small feathery gills, as some of these are poisonous.
4. Remove any creamy meat from inside the shell and the body of the crab, using a teaspoon. Chop the meat well and mix it with the meat from the claws.
5. Add the breadcrumbs to the chopped crab meat; add the vinegar, oil and seasonings.
6. Wash the shell thoroughly, dry it, trim it with scissors if necessary and polish it with a very little olive oil.
7. Fill the shell with the prepared crab mixture.
8. Chop the egg white very finely, sieve the egg yolk; chop the parsley very finely.
9. Decorate the crab by arranging the egg white, egg yolk and chopped parsley in sections.
10. Finally, garnish with the small claws previously washed, dried and trimmed.

LOBSTERS

A live lobster has a dark mottled green shell and, if female, greenish-black coral or spawn. Both shell and spawn become bright red on boiling. The female or " hen " is considered more of a delicacy than the male, but the flesh of the male stays firmer when cooked. The best size is one weighing about $1\frac{3}{4}$–$2\frac{1}{4}$ lbs and will give two servings in the traditional lobster specialities or about 12 ozs meat.

A properly cooked lobster feels heavy in proportion to its size and the tail is curled under the body. When pulled out the tail should roll back into place.

To Prepare a Lobster

All the meat of a lobster is edible with the exception of the spinal cord, a thin black vein which runs through the middle of the under-side of the tail meat, and the stomach which is a hard sack or bag in the right side of the head.

1. Twist off the claws, keep the small ones for garnish.
2. Lay the lobster on its back and cut lengthways from head to tail along the division of the shell. Use a pair of scissors or a sharp knife.
3. Remove the cord in the tail and the bag in the head and discard. Remove the coral, wash and lay aside for decoration or for flavouring sauce or butter.
4. Take care not to break the antennæ as the head shell forms the focal point of the decoration of a lobster dish.
5. Remove the meat from the shell of the body and tail. Crack

the pincer claws with a hammer or nutcracker and pick out the meat. Keep the pieces as large as possible. Include the green meat or liver as this is one of the choicest parts.

Lobster Salad

Method

1. Polish the shell and antennæ with a little oil.
2. Pack the lobster flesh back into the shells and arrange shining side uppermost on a bed of lettuce and watercress.
3. Stand the head in a " rearing " position and decorate the dish with the small claws and the black pincer ends of the large claws.
4. Garnish with cucumber and, if liked, tomato and hard-boiled egg.
5. Serve with mayonnaise dressing.

Lobster Salad 2

Method

1. Arrange a bed of lettuce on a flat dish.
2. Heap the lobster meat, cut in neat dice, in the centre.
3. Coat with mayonnaise.
4. Garnish with small claws, sliced cucumber and sieved hard boiled egg.

Lobster Newburg (A traditional American dish)

$\frac{3}{4}$ lb lobster meat diced $\frac{3}{8}$ pt cream
2 ozs butter $\frac{1}{2}$ teasp paprika pepper
3 egg yolks $\frac{1}{3}$ teasp nutmeg
$\frac{1}{4}$ pt sherry (*not* " cooking " sherry) or Madeira
2 slices hot buttered toast cut into 4 pieces

Method

1. Melt the butter in a double saucepan.
2. Add the lobster meat and heat without colouring for 4–5 mins.
3. Add the paprika and nutmeg and keep hot.
4. Beat the egg yolks and cream. Add to the lobster and stir until the mixture thickens.
5. Add the wine and season with salt to taste.
6. Serve on the 4 pieces of hot buttered toast.

PRAWNS

Several kinds of shell-fish go under this name, many people using the term for large shrimps and also for the Dublin Bay Prawn which is from the same family as the Italian Scampo and the French Langoustine.

Most of the prawns sold in England are imported from Norway, and like shrimps they are cooked on board the trawlers and exported either fresh or frozen or tinned. Fresh prawns can be bought picked or in shell. They should smell fresh and faintly salty and have crisp shells well curled and be a good colour.

Dublin Bay Prawns are caught in the Irish Sea and off the coast of Scotland, and are shelled, de-veined and frozen raw. The fleshy tail only is used.

Dublin Bay Prawns or Langoustines

Allow 4–5 per person

16–20 prawns	2 lemons
fritter batter (see page 192).	deep fat for frying

Brown bread and butter cut thin or split toast (see page 409)

Method

1. Allow to thaw slowly first.
2. Dry the prawns with muslin; dust with flour.
3. Dip in fritter batter.
4. Drop into deep fat from which a faint haze rises.
5. Cook until pale brown (about 3 mins).
6. Drain on absorbent paper.
7. Pile on a hot dish, decorate with quarters of lemon.
8. Serve with brown bread and butter or split toast.

Curried Prawns

$\frac{1}{2}$ lb prawns or 12 Dublin prawns

2–4 ozs rice boiled, strained and kept hot (see page 418).

2 ozs butter	$\frac{1}{2}$ pt vegetable stock
4 ozs shallot	1 tbs (approx) lemon juice
$\frac{1}{2}$ oz curry powder	2 tbs cream or infusion of
1 teasp curry paste	coconut
1 clove garlic (if liked)	$\frac{1}{2}$ teasp salt
6 ozs tomatoes	

Method

1. Melt the butter and add the finely chopped garlic and shallot. Fry until cooked but not coloured.
2. Add the curry powder and paste. Cook for 2–3 mins.
3. Add sliced skinned tomatoes, vegetable stock, lemon juice and salt.
4. Cook for 30 mins, very slowly with the lid on the pan.
5. Test the seasoning, add the prawns and the cream or nut

liquor and heat thoroughly. Take care not to overcook the prawns or they will break up and spoil both in appearance and flavour.

6. Serve with rice, garnish with chopped fennel and strips of lemon rind.

OYSTERS

Oysters are usually eaten raw as hors d'œuvres. It is usual to allow three per person.

1 doz oysters	paprika pepper
lemon juice	little mustard and cress

Garnish

Thinly cut brown bread and butter.
Neatly cut pieces of lemon.

Method

1. Scour the oyster shells. Insert an oyster knife and open each oyster; be careful to keep all the liquid.
2. Remove the hard gristle part (known as the beard) from each oyster and keep the soft cushion part.
3. Put two or three prepared oysters into one shell.
4. Add a little lemon juice to the oyster liquid and pour some of this liquid over the oysters in each shell. Sprinkle a little paprika pepper on each.
5. Serve the shells on an entrée dish covered with a folded napkin.
6. Roll the thinly cut brown bread and butter and serve on a separate dish with neatly cut lemon.

SCALLOPS

Scallops are in season from November to March. They are generally opened and cleaned by the fishmonger, and should be sold with the deep shell in which, if liked, they can be served. If they come unopened, warm with gentle heat until the shell opens, remove the scallop, trim off the beard and black parts. Retain the roe which looks like an orange tongue. Wash well and drain.

Fried Scallops

6 scallops
½ gill white wine or dry cider⎫ or ¾ gill fish stock
1 gill water   ⎭
Seasoned flour, egg and breadcrumbs, or fritter batter to coat.

D

Accompaniments

Thin brown bread and butter, quarters of lemon.

Method

1. Poach the fillets in the fluid.   Use enough liquid barely to cover the fish.
2. Drain and dry in a cloth.
3. Coat with seasoned flour, shake well.
4. Coat with egg and breadcrumbs or fritter batter.
5. Fry in deep fat till golden brown (350° F for 3–4 mins).
6. Drain and serve hot with bread and butter and lemon.

A sauce made with the poaching liquid and ½ oz butter and ½ oz flour, may be served as an additional accompaniment.

Scallops and Mushrooms

6 scallops	4 ozs mushrooms
½ gill white wine or dry cider	1 oz flour
1 gill water	1 oz butter
salt and pepper to taste	½ gill cream or top of milk
sprig of parsley	piece of bay leaf the size of a sixpence
6 peppercorns	1 shallot

Garnish

Browned crumbs
Melted butter
Parsley and lemon

Method

1. Poach the cleaned scallops in the water and wine with the seasoning and flavourings.   Cook for 5 mins.
2. Drain the scallops and cut each into 3 or 4 pieces.
3. Melt the butter in a saucepan, add the shallot chopped finely and the mushrooms sliced.
4. Cook until the shallot is clear but not brown.
5. Stir in the flour and make a coating sauce with ½ pint of the liquor from the fish.
6. When cooked, season carefully and add the cream, taking care not to make the sauce too thin.
7. Add the scallops, reheat but do not reboil.
8. Divide between the shells.   Cover with browned crumbs.
9. Sprinkle with melted butter and brown under the grill.
10. Serve garnished with parsley and lemon.

SHRIMPS

Shrimps are in season all the year round, but are at their best in summer and autumn. There are two kinds on sale in Britain—the pink shrimp which looks like a small prawn, and the brown shrimp which is a pinkish brown speckled with darker brown. Both kinds are sold ready cooked.

" Potted " shrimps are picked, lightly spiced and packed in melted butter. The brown shrimp is used for this dish which is generally sold quick frozen.

Shrimp Creole

1 oz butter
½ oz flour
1 green pepper sliced
1 medium onion chopped
1 stick celery chopped
1 small tin tomatoes
1 teasp salt
⅛ teasp pepper
1 teasp soft brown sugar

½ bay leaf
2 cloves
8 peppercorns
a few drops of Worcester and Tabasco sauce (according to taste)
1 teasp lemon juice
2 tbs white wine or dry cider

½ lb picked shrimps or prawns
¼ lb rice cooked as for curry (see page 418)

Method

1. Sweat the vegetables (except the tomatoes) in the butter until tender, about 15 mins.
2. Stir in the flour and blend thoroughly.
3. Add the tomatoes and liquor, salt, pepper, cloves, bay leaf and sugar.
4. Simmer for 45 mins, add the shrimps and cook for 5 mins.
5. Flavour with Worcester and Tabasco sauce, lemon juice and wine or cider. Check the flavour, which should be hot, sweet and sharp. Correct if necessary.
6. Serve with the hot rice.

CHAPTER IX

MEAT

MEAT is one of the principal body-building foods, and as such takes an important place in planning a well-balanced diet. Choice cuts of meat are very expensive, and it is therefore necessary for the housewife to recognise meat of good quality and to know which cut to buy for satisfactory results which are also economical.

The parts of the animal which do the least muscular work produce the prime cuts. The meat should have a fine grain and be lightly marbled with fat and firm to the touch.

Those parts which do the heavy muscular work have a coarse grain, and gristle fibres may be interspersed. The fat is separated from the meat by a thin tissue.

The quality of the meat varies with the individual animal and is determined by the age and the method of rearing. The fact that the cut is a prime one does not necessarily mean that the meat is of first quality. The only sure guide for the housewife in selecting first quality meat is the fineness of the grain.

Coarser cuts of meat are equal in food value to prime cuts but need long slow cooking by moist methods to make them tender. They are less expensive to buy and produce dishes which are equally appetising and full of flavour.

Beef. The lean is dark red in colour and the fat firm and yellow.
Mutton and lamb. The lean is a lighter colour than beef and the fat is hard and white.
Pork. The lean is pale with a pink tinge and the fat is soft and white.
Veal. The lean is very pale in colour and there is little or no fat. The meat often has bubbles of air enclosed in a thin skin where meat from an older animal would have fat.

Freshly killed meat is tough and should be hung to allow the fibres to become tender owing to the development of lactic acid. The length of time for this process varies according to the animal, and a reliable butcher will offer for sale only meat which has been hung for the right length of time.

Do you know the cuts of Beef?

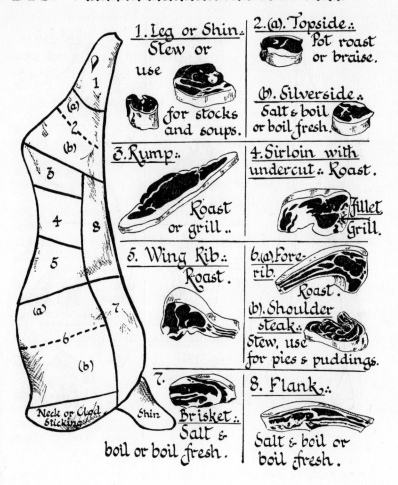

1. Leg or Shin. Stew or use for stocks and soups.

2. (a). Topside. Pot roast or braise.

(b). Silverside. Salt & boil or boil fresh.

3. Rump. Roast or grill.

4. Sirloin with undercut. Roast. Fillet Grill.

5. Wing Rib. Roast.

6. (a) Fore-rib. Roast.

(b). Shoulder steak. Stew, use for pies & puddings.

7. Brisket. Salt & boil or boil fresh.

8. Flank. Salt & boil or boil fresh.

Neck or Clod Sticking. Shin.

Do you know the cuts of Mutton and Lamb?

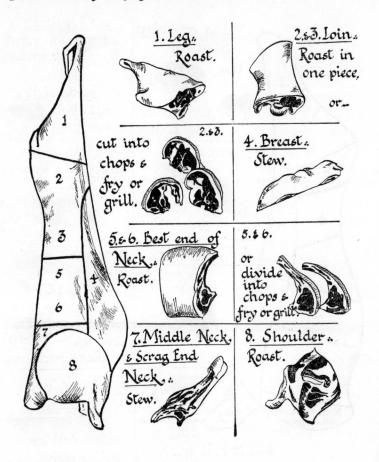

1. Leg.. Roast.

2.&3. Loin.. Roast in one piece, or..

cut into chops & fry or grill.

2.&3.

4. Breast.. Stew.

5.&6. Best end of Neck.. Roast.

5.&6. or divide into chops & fry or grill.

7. Middle Neck, & Scrag End Neck.. Stew.

8. Shoulder.. Roast.

DO YOU KNOW THE CUTS OF PORK?

1. Head.
Salt, boil and make into brawn.

2. & 3. Spare Rib and Blade.
Roast or cut into chops & grill or fry.

4. Hand.
Salt and boil.

5. Loin with Kidney.
Roast or cut into chops & fry or grill.

6. Belly.
Salt and boil or roast (slow method).

7. Leg.
Roast or salt & boil.

8. Foot.
Salt and boil. Use with head for making brawn.

Beef	Mutton and Lamb	Pork	Veal
		Prime Cuts	
Fillet		Fillet or tenderloin	Fillet
Sirloin	Loin	Loin	Loin
Ribs	Best end of neck	Spare rib	
Rump steak	Leg	Leg	Leg
Round			
Topside	Shoulder	Shoulder	
		Medium Cuts	
Shoulder steak	Middle neck	Hand or foreleg	Best end of neck
Silverside	Breast	Belly	
Thick flank			
Aitch-bone			
		Coarser Cuts	
Brisket	Scrag end of neck		Breast
Thin flank			
Neck			Neck
Shin			Knuckle
Clod			
Tail			

The method of cooking meat depends upon the quality and cut. Prime cuts of first quality may be roasted, fried or grilled. Prime cuts of second quality are better pot-roasted or braised but may be roasted slowly. Medium cuts may be pot-roasted, braised or boiled. Coarse cuts should be stewed or boiled.

See also page 135 for cooking of ham and bacon joints.

ROASTING

Roasting is a method of cooking by radiated heat. Correctly used, the term implies hanging the joint on a spit in front of a bright fire, but this method of cooking has been superseded by cooking in a tin in an oven. The tin may be covered or uncovered, and unless the food is very fat, dripping or butter is used to prevent its becoming dry and hard. Some cookers now have electrically rotated spits.

The aim in roasting is to make the meat tender and yet retain the full flavour in the joint. A brown crisp outside looks and tastes appetising and is essential to a good roast.

Methods of Roasting

(a) The meat is seared or browned for 10–15 minutes in a hot oven (450° F) and the cooking finished more slowly (325°–350° F), for the remaining time. This method is suitable for small and medium joints of first quality prime cuts.

(b) The cooking takes place at a moderate even temperature

(350° F) for the whole time. This method is suitable for large joints of first quality prime cuts which are over 5 lbs in weight and where the longer cooking time required would make a seared outside rather thick and hard.

(c) The meat is pot-roasted, that is, cooked in a heavy saucepan with a tightly fitting lid. This method, as for roasting in a solid fuel oven, has no ventilation, and therefore steam from the meat is retained in the pan and the meat does not dry. It is therefore particularly suitable for small pieces of meat and for joints suitable for roasting but not of first quality.

Roasting in a pressure cooker is a form of pot-roasting, but owing to the increase of temperature due to the pressure, the time required for cooking is much less. (See chapter on Pressure Cooking.)

To use a meat thermometer, insert it before cooking into the thickest part of the joint, not touching bone or fat. Cook until the thermometer registers the required temperature. The thermometer reading often rises quite rapidly at the end and therefore careful watch must be kept towards the end of the calculated time.

If a joint is allowed to stand for 10–15 mins before carving, it cuts economically.

Times allowed for roasting

Meat	Minutes per pound	Oven temp. after searing	Meat thermometer reading
Beef . . .	15 mins per lb + 15 mins	350° F	140° F (Rare) 160° F (Medium)
Lamb and Mutton	25 mins per lb + 25 mins	325° F	175° F
Pork . . .	30 mins per lb + 30 mins	350° F	185° F
Veal . . .	30 mins per lb + 30 mins	325° F	175° F

Joints of less than 3 lbs in weight or less than 3 inches in depth cook more quickly than the average type of joint.

Preparation of Meat for Roasting

1. Trim off excess fat, remove any large pieces of gristle if on the outside of the meat.
   In the case of a loin of mutton, remove the skin.
   Remove the spinal cord from the rib or loin.
2. Weigh the joint and calculate the time required for cooking.

3. Wipe with a damp cloth and if necessary tie or skewer to keep a good shape.　If there is any suspicion of taint, wash in vinegar and water using 1 tbs vinegar to 1 pint water.
4. If chilled or frozen meat is used, time must be allowed for complete thawing.　This takes approximately 2 hrs per lb if frozen hard.　Much of the thawing will probably have been done by the butcher.
5. Dust with flour, salt and pepper.
6. Place the joint in the tin or pan and spread generously with dripping, or cooking fat if no dripping is available.　Put on the lid of the roasting tin if used.

Cooking

1. Place in the centre of a preheated oven.
2. If a covered roasting tin is used, basting is not necessary, but if the joint is uncovered or pot-roasted, the meat should be basted every 20–30 mins.
3. The meat should be turned over, using 2 metal spoons, half way through the cooking.
4. Transfer the meat from the tin to a hot flat dish large enough to allow for carving.　Keep hot.

To make Gravy

Pour off the fat from the tin very slowly so that all the sediment and meat juices are retained.

For **clear gravy,** add a sprinkling of salt and a dash of pepper to the sediment, mix well: continue stirring until the sediment is dark brown.　Add $\frac{1}{2}$–$\frac{3}{4}$ pint of hot stock, stir well and bring to the boil. Boil rapidly until the flavour is good.　Skim well.

For **thin gravy,** pour off as much fat as possible and add to the meat juices and sediment 1 teasp flour for every 1 pint of gravy required.

For **thickened gravy,** retain approximately 1 tbs dripping for every pint of gravy and stir in 1 level tbs flour.

Blend the flour and fat together and add the stock gradually (water in which vegetables have been cooked is suitable stock).

Bring to the boil, season and taste.

If not dark enough in colour add a few drops of gravy browning.

Continue boiling rapidly for a few minutes to allow any surplus fat and scum to rise to the surface.　Skim off fat and scum and if necessary remove the last traces of fat by passing a piece of kitchen paper across the surface.　The dull absorbent surface of the kitchen paper acts like blotting paper and absorbs the fat.

Serve in a hot gravy boat.

Joint	Accompaniments	Suitable Vegetables
Beef .	Clear or thin dark gravy, Yorkshire pudding. Horseradish sauce. Roast parsnips.	Baked or boiled potatoes. All vegetables.
Lamb .	Medium brown thickened gravy. Mint sauce.	New potatoes. Peas, french or runner beans.
Mutton .	Medium brown thickened gravy. Onion sauce. Redcurrant or other sharp-flavoured jelly, e.g. Crabapple, cranberry, damson or gooseberry, mint or rowan. Forcemeat stuffing if liked.	Baked or boiled potatoes. All vegetables.
Pork .	Dark brown thin gravy if the stuffing is served separately. Dark brown, thickened gravy if the joint is stuffed. Sage and onion stuffing. Apple sauce.	Cabbage, cauliflower, celery, onions, spinach or sprouts. Boiled potatoes.
Veal .	Medium brown thickened gravy. Veal forcemeat stuffing. Lemon. Bacon rolls.	Green vegetables, onions, tomatoes. Baked or boiled potatoes.

GRILLING

Grilling is a second method of cooking by radiated heat. The food is more closely in contact with the source of heat than when roasting. The heat is very strong, and the grill on the gas and electric cookers should be heated to a bright red glow before cooking is begun.

Cuts suitable for Grilling and times to allow for cooking

Food	Time
Bacon rashers . .	3–5 mins according to thickness
Gammon or Ham rashers	5–10 mins according to thickness
Kidneys (sheep's or pig's)	6–10 mins according to size
Liver	8–15 mins according to thickness
Mutton or Lamb Chops .	10–15 mins according to thickness
Mutton or Lamb Cutlets .	7–10 mins according to thickness
Pork Chops . . .	15–20 mins according to thickness
Sausages . . .	15–20 mins according to thickness and variety
Steak—Fillet . . .	7–12 mins according to thickness of the steak and individual taste. A "rare" steak requires 3–4 mins on either side. This ensures adequate cooking and still leaves the centre red and juicy
Steak—Rump . .	10–15 mins according to thickness and individual taste as to rareness or thorough cooking

Preparation of meat for Grilling

Steak

1. The meat must be of first quality and must be cut across the grain and should be at least $\frac{1}{2}$ inch thick.   If the piece does not fulfil these requirements it *should not be grilled.*
2. The fat on a rump steak should be left on.
3. Beat the meat on both sides.   This should be done on a board, using a rolling pin or a special beating tool called a cutlet bat. Press the meat back into shape and skewer if necessary.
4. Rub lightly with salt and brush with clarified fat or oil.   Allow the steak to stand for 15–20 mins before cooking to allow the salt to penetrate the fibres.

Chops and Cutlets

1. Remove the spinal cord and the outer skin.
2. Trim off excess fat and skewer if necessary.
3. If the chop is a convenient shape, beat as for a steak.
4. Rub with salt, brush with fat and allow to stand 15–20 mins before cooking.

Kidneys

Only kidneys from a sheep or a pig are suitable for grilling.

1. Remove the fat, peel off the skin and remove the core, using a pair of pointed scissors.
2. Split the kidney in half without separating the halves.
3. Soak in salted water (1 teasp salt to 1 pint water) for 15–20 mins to clean thoroughly.
4. Dry well and brush with clarified fat or oil.

Liver

1. Wash thoroughly and remove the skin and larger pipes, using a pair of sharp scissors to cut out the pipes.
2. Dry well and brush with clarified fat or oil.

Preparation of the grill on gas and electric cookers

1. Heat the grill until it glows bright red, put the grill pan underneath for a few moments to heat the rack thoroughly.
2. Brush the rack with clarified fat or oil.
3. Put 1 tbs water in the bottom of the grill pan to prevent burning of the dripping.

Cooking

1. Put the prepared meat on to the greased grill rack and leave the meat under the grill until it changes colour and begins to brown.
2. Turn carefully, using grilling tongs or two wooden spoons or a palette knife and a wooden spoon.   On no account should a sharp or pointed knife or a fork be used for turning the meat, as juices are lost whenever the meat is pierced.
3. Brown lightly on the second side.
4. Reduce the heat and continue cooking for the remainder of the time allowed.
5. Turn at least once more during the cooking.

The finished steak or chop should appear puffy and be elastic to the touch.

Dishing

Transfer on to a hot dish and serve at once with suitable accompaniments:—

Kidneys	Serve on croûtes of fried bread with a pat of maître d'hôtel butter on each kidney.
	Garnish with grilled tomato or fresh watercress.
	They are often served as part of a mixed grill.
Liver	Serve with grilled bacon and tomato. Garnish with parsley or watercress.
Mutton and Lamb Chops, Cutlets	Maître d'hôtel butter, game chips, tomatoes, mushrooms and watercress.
Pork Chops	Hot pineapple slices or apple sauce. Deep fried onion rings (see vegetable cookery).
Sausages	Mashed potatoes, brown thickened gravy, apple or bread sauce.
Steak	Maître d'hôtel butter, game chips, tomatoes, mushrooms, watercress and Worcester sauce.

FRYING

Cuts of meat suitable for frying are the same as those for grilling. Identical preparation is necessary. For times of cooking and method see chapter on Frying.   For preparation of more elaborate dishes using fried meat, see section on entrées.

BRAISING

Braising is a method of cooking combining stewing and roasting. It is a method particularly suitable for second quality prime cuts and middle cuts, the grain of which is too coarse for the dry methods of cooking.

The meat is cooked until tender on a bed of vegetables, bacon and herbs (mirepoix), in a heavy saucepan with a tightly fitting lid and the process completed by browning in a hot oven with the lid off the pan.

Preparation of the Mirepoix

1 medium carrot, an equal amount of onion	$\frac{1}{2}$ rasher of bacon
	bouquet garni
1 piece swede, half the size of the carrot	1 oz dripping
	1 level teasp salt
1 piece of celery approximately equal to the swede	Sufficient stock just to cover the vegetables

Method

1. Prepare the vegetables according to their kind and cut in thick slices.
2. Heat the dripping and fry the bacon until cooked but not brown.
3. Add the vegetables and sauter in the open pan for about 10 mins, when they should be lightly browned and all the fat absorbed.
4. Cover with hot stock, add the seasoning and bring to the boil.

Preparation of meat for braising

1. Trim the meat, wipe with a damp cloth and weigh.
2. If the meat is lean either lard or bard the surface.

   To lard Cut strips of fat bacon 2″ × $\frac{1}{4}$″ × $\frac{1}{4}$″. Push a strip of bacon into the open-pronged end of a larding needle. Make a $\frac{1}{2}$″–1″ " stitch " into the meat, pull the needle through, leaving the two ends of bacon sticking out. The " stitches " should be 2″ apart.

   To bard Tie thin strips of fat bacon over the surface of the meat.

3. Place the meat on the mirepoix, cover with greaseproof paper put on the lid and simmer.

   The time is calculated in the same way as for roasting; rather more than $\frac{2}{3}$ of the total time is required for the simmering or stewing process and the remainder for the roasting process.

4. When the simmering process is complete, remove the lid and the greaseproof paper and put the whole pan into the middle of a hot oven (425° F).

5. Roast in this way for the remainder of the cooking time, by which time the meat will have become brown and fairly crisp.

Dishing

1. Transfer the meat on to a hot dish and keep warm.
2. Strain the liquor from the mirepoix into a small pan and bring to the boil.
3. Skim off any excess fat.
4. Correct the seasoning and, if necessary, add enough gravy browning to make the sauce a rich chestnut colour.
5. Reduce the liquor until it is of a syrupy consistency and pour over the meat.

Accompaniments to serve with a braise

Neat blocks or balls of carrot and swede cooked separately.

If desired, the mirepoix may be served as an accompanying vegetable.

A braise may be enriched by the addition of wine. Dark meat, e.g. beef, rabbit and game, should have red wine.

Light meat, e.g. veal and poultry, should have white wine. Cider can be substituted for wine.

The wine should be added to the mirepoix immediately before the braise is transferred to the oven, or it can be added to the strained stock before it is reduced to a syrupy consistency.

BOILING

Boiling is a method of cooking by moist heat. The meat is covered or almost covered with liquid and the cooking is done in a covered saucepan. After the initial cooking, which varies with the type of meat, the liquid should simmer; that is, bubbles should rise to the surface and break at the sides of the pan only.

The joints suitable are :—

Beef : Topside, Silverside, Thick flank, Brisket, Ox Tongue.
Mutton : Leg, Middle neck.
Pork : Belly (pickled).

Times to allow for Boiling

As for roasting if fresh meat is used. If salt or pickled, add 5 mins per lb to the cooking time.

Preparation of Meat for Boiling

A. *Fresh*

1. Trim off excess fat, remove any spinal cord.
2. Weigh the joint and calculate the time for cooking.
3. Wipe with a damp cloth and if necessary tie or skewer securely to ensure a good shape.
4. If chilled or frozen meat is used, time must be allowed for complete thawing.

B. *Salt or Pickled*

1. Soak overnight in cold water to remove excess salt or pickle.
2. Continue as for fresh meat.

Cooking

A. *Fresh*

1. Put sufficient water into the pan to cover the joint, bring to the boil.
2. Add 1 teasp salt for every lb meat, one onion and a bouquet garni.
3. Put in the prepared meat and allow the liquid to boil rapidly for 3–5 mins. This seals the cut tissue, thus retaining in the joint as much as possible of the flavour and the nutrients.
4. After 5 mins, reduce the heat and allow to simmer for the appropriate length of time.
5. 1–1½ hours before the completion of the cooking, add large pieces of root vegetables.
   Suitable vegetables are: carrot, swede, onion, celery and leek. Care should be taken in the proportion of swede and celery used, as these vegetables have a strong flavour and would dominate the flavour of the liquor if used too freely.
6. If dumplings are to be served, drop them into the liquor 20 mins before serving.

B. *Salt*

1. Put the prepared joint into a pan and cover with cold water.
2. Bring slowly to the boil, and then pour off the liquor.
3. Cover again with cold water, bring to the boil, and then continue as for fresh meat, adding dumplings 20 mins before serving.

Dumplings

For 4 persons

4 oz flour | 1 level teasp baking powder
1½ oz suet | 4 tbs cold water
½ level teasp salt

Method

1. Prepare as for suet pastry (see page 385).
2. Divide the mixture into 8 portions.
3. Knead each portion into a ball.
4. Drop into fast-boiling liquor and boil for 2–3 mins, reduce the heat and simmer for a further 15–18 mins.

Note When adding dumplings to boiled meat, it is important that the liquor should be boiling fast when the dumplings are dropped into it. This means raising the heat during this period of cooking.

Dishing—Fresh and Salt Meat

A. *To serve hot*

1. Remove the meat from the liquor, drain thoroughly and place on a hot dish large enough to allow for the accompaniments and for ease in carving.
2. Place the dumplings and pieces of vegetable round the joint.
3. Additional vegetables may be served in a separate dish either in pieces or mashed together.
4. Strain some of the liquid into a gravy boat and serve with the joint. This liquor is not coloured or thickened.
5. If the joint is mutton, caper sauce (see page 60) should be served either in a separate sauce boat or poured over the joint to coat it.

B. *To serve cold*

1. Remove the pan from the heat and allow the joint to cool in the liquor.
2. When almost cold, remove the joint from the liquor, wrap in a cloth or greaseproof paper and press between two flat surfaces under a weight.

ADDITIONAL RECIPES
Ox Tongue

Preparation

If not pickled by the butcher, wash carefully, remove any discoloured root and soak 10–14 days in a wet pickle, turning daily.

Cooking

As for salt meat.

Dishing

(a) *To serve hot*

As for fresh meat.   It is necessary to remove the bones and skin before serving.

Glaze if liked with a meat glaze.   Garnish with diced vegetables. Serve a thickened gravy made from the liquor in which the tongue was cooked.

(b) *To serve cold*

1. Allow the tongue to cool in the liquor.
2. When almost cold, remove the bones carefully, skin the tongue.
3. Roll, beginning at the root end.
4. Pack into a greased cake tin or meat press.
5. Add enough liquor to moisten the meat.
6. Cover with greaseproof paper.   Put on a saucer or plate small enough just to fit inside the tin.
7. Press under a heavy weight overnight.
8. Turn out carefully and glaze if liked.
9. Serve garnished with greenstuff and white of egg cut into fancy shapes.

STEWING

Stewing is a method of cooking by moist heat in a limited amount of liquid.   It implies long slow cooking in a pan or casserole with a tight-fitting lid.   In this method of cooking, flavour and nutrients are extracted into the liquid, and therefore it is important that the amount of liquid used should not exceed the amount which can conveniently be served.   Provided that the lid fits tightly there is little evaporation, and therefore little risk of burning if the food is cooked slowly.   Long slow cooking in liquid makes it possible to produce appetising and attractive dishes from the cheaper, coarser cuts of meat.   Medium cuts are preferred for the richer stews.

	Medium Cuts	*Coarser Cuts*
Beef	Shoulder steak, thick flank.	Neck, shin, clod, thin flank.
Mutton	Middle neck.	Scrag end of neck.
Pork	Hand or foreleg.	Belly can be used if it is not considered too fat.
Veal	Best end of neck.	Breast, neck and knuckle.

Times to allow for cooking

Beef and Pork   Medium cuts 2–2½ hours.   Coarser cuts 3–4 hours.

Mutton ⎫
Veal   ⎬   1½–2 hours for all cuts.

Classification of Stews

1. Simple stews, where the vegetables cooked with the meat are served as part of the dish.
2. Richer stews, where the flavouring vegetables are strained off and the liquid made into a sauce.   Fresh vegetables are separately cooked for garnish.

Simple Stews

Preparation of meat

1. Wipe the meat, remove pieces of solid fat, spinal cord and gristle.
2. Cut into pieces of convenient size.   Mutton is cut according to the jointing of the bone and is left on the bone.

Beef and **veal** are cut in pieces the size of a large walnut, except for shin of beef which is cut to about half this size.

Brown Stew

¾ lb shin, neck or clod of beef	1 teasp salt
1 medium onion	¾ oz seasoned flour
1 large carrot	¾ pt stock or water
1 small piece swede or celery	Gravy browning

Garnish   Chopped parsley

Method

1. Prepare the meat and toss in seasoned flour.
2. Prepare the vegetables and cut into neat pieces.
3. Put into the pan in alternate layers of meat and vegetables.
4. Cover with stock or water, add the salt.
5. Put the lid on the pan and bring slowly to the boil.
6. Reduce the heat and simmer gently for 2–3 hours.
7. When the meat is tender, taste and season as necessary.   Add enough gravy browning to give a rich dark brown colour.

Dishing

1. Lift the meat out of the liquid with a perforated spoon.
2. Pile on a hot dish deep enough to hold the gravy and vegetables.
3. Pour the gravy and vegetables round the meat.
4. Garnish with parsley.

Fresh Meat Mince

¾ lb minced beef (shin, neck or clod)
1 medium onion
1 oz dripping

2 teasp salt
¾ oz medium oatmeal
½ pt stock or water
Gravy browning

Garnish

Sippets of toast
Baked tomatoes cut in half

Parsley

Method

1. Chop the onion finely and add to the minced meat.
2. Heat the dripping to hazing point.
3. Fry the meat and the onion until all the fat is absorbed.
4. Stir almost continuously to prevent the meat from clogging into lumps.
5. Cover with hot stock, season and bring to the boil.
6. Sprinkle in the oatmeal while the liquid is boiling.
7. Reduce the heat and simmer for 1 hour.

Dishing

1. Pour on to a hot dish.
2. Decorate the edge with sippets of toast.
3. Place halves of grilled or baked tomatoes down the centre of the dish.
4. Garnish with parsley.

Haricot Mutton

1 lb middle neck of mutton
1 oz dripping
1 oz flour
1 medium carrot
1 medium onion

1 small piece turnip
2 teasp salt
⅛ teasp pepper
2 oz haricot beans
¾ pt stock

Garnish

Parsley

Variations in flavour

(a) Add 2 sliced tomatoes.
(b) Use 1 dessertsp coralline pepper in place of ⅛ teasp pepper.
(c) Garnish with chopped savory or tarragon in place of parsley.

Method

1. Soak the beans overnight.   Cook in salted water until tender.
2. Prepare the meat and the vegetables and cut into neat pieces.
3. Heat the fat to hazing point.

4. Fry the meat until light brown.   Remove from the fat.
5. Fry the onion carefully to avoid burning.
6. Return the meat to the pan, add the other vegetables.
7. Cover with hot stock, season and bring to the boil.
8. Reduce the heat and simmer for 1½ hours.
9. Blend the flour with a little cold water, add to the stew, stirring well.
10. Continue cooking for a further 10 mins.
11. Taste, and if necessary correct seasoning and colour.

Dishing

As for a brown stew.

Hot Pot

1 lb neck of mutton or beef	⅛ teasp pepper
2 medium onions	¾ pt stock or water
1 medium carrot	2 lbs potatoes
2 teasp salt	

Garnish

Parsley

Method

1. Prepare the meat and the vegetables.
2. Cut the onions and carrot in thin slices and the potatoes in thick slices (⅜″).
3. Put alternate layers of vegetables, meat and seasoning into a casserole.   Start and finish with a layer of vegetables.   The top layer should be potatoes only and should be neatly arranged.
4. Add sufficient stock to reach the bottom of the layer of potatoes.
5. Cover with the lid.
6. Cook in the centre of a moderate oven, 350° F, for 1½–2 hrs if mutton is used, 2½–3 hrs if beef is used.
7. About ¾ hr before the completion of the cooking, remove the casserole lid and allow the potatoes to brown.

Dishing

Serve in the dish in which it was cooked.

Irish Stew

1 lb neck of mutton	$\frac{1}{8}$ teasp pepper
2 medium onions	$\frac{3}{4}$ pt stock or water
2 teasp salt	2 lbs potatoes

Garnish Parsley

Method

1. Prepare the meat and vegetables.
2. Cut the onions into five rings and half the potatoes in thick slices, leaving the remainder in large pieces.
3. Put the meat and the sliced vegetables in alternate layers in a saucepan. Add the seasoning with the meat.
4. Just cover the meat with stock, put on the lid of the pan and bring to the boil.
5. Reduce the heat and simmer for 1 hr.
6. Add the pieces of potato, placing them so that they rest on the meat and sliced vegetables.
7. Continue cooking for $\frac{3}{4}$ hr or until the potatoes are soft but not broken down. The sliced potatoes will be a mash by the end of the cooking and so thicken the gravy.
8. Taste for seasoning.

Dishing

1. Remove the potato pieces and place round the edge of a hot dish.
2. Pile the meat in the centre of the dish.
3. Pour the gravy over the meat.
4. Garnish with parsley.

Sea Pie or Rabbit Casserole

1 rabbit cut up and blanched *or*	1 oz seasoned flour
$\frac{3}{4}$ lb neck or clod of beef	1 teasp salt
1 medium onion	$\frac{3}{4}$ pt stock or water
1 medium carrot	$\frac{1}{2}$ lb suet pastry or plain un-
1 small piece swede or celery	sweetened scone mix

Garnish Parsley

Method

1. Toss the cut-up meat or rabbit in the seasoned flour, continue as for a Hot Pot and put to cook $2\frac{1}{2}$ hrs.
2. Make the suet pastry (see page 385 or scone mix, p. 335). Roll out to fit the top of the casserole.
3. Remove the lid of the casserole, cover the meat with suet pastry or scone mixture.

4. Raise the oven temperature to 400° F and return the casserole to the top third of the oven.
5. Cook for 45 mins until the pastry is brown and well risen. A scone topping will take 20–30 mins.

Dishing

1. Sprinkle the pastry crust with chopped parsley.
2. Dish in the casserole.

Kidney

¾ lb ox or sheep's kidney	1 teasp salt
1 oz flour	⅛ teasp pepper
1 medium onion	¾ pt stock

Garnish

1 lb cooked sieved potato	2 tbs hot milk
1 oz butter	chopped parsley

Method

1. Remove the fat from the kidney.
2. Peel off the skin and remove the core.
3. Split the kidney in half without separating the halves.
4. Soak in salted water (1 teasp salt to 1 pt water) for 20 mins.
5. Dry and cut the ox kidney into neat pieces.
6. Toss in the seasoned flour.
7. Put in the pan with the chopped onion.
8. Cover with the stock and put on the lid.
9. Bring to the boil and simmer gently for 2–3 hrs.
10. When the kidney is tender correct the seasoning and colour.
11. Thicken with cornflour to a pouring consistency.

Dishing

1. Beat the butter and the hot milk into the hot mashed potatoes.
2. Arrange as a border round a hot dish.
3. Pour the kidney into the centre.
4. Sprinkle with chopped parsley.

Ox-tail

1 ox-tail	6 peppercorns
1 medium onion	2 teasp salt
1 medium carrot	1 pt stock or water
small piece swede	1 oz flour
1 blade mace	2–3 teasp ketchup

Method

1. Wipe the tail and cut into neat joints.

2. Blanch the joints.
3. Prepare the vegetables and put into a pan with the joints.
4. Add the mace and seasonings.
5. Cover with stock or water and bring to the boil.   Skim and cover the pan.
6. Reduce the heat and simmer 2–3 hrs.
7. Leave to cool overnight.
8. Remove any fat from the surface and bring to the boil.
9. Simmer for a further 2 hrs.
10. Blend the flour with a little water and add to the stew.   Boil for 3–5 mins.
11. Taste and correct the seasoning and colour.

Dishing   Finish as for a simple brown stew.

Richer Stews

A. White stews

Preparation of *meat*: as for simple stews.

Preparation of *rabbit*:

1. Wash thoroughly in salt water.
2. Cut out the tail using a pair of sharp scissors.
3. Cut into neat joints, removing the flap skin, kidney and head.
4. Cut off the shank bone from the leg.
5. Blanch (see page 26).

Fricassée of Veal or Rabbit

(to serve 6 portions)

1 lb fillet of veal or 1 rabbit
1 small onion
Stalks and skins from the mushrooms used in the garnish

Bouquet garni
2 strips lemon rind
1 pt stock

Sauce

2 oz margarine or butter
2 oz flour
½ pt liquid from the meat
½ pt milk

2 tbs cream or evaporated milk (if liked)
½ teasp lemon juice

Garnish

6 small mushrooms
6 bacon rolls
6 crescents of fried bread

parsley
6 butterflies of lemon

Method

1. Stew the meat and flavourings in the stock until tender, 1–1½ hrs.
2. Strain off ½ pt of liquor from the meat.   Keep the meat hot in the remaining liquor.
3. Make the sauce, flavour carefully and keep hot.
4. Remove the meat from the liquor and flavourings, add to the sauce.
5. Reheat but do not reboil.
6. Pour on to a deep dish, taking care that the meat is thoroughly coated with the sauce.
7. Arrange the cooked garnish on the meat.

Cheaper cuts of meat may be used but will need longer cooking.

Blanquette of Veal or Rabbit

Prepare as for a Fricassée with the addition of 2 egg yolks to the sauce.   Care must be taken not to overheat the sauce after the egg yolks have been added, to avoid curdling the eggs.

B. Brown Stews

The colour of the stew is obtained by the browning of the roux rather than the addition of gravy browning.   A fuller, richer flavour is obtained by browning the meat, vegetables and flour. It is because the meat is fried to produce the good flavour that the medium cuts are preferred.

Varieties of Brown Stew
Brown Stew (Rich)

¾ lb shoulder steak	small piece swede
1 oz dripping	2 teasp salt
¾ oz flour	⅛ teasp pepper
1 medium onion	¾ pt hot stock
1 medium carrot	

Garnish

Strips or dice of carrot and swede
Parsley

Preparation of Meat

1. Wipe and trim off large pieces of fat.
2. Cut into neat pieces.

Method

1. Chop the onion.
2. Prepare the root vegetables, shape into blocks and reserve the blocks for garnish.

3. Cut the trimmings into small pieces and use for flavouring.
4. Heat the dripping to hazing point, fry the meat lightly on both sides and remove from the pan. Fry, at one time, not more meat than covers the bottom of the pan.
5. Fry the onion until it begins to brown.
6. Add the flour and continue frying slowly until a rich brown colour is obtained. Stir this roux slowly with a metal spoon to prevent scorching.
7. Add the hot stock gradually, stirring all the time.
8. Season.
9. Bring to the boil, skim and add the meat and the flavouring vegetables, i.e. the trimmings from the garnish.
10. Simmer gently for 2–2½ hours or until the meat is tender.
11. Cut the prepared blocks of carrot and swede into strips or dice.
12. Cook in boiling salted water for 15 mins or until tender.
13. Strain and keep hot. The completion of the cooking of the garnish should coincide with the finish of the cooking of the stew.
14. When the cooking is complete, taste the sauce and correct the seasoning, colour and consistency, which should be that of a pouring sauce.

Dishing

1. Remove the meat from the sauce with a perforated spoon.
2. Pile on a hot dish.
3. Strain the sauce over the meat.
4. Arrange the garnish attractively at either end of the dish.
5. Sprinkle the vegetable garnish with finely chopped parsley.

Beef Stewed in Red Wine

1½ lbs shoulder or chuck steak	*Marinade*
3 ozs salt pork or streaky bacon	¼ pt red wine
	sprig of thyme and parsley
1½ tbs flour	2 tbs olive oil
1 pt stock	1 large onion sliced
1 oz dripping	2 teasp salt
	⅛ teasp pepper

Garnish

6 ozs small mushrooms
12–18 small round onions

Method

1. Cut the meat into strips ¼″ thick. Put into a deep dish.
2. Sprinkle with salt, pepper and herbs.

3. Pour over the wine and oil and cover with the sliced onion.
4. Leave for 3–6 hours to marinate.
5. When the meat is ready, melt the dripping and fry the bacon until the fat is clear. Remove and set aside.
6. Fry the small onions until brown and remove; set aside.
7. Drain the pieces of meat and brown quickly in the dripping.
8. Sprinkle the flour over the meat and allow it to absorb the fat.
9. Strain in the marinade.
10. Tie the herbs and garlic in muslin and add with the stock. Season.
11. Cover the pan and cook slowly for 2 hours.
12. Add the browned small onions, the mushrooms sliced but not peeled, and cook for another $\frac{1}{2}$ hour.
13. Remove the herbs and garlic, test the seasoning.
14. Dish the meat in the centre of a hot dish and arrange the mushrooms and onions at each end.

Goulash

$1\frac{1}{2}$ lbs lean stewing meat: beef or a mixture of beef and veal or pork

2 ozs dripping	1 lb tomatoes or 1 small tin
1 lb onions	tomatoes
2 tbs flour	2 teasp salt
1 clove garlic	$\frac{1}{4}$ pt red wine or tomato juice or
$1\frac{1}{2}$ pts stock	a mixture of both
	2 teasp paprika

Method

1. Cut the meat into cubes about $1\frac{1}{2}$ ins.
2. Slice the onion and fry in the fat until cooked, but only slightly brown.
3. Add the meat and fry until brown.
4. Stir in the flour and paprika.
5. Add the stock and wine or tomato juice and bring to the boil. Skim. Add the clove of garlic, skinned tomatoes and salt.
6. Cook slowly until tender: 2 hours will be necessary if shin of beef is used.
7. When the meat is tender, remove the garlic, check the sauce for seasoning. Note that no ordinary pepper is used.
8. Pile the meat on a hot dish, serve the sauce round it.

Variations

1. Just before serving stir in $\frac{1}{4}$ pt cream, preferably sour, reheat and dish.
2. Twenty minutes before serving add prepared vegetables such as small new potatoes, carrots or haricot beans.

3. Five minutes before serving add 1 tbs chopped green pepper and 1 tbs chopped parsley.

Ragoût of Rabbit or Veal

¾ lb fillet of veal *or*	1 medium carrot
1 rabbit	small piece of swede
1½ oz dripping	2 teasp salt
¾ oz flour	⅛ teasp pepper
1 medium onion	¾ pt hot stock

Garnish

6–8 bacon rolls	parsley
diced carrot and swede	

Method

1. Follow instructions for rich brown stew.
2. Prepare and cook the vegetables as for a rich brown stew.
3. Bake or grill the bacon rolls.

Dishing

As for a rich brown stew.

Beef or Veal Olives

¾ lb topside *or* rump of beef *or*	1 medium carrot
¾ lb fillet of veal	small piece of swede
1½ ozs dripping	2 teasp salt
¾ oz flour	⅛ teasp pepper
1 medium onion	⅝ pt hot stock

Forcemeat

3 tbs fresh breadcrumbs	¼ teasp grated lemon rind
1 tbs chopped suet	1 teasp salt
2 teasp chopped parsley	⅛ teasp pepper
pinch of powdered herbs	a little beaten egg

Garnish

Diced carrot and swede and/or peas and potato purée.

Potato Purée

1 lb cooked sieved potatoes	2 tbs hot milk
1 oz butter	

Preparation of Meat

1. Buy the meat if possible in a thick piece (3″ deep across the grain). Wipe and trim.

2. Cut across the grain in thin slices, approx 3″ × 4″ in size.
3. Flatten by beating with a cutlet bat or rolling pin.

Method

1. Prepare the forcemeat.
2. Spread each piece of meat with a little of the forcemeat.
3. Roll up neatly and tie with cotton or skewer with a pointed matchstick.
4. Continue as for a brown stew.
5. Prepare and cook the garnish vegetables as for a rich brown stew.
6. Sieve the potatoes and whilst hot beat in the butter and hot milk. Season carefully.

Dishing

1. Arrange the potato purée in a rectangular block down the centre of a hot dish.
2. Remove the cotton from the olives and place them on the potato.
3. Strain the sauce over the meat.
4. Garnish with the vegetables cooked as for a rich brown stew.

Mock Game

¾ lb topside or rump of beef	¾ pt hot stock
2 rashers of streaky bacon	1 teasp chopped capers
1 oz dripping	1 teasp redcurrant jelly
1 medium onion	¼ teasp lemon rind
1 medium carrot	2 teasp cornflour
⅛ teasp pepper	⅜ pt red wine
2 teasp salt	

Garnish

½ lb potato purée	parsley
8 crescents fried bread	

Preparation of Meat

As for beef olives.

Method

1. Remove the rust and rind from the rashers and press them out thinly.
2. Divide the bacon into the same number of pieces as the meat.
3. Lay a piece of bacon on each piece of meat and tie or skewer as for beef olives.
4. Fry the meat and vegetables as for a brown stew, add the stock and seasonings and simmer 2–2½ hours.

5. Halfway through the cooking add the finely grated lemon rind, the chopped capers and the jelly.
6. Blend the cornflour with the red wine and use it to thicken the strained sauce.
7. Taste and correct seasoning and colour.
8. Prepare the potato purée as for beef olives.
9. Divide into portions the size of a small walnut.
10. Roll into balls and coat with egg and breadcrumbs.
11. Fry in deep fat.
12. Fry the crescents of bread in the deep fat.

Dishing

1. Remove the cotton or matchstick from the meat and arrange neatly down the centre of a hot dish.
2. Pour the thickened sauce over the meat.
3. Garnish with the potato balls and crescents of bread and small sprigs of parsley.

ENTRÉES

An entrée is a savoury dish which is complete in itself, that is, the sauce and the garnish of vegetables and other accompaniments are served in the dish with the meat or fish. The sauce is a very important part of an entrée and it should be well flavoured, of a good colour and of the correct consistency. The garnish should all be edible and there should be enough for each person to take an adequate portion. Too much, however, would spoil the smartness of the dish. It is usual to dish an entrée so that each portion is clearly defined, as when served at a dinner party the dish is handed to each guest to help himself.

Before the dishing of an entrée is actually started, all the component parts must be prepared so that the entrée does not get cold. If the dish is placed in a shallow tin of very hot water and is kept there during the dishing and garnishing processes, the finished entrée can be served really hot.

Entrées may be classified:—

(A) *Hot*

   (a) Heavy; such as cutlets, fillets, fricassées, ragoûts, rissoles, sweetbreads, tournedos, salmi of game.
   (b) Light; such as beignets, croquettes, kromeskies, patties, quenelles, soufflés, vol-au-vents.

(B) *Cold*

Such as chaudfroids, galantines; pies such as game, veal and ham or steak.

Many of these dishes appear in other sections of this book and will not be included in this section. Recipes for chicken and game entrées will be found in the chapter on Poultry and Game.

The most suitable cuts for meat entrées are fillet of beef or veal served as fillets or tournedos of beef or escalope of veal and the best end of neck of mutton which is trimmed and served as cutlets.

Fillets of Beef

Choose a piece of meat thick enough to cut into the required number of $\frac{3}{4}''$ thick slices. These slices *must* be cut *across* the grain of the meat. It is usual to cut each piece into a round shape, using a 2″ cutter to mark the shape and size. A sharp-pointed knife is needed to cut the meat cleanly. This leaves a certain amount of unused meat and this should be made into another entrée as the meat is expensive. It is more economical, but not so attractive, to leave the fillets in the shape of the slice. This is possible if the original piece of meat is of a good shape.

After slicing and trimming where necessary, beat each slice with a cutlet bat or rolling pin and reshape the fillet or tournedos.

Fillets and tournedos are fried or grilled according to the entrée. They are dished on croûtes of fried bread cut the same size and shape as the fillet.

Lamb or Mutton for Cutlets

Only the very choice part of the neck produces real cutlet mutton, each side of the animal giving only 4 " bones ". Buy according to the number of bones without the meat's being chined or chopped. Remove the backbone or chine by sawing through the rib bone as near to the backbone as possible. Avoid cutting the fillet, that is, the large lean piece in the cutlet. Cut off any long rib bone, leaving the cutlet bone 4″–4½″ in length. Cut between each rib bone to obtain the cutlets. As the backbone has been removed this is a simple process. Trim off the outside skin and a little of the outside layer of fat so that the cutlet is a neat pear shape. It is important to use a very sharp knife and to cut cleanly. Free the end of the bone from meat, leaving $\frac{3}{4}''$ bone protruding. Scrape the skin from the inside of the bone. Beat each cutlet with a bat or a rolling pin.

Cutlets may be grilled or fried in shallow fat, preferably butter. If they are to be coated with egg and crumbs, they should be steamed or baked between two tin or enamel plates until tender. When cold they should be coated with egg and crumbs in the usual way and fried in deep or shallow fat until a good colour.

RECIPES FOR ENTRÉES

NAME	MEAT AND ITS PREPARATION	ACCOMPANIMENTS AND GARNISH	SAUCE	DISHING
A. Beef	½ lb of fillet of beef should be cut into 6 fillets, and trimmings should be used for Vienna Steaks or Patty fillings. Recipes for sauces and potato mixture will be found in the appropriate sections of the book.			
Fillets of beef Duchess	1 lb fillet of beef Melted clarified fat for brushing *Method* 1. Cut the fillets in circles 2" across. 2. Trim and beat. 3. Grill lightly on both sides.	½ lb duchess potato mixture, paprika pepper *Method* 1. Use a star vegetable forcer and pipe the mixture on to a greased baking tray in rounds 2", across. Keep the piles the same height and finish with a star on the top of each. 2. Allow to cool. 3. Brush with beaten egg and bake in the top of a hot oven, 450° F., until brown (10 mins).	½ pt espagnole sauce	1. Arrange the fillets in a half circle on a hot entrée dish. 2. Put a duchess potato on each. 3. Sprinkle with paprika pepper. 4. Pour the sauce round.
Fillets of beef Madeleine	1 lb fillet of beef 2 ozs clarified butter *Method* Fry the prepared fillets in the butter.	12 small new potatoes 6 croûtes of fried bread 3 tbs meat glaze 2 oz fresh butter juice of ½ lemon 1 shallot 2 tbs of a mixture of chopped chervil, chives, parsley, tarragon and thyme ¼ teasp salt dash of black pepper Cayenne to taste *Method* 1. Parboil the potatoes, drain and fry in deep fat until golden brown. 2. Fry the croûtes. 3. Warm the meat glaze over hot water. 4. Gradually beat in the butter. 5. Add the lemon juice, finely chopped shallot and herbs. 6. Season.	—	1. Arrange the croûtes diagonally across a hot dish. 2. Put a fillet on each. 3. Arrange the potatoes in piles on either side of the fillets. 4. Sprinkle with chopped parsley. 5. Divide the herb glaze between the six fillets. 6. Put under a hot grill for a moment or two to allow the glaze to run over the fillets.
Fillets of beef Pompadour	1 lb fillet of beef 2 oz clarified butter 2 tbs liquid meat glaze *Method* 1. Fry the prepared fillets. 2. Brush with glaze when dished.	6 croûtes of fried bread 6 slices of skinned tomatoes cut ⅜" thick 3 teasp maître d'hôtel butter 3 tbs macédoine of vegetables *Method* 1 Cook the vegetables in boiling	½ pt espagnole sauce	1. Arrange the croûtes in a circle or a straight line on a hot dish. 2. Put a fillet on each. Glaze. 3. Cover each fillet with a slice of tomato and a pat of butter. 4. Pour the sauce round the meat. 5. Garnish with piles of vegetables.

Dish	Ingredients and Method	Garnish	Sauce	Serving
Fillets of beef Russian	1 lb fillet of beef 1 tbs olive oil 2 tbs meat glaze *Method* 1. Brush the prepared fillets with oil 2. Grill and glaze.	2. Prepare the maitre d'hôtel butter. 3. Bake or steam the tomatoes. 4. Fry the croûtes. 1 doz small onions 6 teasp grated horseradish 1–2 oz clarified butter *Method* 1. Slice the onions evenly. 2. Fry in butter until golden brown. Drain well.	$^{1}/_{2}$ pt good brown sauce, flavoured with madeira if possible	1. Arrange the fillets in a circle on a hot dish. 2. Put 1 teasp grated horseradish on each. 3. Pour the sauce round the meat. 4. Pile the onions in the centre of the dish.
Vienna steaks	Trimmings from fillets made up to 1 lb in weight with lean steak 2 oz unsalted butter 1 teasp chopped parsley 1 egg yolk Stock 2 teasp salt $^{1}/_{8}$ teasp nutmeg $^{1}/_{8}$ teasp pepper *Method* 1. Pass the meat twice through a mincer. 2. Add all the seasonings and the onion. 3. Bind to a stiff mixture with egg yolk and stock. 4. Shape into neat cakes, using the inside of a 2″ cutter as a mould. 5. Fry in the clarified fat for 7–10 mins.	3 medium onions 2 teasp seasoned flour *Method* 1. Slice the onions evenly, retain all the well-shaped rings and use the trimmings to flavour the steaks. 2. Toss the separated rings in seasoned flour. 3. Fry until golden brown in deep fat.	$^{1}/_{2}$ pt espagnole	1. Brush the meat cakes with glaze. 2. Arrange in a block down the centre of a hot dish. 3. Pour the sauce round. 4. Pile the onion rings on the meat cakes.
B. Mutton				
	1¼ lbs best end neck of mutton should cut into 4 cutlets.			
Cutlets Milanaise	1¼ lbs best end of neck of mutton *Coating* Egg and breadcrumbs 4 ozs clarified mutton fat or butter *Method* 1. Trim the cutlets. 2. Bake between 2 plates, cool, coat with egg and crumbs. 3. Fry in the fat.	1 lb duchess potato mixture 1 tbs strips of cooked tongue 1 tbs strips of cooked macaroni 1 tbs strips of truffles (or pickled walnuts) *Method* 1. Prepare the strips of tongue, macaroni and truffle. 2. Heat in a little stock or sauce.	$^{1}/_{2}$ pt tomato sauce	1. Pipe a block of the potato mixture 2$^{1}/_{2}$″ wide down the centre of the dish. 2. Stand the cutlets on this block with the bone curving over to the left. 3. Put a cutlet frill on each bone. 4. Pour the sauce round. 5. Pile the garnish on each side.

E

RECIPES FOR ENTRÉES *continued*

Name	Meat and its Preparation	Accompaniments and Garnish	Sauce	Dishing
Cutlets Réforme	1¼ lbs cutlet mutton *Coating*: beaten egg 2 tbs finely chopped ham 3 tbs breadcrumbs 4 ozs clarified fat for frying *Method* 1. Bake the cutlets as for milanaise cutlets. 2. Mix the breadcrumbs and ham. 3. Brush the cutlets with egg and coat with the ham and crumb mixture.	1 lb duchess potato mixture 1 tbs strips of carrot 1 tbs strips of truffle 1 tbs strips of gherkin 1 tbs strips of hard boiled egg white 1 tbs strips of mushroom 1 tbs sherry *Method* 1. Prepare the strips of carrot and cook in boiling salted water and drain. 2. Heat with the other garnishes in the sherry and a little stock.	½ pt réforme sauce	As for Cutlets Milanaise.
Cutlets Soubise	1¼ lbs cutlet mutton 2 tbs meat glaze 2 ozs unsalted butter *Method* 1. Fry the cutlets in the butter. 2. Glaze just before serving.	12 potato balls prepared *either* from duchess potato mixture formed into balls, coated with egg and crumbs and fried in deep fat *or* small balls scooped from a raw potato, parboiled, dried, coated in egg and breadcrumbs and fried in deep fat.	½ pt Soubise sauce	1. Arrange the cutlets down the centre of a hot dish. 2. Put a cutlet frill on each. 3. Pour the sauce round. 4. Garnish with potato balls.
Tomato cutlets	1¼ lbs cutlet mutton prepared as for Cutlets Soubise	4 small tbs cooked fresh or frozen peas *or* small brussels sprouts.	½ pt tomato sauce	1. Arrange the cutlets down the centre of a hot dish. 2. Put a cutlet frill on each. 3. Pour the sauce round. 4. Pile the vegetables on both sides.
Veal	1 lb fillet of veal should cut into 6 fillets and trimmings should be used for patty fillings or fricassées or curry.			
Escalope Talleyrand	1 lb fillet of veal 1 oz butter 3 mushrooms finely chopped 1 shallot finely chopped *Method* 1. Prepare the fillets, fry gently in the butter, but do not allow to brown. 2. Add the chopped shallot and mushrooms. 3. Put the lid on the pan and allow to sauter until almost tender, ¾ hr. 4. Pour off any remaining fat. 5. Add the white sauce and simmer for 15–20 mins.	1 lb duchess potato mixture 6 bacon rolls 6 lemon butterflies 3 tbs green peas	¾ pt white sauce 1 tbs chopped parsley 2 teasp lemon juice 1 egg yolk	1. Arrange a potato border on the dish. 2. Lift out the fillets and place on the border. 3. Add the parsley, lemon juice and yolk of egg to the sauce. 4. Cook *without boiling* for 5 mins. 5. Coat the cutlets with the sauce. 6. Garnish with bacon rolls, lemon butterflies and green peas.

Fresh meat Curry	1 lb fillet trimmings or lean beef, mutton or veal *Method* 1. Cut the meat into neat pieces. 2. Put the meat into the curry sauce and allow to simmer for 1½ hrs. Use a casserole for cooking. 3. Cool the curry and stand overnight. 4. Reheat when required.	*Side dishes* (a) 4–6 oz. cooked Patna rice. (b) 2 sliced skinned tomatoes served with French dressing and chopped parsley. (c) 1 onion, finely chopped, mixed with 1 tbs evaporated milk and 2 teasp white vinegar. (d) 1 tbs desiccated coconut mixed with 2 tbs evaporated milk. (e) 1 lemon, cut in quarters. (f) Mango chutney.	³/₄ pint curry sauce	1. Serve the curry in the casserole in which it is cooked. 2. Pile the rice in a separate dish. Sprinkle with cayenne pepper. 3. Serve each side dish separately. See also p. 244.
Sweetbread Italian	1 ox sweetbread Strips of larding bacon Mirepoix for braising (page 110) 2 tbs liquid glaze *Method* 1. Soak the sweetbread in salt water for 1 hour. 2. Rinse, blanch and remove any fat. 3. Press between 2 plates until cold. 4. Insert the lardoons of fat. 5. Prepare the mirepoix, add the sweetbread and cook for 1–1½ hours. 6. Remove the lid of the pan and bake the sweetbread in a hot oven until the lardoons are crisp.	1 croûte of fried bread similar in size to the sweetbread 1 oz macaroni, cooked 2 tbs button mushrooms fried in 1 tbs butter	½ pint espagnole	1. Lift the sweetbread on to the croûte of bread. 2. Glaze and put to keep hot. 3. Strain the liquid from the braise. Reduce to a syrupy consistency and skim. 4. Add the espagnole sauce and reheat. 5. Pour round the sweetbread. 6. Garnish with macaroni and button mushrooms.
Farced liver	1½ lbs calf's liver Bacon, ½ rasher to each piece of liver ½ pint stock Worcester sauce to taste (approx 1 tbs) *Method* 1. Clean and skin the liver and remove any pipes. 2. Cut into slices half an inch thick. 3. Lay the slices in a greased baking tin. 4. Cover each strip with farce and a strip of bacon. 5. Pour the stock round and cook in the centre of a moderate oven, 350° F for 30–40 mins.	*Farce* 3 ozs fresh breadcrumbs 1 small onion chopped finely 1 tbs chopped parsley ½ teasp grated lemon rind ½ teasp salt ⅛ teasp pepper Yolk of egg to bind	—	1. Lift the pieces of liver on to a hot dish. 2. Add the Worcester sauce to the gravy and boil up. 3. Strain the gravy round the liver.

MEAT PIES AND PUDDINGS

Reference should be made to the Chapters on Pastry and Puddings

Name	Recipe for the Filling	Preparation of the Filling	Types of Pastry Used	Cooking Instructions
Beef Steak and Kidney Pie	1 lb rump steak ¼ lb kidney 1 oz seasoned flour ¼ pt stock	1. Clean the kidney and cut into dice. 2. Wipe the meat and cut into thin slices or neat pieces. 3. If the meat is sliced, wrap each slice round 2 or 3 dice of kidney. 4. Toss the meat and the kidney in seasoned flour. 5. Pack neatly into a one-pint pie dish. 6. Pour the stock over the meat.	4 ozs flaky or rough puff If thicker pastry is liked use 6 ozs.	1. Bake in the centre of an oven preheated to 450° F for 15 mins. 2. Reduce to 350° F for a further 2–2½ hours, or until the meat is tender. 3. After 1½ hours' cooking, cover the pie with kitchen paper to prevent scorching.
Beef Steak and Kidney Pudding	As for Beefsteak and Kidney Pie	1. Prepare the meat as for a pie. 2. Pack into a pint basin lined with suet pastry. See page 260 for this method.	6 ozs suet pastry	Steam for 3–4 hours.
Meat and Vegetable Pudding	¾ lb shoulder steak 1 oz seasoned flour 1 large onion 2 potatoes 1 carrot 1 teasp salt ½ teasp meat or vegetable extract if liked ¼ pt stock	1. Wipe the meat and cut into neat pieces. 2. Toss in seasoned flour. 3. Dice the prepared vegetables. 4. Fill the lined basin with the mixture. 5. Add the stock.	6 ozs suet pastry	Steam for 3–4 hours.

Pork Pie	8 ozs lean pork 4 ozs pork fat 2 teasp salt ½ teasp black pepper ⅛ pt stock ½ teasp powdered sage or ⅛ „ ground mace if liked ⅛ pt jellied stock for filling	1. Wipe the meat and cut into neat small pieces. 2. Mix thoroughly with the seasonings. 3. Pack into the piecrust with the stock.	½ lb hot water crust pastry	See instructions for raising a pie (page 401). When cold, fill up the pie with warm stock. To do this put a small funnel into the hole in the pie, and pour the warm stock gently in.
Rabbit	1 rabbit ¼ lb bacon or pickled pork 2 hard-boiled eggs 2 tbs seasoned flour 2 teasp salt ¼ pt stock	1. Wash, trim, joint and blanch the rabbit. 2. Cut the bacon or pork into small thin pieces. 3. Halve the eggs. 4. Toss all the ingredients in the flour. 5. Pack into a one and a half pint pie dish. The egg should be covered with meat. Season. 6. Pour the stock into the dish.	6–8 ozs flaky or rough puff pastry	As for Beefsteak and Kidney Pie.
Veal and Ham	¾ lb fillet of veal 2 ozs raw ham 1 or 2 hard-boiled eggs ¼ teasp grated lemon rind 1 teasp salt ⅛ teasp pepper ⅛ „ ground mace if liked ¼ pt stock	1. Wipe the meat and cut into neat pieces. 2. Mix thoroughly with the seasonings. 3. Pack into a one pint pie dish, taking care to cover the hard-boiled eggs with meat. 4. Add the stock.	4–6 ozs flaky or rough puff pastry or 8 ozs hot water crust pastry	As for Beefsteak and Kidney Pie or as for Pork Pie.

Kidneys

Kidneys should be obtained from a sheep or a pig. They should be prepared as for grilling and sautéd in clarified fat for 20 mins until tender.

They can replace beef, mutton or veal in any entrée for which meat is not coated with egg and crumbs.

ADDITIONAL RECIPES

Dressed Sheep's Head

1 cooked sheep's head (see Sheep's Head Broth, page 49)
1½ ozs flour   1½ ozs butter
¾ pt liquid (½ milk ½ stock from the head)
⅛ teasp pepper   ¼ teasp salt
2 tbs chopped parsley   crescents of toast
chopped cooked brains (if liked)

Method

1. Remove the head from the broth. Slice the meat neatly and place in a hot fireproof dish.
2. Skin and slice the tongue, add to the meat. Keep hot.
3. Make a sauce from the flour, butter and liquid. Season carefully and add the chopped parsley and brains if liked.
4. Pour over the sliced meat.
5. Garnish with crescents of toast and parsley.

Brain Cakes

If the appearance of brain sauce is not attractive, the brains may be chopped up and mixed with enough breadcrumbs to make the mixture of croquette consistency. This mixture can be seasoned to taste and made into small round cakes which, fried in hot fat, make an alternative garnish to crescents of toast.

Roast Heart

Choose either an ox heart or a sheep's heart. Allow 1¼–1½ lbs of meat to 4 persons (1 ox or 3 sheep's hearts).

Cut away the thick muscular arteries and the veins. Do not divide the heart completely.

Soak well in salt water (1 teasp to 1 pt water) or vinegar water (1 tbs to 1 pt water) for ½–1 hour according to the size of the heart. This will draw out the blood. Clean thoroughly and soak again for 15–20 mins in clean water.

Stuffing

4 ozs breadcrumbs	1 teasp powdered sage
2 ozs dripping or suet	$\frac{1}{2}$ teasp salt
2 cooked chopped onions	egg or milk to bind

Method

1. Mix all the ingredients together until the dripping is thoroughly dispersed through the mixture.
2. Bind with egg or milk.
3. Dry the hearts and fill the cavity with stuffing.
4. Sew up the flesh to enclose the stuffing.
5. Put the hearts in a heavy pan with $\frac{1}{2}''$ hot dripping.
6. Baste well and cover with greaseproof paper. Put on the lid.
7. Cook a sheep's heart for 50–60 mins and an ox heart for $1\frac{1}{2}$–2 hours, keeping the fat sizzling gently all the time. Baste well every 20 mins. As the fibre of the meat is close, this basting is essential to make the flesh tender.
8. When tender, put the heart on to a hot dish and remove stitches.
9. Make a good thick brown gravy with 1 tbs of the fat + 1 tbs flour + $\frac{3}{4}$ pt stock (see page 106).
10. Serve the hearts with roast or mashed potatoes, root or green vegetables and a sharp jelly such as redcurrant, gooseberry or rowan.

Liver with Herbs

1 lb lamb's or calf's liver
3–4 ozs mushrooms
1–2 tbs chopped herbs such as parsley and chives with a little tarragon or thyme or rosemary added

1 tbs olive oil	1 tbs seasoned flour
1 tbs chopped shallot	2 ozs butter

Method

1. Slice the liver after removing the pipes. Dip in the flour.
2. Melt the butter and olive oil in a frying pan.
3. Fry the liver quickly on both sides so that it is brown.
4. Add the mushrooms, herbs and shallot all very finely chopped.
5. Fry for 3–5 minutes over a low heat, stirring to prevent sticking.
6. Dish on a hot serving dish, garnished with lemon.

Cooking Ham and Bacon Joints

Cuts suitable for boiling or baking.

Ham. The ham is the back leg together with part of the loin, and is taken from a specially bred pig before any curing has been done. Generally hams are cured by dry salting, but there are many local and traditional cures which are prized by those skilled in using them. Most country housewives have a family recipe which they use, but the hams bought in the shops are nearly all cured by " salting ".

Bacon. The neck or " collar " and the forehock (which is the top of the front leg) make excellent joints for boiling or baking. " Gammon ", like ham, comes from the hind leg, but is cut from a side of cured pork. A " corner " is the part which joins on to the " long back " cut of bacon.

To Boil Ham or Bacon

1. Weigh the joint and calculate the time required for cooking, allowing 15 mins to every 1 lb meat plus 15 mins if the piece weighs more than 12 lbs. If less than 12 lbs in weight allow 20 mins per lb plus 20 mins.
2. Soak overnight in cold water.
3. Rinse the joint and put into a saucepan with enough cold water to cover completely. Add a bouquet garni.
4. Bring *slowly* to the boil, skim well and *simmer* for the required length of time, keeping the lid on the pan.
5. Allow to cool in the liquor.
6. Take the joint out of the cold liquor, dry and peel off the skin.
7. Sprinkle the fat with brown raspings.

To Bake Ham

1. Prepare the joint as for boiling and follow the instructions for boiling until the joint has cooked for half the allotted time.
2. Remove the ham from the hot liquid—dry and cover completely with a " dough " made from flour and water. This dough should be slightly sticky and must cover the joint completely. The covering is specially important if the joint is a piece of a ham, i.e. it has a cut surface.
3. Put in a baking tin and cook at 350° for the remainder of the cooking time less 20 mins. No fat is needed.
4. Take the ham from the oven, break the crust of paste and remove.
5. Strip off the skin and score the fat in diamond shapes.
6. Stud each diamond with a clove and sprinkle the fat with brown sugar.
7. Put the ham back in the oven (temperature 425°) and allow to brown. This will take the remaining 20 mins.

Serving

1. If it is to be served hot with either peaches, pineapple or oranges, the sugar coating is brushed with the appropriate juice and the fruit is heated in the oven during the browning period. Serve the joint on a hot dish surrounded by the fruit garnished with halved walnuts or hot maraschino cherries. If the ham is whole put a paper frill round the hock joint.

2. Boiled or baked ham or bacon may be served hot with piquant, tomato or Cumberland sauce or with broad beans coated with parsley sauce.

Baked Bacon

1. Weigh the joint and calculate the cooking time, allowing 20 mins per lb plus 20 mins.

2. Soak overnight if dry salted, but a normal mild cure will not need this.

3. Cover with a paste made from flour and water. Cover completely.

4. Bake in the centre of a moderate oven (350° F) for the necessary time. Basting is not necessary.

5. When cooked, remove the crust and strip off any skin.

6. Coat the fat with brown crumbs.

7. Serve hot or cold.

COLD MEATS

Aspic Mould

Aspic Jelly (see p. 292).

Suggestions for suitable combinations of food.

1. Prawns or shrimps with peas, radishes, egg white cut into fancy shapes or slices of hard boiled egg.

2. Crayfish or lobster claws with leaves of watercress.

3. Hard-boiled egg and cucumber.

4. Slices of chicken breast with tomato and hard-boiled egg and pieces of chive.

Method

1. *Either* set in jelly as on page 294

   or ¾ fill a rinsed plain mould with jelly and when beginning to set drop in the fillings
   or arrange the fillings in a rinsed plain mould and cover with cool jelly.

2. Allow to set.
3. Turn out (see page 289) and serve with salad.

Brawn

1 pig's head
and 1 or 2 trotters or a cowheel
1 or 2 onions
12 peppercorns ⎫
1 or 2 blades mace ⎬ tied in muslin
parsley and thyme ⎭

Method

1. Soak the head in brine from 3 to 5 days unless already pickled.
2. Clean the head thoroughly (see sheep's head).
3. Cover with cold water and bring to the boil, add seasonings and simmer until tender (2–3 hours).
4. Remove the tongue, skin it and leave until required.
5. Remove all the meat from the bones and cut into dice.
6. Put the bones back into the pan and add 1 quart of the liquor, the onions and seasonings; allow to simmer about 1 hour.
7. Strain this liquid and reduce it until it will form a jelly when cold.
8. Add the diced meat, check the seasoning.
9. Decorate a rinsed mould or basin with sliced tongue and slices of hard-boiled egg if liked.
10. Pour the meat mixture into the prepared mould and leave until set.
11. When set, turn out and garnish with parsley.

Potted Hough (Shin of Beef)

½ lb hough (shin of beef)
1 lb knuckle of veal or a nap-bone
1 level teasp salt
1 or 2 blades mace ⎫
¼ teasp mixed spice ⎬ tied in muslin
12 peppercorns ⎭
1 quart water

Method

1. Wipe the meat and cut into 1″ cubes.
2. Wash the bones well.
3. Put the water and salt into a pan and add the meat and the bones, bring to the boil, simmer 2 to 3 hours.

4. Remove the meat, add the spices and herbs and simmer from 1–1½ hours.
5. Shred the meat finely and put it into a basin or mould rinsed with cold water.
6. Strain the stock and reduce it until, when cold, it shows signs of setting.
7. Pour some of this stock over the meat, stir frequently until it shows signs of setting.
8. Leave until set.

Note If the stock does not show signs of jellying add gelatine, using ¼ oz gelatine to 1 pt stock. See notes on dissolving gelatine page 288.

Galantine of Veal

1 lb stewing veal	2 teasp finely chopped parsley
½ lb lean ham	1 ,, grated lemon rind
6 ozs breadcrumbs	1 egg
3 level teasp salt	¼ to ½ pt stock
¼ teasp pepper	

Garnish

Meat glaze
Cooked carrot
Hard-boiled egg white and little yolk

Method

1. Wipe and trim the veal, pass it twice through the mincer.
2. Trim the rind from the ham and mince it with the veal.
3. Add the breadcrumbs and seasonings to the prepared meat.
4. Beat the egg and add to it about ¼ pt stock. Add to the dry ingredients and mix all together to a soft consistency.
5. Turn out on to a floured board and roll into a neat shape, using the hands. Weigh the galantine.
6. Roll in a clean cloth, tie the ends securely.
7. Put into a pan containing sufficient boiling water or stock to cover the roll. Simmer very gently, allowing 30 minutes to each lb. Allow at least one hour. The simmering must be very gentle to prevent the galantine from cracking on the surface.
8. When cooked, remove the galantine, untie and transfer it to a clean cloth. Tie both ends tightly and press the galantine between two plates under weights. Leave until cold.
9. When quite cold, remove the cloth, and if the surface is very greasy wring a clean cloth in very hot water and place over

the galantine for a few minutes to help to remove surface grease.
10. Glaze the roll with a little hot glaze (see page 45).
11. When sufficiently glazed decorate suitably with hard-boiled egg and/or cooked carrot and parsley.
12. Serve cold with a suitable salad.

Beef Roll

Instead of veal and ham use
    1 lb stewing beef and
    ½ lb sausage meat *or* ¼ lb lean bacon

Vary the flavour by using, instead of lemon and parsley, *either* ⅛ teasp ground mace and 2 teasp mixed chopped herbs, *or* a row of stoned black olives down the centre of the meat.

Stock can be replaced by white wine or dry cider in either recipe.

Pâté of Pork

½ lb pig's liver (calf's liver can be used)	2 shallots
	4 ozs breadcrumbs
1½ lbs lean pork	1 teasp black pepper
½ lb pickled pork	1 teasp chopped herbs (sage and
salt as necessary	rosemary)
¼ teasp ground mace	1 egg

Method

1. Mince the meats with the shallots, passing them twice through the mincer so that the meat is ground really fine.
2. Add the breadcrumbs and seasonings and bind with beaten egg and if necessary a little stock. The consistency should be such that the mixture just drops off the spoon. Taste and check the seasoning.
3. Press into a deep casserole or terrine. Cover with greaseproof paper and put on the lid.
4. Stand the terrine in a meat tin of water and cook in a moderate oven (325°) for 3½ hours. The pâté is cooked when the juice pressed out from the centre is no longer pink.
5. Remove the lid, add a clean piece of paper, cover with a weight to press and leave to cool.
6. When cold, remove the weight and paper, pour melted lard over the top and keep in a cool place.
7. Serve cold with hot toast, as a first course, or hot with vegetables or salad as an entrée.

Pâté of Chicken Livers

1 lb chicken livers
8 ozs fat pork meat
2 small eggs
1 clove garlic
4 ozs sieved fresh breadcrumbs
$\frac{1}{8}$ teasp each nutmeg and cinnamon
2 level teasp salt
$\frac{1}{8}$ teasp freshly ground black pepper
2 tbs brandy
8 rashers streaky bacon

Method

1. Pass the liver, garlic and fat pork twice through the mincer.
2. Rub through a sieve.
3. Add the breadcrumbs, seasonings, brandy and beaten eggs. Beat well. The mixture should just drop off the spoon.
4. Line a 1 pt terrine or casserole with bacon.
5. Pack the liver mixture into the casserole. Cover with bacon and put on the lid.
6. Stand in a baking tin of water and cook at No. 3 for $2\frac{1}{2}$ hours in the centre of the oven.
7. Allow to cool with the lid on.
   If the terrine is to be kept for long, cover the top with a layer of melted lard.
8. Serve cold with split toast or hot (reheated in the oven in a tin of water) with vegetables.

Pressed Beef (Brisket)

3 to 4 lbs pickled brisket or silverside.

Method

1. Wipe the joint or wash it thoroughly after removing from the brine.
2. Soak overnight or several hours in cold water to remove excess salt and to soften the meat fibres.
3. Put into a pan of warm water, bring to the boil and allow to simmer very gently until the meat is tender (allowing at least $\frac{1}{2}$ hour to each lb plus $\frac{1}{2}$ hour over).
4. Remove from liquid, tie securely in an old clean cloth and press between two boards until cold. When cold, coat with either meat glaze or browned breadcrumbs.
5. Serve cold with a suitable salad.

Wet Pickle for Meat

Suitable cuts: silverside, topside, brisket.

3 lbs common salt	1 lb moist sugar or treacle
1 gallon boiling water	1 oz peppercorns
1 oz saltpetre	

Method

1. Put all the ingredients into a large pan, bring to boiling point and boil for 5 minutes.
2. Skim well; strain into a large basin or a deep crock and leave until cold.
3. Before putting meat into this pickle, remove any discoloured parts from the meat and wipe thoroughly with a damp cloth.
4. Put the meat into the liquid; cover, turn the meat every day and leave it from 10 to 14 days.

FILLINGS FOR PATTIES AND VOL-AU-VENTS

8 ozs puff pastry will make 6 patties cut with a two and a half inch cutter *or* 1 vol-au-vent case cut with a seven-inch oval cutter.

The basis of all these fillings is a good white sauce, and the variety chosen depends upon the preference of the cook. Generally, a Béchamel sauce is used where the added main ingredient has a pronounced flavour, e.g. salmon, lobster, game, oysters.

Velouté sauce is used when a more delicately flavoured main ingredient is used, e.g. crayfish, chicken, veal or sweetbread.

As when making savouries, the flavourings added to the sauce and meat or fish can be varied, but they must be added skilfully so that the flavour of the main ingredient is enhanced and not over-whelmed. A little cream added to the sauce improves the flavour.

The ingredients for the filling must be cooked before they are added to the sauce. They must be well blended together and made thoroughly hot in the sauce before being put in the hot pastry cases.

If to be eaten cold, the mixture should be allowed to cool before filling the cold pastry cases.

To fill 6 patty cases or seven-inch vol-au-vent case use 1 gill (¼ pint) sauce and any of the following additions:

A. *Filling*

5 ozs cooked white fish + 1 oz picked chopped shrimps or prawns
1 teasp anchovy essence
2–3 teasp lemon juice
1 teasp coralline pepper

Garnish

Prawns or shrimp heads, lemon butterflies, chopped parsley

B. *Filling*

6 ozs flaked tinned or fresh lobster, salmon, crayfish or 6 ozs picked
   prawns
⅛ teasp cayenne pepper
1–2 teasp lemon juice

Garnish

Salmon; cucumber or fennel   Well-shaped pieces of meat if
Shellfish; claws and heads of   tinned
   fish   Chopped parsley
        Lemon butterflies

C. *Filling*

4 ozs cooked chopped chicken or 3 of chicken and 1 of ham
4 mushrooms chopped and fried in butter
2 sliced skinned tomatoes cooked with the mushrooms
2 teasp lemon juice
⅛ teasp cayenne pepper
salt and pepper to taste

Garnish

Lemon butterflies and chopped parsley
or pieces of tomato-skin and slices of truffle

D. *Filling*

2 hard-boiled eggs chopped
2 ozs minced ham or tongue
2 chopped mushrooms fried in butter
⅛ teasp cayenne pepper *or* 1 teasp coralline pepper

Garnish

Sieved hard-boiled yolk of egg
White of egg cut into fancy shapes
Coralline pepper and chopped parsley

E. *Filling*

2 tomatoes skinned and chopped, using the pulp only and discarding seeds and juice
3 ozs grated hard cheese, preferably Parmesan
½ teasp made mustard
½ teasp salt
⅛ teasp cayenne pepper

Garnish

Sprigs of parsley or other green herbs

Game Vol-au-Vent or Patties

F. *Filling*

¼ pt espagnole sauce in place of Béchamel
4 ozs cooked game: pheasant, partridge, pigeon etc.

2 tomatoes	½ oz butter
6 mushrooms	⅛ teasp cayenne pepper
a very little grated lemon rind	½ teasp salt

Garnish

The feet and a few feathers saved from the bird

Method

1. Skin and cut up the mushrooms and tomatoes.
2. Fry in the butter until tender.
3. Add the seasoning and the sauce.
4. Taste and correct the flavour.
5. Add the chopped game. Place in the prepared pastry cases and serve hot.

Oyster Patties

Filling

12 raw oysters	1 teasp lemon juice
⅛ teasp cayenne pepper	1 teasp cream

Garnish

Sprigs of parsley

Method

1. Blanch and beard the oysters, using their own liquor for heating.
2. Cut each oyster into 2 or 3 pieces.
3. Add the oysters, cream and seasoning to the sauce.
4. Reheat but do not reboil.
5. Fill the pastry cases.
6. Garnish with the parsley and serve hot.

CHAPTER X

POULTRY AND GAME

Poultry

POULTRY includes chickens, hens, turkeys, geese and ducks.
Chickens are usually classified as follows:

Poussins i.e. very young birds 1 to 1½ lbs weight. These are usually served whole or in halves.

Spring Chickens i.e. very young birds which may weigh from 1½ to 3 lbs.

Surrey Fowls i.e. specially fed kinds which are regarded as some of the finest chickens. Average weight approximately 6 lbs.

Capons i.e. neutered cockerels. These usually weigh from 7 to 8 lbs each.

Hens are the older birds which have had one or two laying seasons.

Choice of Poultry

Choose only birds which are free from smell and avoid those with a bluish tint near the vent.

Chickens

1. The breast bone and the beak should be pliable.
2. The bird should have smooth legs, short spurs, soft feet.
3. The breast should be plump.

Turkeys

1. The flesh should be firm and white.
2. The legs should be firm, plump and smooth, the spurs short and the feet supple.

Geese and Ducks

1. The skin should be white and the breast plump.
2. The bird should have a yellow bill and soft, pliable, yellow feet.

Methods of Cooking

Young birds are roasted, but older chickens and hens may be boiled, braised, steamed, cooked in a pressure cooker or " en casserole ".

Storing and Hanging

A bird should be stored for at least 24 hours before trussing, and after " shaping " should be put on a shelf with the head hanging down, in a cool, dry place. The legs are tied so that they lie alongside the carcase.

To Draw a Chicken

1. Single the carcase over burning methylated spirits or a gas ring.
2. Remove the sinews by cutting round the legs one inch below the hock joint, taking care not to cut the sinews. Break the bone at the cut, twist the foot and draw out the sinews by pulling the foot away from the leg. Attach a loop of stout string to the middle toe, looping the other end of the string over your shoe and, using it as a lever, pull the bird upwards, so removing the foot, shank and sinews.
3. If the bird is old and the sinews tough, it is often easier to remove the sinews one at a time.
   Bend back the broken bone so that the sinews are exposed. Put a trussing needle or a skewer under one sinew, twist and pull the skewer away from the leg without tearing the flesh of the drumstick. Treat each sinew separately and count them to see that there is one for each toe.
4. Trim the extreme ends of the wings and cut off the " thumbs ".
5. Place the bird on the table, breast down and head towards the worker. With one hand, pinch up a portion of the skin along the back of the neck, and slit by cutting from the shoulders up to the feathers close to the head. Sever the neck between the shoulders; retain the neck, cut off the neck skin, leaving a good flap.
6. Peel the crop, the food pipe, and the windpipe from the neck skin by pulling or cutting them as close to the body as possible. Remove. Insert the second finger into the body cavity along the backbone, and loosen the lungs and other organs.
7. Fold the flap of skin over the opening, on to the back, and hold it down by bending the wings under the body.
8. With the bird upright on its shoulders, and using a sharp pointed knife, grasp the tail, and make an incision between the vent and tail, taking great care not to cut into the intestines. Hook up the last portion of these with the first finger, and, inserting the knife between the intestines and the uncut skin, cut out the vent.

9. The bird should be placed on its back, with the tail towards the worker. Ease out the internal organs by pressing the carcass with the left hand and grasping the gizzard with the right hand. If the organs were well loosened at the neck end, they should pull out quite easily. Remove the ovary or testes, which lie against the centre of the backbone. Make sure that the pink, spongy lungs have been removed from the region of the ribs.

10. Wipe the bird inside with a clean damp cloth.

11. Cut the giblets away from the organs. The giblets consist of the heart, neck, gizzard and liver. Trim the heart by cutting off the fat and tubes.

    Cut the gizzard open and remove the horny lining and contents; cut the gall bladder carefully from the liver.

    The giblets should be kept separate from the bird so that they do not discolour the flesh of the bird.

Roast Chicken

To Truss

Thread and knot a trussing needle with about 18 inches of string. Laying the bird on its back, neck end nearest to the worker, hold the thighs upright. Pass the needle through the top of one thigh, just behind the joint, through the carcass, and out through the other thigh. Turn the bird over. Pass the needle through the " elbow " of the wing, over the back to hold down the flap of skin, and out through the other wing " elbow ". Untie the string from the needle, pull the two ends tightly, and tie with a double knot.

Lay the bird on its back, in the same position as before. Thread a trussing needle with about 12 inches of string. Holding the skin tightly over the tip of the breastbone, pass the needle through this. Unthread it, and, taking hold of the two ends, pass them round the hock end of the " drumsticks ", cross the string over the vent cavity, and tie down tightly behind the tail, so that the legs are pulled down over the opening, and the breast muscles pushed up to give a plump finish.

To Stuff

The addition of stuffing alters the flavour of the meat and many people prefer not to stuff a chicken for this reason.

Use 2–3 ozs veal forcemeat or a mixture of forcemeat and sausage meat.

1. Loosen the skin at the neck of the bird over the " wishbone ".

2. Push the stuffing between the skin and the flesh until a plump curve is obtained.

3. Draw the neck skin tightly over to the back of the bird and clip it firmly into place with the tips of the wings. Surplus stuffing may be shaped into balls, coated, and either fried in deep fat or baked round the bird. (See also pp. 412–14.)

To Cook

1. Prepare an oven, preheated to 425° F. After 15 mins reduce to 350° F.
2. Put the trussed chicken in a roasting tin. Cover the breast of the chicken with strips of fat bacon and a little dripping, or cover with foil and leave until the bird is frothed.
3. Place in the middle of the oven and baste every 20 minutes during cooking if not covered.
4. Allow 20 minutes to every pound + 20 minutes, calculating the time from the weight of the bird after trussing.
5. During the last 15 minutes before dishing remove the bacon from the breast of the chicken. Dredge the bird with flour, baste with hot fat and place at the top of the oven to brown and crisp the breast; this is known as frothing.
6. While the bird is in the last stage of cooking, bake the bacon rolls and fry in deep fat any surplus stuffing, made into force-meat balls.

To Dish

1. Remove the string from the chicken and place on a hot meat dish large enough to permit easy carving. Keep hot.
2. Strain the fat from the roasting tin, leaving the sediment in the tin.
3. Add 1 teasp flour and $\frac{1}{4}$ teasp salt and heat until the flour has absorbed all the fat and sediment, and the mixture is a good chestnut brown colour.
4. Strain $\frac{1}{2}$ pint of giblet stock into the tin, stir well, bring to the boil and allow to evaporate for about 5 minutes.
5. Pass a piece of kitchen paper or clean tissue paper over the surface to absorb any globules of fat.
6. Strain into a hot gravy boat and serve with the chicken.
7. Garnish the chicken with bacon rolls and forcemeat balls if liked.
8. Serve with bread sauce.

How to prepare

Turkey

1. Draw and truss as for chicken.
2. Stuff the breast with veal, oatmeal and/or chestnut stuffing.
3. Cover the breast with fat bacon.
4. Spread the top with dripping. Cover with foil.

5. Place in a hot oven, 425° F for the first 15 minutes, then reduce the heat to 350° F.   Baste frequently if not covered.
6. Cook a small turkey 1½ to 2 hours.   Allow 12 minutes to the pound and 12 minutes over for a large turkey.
7. Serve the turkey.

Goose

1. Draw and truss as for chicken but cut off the wings at the first joint and do not cross them at the back.
2. Stick the legs down by the side of the body.
3. Stuff the body of the bird with sage and onion stuffing (page 414).
4. Roast as for turkey, using greaseproof paper on the breast in place of bacon.
5. Allow 2–2½ hours according to size.
6. Garnish with watercress when dishing.

Duck

1. Truss as for goose, leaving on the feet, and turn these close to the legs.
2. Stuff with sage and onion stuffing, or put a piece of butter and seasoning inside.
3. Cover with a piece of greased paper before roasting.
4. Proceed as for goose, allowing 1½–2 hours for cooking.
5. Dish and garnish with watercress.

Accompaniments for Poultry

Poultry	Potatoes	Other Vegetables	Sauces and Accompaniments
Roast Chicken	Baked, fried, or boiled new potatoes	Cauliflower, peas, new carrots, green beans, celery, green salad	Veal forcemeat, bread sauce, bacon rolls, thin gravy
Roast Duck	Roast or boiled	Peas, carrots, any green vegetable Orange salad (see page 187)	Apple sauce, sage and onion stuffing, thin gravy, flavoured with orange juice if liked
Roast Goose	Roast or boiled	Onions, carrots, any green vegetable	Sage and onion, or savoury apple and prune stuffing Apple sauce Thickened gravy
Roast Turkey	Roast, fried or boiled	Onions, peas, pumpkin, brussels sprouts	Sausages, chestnut sausagemeat or veal stuffing Bacon rolls Bread sauce, cranberry or celery sauce Thickened gravy

Boiled Chicken

Draw as for a roasting chicken.

To Pocket the Legs

1. Place the bird on its back with the tail towards the worker. Starting just above the vent, separate the skin from the flesh until two fingers can be inserted between the skin and the flesh. Work these two fingers under the skin towards the leg.
2. Loosen the skin round the drumstick, keeping the fingers between the skin and the flesh. Leave the skin firmly attached to the flesh over the breast and wish bones. Bend back the hock joint of the leg and cut through the skin and the tendon just below the joint.
3. Remove the shank and the wide tendon at the joint. This leaves the round bone clear.
4. Insert the two fingers of the right hand inside the skin above the vent and gather the loose skin into folds. Press the thumb on the end of the hock bone, pushing the drumstick towards the wing and close to the body. Then push the hock bone towards the end of the breast bone nearest the vent until it is pocketed between the skin and the flesh.
5. Repeat on the other side of the bird.

To Truss

1. Thread and knot a trussing needle with 18″ string. Lay the bird on its back, neck end nearest the worker, holding the thighs close to the body. Pass the needle through the thigh, just behind the joint, through the carcase and out through the other thigh.
2. Turn the bird over. Pass the needle through the " elbow " of the wing, over the back to hold down the flap of skin and out through the other wing " elbow ". Untie the string from the needle, pull the two ends tightly, and tie a double knot between the wing and the thigh.
3. Press the tail or " parson's nose " inside the body cavity, and tuck in the loose skin from the drumsticks.
4. Smooth the skin from the breast bone over the vent, and pull to the back of the bird.
5. Thread a needle with 18″ string and pass the needle through the flesh under the tip of the breast bone.
6. Cross the string under the bird and, holding the ends of the drumsticks as close to the body as possible, bring the string to the top of the bird and tie securely.
7. Tuck in any surplus skin under the drumsticks and smooth the skin all over the bird, making sure that the flap of skin under the body is held in place by the string.

To Boil a Fow

1. Rub the breast with a cut lemon, wrap the bird in a clean cloth and put into a pan of boiling water.

   See that the water covers the bird and add to it the giblets, an onion stuck with 3 or 4 cloves, a piece of carrot and a bouquet garni.

2. Boil for 5 minutes, then reduce the heat and simmer for 2–3 hours, according to the age of the bird.

To Dish a Boiled Fowl

1. Remove the cloth from the bird, cut and remove the trussing strings.
2. Dry the bird with a clean cloth, put on a hot dish and put aside to keep hot.
3. Make a rich coating sauce with ½ chicken stock and ½ milk.
4. Coat the bird with the sauce.
5. Decorate with sieved yolk of egg and finely chopped parsley.

ENTRÉES USING CHICKEN
Fricassée of Chicken

1 partially cooked boiling fowl or 1 raw chicken
2 oz butter
2 ozs flour
1 pt chicken stock or ½ pt chicken stock + ½ pt milk
A few mushroom stalks
6 peppercorns
2 or 3 strips lemon rind
1 small onion
1 teasp lemon juice, if desired

Garnish

6 or 7 bacon rolls
2 or 3 teasp green peas (fresh, tinned or frozen)
or butterflies of lemon
6 or 7 crescent shape croûtons fried bread
Parsley sprigs

Method

1. If a boiling fowl is used, partially steam it for approximately 1½ hours, or cook it in a pressure cooker for ½ hour.
2. Cut the partially cooked fowl or raw chicken into neat joints, remove the skin from each. Use this and the carcase for making chicken stock.
3. Put the prepared joints into a white-lined pan or casserole, add the salt, strips of lemon rind, peeled mushroom stalks, washed parsley and chicken stock.

4. Bring to the boil and leave to simmer for approximately 1½ hours, i.e. until the chicken is tender.
5. When tender, strain off the liquid; keep the joints hot.
6. Make the sauce, using the butter, flour and chicken stock.
7. Put the joints of chicken into the sauce and heat gently until the chicken is piping hot.
8. Turn on to a hot dish, garnish with bacon rolls, crescents of fried bread and either green peas or butterflies of lemon.

Chicken Casserole

Follow the recipe and method for Fricassée of Chicken, using a young bird which does not need to be previously cooked. Add 2 tbs cream to the sauce and garnish with 6–9 grilled or fried button mushrooms in addition to the crescents of fried bread, bacon rolls and green peas or lemon butterflies.

Chicken Marengo

1 uncooked chicken	¼ pt cooking sherry
2 tbs salad oil	1 croûte fried bread
½ pt tomato sauce	3 or 4 mushrooms cut into strips
½ pt espagnole sauce	1 truffle cut into strips

Garnish
Fleurons of pastry or crescents of fried bread, and button mushrooms

Method
1. Cut the chicken into neat joints and remove the skin from each.
2. Fry the joints in oil until a light brown colour. Drain them and trim if necessary.
3. Mix the tomato and espagnole sauces and bring to the boil, add the fried joints of chicken, and any mushroom or truffle trimmings. Simmer very gently until tender.
4. Dish the chicken on a croûte of fried bread.
5. Thicken the sauce if necessary, using a little blended cornflour or arrowroot. Strain it through muslin or tammy.
6. Add the sherry, reheat the sauce, add the strips of mushrooms and truffle and pour over the joints of chicken previously arranged on the croûte of fried bread.
7. Garnish with fleurons of pastry and button mushrooms.

Note A boiling fowl may be used if it is steamed or pressure cooked, and allowed to cool before carving.

Chicken Maryland (for 2 persons)

1 poussin
2 ozs flour seasoned with ½ teasp salt, ¼ teasp paprika
egg and breadcrumbs to coat
2 ozs bacon dripping
2 tbs cream
½ pt stock

Garnish

Corn fritters, fried bananas, potato croquettes (see page 219). Watercress.

Method

1. Split the poussin by cutting down the breast-bone and the back with scissors.
2. Coat each half with seasoned flour.
3. Dip in egg and fresh crumbs.
4. Shake off the surplus crumbs and press firmly those adhering.
5. Leave to set for 1 hour.
6. Heat the dripping in a shallow but heavy pan until a faint haze rises.   There should be 1″ depth of fat in the pan.
7. Brown the halves of chicken, then reduce the heat and cook slowly for 30 mins or until it is tender.
8. Remove the chicken and keep hot.   Pour off the fat leaving 2 tbs in the pan.
9. Add 2 tbs of the remainder of the seasoned flour.   Blend carefully and allow to colour to a light chestnut shade.
10. Add the stock slowly, stirring all the time.   Boil up.   Cook 5 mins and skim well.   Test for flavour.
11. Add the cream slowly and reheat but do not boil.
12. Serve the chicken on a hot dish, garnished with watercress, corn fritters, fried bananas and potato croquettes.
13. Serve the gravy separately.

Corn Fritters

8 ozs flour	1 tbs melted butter
2 teasp baking powder	⅜ pt milk
¾ teasp salt	⅜ pt corn (tinned corn well drained)

Method

1. Sieve together all dry ingredients.
2. Add the drained corn.   Mix.

3. Mix in the melted butter and milk. The consistency should be slack enough to drop off the spoon.
4. Fry teaspoonfuls of the mixture in fat from which a faint haze rises.
5. Cook 3–5 mins until golden brown. Drain well.

Fried Bananas

1. Cut the bananas lengthways and then across to a convenient size.
2. Drop into the hot fat round the chicken or fry after the chicken has been lifted out of the fat before making the gravy.
3. Fry for 3–5 mins until soft and delicately brown.
4. Drain and keep hot.

Horseradish sauce may be served instead of fried bananas.

Chaudfroid of Chicken

1 chicken boiled or steamed and allowed to become cold

Chaudfroid Sauce

$\frac{1}{2}$ pt Béchamel sauce	1 tbs cream
$\frac{1}{4}$ pt aspic jelly	aspic jelly for glazing

Garnish

Neatly cut pieces of tomato or pimento skin, truffle or pickled walnut, leaves of chervil or other fine green herbs
Chopped aspic jelly
Green salad plants

Method

1. Divide the chicken into joints, carving each side of the breast as a whole piece.
2. Trim into portions and remove any protruding pieces of bone.
3. Skin the joints.
4. Wipe the joints with muslin wrung out in boiling water to remove any grease.
5. Wipe with dry muslin.
6. Put the pieces of chicken on a wire cooling tray.
7. Prepare the Béchamel sauce of a coating consistency. Cool to blood heat.
8. Warm the aspic jelly and when just liquid add it gradually to the sauce, stirring well.
9. Correct the flavour.

10. Wring through a tammy cloth or strain through scalded muslin.
11. Add the cream.

To coat the chicken

1. Have ready a bowl of ice and a bowl of hot water so that the temperature of the sauce may be corrected if necessary.
2. The sauce should flow over the food so that the surface is smooth, but it must be thick enough to mask the food completely.

 If it becomes too cool, the aspic will begin to set and the sauce will not flow smoothly. If this happens, warm the basin of sauce in the bowl of hot water.

 If the aspic is too warm, the sauce will not completely mask the meat. If this is so, cool the basin of sauce in the ice.

3. Use a large metal spoon to pour the sauce over the pieces of chicken meat. If a large galantine or whole chicken is masked, pour from the basin.
4. When the sauce is cool and just set, put on the decoration and allow to become really cold. It is convenient to use two hat-pins to place the decoration in position.
5. Baste the pieces of chicken meat with clear aspic jelly which is just liquid, to give a gloss.

Chaudfroid sauce may be used to coat slices of galantine, pieces of cooked fish, meat or game or for whole cooked poultry or game.

Variations of Chaudfroid Sauce

TYPE	RECIPE	USES
Brown . .	½ pt espagnole sauce ¼ pt aspic	For coating cutlets previously braised and pressed, or pieces of game.
Cardinal .	½ pt Béchamel sauce 1 lobster coral ¼ pt aspic	For coating lobster meat.
Green . .	¼ pt Béchamel sauce ¼ pt purée of green peas or spinach ¼ pt aspic	For coating cutlets.
Mayonnaise .	See Variations of Mayonnaise Sauce (p. 69)	For coating salmon, lobster, halibut or chicken.
Terracotta .	¼ pt espagnole sauce ¼ pt tomato sauce ¼ pt aspic	For coating meat, chicken or game.

Braised Duck

Ingredients

1 duck	1 orange
1 large onion	stock
2 carrots	seasoning
2 ozs mushrooms	1 bayleaf (very small)
1 oz bacon scraps	sprig winter savory
2 ozs butter or dripping	½ teasp sage or 1 sprig if
1 gill red wine	freshly gathered
1 croûte fried bread	parsley to garnish

Method

1. Cut the vegetables into thick slices and roughly chop the bacon.
2. Heat the fat in a saucepan large enough to hold the duck.
3. Fry the vegetables and bacon till lightly brown.
4. Add the grated rind of the orange, the bayleaf, winter savory and sage.
5. Barely cover with stock and season.
6. Place the trussed duck on the bed of vegetables, cover with greaseproof paper and put on the pan lid.
7. Simmer gently three-quarters to one-and-a-half hours, depending on age and size of the duck.
8. Add the wine and cook in a moderate oven 350° F for a further half to three-quarters of an hour.
9. Remove the duck, carve off the leg with the thigh, remove the skin and fillet off the breast in one piece. Keep warm.
10. Strain the stock and skim off surplus fat.
11. Thicken, allowing one-and-a-half ounces flour to each pint of liquid. Correct the seasoning.
12. Dish the duck on a croûte of fried bread.
13. Pour over the sauce and garnish with segments of orange and parsley.

If liked the duck may be divided before cooking, in which case the time of simmering can be reduced. This recipe can be used for older ducks that are too tough for roasting.

Normandy Roast Duck

1 duck trussed for roasting	¼ teasp ground cinnamon
½ pt dry cider	salt and pepper
1 pt sour apples diced	2 tbs brandy
¼ pt diced bread	2 tbs thick cream (optional)
2 ozs butter	

Method

1. Melt the butter in a frying pan. Before it colours, add the diced bread and fry until lightly brown.
2. Add the diced apple and cook till soft. Season and add the cinnamon.
3. Moisten with some of the cider.
4. Use this to stuff the body cavity of the duck.
5. Roast *uncovered* in an oven preheated to 350° F, allowing 25 mins per lb.
6. After 15 mins, prick the skin several times to let the fat run.
7. Half way through the cooking, transfer the duck to a clean hot baking tin and pour over it the rest of the cider.
8. Continue the cooking, basting from time to time.
9. When the duck is cooked, lift it on to a hot dish and keep hot.
10. Skim as much fat as possible from the juices in the pan, test for seasoning and add 2 tbs of brandy and cream if liked.
11. Reheat the sauce, stirring all the time. Do not reboil.
12. Strain into a sauceboat.

This dish is especially good served with celery either braised or poached and served with melted butter.

Game

The term " Game " is applied to:—

1. Certain birds e.g. grouse, pheasant, ptarmigan, blackcock, partridge, woodcock, snipe, plover.
2. Certain four-footed animals, e.g. deer (venison) and hare.

Game	Season
Grouse	August 12th–December 10th
Blackcock	August 20th–December 10th
Ptarmigan	September–May
Partridge	September 1st–February 1st
Pheasant	October 1st–February 1st
Woodcock ⎫ Plovers ⎬ Snipe ⎪ Wild Duck ⎭	November–March

Quails are at their best during July and August and may be obtained all the year round.

Guinea Fowl	Late Spring to early Summer
Buck Venison	June–September
Doe Venison	October–December
Hares	August–March

To Choose Winged Game

1. Choose birds with plump breasts and small bones in proportion to the size of the birds.
2. Choose birds with short round spurs, tender pinions, soft quills.
3. Avoid birds which are mutilated by shot.

" Hanging " of Game

Hanging is necessary in order to develop the full flavour of the bird, and make it tender. The length of time depends on the age and kind of bird and the taste of the consumer. The bird should hang undrawn in a cool larder, preferably in a current of cold air, until blood drops from the bill, and the feathers can easily be plucked from the breast. Pheasants should hang slightly longer than any other game, otherwise the flavour of the pheasant is insufficiently developed and is too much like the flavour of chicken.

Wild Duck and Widgeon

Hang these birds for two days only, otherwise a rancid flavour may develop.

Methods of Cooking Game

Young birds are roasted. This is probably the most popular method of cooking game.

Older and consequently tougher birds are braised, cooked in a casserole or put into pies.

To prepare Game for roasting

1. Pluck; reserve one or two tail feathers if required.
2. Do not draw any sinews; leave on the feet but remove the claws.
3. Scald the legs.
4. Draw the bird as for drawing a chicken.
5. Wipe inside the bird with a clean damp cloth but do not wash it. Insert a piece of butter or steak to keep the bird moist.
6. Cut off the wings at the first joint, then truss as for roast chicken.
7. Cover the breast of the bird with strips of fat bacon. This is known as " barding ".

Roast Pheasant

1. Have ready an oven preheated to 400° F.
2. Stand the prepared bird in a roasting tin, add one tablespoonful good dripping or butter and cover the roasting tin with the lid. Or wrap the bird in aluminium foil.

3. Roast a very young bird from 40 to 50 minutes, an older bird from 1 to 1½ hrs. Reduce the temperature to 350 °F after ten minutes.
4. If the bird is cooked in an open tin, baste frequently during the cooking to prevent it from becoming dry.
5. About 10 minutes before the bird is cooked, froth the breast. To do this remove the bacon, baste the bird with the hot dripping, dredge it with flour and baste again. Return the bird to the oven (temperature 400° F) and leave it until it is a good brown colour and frothy.

To Dish the Bird

1. Place on a hot dish a croûte of fried bread large enough to support the bird (about ½″ thick on the outside and hollowed slightly to hold the bird steady).
2. Arrange fried breadcrumbs round the bird, put a little watercress in the vent and garnish with one or two tail feathers.
3. Serve fried game chips or straws, green salad, bread sauce and clear brown gravy.

To fry breadcrumbs

1. Heat 1 oz clarified butter in a heavy frying pan.
2. Add ¼ pt freshly made breadcrumbs and stir with a fork until the crumbs absorb all the melted butter.
3. Continue stirring over gentle heat until the crumbs are a good chestnut-brown colour.

Hare

To prepare for roasting

1. Cut off the legs at the first joint.
2. Slit the skin along the belly and loosen it from the body.
3. Draw it over the hind legs by pulling away inside out. Pull towards the tail.
4. Pull the skin towards the head and off the forelegs.
5. Draw the skin towards the neck, then, with a sharp knife, remove it from the head.
6. Slit the belly and draw out the entrails. Reserve the heart and liver and collect in a basin the blood from the hare.
7. Wash the hare thoroughly in tepid water containing salt. Rinse and dry it well.
8. Take out the eyes but leave the ears and tail.
9. Fill the body cavity with forcemeat (see below).
10. Sew up the body slit and truss into shape.
11. Brush the back with clarified butter or dripping and lay

pieces of fat bacon over the back of the hare. Tie these on with string.

12. Have ready an oven preheated to 425° F.

To Roast a Hare

1. Put the hare into a roasting tin. Add 1 to 2 tbs clarified dripping and roast as for meat from 1½ hours to 2 hours according to the weight of the hare. Reduce the oven temperature to 375° F after 10 minutes.
2. Baste frequently throughout the roasting to prevent the skin becoming hard.
3. Approximately 10 minutes before it is cooked, baste, dredge with flour, baste again and return to a hot oven to become brown.
4. Serve the hare on a large hot meat dish.
5. Make a thickened chestnut-brown gravy (see page 106).
6. Serve with red currant jelly and small stuffing balls made from surplus stuffing.

Forcemeat for Hare

3 to 4 ozs breadcrumbs	parboiled liver from the hare
1½ to 2 ozs shredded suet	⅛ teasp pepper
1 shallot	1 level teasp salt
2 teasp herbs (a mixture of parsley, marjoram, lemon thyme, grated lemon rind)	1 egg
	1 anchovy if liked

Method

1. Mix together the breadcrumbs and suet.
2. Chop finely the shallot and liver.
3. Chop all the herbs finely.
4. Bone or chop the anchovy.
5. Mix all the ingredients together and bind with beaten egg or a mixture of beaten egg and stock.

Jugged Hare

1 hare	1 pt stock
1 onion stuck with cloves (approximately 8)	1 bouquet garni
	⅛ teasp cayenne pepper
2 ozs butter	2 teasp salt

Thickening

1 oz butter	¼ pt port wine
1 oz flour	1 tbs red currant jelly

Garnish

Fleurons of puff pastry or crescents of fried bread
Cherries
Forcemeat balls

Method

1. Skin and paunch the hare. Wipe, but do not wash it because washing removes flavour.
2. Cut the hare into neat joints.
3. Fry the joints in the butter.
4. Heat the stock in a fireproof stew jar.
5. Drain the joints and add to the stock; add the onion and seasoning.
6. Cook very gently in a moderately hot oven from 2½ to 3 hours. Allow to cool overnight. Reheat and cook for 15–20 minutes or until the flesh is ready to leave the bones.
7. Knead together the flour and butter and make into small balls.
8. Stir these into the stew half an hour before serving. Add the port wine and red currant jelly.
9. Heat the fleurons of pastry *or* fry the crescents of bread.
10. Heat the cherries, fry the forcemeat balls.
11. Arrange the joints of hare in the centre of a large dish and strain the gravy over them.
12. Garnish with fleurons of pastry or fried bread.
13. Pile the heated cherries on top of the hare.
14. Arrange a few fried forcemeat balls around the hare.
15. Serve additional red currant jelly separately.

Venison

1. Hang the venison from 14 to 20 days in a dry larder where there is a current of air.
2. During the hanging, wipe the venison every day and occasionally dust it with pepper and ginger.
3. Weigh, wipe and trim the venison.
4. Make a thick paste of flour and water, using approximately ½ pint water to 1 lb flour. Encase the piece of venison in the paste.
5. Cook in an oven preheated to 450° F for 10 minutes. Reduce the heat to 375° F for the required time. Allow 30 minutes to each lb and 30 minutes over.

No additional dripping is needed as the paste prevents any drying of the meat.

F

To Serve

1. Remove the flour casing.
2. Make a good clear gravy (see page 106).
3. Serve with red currant jelly (see page 465).

Accompaniments for Game

Game	Preparation	Potatoes	Other Vegetables	Accompaniments and sauces
Grouse	Prepare as for pheasant. Instead of steak insert a piece of butter inside the bird, and follow instructions for pheasant.	Game chips, roast, or mashed	Cauliflower, onions, celery, green beans	Green salad, fried bread-crumbs, bread sauce, clear brown gravy
Wild Duck and Widgeon	Prepare as for pheasant. Insert piece of butter instead of steak. Roast for ¾ hr to 1 hr.	Game chips, roast or mashed	Cauliflower, celery, onions, green peas or beans	Orange salad, watercress, bigarade sauce
Snipe, Plover, Woodcock	Do not draw before cooking. Place a slice of toast under each bird during the cooking to catch the juices. Roast ¾–1 hour.	Game chips, roast or mashed	Orange salad Green salad	Serve on the pieces of toast with slices of lemon, fried crumbs, good clear gravy
Roast Venison	See instructions above.	Roast or boiled	Any green vegetable, carrots, onions, celery	Clear brown gravy and red currant jelly
Roast Hare	See instructions above.	Baked jacket, roast or boiled	Carrots, onions or any green vegetable	Savoury stuffing, redcurrant jelly, brown gravy

Note Recipes for sauces, salads etc will be found in the appropriate sections of this book: page numbers are given in the index.

PIGEONS

Roast Pigeon

To each person allow:

Stuffing

1 young plump bird
1 rasher bacon
1 oz dripping
flour for dredging

pigeon liver
a piece of butter the size of a walnut
2 teasp breadcrumbs
1 mushroom if liked

Method

1. Clean and truss the bird, leaving the feet on.
2. Melt the nut of butter in a thick pan; sauté the cleaned liver slowly, with the mushroom if used, until cooked.
3. Mash the liver and mushroom with the breadcrumbs and bind with the butter and if necessary a little sherry or brandy.
4. Stuff the bird at the neck end. Cover the breast with the bacon.
5. Roast at 400° F for 25–40 minutes according to size.
6. After 15 minutes, remove the bacon, put it aside to keep hot, dredge the breast with flour, baste well with dripping and continue cooking.
7. Serve with thin gravy (see page 148 for gravy for chicken) and watercress and fried crumbs.

Casserole of Pigeons

2 large pigeons	$\frac{1}{8}$ teasp black pepper
1 oz butter	1 level teasp salt
$\frac{1}{4}$ lb diced fat bacon or fat from a cooked ham	$1\frac{1}{2}$ small onions or shallots about the size of a hazelnut
2 tbs flour	$\frac{1}{4}$ lb mushrooms
$\frac{3}{4}$ pt stock	bouquet garni

To garnish: 8 fleurons of pastry or sippets of fried bread
8 stoned olives or cherries heated in stock
parsley
forcemeat balls if liked

Method

1. Split the cleaned birds in half and remove the feet.
2. Heat the butter until it begins to brown.   Add the diced bacon fat and fry till crisp.   Remove the bacon.
3. Brown the halved birds on both sides.   Remove from the fat.
4. Stir the flour into the fat—brown slowly.
5. Add the stock, seasonings and bouquet garni.   Boil up.
6. Add the onions; replace the bacon and pigeons and cook tightly covered for 30 minutes or until the birds are tender.
7. Add the sliced mushrooms and forcemeat balls if used, and cook a further 15 minutes.
8. Dish the birds on a hot dish, taste the sauce, correct the seasoning if necessary and strain a little round the bird.   Serve the remainder in a hot sauce boat.
9. Garnish the birds with fleurons of pastry, olives or cherries, and the forcemeat balls.   Sprinkle chopped parsley over the piles of garnish.

Braised Pigeons

To each person allow:

1 pigeon
4 small shallots or spring onions
1 oz carrot and celery chopped coarsely
1 rasher bacon cut into dice
½ oz butter
1 dessertsp tomato purée or ¼ lb skinned tomatoes
1 level tbs flour
sprig of parsley, rosemary and thyme
1 wineglass of red wine if liked

Method

1. Melt the butter and fry the dice of bacon.
2. Brown the pigeons (left whole) in the fat.   Remove.
3. Sweat the vegetables in the fat until as much fat as possible is absorbed.
4. Add the flour to absorb the remainder of the fat.
5. Add the stock slowly, stirring well, boil up.   Skim.
6. Season and add herbs.
7. Put the birds on to the bed of vegetables.   Pour the wine over the breasts of the birds.
8. The liquid should cover the vegetables but the birds should sit above it.
9. Cover the birds with greaseproof paper.   Put on a tightly fitting lid.
10. Cook slowly at simmering point or in a slow oven (325°–350°) for 1½ hours.

If the cooking has been done in a casserole, the dish, after removing the greaseproof paper, can go straight to table.

To serve, cut the birds in half with a pair of poultry or kitchen scissors and serve with the vegetables and gravy from the dish.

Hand hot toast or crispbread instead of potatoes and a sharp sweet jelly such as red currant, rowan or cranberry.

Salmi of Game

1 lightly roasted bird
¾ pt espagnole sauce
⅛ pt port wine
2 teasp red currant jelly

a few button mushrooms
a few glacé cherries
fleurons of pastry

Method

1. Divide the bird into neat joints, removing the skin from each joint.

2. Put the joints into a stewpan or casserole. Add the sauce, jelly, wine and mushroom stalks.
3. Simmer gently until tender, ¾–1½ hours according to the age of the bird.
4. When tender arrange the joints neatly on a hot dish and strain the sauce over and around them.
5. Garnish with button mushrooms, cherries and fleurons of pastry.

Note The joints of any cold roast game may be utilised.

Raised Game Pie

Filling

1 large pigeon or other bird	1 or 2 pickled walnuts, if liked
6 ozs sausage meat	¼ pt stock (jellied if possible)
4 ozs lean steak	1 teasp gelatine, if necessary
1–2 ozs raw ham	
1 teasp salt	*Garnish*
¼ „ pepper	aspic jelly
	sausage meat balls (about 9)
	glaze

Hot Water Pastry

8 ozs flour	3 ozs lard
1½ teasp salt	1 egg yolk
⅛ pt milk or milk and water	

Method

1. Sieve the warmed flour and salt into a warm basin.
2. Melt the lard in the milk and water and pour over the egg yolk, and mix well together.
3. Make a well in the centre of the flour, add the liquid and beat into the dry ingredients, using a wooden spoon. Knead well until smooth. Leave to cool.
4. Grease a raised pie mould and line it with ¾ of the prepared pastry, pressing the pastry to the sides of the tin so that there are no cracks or wrinkles.
5. Line the pastry with sausage meat, reserving some for the small balls for garnishing.
6. Divide the pigeon into neat joints, reserving the feet and legs. Cut the steak and ham into neat pieces.
7. Mix the prepared meats with the seasoning and fill up the pie mould.
8. Add a little stock and cover the pie with the remaining pastry.
9. Make a hole in the centre for the escape of steam, bake the pie in a hot oven for the first ½ hour (approx 425° F). Then

reduce the heat to 375° F for the next ¾ hour and to 350° F for another ½ hour.

10. Remove the pie from the oven, fill up with hot stock, leave to cool. Remove the tin mould when the pie is cold.

11. Remove the pastry lid and glaze the pie. Glaze the sausage meat balls and the pigeon's feet.

12. Fill the top of the pie with chopped aspic jelly.

13. Arrange the sausage meat balls round the top of the pie and the pigeon's feet in the centre.

CHAPTER XI

VEGETABLES AND SALADS

VEGETABLES of all types, including salad stuffs, form a most valuable part of our diet. They play an important part in maintaining general good health, owing to the presence of mineral elements and vitamins. Their contribution to good health depends upon the retention of these mineral elements and vitamins which help to protect the body from disease and to regulate the body processes, on which vitality and good health depend. The presence of indigestible cellulose or roughage helps to keep the large bowel functioning regularly in the elimination of unwanted matter from the body.

Most mineral elements are soluble in water; therefore, if these are to be retained, as little water as possible should be used for cooking. A small quantity of water will soon become saturated with minerals and will therefore dissolve no more, and the remainder of the minerals will be left in the vegetables. The small amount of liquid left over when cooking is complete is full of flavour and can be used for soups, sauces and gravies.

The vitamins present are A, C and several from the B group. A is not much affected by cooking, B is partially affected, and C is readily destroyed.

Vitamin A is found as a carotene in carrots, swedes, beetroot and tomatoes. These vegetables are eaten mainly for the value of this carotene, as they are not rich in Vitamin C.

B Vitamins are found in the dark green leaves of green vegetables and in legumes and pulses.

Vitamin C is found in green vegetables and in potatoes.

As these vegetables are one of the best sources of Vitamin C in the normal diet, it is essential to consider its retention in deciding how best to cook and serve vegetables. Vitamin C is present to a considerable extent in *fresh* green vegetables but is destroyed by exposure to the air after gathering. An enzyme which destroys the vitamin is freed as soon as the cell structure is broken, as in cutting, shredding and peeling. It is killed as soon as the vegetable is put into boiling water. Long cooking exposed to the air, that is, with the lid off the pan, also destroys the vitamin.

167

BUYING AND STORING OF VEGETABLES

A. *Buy*, if possible, from the person who grows the vegetables so that they may be freshly gathered. Choose:—

1. Greens of a good colour, with crisp leaves and firm heart. A cabbage or lettuce consisting only of heart may be a stale one with the outside leaves removed and the stalk cut off. If the leaves feel crisp the lettuce or cabbage is fresh.
2. Green peas and french or runner beans which are firm and crisp and look faintly moist.
3. Roots and tubers which are free from excess of earth (it weighs heavy), are of a good colour and feel firm to the touch. Flabby roots and tubers have been exposed to the air for some time.
4. Vegetables of an even size, as they are more economical to cook and are generally of the best flavour. Very large vegetables are often coarse in texture and poor in flavour.

B. *Store* roots and tubers in a dark, cool, airy place, preferably on wire racks.

Store green vegetables, wrapped in polythene, in the refrigerator if possible. They can be kept crisp and firm if put at once into an air-tight tin or a saucepan with a well-fitting lid. Water-cress and mustard and cress do not keep well even in these conditions: it is advisable to buy only as much as can be used within 24 hours. It should be inspected the next day and any decaying leaves or stalks removed so that they do not spoil other parts of the cress.

PREPARATION OF VEGETABLES

A. **Roots and Tubers** such as carrots, turnips, swedes, beetroot, parsnips, salsify and celeriac, potatoes and Jerusalem artichokes.

1. Scrub to remove earth.
2. Scrape or peel thinly for economy and remove any eyes or discoloured portions.
   Turnips and swedes must be peeled thickly enough for all the skin to be removed.
3. Cut into even-sized pieces so that cooking is even.
4. Beetroot should be washed carefully, and the stalks cut off to within 1–1½″ of the vegetable.
   Peel after cooking.

B. **Green vegetables** such as all members of the cabbage family, kale, lettuce, water-cress, endive, mustard and cress.

1. Wash thoroughly and soak for a short time if necessary and not longer than 20 minutes. Water-cress must be carefully picked

over to remove little snails etc., and mustard-cress to remove seeds.

2. Discard only discoloured leaves as the outer leaves are richer in the B vitamins and carotene than the pale inner leaves. The inner part of the lettuce or cabbage is rich in Vitamin C as this is the " growing tip ".

3. Use lettuce uncooked as far as possible, leaving the leaves whole except for the coarse outer leaves which look unappetising. These can be shredded finely with a sharp knife and used as a basis for the salad.

4. Shred cabbage, break up cauliflower unless particularly wanted whole for the appearance, as the smaller portions cook more quickly. Shred just before cooking.

5. Spinach needs very careful washing as it tends to be gritty. The leaves are left whole after removing the coarse vein of each.

C. **Legumes** such as fresh peas and beans, and **Pulses** such as dried peas, beans and lentils.

1. Peas, broad beans. Remove the shells.

2. French and runner beans. Cut off the ends and the strings from the sides. Leave whole if small, shred thinly if larger.

3. Dried peas, beans, lentils. Wash and soak overnight.

D. **Marrow or Pumpkin**

1. Peel thickly to remove all the hard skin.

2. Cut into pieces and remove seeds.

E. **Onion family** such as onions, leeks, shallots.

1. Remove the root first and peel off the outer skin. Doing this under water reduces the strong aromatic smell to a minimum and saves the eyes from watering.

2. Leeks should be cut in half lengthways so that dirt can be removed from between the layers. Some of the green part of the stem should be retained.

F. **Blanched stems** such as celery, seakale, chicory.

1. Remove any discoloured portions. Green stems have a bitter flavour when raw. If the colour is only pale green they may be used as the bitterness is removed by cooking.

2. Scrub to remove dirt and scrape off any brown pieces.

3. Cut into even lengths and if liked tie into bundles for convenience in cooking.

G. **Asparagus**
1. Cut into even lengths.
2. Scrape the white part of the stem.
3. Wash carefully to prevent damage to the tips.
4. Tie into bundles for convenience in cooking.

WAYS OF COOKING VEGETABLES

A. **Baking** in a casserole or covered dish. Suitable for all except potatoes and green vegetables.
1. Prepare the vegetables according to their kind and slice or dice.
2. Put into a casserole with 1 tbs water and $\frac{1}{2}$ oz butter to every 1 lb vegetable. There should be sufficient liquid just to cover the bottom of the casserole. Add 1 teasp salt to every 1 lb vegetable.
3. Cover with a well-fitting lid.
4. Bake in a moderate oven (350° F–375° F) until tender. This will take from $\frac{1}{2}$–1 hour according to the size of the pieces and the age of the vegetables.
5. Serve sprinkled with chopped parsley, in the dish in which the food has been cooked. This method may be carried out in a saucepan. It is usual to melt enough fat to cover the bottom of the pan, then add the vegetables, water and salt.

B. **Baking in Fat** Suitable for all roots, tubers and onions.
1. Prepare the vegetable as for boiling.
2. Parboil by covering with boiling salted water and allowing to boil for 3–5 minutes.
3. Strain carefully.
4. Heat sufficient dripping in a tin to give $\frac{1}{4}$–$\frac{1}{2}$ inch depth when melted.
5. When smoking hot, put in the vegetables. Baste with dripping.
6. Cook at 425° F for $\frac{3}{4}$–1 hour or until brown and tender.
7. This cooking can take place round a joint of meat.

C. **Boiling**
Green Vegetables
1. Prepare just before cooking.
2. Boil $\frac{1}{4}$ pint water for every 1$\frac{1}{2}$–2 lbs vegetable.
3. Add 1 teasp salt for every 1 lb vegetable.
4. Put in the prepared vegetable. Put the lid on the pan and boil rapidly for 10–15 mins or until just tender.

5. If there is any liquid left, strain well and serve the vegetable at once, as Vitamin C is lost if the vegetable is kept hot after cooking.

Root Vegetables, Tubers, Stalks, and Bulbs

1. Prepare according to kind and cut to an even size.
2. Cook in sufficient boiling water to partially cover the vegetables (approximately $\frac{1}{2}$ pint water to 2 lbs vegetables).
3. Boil rather slowly to prevent the vegetables from breaking up. Keep the lid tightly on the pan.
4. When tender strain off any liquid and use for stock.
5. Serve at once to prevent loss of Vitamin C.

D. Frying—Deep Fat
Root Vegetables, Tubers, Cauliflower

1. Prepare according to kind.
2. Parboil and drain well.
3. Coat in batter or egg and breadcrumbs.
4. Fry in deep fat at hazing point until brown (380° F).
5. Drain and serve at once.

Onions

1. Cut into rings. Parboil.
2. Drain well, coat with flour.
3. Lower carefully into hazing fat and fry until a good brown colour.
4. Drain.

Potatoes (Chips)

1. Have the fat hot enough for a faint haze to rise (375°–380° F).
2. Place the well-dried chips in a wire basket and *lower gently* into the fat, which will bubble and froth.
3. After 3 mins. lift out the potatoes.
4. Reheat the fat to hazing point.
5. Lower the basket of chips into the fat and continue cooking until the chips are golden brown and tender.
6. Drain on absorbent paper.

E. Frying—Shallow Fat
Onions

1. Slice about $\frac{1}{4}''$ thick.
2. Fry in smoking hot fat, turning frequently to keep an even brown.
3. Shut the kitchen door and open the windows to allow the very penetrating smell to escape.

Potatoes

1. Fry slices in sufficient smoking fat to cover ($\frac{1}{4}''$).
2. Turn when the underneath side has browned.
3. Drain well.

Cold cooked potatoes may be used up in this way either sliced or mashed. If mashed, incorporate grated onion or garlic or chopped chives for flavour.

F. Roasting Suitable for beetroot, onions and potatoes.

Beetroot

1. Wash and trim the stalks to within 1 inch of the vegetable.
2. Do not pierce the skin in any way or the juice of the beetroot will run out and colour will be lost.
3. Place on the oven shelf in the middle of the oven.
4. Cook until tender—1–2 hours according to size and age—at a temperature 350–375° F.

Onions

1. Trim off the root and any sprouts.
2. Cook as for a beetroot. Time: $\frac{3}{4}$–1 hour.

Potatoes

1. Scrub until the skin is really clean.
2. Remove eyes and discoloured parts.
3. Prick the skin or slit one side of the potato if no eyes or discolouration have been removed. This prevents the potato from bursting in the oven.
4. Brush over with dripping.
5. Cook as for beetroot, $\frac{3}{4}$–1$\frac{1}{2}$ hours according to size.
6. When dishing break the skin by squeezing to allow some steam to escape. This keeps the potato floury.
7. Serve in an *uncovered* dish, if possible in a napkin to keep the potato hot. A lid on the dish would make the potatoes go waxy or " sad ".

TABLE OF VEGETABLE COOKERY

Type	Method of Cooking	Time	Special Points in Preparation or Cooking	Method of Serving
Artichokes Globe	Boiling	30–40 mins	Cut off the stalk. Trim off any brown or coarse leaves. Trim off any brown tips to the leaves, using a pair of scissors.	Remove the centre cluster of leaves. Serve hot with melted butter or hollandaise sauce. Serve cold with vinaigrette sauce (see page 186).
Artichokes Jerusalem	Boiling	20–30 mins	Scrape or peel thinly. Drop into a basin of water adding 1 tbs vinegar to every quart of water. Leave in vinegar water until needed.	Toss in butter or coat with sauce made from $\frac{1}{2}$ milk + $\frac{1}{2}$ water from the cooking. Serve with a roast. Serve with fried dishes or with réchauffés.
Asparagus	Boiling	15–20 mins	Tie into bundles so that it is easy to remove the vegetables when cooked. If possible stand the vegetable upright to keep the tips out of the water as these drop off easily when cooked.	Serve with melted butter sauce or Hollandaise Sauce.
Beans Broad	Boiling	15–20 mins		Serve with parsley sauce.
French	Boiling	10–20 ,,	If young and small leave whole. If large shred finely just before cooking.	Toss in butter.
Runner	Boiling	10–20 ,,		Toss in butter.
Dried (Haricot)	Boiling	$\frac{1}{2}$–1$\frac{1}{2}$ hours	See cooking of dried peas.	
Beetroot	Boiling	1–1$\frac{1}{2}$ hours	Do not damage the skin before cooking. The skin will peel off easily when cooked.	Serve cooked with white sauce or allow the juice from the peeled beetroot to run into the sauce to colour it.
	Baking	1–1$\frac{1}{2}$ hours	As above	As above
Broccoli Purple			As for cabbage but leave the leaves and stems whole.	
,, White			As for cauliflower.	

TABLE OF VEGETABLE COOKERY *continued*

Type	Method of Cooking	Time	Special Points in Preparation or Cooking	Method of Serving
Brussels Sprouts	Boiling	7–15 mins	Cut the stalks across after removing outer leaves.	Toss in butter if liked.
Cabbage, Savoy or Spring Greens	Boiling	10–15 mins	Shred finely just before cooking.	Toss in butter if liked.
Carrots	Boiling	15–30 mins according to age	Very young carrots need only be scrubbed. Older ones should be scraped. Large carrots should be cut into rings or diced, small ones left whole.	1. Toss in butter and sprinkle with chopped parsley. 2. Coat with parsley sauce, *or* 3. Serve cold in salad coated with mayonnaise or salad dressing.
Cauliflower	Boiling	10–20 mins if sprigs, 20–30 mins if left whole	Remove unwanted outer leaves, leaving green outer ring especially if the vegetable is cooked whole. Cut stalks across.	1. Coat with white sauce made from $\frac{1}{2}$ milk + $\frac{1}{2}$ water from the cooking. 2. Coat with cheese sauce and if liked sprinkle with cheese and browned crumbs, brown under grill. 3. Serve cold divided into sprigs and coat with mayonnaise. 4. See "Supper Dishes" for Broccoli and bacon sauce.
	Frying	10 mins	Divide into sprigs. Parboil and coat with coating batter. Cook in deep fat with a faint haze rising from it.	Serve very hot as an accompaniment to roasts or réchauffé dishes.
Celeriac	Boiling	15–30 mins according to size	Wash and brush to remove outer skin. Slice.	Coat with white or egg sauce.

Vegetable	Method	Time	Preparation	Sauce / Serving
[Celery]	Boiling Braising	½-1 hour	Leave whole as far as possible.	Coat with white, parsley or cheese sauce. Cook on a bed of vegetables (see chapter on Braising). Remove from the pan. Strain off the liquid and reduce by fast boiling until it thickens, or thicken with a little arrowroot. Coat the vegetable with this " glaze ".
Chicory	Boiling	15-20 mins	Wash very carefully. Add lemon juice and butter or margarine to the cooking water to counteract the bitter flavour.	Serve with good white, parsley or tomato sauce.
	Braising	30-40 mins	As for celery.	As for celery.
Corn on the Cob	Boiling	10-15 mins	Use very young. Keep whole.	Serve with melted butter sauce.
Cucumber	As for marrow	—	—	—
Endive	As for spinach	—	—	—
Leeks	Boiling	15-20 mins	Cut lengthways to remove any grit, but keep some of the green stem.	Serve with white, cheese or tomato sauce.
	Braising	30-40 mins	As for celery.	—
Lentils	Boiling	—	See cooking of dried peas.	
Marrow	Steaming	20-30 mins	Sprinkle with salt and place in the steamer over boiling water. Steam until ½ cooked, then bake in fat according to instructions for baking vegetables.	Coat with white, cheese or tomato sauce or serve au gratin.
	Baking	20-30 mins	See Supper Dishes, page 242.	Serve with brown, espagnole or tomato sauce or as an accompaniment to roasts and savoury dishes.
	Stuffed			—
Mushrooms	Baking	10-15 mins	Remove the stalks and peel off the outer skin, beginning from the edge and pulling towards the centre. Use the stalks and peel to flavour stock for soups, stews, gravies and sauces. Bake as for Vegetables baked in fat.	—

TABLE OF VEGETABLE COOKERY *continued*

TYPE	METHOD OF COOKING	TIME	SPECIAL POINTS IN PREPARATION OR COOKING	METHOD OF SERVING
Mushrooms (*cont.*)	Grilling	7–10 mins	Put a piece of butter the size of a pea on each mushroom (in the hollow where the stalk was attached). Cook under a medium grill.	
	Frying	7–10 mins	Fry in *butter* as for shallow frying.	
	Stewing	10–15 mins	Stew in milk with the lid on the pan. Season carefully.	
	Stuffed		Careful seasoning is necessary to avoid losing the delicate natural flavour of the mushroom. See Supper Dishes, page 240.	
Dried Mushrooms			Should be soaked in water overnight and cooked in the same water until it is all evaporated. They can then be used in the same way as fresh ones and have an excellent flavour.	
Onions	Boiling	15–30 mins according to size	—	Serve with white, cheese or tomato sauce.
	Braising	30–40 mins		
	Frying: deep fat	10 mins	As for celery. Cut into rings, separate, dip in beaten white of egg and toss in seasoned flour.	Use as a garnish to entrées, such as tournedos or cutlets and with chops and steak.
	Shallow fat	20–30 mins	Slice about ¼″ thick.	Serve with steak or liver.
	Stuffed		See Supper Dishes, page 241	
Parsnips	As for carrots	—	—	—
Peas, Fresh	Boiling	10–15 mins	Shell just before cooking. To every 1 lb peas add 1 teasp salt, 1 teasp sugar, sprig of mint and a knob of butter the size of a walnut. Cook as for boiling vegetables.	Remove the mint. Strain well and serve. Chopped parsley may be sprinkled over if liked.

	Method	Time	Preparation	
Potatoes, New	Boiling	10–20 mins according to size	Scrub, then scrape.	Drain thoroughly, toss in butter and sprinkle with chopped parsley.
Old	Boiling	15–20 mins according to size and age	Prepare according to instructions for the preparation of root vegetables. Take care to cut off any green parts.	Strain and then return to the pan placed near heat in order to dry off the vegetables, or
	Mashing and creaming			Mash with a fork or vegetable ricer and mix with butter and milk. Beat well and reheat before serving.
	Baking	45 mins–1 hour	See instructions for baking in fat.	
	Roasting (in jackets)	45 mins–1¼ hours	See instructions for roasting vegetables.	Drain well. Serve with fried food. Fry until brown and dry. Unless the fat is really hot the potatoes will be greasy and indigestible.
	Frying: Shallow Fat		Peel and cut into thin slices.	
	Deep Fat	20–30 mins	Peel thinly and cut into strips. For serving as chips cut about ⅜ inch both ways and as long as the potato. For "straws" to be served with game cut ⅛" thick by 1½"–2" in length. Wash well under running water after cutting and then dry carefully in a cloth.	Drain well in the basket and again on absorbent paper. Serve hot with *no lid* on the dish with fried foods.
Pumpkin	Boiling or steaming as for Marrow	—	—	—
Red Cabbage	Boiling	30–40 mins	See additional recipes, page 181.	—
Salsify	Boiling	20–30 mins	As for Jerusalem Artichokes.	—
Seakale	Boiling or Braising	15–25 mins 30–45 mins	Cut off the root and prepare, cook and serve as celery.	—

TABLE OF VEGETABLE COOKERY *continued*

TYPE	METHOD OF COOKING	TIME	SPECIAL POINTS IN PREPARATION OR COOKING	METHOD OF SERVING
Spinach	Boiling	10–15 mins	Wash very thoroughly. Remove coarse veins and stalks. Add no water, as there will be enough clinging to the leaves.	When cooked, strain, pressing out the liquid. Chop very finely or sieve. Reheat with butter and seasonings. Serve plain or garnished with sippets of toast or fried bread or with sieved hard-boiled egg.
Swedes or Turnips	Boiling	20–40 mins	Peel thickly to remove all the outer skin. Cut into pieces.	Mash with carrots and potatoes or leave plain, add 2 tbs cream + 1 teasp butter to each 1 lb vegetables, reheat and serve garnished with parsley or chopped green herbs.
Tomatoes	Baking	10–20 mins according to size	Choose even-sized firm tomatoes, leave whole or cut in halves. Brush with melted margarine and bake in a fireproof dish, or scoop out the centres and stuff (see Supper Dishes, page 241) or remove the top by taking out a cone-shaped piece round the stalk. Insert a piece of bay leaf, $\frac{1}{4}$ a clove of garlic and $\frac{1}{4}$ teasp brown sugar. Replace the lid and bake.	Serve with any dish.
	Steaming	10–20 mins	Cut in half or slice and steam between two plates.	Serve with baked, steamed or fried fish. As a garnish or a vegetable. May be sprinkled with chopped parsley or green herbs.
	Frying Grilling	5–10 mins 5–7 mins	In slices in shallow fat. Sprinkle with salt and a little sugar. Cut in half crossways. Put on a piece of butter or margarine the size of a pea. Cook under a medium grill until the centre core is tender.	Garnish with chopped parsley, a leaf of parsley or chopped green herbs.

Dried Peas

3 ozs dried peas equals 1 lb fresh peas.

Method

1. Soak overnight in water.   Add a pinch of soda if the water is hard.
2. Rinse very thoroughly.
3. Cook in boiling water until tender ($\frac{1}{2}$–$1\frac{1}{2}$ hrs).
4. Keep the lid on the pan and take care to prevent the pan from boiling dry.
5. Flavour with garlic, mint or onion.
6. Strain, toss in butter and sprinkle with chopped parsley.

Duchess Potato Mixture

1 lb cooked potato
1 oz butter
1–2 egg yolks
2 teasp salt
$\frac{1}{8}$ teasp pepper
a little hot milk (1–2 teasp) if the egg yolks are small

Method

1. Rub the hot potato through a sieve.
2. Melt the butter in a saucepan.
3. Add the beaten egg yolks and hot milk if used.   Beat well
4. Put into a forcing bag with a star vegetable forcer.
5. Pipe in piles on to a greased baking sheet.
6. Allow to cool and *when cold* brush over with egg and water glaze.   (Rinse out the basin in which the eggs were beaten to provide the glaze.)
7. Bake in the top third of an oven 400°–425°F until brown and crisp on the edges.

Egg Plant or Aubergines

To prepare

Peel off the dark purple skin, and if the seeds are formed in the centre, remove.   If very young, the seeds can be left in.

(a) *Fried*

Slice about $\frac{1}{2}''$ thick.   Steam for 5–10 mins until almost soft. Fry in shallow or deep fat until brown.

(b) *Stuffed*

Treat as vegetable marrow (page 242).

(c) *Stewed*

1. Cut into thin slices.
2. Soak for 1 hour in a marinade of equal quantities of olive oil and lemon juice with ⅛ teasp salt, ⅛ teasp sugar and a pinch of black pepper to every tbs oil.
3. Allow sufficient marinade to cover the vegetable, and after soaking:—
4. Stew in this liquor until tender (10–30 minutes according to size).
5. Sieved tomatoes may be added when cooking.
6. Serve with crisp brown toast.

Peppers or Pimientos

These vegetables can now be bought in any good greengrocer's shop. The small red ones, known as chillies, are used dried in pickles and it is from these that cayenne pepper is made. The large sweet ones, known as capsicums or pimientos, are either green or red in colour. They have a fairly strong flavour and should be used sparingly until a taste for them is acquired.

To prepare peppers

Scald in boiling salted water.

Remove the stalk or slit the side and scoop out the seeds and the veins. The seeds are very hot indeed and should be removed carefully before cooking. A few may be tied in muslin and used in stews to give a peppery flavour.

(*a*) *Salads.* Remove from the water after one minute. Rinse in cold water. Slice thinly and serve with French dressing in any green salad. It is particularly good with lettuce and chicory as an accompaniment to a plain roast chicken.

(*b*) *Stuffed.* Scald for 5 minutes; scoop out the centre and stuff with one of the following:

     i. The filling for stuffed tomatoes (p. 241).
     ii. The filling for vegetable marrow (p. 242).
     iii. Risotto mixture (using 1 oz rice to each pepper) (p. 238)
     iv. A mixture of cooked rice, picked shrimps or prawns, anchovy sauce and seasoning.

Arrange any surplus filling in a deep fireproof dish; place the stuffed peppers on the top. The peppers should almost fill the dish. Add enough tomato or brown sauce to keep the dish moist throughout the cooking. Approximately ¼ pt sauce to each pepper will be needed, but the quantity is affected by the number of peppers and the size of the dish. Cover with greaseproof paper and bake for 30 minutes in a moderate oven (375° F).

(c) *In Stews.* Scald and slice as for salads and add to a stew 20 minutes before serving.

Red Cabbage

1 lb shredded heart of red cab- bage	1 tbs brown sugar
1 onion finely chopped	1 tbs white vinegar
1 apple coarsely chopped	½ teasp black pepper
1 oz dripping or butter	1 teasp salt
⅛ pt stock or water	pinch of powdered mace

Method

1. Melt the dripping.
2. Add all the other ingredients.
3. Put the lid on the pan and cook, shaking from time to time until the cabbage is tender but still crisp and the pan is dry but not burnt.

Sour Cabbage

1 lb shredded cabbage cooked in the usual way
1 oz bacon dripping
6 tbs white vinegar
pinch of ground cloves and nutmeg
1 tbs brown sugar

Method

1. Strain the cabbage, which should be crisp.
2. Melt the bacon fat, add the vinegar, sugar and spices. Cook for 3 mins.
3. Add the cabbage and reheat.

SALADS

Some of the protective nutrients found in vegetables are inevitably lost in cooking; therefore eating them uncooked, especially green vegetables, is to be encouraged. Raw vegetables therefore should be served all through the year as an accompaniment to hot and cold savoury dishes or as a separate course. Many people find raw vegetables other than the accepted " salad stuffs " distasteful, but vegetables play such an important part in protecting the body from illness that a liking for some raw vegetables such as carrot, cabbage, sprouts, cauliflower, is to be encouraged. If these are carefully prepared in as fine a state as possible and are delicately flavoured with dressings of various kinds they prove acceptable to most people, especially if given, at first, in very small quantities.

Except for carrots, which most people enjoy finely grated, root vegetables and tubers such as potatoes and artichokes will be found more palatable if cooked and, when cold, diced and mixed with a salad dressing. Beetroot and swedes can be served raw if coarsely grated. The blending of flavour is a matter for personal taste, and only experience will prove to the housewife what is popular with her family.

Preparing Salad Ingredients

A. **Raw green vegetables** such as lettuce, cress, cabbage heart, brussels sprouts, chicory, endive, spinach.

   1. Use as soon after picking as possible.
   2. Handle as little as possible, so that delicate leaves are not bruised, to the detriment of their appearance, flavour and vitamin C content.
   3. Wash under running water to free from dust and dirt.
   4. Discard discoloured leaves.
   5. Shake lightly and drain, either on a clean cloth or on a sieve or cake cooling tray.
   6. If the leaves seem rather limp, they may be crisped by drying in a cloth and putting in a covered container in the least cold part of the refrigerator for about 30 mins.
   7. Wherever possible use the leaves whole, but if any are coarse in texture such as outside leaves of lettuce, cabbage or sprouts, they should be shredded finely, using a very sharp knife, or if the hearts are firm they may be grated on a coarse grater. This should be done just before serving so that the loss of Vitamin C is as small as possible.

B. **Raw root vegetables** such as carrots, swedes, beetroot, radishes, and celery.

   1. Wash free from dirt, scrape or peel.
   2. Grate carrots and swede finely and beetroot coarsely.
   3. Top and tail radishes. If required as " roses " slit halfway down from top to root several times and leave to soak in water to open out.
   4. Scrub the celery sticks, leave in convenient lengths. Dice or shred lengthways and leave in cold water for $\frac{1}{2}$ hour to curl.

Use in small quantities mixed with lemon juice and cream, french dressing or salad cream until the taste for raw vegetables has been developed.

C. **Cooked vegetables** such as potatoes, beetroot, swedes, peas, beans, artichokes, celery, cauliflower.
1. Drain very thoroughly after cooking.   Cool.
2. Slice or dice.
3. Serve with a suitable dressing or leave plain.

D. **Flavourings** such as chives, spring onions, green herbs, including parsley and nasturtium leaves, young dandelion leaves, cucumber.
1. Wash carefully, and chop all the green leaves.
2. Use sparingly if a new flavour is being introduced.
3. Slice cucumber with or without the peel according to taste.

E. **Gherkins, pickles and chutneys.**

Serve pickles and chutneys in separate dishes and in small quantities so that their strong flavour does not overwhelm the more delicate flavours of the green ingredients.

F. **Fruit** (fresh or dried) and **tomatoes.**
1. Wash and peel if liked.   Cut up as required.
2. Tomatoes may be skinned by pouring boiling water over, leaving for 2 minutes and then covering with cold water.   The skin then peels off without damaging the fruit.   With or without the peel, tomatoes can be sliced easily with a serrated knife.

G. **Eggs**   Hard boiled or scrambled.

H. **Meat, Fish and Poultry**   Tinned or cold cooked meat, fish or poultry.   Slice, chop or mince and serve plain or mixed with a suitable dressing.

I. **Cheese**   Cream or hard cheese, grated or cut into cubes or slices according to kind.

Sour milk cottage cheese can be mixed with chopped herbs, such as chives, savory, lovage, grated onion or Worcester sauce and made into a block or into balls.

Hints for Assembling a Salad

1. If the salad is to be served with hot poultry, game or meat, serve a green leafy salad such as lettuce, endive, chicory or cress. Toss in french dressing just before serving.

When served with duck, slices or segments of orange, carefully freed of pith, are added to the green vegetable.

2. If the salad is to be served in a large bowl, it is easier to use a

few ingredients only so that they can easily be distinguished when serving. A mixture of chopped ingredients may, however, be sprinkled throughout the layers of vegetables in the bowl.

3. A salad on a flat dish or tray. The ingredients can be kept separate by arranging them geometrically, taking care to blend the colours tastefully and keeping the proportions of the various ingredients balanced. At least half of the salad should consist of green vegetables.

If members of the family have varying tastes, it is easier to serve a salad from a flat dish than from a bowl.

Individual salads give a great deal of scope for attractive arrangement and for studying individual likes and dislikes.

Note All salads should be served as soon as possible after preparation.

SALAD DRESSINGS

Boiled Salad Dressing

$\frac{1}{2}$ oz flour	1 teasp sugar
$1\frac{1}{2}$ gills milk	$\frac{1}{4}$ teasp pepper
$\frac{1}{2}$ gill mixed vinegar	1 teasp salt
1 yolk egg	$\frac{1}{2}$ teasp dry mustard
$\frac{1}{2}$ oz butter	

Method

1. Mix all the dry ingredients.
2. Add the yolk and milk, stirring all the time.
3. Add the vinegar a little at a time.
4. Melt the butter in a double saucepan, add the mixture and cook until it thickens.
5. Beat well and cool before use.

If the dressing is to be kept, bottle when cold.

Cream Salad Dressing

1 dessertsp cream or evaporated milk	$\frac{1}{2}$ teasp made mustard
	$\frac{1}{8}$ teasp salt
1 tbs salad oil	pinch of pepper
1 teasp mixed vinegars or lemon juice	1 teasp sugar

Method

1. Mix the cream with the mustard, salt and pepper.
2. Add the oil drop by drop, stirring all the time.
3. Add the vinegar gradually.

French Dressing

1 tbs salad oil	$\frac{1}{8}$ teasp salt
1 dessertsp wine vinegar or	$\frac{1}{8}$ teasp sugar
1 teasp vinegar + 1 teasp	pinch black pepper
lemon juice	squeeze of garlic juice, if liked

Method

1. Mix the seasonings with the oil.
2. Add the vinegar drop by drop, stirring all the time.
3. When the mixture has formed an emulsion, it may be bottled for storage, but is better freshly made.

Mayonnaise

See chapter on Sauces.

Plain Dressing

$\frac{1}{2}$ pt good white sauce of coating consistency	1 teasp salt
$\frac{1}{4}$ teasp pepper	1–2 teasp sugar
$\frac{1}{2}$ teasp dry mustard	$\frac{1}{2}$ gill vinegar

Method

Mix the seasonings with the vinegar and then add gradually to the sauce.

Sweet Salad Dressing

1 tin condensed milk	1 dessertsp mustard
2 tins vinegar (using the milk tin to measure)	2 teasp salt
	$\frac{1}{4}$ teasp pepper

Method

Blend all together and store in bottles.

Summer Cream Dressing

2 tbs cream or evaporated milk	$\frac{1}{4}$ teasp sugar
2 teasp lemon juice	pinch salt
$\frac{1}{8}$ teasp cayenne pepper	1 egg white

Method

1. Half whip the cream and mix with the seasonings and lemon juice.
2. Beat up the egg white and fold into the cream mixture.

Vinaigrette Dressing

4 tbs salad oil	½ teasp made mustard
2 tbs mixed vinegars	¼ teasp salt
1 teasp each gherkins, parsley and shallots, finely chopped	¼ teasp pepper

Method

1. Mix the ingredients well, dissolving the salt in the oil.
2. Serve at once.

Additional Recipes for Salads
Banana and Nut Salad

Method

1. Arrange a bed of young lettuce or water-cress on a platter.
2. Lay over it whole peeled bananas, surrounded with chopped apple, orange or pineapple.
3. Coat with a dressing made from half-whipped cream flavoured with lemon juice and black pepper. (1 tbs cream, 1 teasp lemon juice and pinch cayenne pepper and sugar to each banana.)
4. Sprinkle with chopped walnuts.

Carrot and Apple Salad

4 tbs grated raw carrot	½ teasp salt
4 ,, chopped apple	pinch of pepper
1 ,, seedless raisins	green stuff for the bed on which
2 teasp lemon juice	to serve
2 tbs half-whipped cream	

Method

1. Blend the lemon juice and seasonings with the half-whipped cream.
2. Add the grated carrot, diced apple and raisins. Mix.
3. Pile on a bed of green stuff.

Cucumber Salad

1 cucumber of medium size	⅛ teasp pepper
1 tbs coarse salt	1 tbs sugar
2 tbs vinegar	1 tbs chopped chives and/or
1 dessertsp water	sliced spring onions

Method

1. Slice the cucumber, peeled or not as liked.
2. Sprinkle with salt in between the layers. Leave for 2 hours.

3. Rinse well to remove salt liquor.   Drain thoroughly and lay in a flat dish.
4. Mix water, vinegar and seasonings.   Pour over the cucumber.
5. Sprinkle with chopped chives and thin slices of spring onion.

Orange Salad

2 oranges

2 tbs chopped apple

2 tbs chopped celery or pine-apple

1 tbs chopped nuts

lettuce leaves

salad dressing (either cream dressing or mayonnaise)

Method

1. Cut the oranges across and remove the pulp with a grapefruit knife.
2. Reserve the juice and use in place of lemon juice in the dressing.
3. Clear the skins of pith without breaking.
4. Mix the chopped fruit with the dressing.   Pile into the shells of orange skin, which have been lined with the lettuce leaves.
5. Sprinkle with nuts.

Pineapple and Cream Cheese Salad

1 small pineapple or 1 tin (small) pineapple slices

¼ lb cream or cottage cheese or 2 ozs grated hard cheese

1 tbs half-whipped cream

1 teasp lemon juice

pinch of cayenne pepper

1 dessertsp chopped walnuts

coralline pepper to garnish

lettuce leaves

Method

1. Make a dressing from the cream, lemon juice, salt and pepper.
2. Mash up the cheese with the dressing.
3. Lay the lettuce leaves in a bed on each plate.   Put one ring of pineapple on each plate.
4. Pile on the mashed cheese to which has been added any surplus pineapple chopped coarsely.
5. Sprinkle with chopped nuts and coralline pepper.

Potato Salad

1 lb cooked cold potato; new ones if possible or waxy old potatoes

1 tbs chopped chives or finely chopped raw onion

¼ pt salad cream, mayonnaise or thick salad dressing

1 tbs chopped parsley, chervil, mint, savory or other green herbs

Method

1. Dice the vegetables, add the chopped chives or onions.
2. Mix with the dressing.
3. Put in a dish and sprinkle with the chopped herbs.

Red Apple and Nut Salad

4 small red apples	water-cress
1 small banana	summer cream dressing
1 tbs chopped walnuts	(p. 185)
lettuce leaves	

Method

1. Wash the apples.
2. Cut off the tops of the apples.   Remove the core and scoop out the fruit, leaving a thin casing.
3. Chop up the apple, banana, nuts and water-cress.
4. Mix with the dressing made by adding all the seasonings to the cream and stirring in the stiffly whipped egg white.   Fill the apple cases.
5. Replace the top of the apple as a cap.
6. Garnish with sprigs of water-cress.
7. Lay each apple on a lettuce leaf.

Russian Salad (suitable for winter)

1 small heart celery
1 small cooked beetroot diced
4 tbs cooked peas (tinned or frozen)
4 tbs diced raw apple
1 tbs chopped capers or gherkins ⎫ for garnish
1 tbs chopped pickled walnuts   ⎭
water-cress, mustard and cress or endive as available
mayonnaise dressing to moisten.

Method

1. Wash the celery, reserve the pale leaves for garnish.
2. Shred some of the outer stalks—soak in cold water.   Dice the remainder.
3. Mix the diced celery, apple and beetroot with the mayonnaise.
4. Put this mixture into a shallow bowl.
5. Decorate the top with a geometrical design of the celery shreds and peas, using the chopped capers and walnuts to make dividing lines.
6. Surround the mixture with sprigs of water-cress, bunches of fine cress or shredded endive and add the celery leaves if liked.

Tomato Salad

1 lb firm tomatoes
2 heaped teasp chopped onion or chives
chopped parsley
french dressing

Method

1. Scald and peel the tomatoes, cut into slices and lay on a flat dish.
2. Sprinkle with chopped onion.
3. Mix the oil and the seasonings, add the vinegar drop by drop, stirring vigorously.
4. Pour over the vegetables and garnish with chopped parsley. The onion may be omitted, in which case rub the dish with a crushed clove of garlic.

Winter Salad

2 tbs cooked diced potato	*Dressing*
2 tbs „ beetroot	2 hard-boiled eggs
2 tbs „ carrot	3 tbs vinegar
2 tbs cooked or tinned peas	$\frac{1}{4}$ pt cream or top of the milk
2 tomatoes	or evaporated milk
1 teasp chopped capers or gherkins	1 teasp sugar
	$\frac{1}{4}$ teasp salt
2 teasp chopped parsley, watercress or grated sprouts or cabbage	$\frac{1}{4}$ teasp black pepper
	1 clove garlic

Method

1. Slit the eggs and reserve the whites for garnish.
2. Pound the yolks, add the seasonings and vinegar, mixing well.
3. Stir in the cream.
4. Reserve some of the peas for garnish and mix the remainder with the diced potatoes, beetroot and carrots. Stir in the dressing.
5. Bruise the garlic clove and rub the bowl with the crushed part.
6. Put the vegetables in a bowl; surround with a border of watercress, cabbage or sprouts. Garnish with peas, tomato, capers and parsley.

CHAPTER XII

FRYING

THIS is a comparatively quick method of cooking, but it requires constant care in both preparation and cooking of the foods.

The cooking takes place in heated oil or fat, and the first point to consider is the suitability of the fat. It should be free from moisture so that spluttering is avoided, and should have a high smoking temperature. Fat reaches its smoking temperature at between 350° and 400° F, a temperature that is much higher than that of boiling water (212° F). A good fat does not smoke below 360° F.

Vegetable oils, hard beef or mutton dripping, lard and some cooking fats are suitable for all frying. Soft fats such as margarine and butter can be used for shallow frying. Butter is essential for such dishes as omelets. It gives a better flavour than any other fat but burns easily. The fat must be hot enough to seal the outside of the food when it is put in. It must be heated long enough to drive off any moisture, that is, it must have ceased to bubble, it should be quite still and a faint blue haze should rise from the surface of most fats and oils but not corn oil. Corn oil added to butter prevents burning because of its high hazing temperature.

Because the temperature is very high, cooking is rapid and only certain foods are suitable for frying:—best quality meat, most fish, réchauffés, made-up meat such as sausages, bacon, root vegetables, batter mixtures used for pancakes and fritters, yeast doughs as for doughnuts, pastry for rissoles or fleurons for garnish, choux pastry as for cheese aigrettes.

There are two methods:—

1. *Shallow frying*, when a frying pan is used and the food is fried with no fat, with very little fat or with sufficient fat to come half way up the food.
2. *Deep frying*, when a pan at least 6″ deep is used with sufficient fat completely to cover the food.

Pans for frying must be heavy in the base to prevent tipping and to give an even heat.

DRY SHALLOW FRYING

This is suitable for bacon, sausages and oily fish such as herrings. The foods contain so much fat that enough is drawn out to prevent sticking. Additional fat would make them greasy and indigestible.

1. Prepare the food as required, e.g. cut off rind and rust of bacon, prick sausages and clean fish.
2. Heat the pan before putting in the prepared food, and then reduce the heat under the pan and cook gently until the food is tender, turning to prevent burning. Bacon rashers should overlap in the pan so that only the fat touches the pan and the lean lies on other pieces, so that it does not dry.

Time

Bacon rashers	3–5 minutes according to thickness
Ham rashers	5–15 minutes according to thickness
Herring and mackerel	15–20 minutes
Sausages	15–20 minutes
Sprats	5–10 minutes

SHALLOW FRYING WITH FAT

(*a*) With only sufficient fat to cover the pan as for pancakes (see chapter on batters).

(*b*) Sautéing or cooking in just sufficient fat to be absorbed by the food, as in preparing vegetables for soups and sauces.

(*c*) With sufficient fat to come half way up the food as for chops, steak, liver, meat or fish cakes, steaks and fillets of fish.

1. Prepare the food according to its kind and coat as necessary. (See below for coatings.)
2. Heat the fat in the pan until a faint haze rises.
3. Lower the food one piece at a time into the fat and cook with sufficient heat to keep the fat hazing until the underside is lightly brown.
4. Turn the food over using a palette knife and fish slice and repeat until the second side is brown.
5. Reduce the heat and continue cooking *slowly* until the food is tender.

Time

Beef steak	10–20 mins. according to thickness.
Chops	10–20 mins. ,, ,,
Fish cakes or cutlets	10 mins.
Fish fillets	5–10 mins.
Fish steaks	10–15 mins.
Liver	15–20 mins.
Meat cakes or cutlets	10 mins.

6. Remove from the pan and drain on absorbent paper such as tissue or kitchen paper, *not* greaseproof paper.

COATINGS FOR FRIED FOODS

Seasoned Flour or Fine or Medium Oatmeal

2 oz flour or oatmeal　　　　　$\frac{1}{8}$ teasp pepper
$\frac{1}{4}$ teasp salt

This is used for fish steaks or fillets, including herring, mackerel and liver.　As the surface of the fish or liver is damp, the food should be pressed on to the flour or oatmeal, reversed and pressed again and the surplus meal shaken off.

The surface is then sealed and dried and suitable for simple shallow frying.

Batter of Flour and Milk

2 oz flour　　　　　　　　　1 level teasp baking powder
$\frac{1}{4}$ teasp salt　　　　　　　　$\frac{1}{8}$ pint milk
$\frac{1}{8}$ teasp pepper

Mix to a smooth paste.　This mixture should be used at once so that the baking powder does not begin to work before the food is cooked.　It is suitable for fish fillets and steaks, fish or meat cakes.

The food is passed through dry flour and then through the batter and put immediately into the hot fat.

Whole Egg Batter

1 egg　　　　　　　　　　　$\frac{1}{4}$ lb flour
$\frac{1}{4}$ pt milk　　　　　　　　　$\frac{1}{4}$ teasp salt

Make as for Yorkshire Pudding (see chapter on batters).　This is an alternative to the flour and milk batter and is used in the same way.　It has more flavour than the previous mixture and is more nourishing because of the egg content.

Fritter Batter

2 oz flour　　　　　　　　　1 dessertsp salad oil
$\frac{1}{8}$ teasp salt　　　　　　　　1 egg white
$\frac{1}{8}$ pt tepid water

Mix the flour, salt, water and oil to a smooth paste and then lightly fold in the stiffly beaten white of egg.

This is used for fruit fritters, kromeskies, small fillets of fish.　It is used as are the other two flour batters, but gives a lighter, crisper result and a different flavour.

Egg and Breadcrumbs

1 well beaten egg $\frac{1}{4}$ teasp salt
2 teasp milk   crumbs

The egg, salt and milk are mixed together. Milk up to an amount equivalent to the egg may be used, but the resulting coating is not so satisfactory as it is generally less even.

Method

1. Put the egg mixture into a shallow dish or deep plate.
2. Put fine white breadcrumbs or sieved raspings on to a paper or into a shallow dish. If the crumbs are scarce, a paper will be found more suitable, but if there is a good supply of crumbs a dish containing a depth of crumbs sufficient to immerse the food completely is desirable as this makes the process quicker.
3. Put the food into the egg and milk, brush over with egg making sure that the coating is even all over.
4. Lift the food with a fork in the left hand, steadying it with a palette knife or the brush in the right hand.
5. Allow surplus egg to run off. This is important as uneven coating of egg gives uneven finish.
6. Drop the food into the crumbs. Toss the crumbs over all the coating.
7. Lift out with the fingers and toss from one hand to another to remove the surplus crumbs.
8. Pat the surface with a palette knife to make it smooth and even.
9. It is advisable to keep clean the surface on which the final patting takes place as only in this way can the coating on several pieces of food be kept smooth and even.

This is used for mutton or veal cutlets, fish and meat cakes, cutlets or croquettes, fish fillets, whole fish, rissoles, scotch eggs, potato croquettes.

Fish fillets, steak and Dublin prawns should be dusted with seasoned flour before coating with egg and crumbs. This ensures a dry surface to which the egg mixture will adhere and so give a satisfactory coating.

DEEP FAT FRYING

This is suitable for choux pastry, all croquette mixtures, cutlets, doughnuts, white fish of all types, fritters, vegetables.

G

A special pan is necessary, one in which a depth of 4″–5″ of fat can be safely heated. The pan should not be more than ⅔ full when the fat is melted. This allows the food to be immersed in the fat without any danger of the fat bubbling up over the edge. Bubbling occurs because the food is slightly damp when put in and the moisture is driven off. It is particularly noticeable when frying chips. The pan should have a firm heavy base, and be thick enough to prevent burning of the fat.

Because of the great heat of the fat, the surface of the food is sealed immediately and no flavour from the food is absorbed by the fat. Thus it can be used for all kinds of food and very little fat is absorbed by the food so it is an economical way of cooking once the initial outlay for fat has been made, and provided the fat is kept clean and not allowed to burn. A frying basket with a diameter of 1 inch less than that of the pan is used to lower the food into the fat. Draining can be done in the basket when it is lifted out. The food can then be removed from the basket with the fingers. Further draining on paper as for shallow frying is necessary.

Certain uncoated foods such as cheese aigrettes, doughnuts, fritters and parsley would stick to the basket and lose their shape, so these are fried directly in the fat and a wire spoon used to turn and remove them. (See chapter on Fish for the frying of Parsley.)

It is inevitable that some crumbs from coated foods are left in the fat after frying, and therefore the fat should, after use, be passed through a strainer lined with clean dry muslin. It is essential that the fat is not allowed to burn. Burnt fat produces a dark colour and a bitter flavour, while fat of the correct temperature gives a golden brown colour and an appetising flavour.

To test the fat for correct heat

1. No bubbles should rise from the surface; a quiescent fat indicates that it contains no water.
2. A faint blue haze should rise from the surface, very faint if the food is to be cooked in a raw state, rather more haze if the food is already cooked as in réchauffé dishes.

    On no account should smoke rise—the fat is then too hot. This smoke is opaque and has an acrid smell.
3. A cube of bread dropped into the fat should rise to the surface at once and become crisp and a golden brown in 1 minute. This is the temperature for réchauffé dishes.

Essential points for success in frying

1. The fat must be clean and light in colour.

2. The correct heat must be used. If a thermometer is available the following temperatures can be checked. If corn oil is used a temperature check is essential, as the oil does not smoke until it is too hot to use for frying.

Réchauffé dishes 360–380° F

Potato chips 370–390° F
(although raw, there is a good deal of moisture on the surface and this cools the fat rapidly)

Fillets of fish ⎱
Fritters ⎰
Doughnuts ⎱ 350–360° F
Cheese aigrettes ⎰
Cutlets of meat ⎱

Only a little food should be put into the fat at a time so that the fat does not cook unduly.
3. When the food is coated, the coating must be of even thickness all over.
4. If the fat is not hot enough, the surface of the food is not sealed and portions of meat and fish escape and the food becomes greasy and sodden. If too much food is put into the pan at one time, the fat may flow over the sides of the pan and catch fire. This is dangerous as well as wasteful.
5. The food should be turned when necessary. This occurs in shallow frying and in the cooking of fritters and doughnuts in deep fat. These foods float in the top of the fat and so the upper side does not brown.
6. Food must be drained on absorbent paper to remove traces of surface fat which would be reabsorbed into the fried food causing greasiness.

WHAT WENT WRONG—AND WHY

Fried food is dark brown in colour or has a bitter flavour

(a) The fat was too hot when the food was put in, so that the outside became brown quickly, and, while the inside was cooking, the outside became very dark in colour and bitter in flavour.
(b) The fat had been burnt and was therefore dark in colour.
(c) The fat used was unsuitable, probably too soft a fat which would reach smoking point at too low a temperature and the food would be immersed too long.

Black specks appear on the finished coating

The fat was unstrained and contained crumbs or specks of batter from previous fryings.

Food is raw inside

The fat was too hot, giving a brown coating outside before the inside had been cooked through.

Croquettes or rissoles burst

    (*a*) The coating was not applied evenly so that it did not seal immediately all over.   The high temperature of the fat caused the heat to reach the food where the coating was too thin or missing, the food swelled and burst through.

    (*b*) The fat was not hot enough to seal the coating evenly, so that the fat penetrated making the inside soggy and, because there was no firm seal, the food broke up.

Results are greasy

    (*a*) The fat was not hot enough.

    (*b*) When removed from the fat the food was not drained on absorbent paper and so surface fat clung to the coating.

CHAPTER XIII

STEAMING

STEAMING is a means of cooking by the vapour from boiling water and is a slow, gradual method of cooking. Food steamed takes approximately half as long again as food boiled, but there is less risk of overcooking, and food does not become broken up so readily. Nutrients are not lost as readily as when food is boiled. In the case of vegetables, more of the mineral elements are retained but almost all of the vitamin C is lost. Many vegetables, particularly greens, are unpalatable when steamed. All puddings are lighter and more digestible if steamed; meat and fish are more tender than when boiled and have a better flavour. The flavour of all steamed foods is delicate; hence the use of this method of cooking for invalids and those who do not like strongly flavoured foods.

For steaming the food may be placed :—

1. In a steamer over boiling water, when the food is in direct contact with the steam. This is used for most vegetables, joints of meat, poultry or large pieces of fish or for pudding mixtures enclosed in a basin or tin. When the steam comes into direct contact with the food, some of the soluble nutrients are dissolved and lost into the water below. In the case of meat, poultry and fish, some conservation can be assured if the food is wrapped in greaseproof paper.

2. In a covered receptacle placed over boiling water when the food does not come into contact with the steam, but cooks in its own juices. This is used for thin fillets of fish, chops, vegetables and tomatoes.

   This method retains all the juices and flavours.

3. In a covered receptacle placed in a pan of boiling water. The water should come $\frac{1}{3}-\frac{1}{2}$ way up the side of the receptacle. Again, all the nutrients are preserved as in method 2. In both these methods, longer cooking is required than when the steam comes into direct contact with the food.

Points to remember when steaming

1. The steamer must fit the pan and the lid must fit tightly to prevent undue escape of steam.

2. The water in the lower container or round the vessel containing the food must boil *all the time*.

    If the food cooked consists of vegetables, meat, fish, poultry or a pudding, the water must boil rapidly, but for egg dishes or soufflés, it should simmer only.
3. All foods other than vegetables should be protected by covering with greaseproof paper or vegetable parchment to prevent condensed steam from making the food sodden.
4. The water must be replenished as it boils away and boiling water must be used in order that the cooking of the food is not interrupted.
5. The time of cooking must be calculated according to the type of food cooked; see cooking instructions with the recipes.

CHAPTER XIV

EGG COOKERY

EGGS are important in cookery both for their food value and for the part they play in many recipes. They are one of the most digestible forms of protein and contain also fat, iron and vitamins A and B. Hen, duck, and goose eggs are all valuable, but most recipes refer to hen eggs. Duck eggs are larger than hen eggs, and as a rule one duck egg is considered to be equivalent to 1½ hen eggs, while one goose egg will replace 2½ hen eggs.

Duck eggs must be cooked thoroughly when used, as they sometimes contain harmful bacteria. Consequently they are not recommended for dishes in which the egg is uncooked as in cold soufflés, nor for dishes in which the egg is lightly cooked, such as poached, scrambled or coddled egg, batters, custards and omelets. They are particularly suitable for cakes and puddings.

All eggs are more easily digested when new laid, i.e. within 7 days of laying. During this time the shell is slightly rough to the touch, and if held against a strong light, the egg is translucent and shows no black specks inside.

When broken, a fresh egg smells pleasant, the yolk is firm and curved and the white is viscid and keeps a definite shape round the yolk. When the yolk is flat and breaks readily and the white is watery and spreads easily, the egg is stale.

A stale watery egg white will not whip easily; that is why it is difficult to whip the white of a preserved egg, although such an egg has excellent food value, and is satisfactory for cakes and puddings. It is advisable to break each egg separately when several are being used in a dish, in order to test the freshness of each one and prevent a tainted egg from spoiling the other ingredients.

To separate the Yolk from the White

Eggs should be at least 24 hours old before being separated. Have ready two small basins. Tap the shell smartly with a knife in order to make a break in the shell. Insert the thumbs into the crack and break the egg apart, while holding the egg over one of the basins. As the shell parts, tip the yolk into one piece of the shell, allowing part of the white to run into the basin. Pass the yolk from one half of the shell to the other until all the white has run into the basin. Remove the last traces of white from the shell with the tip of the little finger. The whole yolk should now be in one piece of the shell. If it breaks do not try to remove any more white as streaks of yolk may drop into the basin and this, because of its fat content, would prevent the white from whisking. Drop the yolk into the other basin and remove the speck.

To Whisk an Egg White

In whisking, the albumen is distended, and in this condition it is capable of holding the air introduced by the action of whisking. The colder the air whisked in, the greater will be the expansion on heating; therefore an egg white should be beaten in a cool place.

In order to avoid any loss of air which would occur if the whipped white were to stand in a warm place, the egg should be used immediately after beating. If beaten egg white is left to stand it loses volume and goes watery, because the albumen has been stretched during beating and has become thin and frail. If the air begins to expand, the albumen collapses because it cannot stand any further expansion until it has been subjected to heat, when it coagulates and becomes stronger. (See notes on effect of heat on eggs.) For the same reason, i.e. the thinness of the distended albumen, beaten egg white, when added to a mixture, should be folded in very lightly to avoid the loss of air that occurs if the albumen is ruptured by heavy handling. The mixture should be cooked at once so that the albumen becomes set and the mixture retains its shape and its open texture.

When whisking, use a basin and whisk which are free from grease, as grease would weaken the albumen and prevent the egg from whisking. If a flat type of whisk is used the basin should be wide and shallow, but if a rotary one is preferred, a narrow deeper basin should be used. Salt or sugar, when used in very small quantities, strengthens the albumen and helps to speed up the process. A very small pinch is sufficient; too much makes the egg go watery.

Some recipes call for " stale egg whites ". This means egg whites from new laid or fresh eggs which have been separated and the whites left to stand in a cool place for 48 hours. During this time, some of the water content of the albumen evaporates, leaving a more gelatinous mass which will, because of its elasticity, hold more air and consequently will whip up better.

For mixtures in which beaten egg white is one of the main ingredients, e.g. meringues and soufflés, the eggs should preferably be 2–4 days old, and they should be separated the day before they are to be used. (See chapter on Cakes.)

The Effect of Heat on Eggs

Egg white is soluble in cold water, but when heat is applied, either to the egg as it comes from the shell or when it is mixed with liquid, the white begins to coagulate. The higher the temperature, the tougher the white becomes.

An egg will set and cook at a temperature much lower than boiling point; therefore sauces and custards to which eggs have been added should be cooked slowly and kept below boiling point. If too high a temperature is reached the egg sets quickly and unevenly in small hard flakes. It shrinks, squeezing out some of the liquid with which it has been mixed, and as a result gives a cracked or curdled appearance to the custard or sauce.

The Uses of Eggs in Cooking

1. As a main dish e.g. boiled, scrambled, poached, fried, baked and in omelets.
2. As a thickening agent as in sauces, custards, and puddings with a custard base.
3. As a means of introducing and retaining air in mixtures such as cakes, puddings and sweets, and batters.
4. As a binding agent to hold various ingredients together as in réchauffé dishes.
5. As an agent for coating as in egg and breadcrumbs (see chapter on frying).

To Store Eggs

1. Eggs should be kept in a cool place away from strong-smelling foods; these might taint the eggs, because the shells are porous.
2. If the white of the egg has been used and the yolk is kept unbroken, such a yolk may be put into a cup, covered with cold water and kept in a cool place for several days. It should be protected from dust. Broken yolks should be put in a container with a closely fitting lid, and used as soon as possible.
3. If the white of the egg is left, it should be stored in a covered container in a cool place.
4. A refrigerator is ideal for the storage of opened eggs, and may be used for keeping eggs in their shells provided that air can circulate round them, and they are taken from the refrigerator some time before using so that they are at room temperature when broken.

To Preserve Eggs

The porous shell must be coated with a substance to render it non-porous, and so prevent evaporation and exclude air.

This may be done :—

1. By packing tightly in bran or sawdust.
2. By coating with liquid wax, fat, or any of the commercial varnishes sold for the purpose.
3. By packing pointed end down in a cold solution of waterglass.

Eggs should be preserved when they are 1–2 days old. They should be clean, but must not be washed as this removes a very thin natural varnish. If dirty the egg should be wiped with a soft damp cloth.

To Boil an Egg

1. Boil enough water to cover the egg completely.
2. Lower the egg gently into the water, using a spoon to prevent cracking.
3. The water should bubble gently for the required length of time :—

   (a) Soft boil, i.e. the white opaque but still very soft—$3\frac{1}{2}$ mins.
   (b) Moderately soft, i.e. the white opaque and set but soft—4–$4\frac{1}{2}$ mins.
   (c) Hard boil, i.e. the white and the yolk very firm—10 mins. Eggs which are more than 7 days old will take a little less time.

4. When the eggs are removed from the water, the shell should be lightly cracked at one end to prevent further cooking.
   If hard boiled, the eggs should be cooled in cold water immediately after cooking. This helps to prevent a dark ring round the yolk; often a sign of over-cooking, sometimes a sign that an egg is not new laid.

To Coddle an Egg

1. Boil enough water to cover the egg.
2. Lower the egg into the water, put the lid on the pan and leave in a warm place for 7 mins. The water must be kept hot, but not allowed to boil.

To Fry an Egg

1. Break the egg into a saucer.
2. Heat enough dripping in a frying-pan to give $\frac{1}{8}''$ depth.
3. When the fat is faintly hazing, tip the pan so that the fat flows to one side.
4. Slide the egg into the hot fat. This keeps the egg in a good shape as the heat of the fat sets the white quickly.

5. Straighten the pan and allow the egg to cook gently until the white is firm. Baste with hot fat to cook the top of the egg.
6. Remove the egg from the pan with a fish slice and drain well.

To Poach an Egg

1. Half fill a frying-pan with water.
2. Bring to the boil and add 1 teasp salt and 1 dessertsp vinegar to every pint of water.
3. Break the egg into a saucer and slide into the boiling water.
4. Simmer, but do not boil, for 5 mins or until the white is opaque.
5. Lift out with a fish slice and drain well.
6. Serve on hot buttered toast.
7. A neat shape can be obtained by sliding the egg into a greased plain pastry cutter placed in the frying pan.

To Scramble an Egg

1. Break the egg into a basin, add $\frac{1}{2}$ level teasp salt and a pinch of pepper.
2. Beat with a fork until all traces of ropiness are removed.
3. Stir in 1 tbs milk.
4. In a small saucepan, melt a piece of butter the size of a walnut ($\frac{1}{2}$ oz); do not allow it to brown or haze.
5. Add the egg and cook *gently*, stirring all the time, until the mixture is almost set but is still creamy. Remove from the heat while the mixture is still soft as the heat of the pan will finish the cooking. If overcooked the egg will become tough and hard, and a watery liquid will separate out.
6. Serve on buttered toast.

Custards

Proportions

Type	Milk	Sugar	Eggs	
Baked	1 pint	1 oz	2 or 3 according to the firmness required	2 whole eggs plus 1 yolk make a very good custard, firm enough just to retain its shape when cooked.
Cup or pouring	1 pint	1 oz	2–3 according to the consistency required	2 eggs will thicken 1 pint milk just enough for a thin pouring sauce.
Steamed (and see p. 207)	1 pint	1 oz	4–6	This is generally turned out when cooked and must be firm enough to support its own weight; hence the high proportion of eggs to milk.

PUDDINGS WITH A CUSTARD FOUNDATION

Name	Additions and Flavourings	Custard	Method	Serving
Bread and Butter Pudding	2–3 thin slices of bread and butter 1 oz currants or sultanas Nutmeg	1 egg 1/2 pint milk 1/2 oz sugar	1. Grease a pie dish (1 pint). 2. Lay half the bread and butter in the dish. Sprinkle over the washed fruit. 3. Cover with the remaining bread and butter. Sprinkle on the sugar. 4. Strain over the prepared custard. Grate the nutmeg on the top. 5. Cover and leave for 20–30 minutes. 6. Bake in the middle of a moderate oven, 325° F, for 20 minutes or until the custard is set, and the top of the pudding is crisp and brown.	—
Cabinet Pudding, Plain	3 ozs bread and butter 1 oz stoned raisins 1/4 teasp almond or ratafia essence 1/2 teasp vanilla essence	1–2 eggs 1/2 pint milk 1 oz sugar	1. Grease a pudding basin (1 pint) and prepare a steamer. 2. Lay some of the raisins on the bottom of the basin. 3. Put the rest of the raisins with the diced bread and butter, essences and sugar, in a bowl. 4. Strain over the custard and allow to stand for 15 minutes. 5. Pour into the prepared basin, cover with greased paper. 6. Steam very gently for 1 hour with the water at simmering point. 7. Turn on to a hot dish and serve.	Jam Sauce
Cabinet Pudding, Rich	2 sponge cakes (3 ozs) 1/2 oz ratafia biscuits 1 teasp vanilla essence 2 ozs glacé cherries Angelica to decorate	1/2 pint milk 2 eggs 1 oz sugar	1. Grease a plain tin mould. Cover the bottom with a piece of greaseproof paper. Prepare the steamer. 2. With pieces of cherry and angelica, make a design on the greased paper. 3. Crumble the cake and biscuits, add the remainder of the cherries cut up, the sugar and the essence. 4. Strain over the custard. Stand until cool. 5. Pour gently into the mould. Do not disturb the decoration. 6. Cover with greased paper and steam very gently for 1 hour or until firm. 7. Turn out on to a hot dish and serve.	Raspberry Jam Sauce
Caramel Custard or Cream	Caramel 3 ozs sugar 3/4 gill water	3 eggs or 2 whole eggs plus 2 yolks 1 oz sugar 1 1/2 pt milk 1 teasp vanilla essence	1. Prepare a steamer or pan with a folded cloth at the bottom. 2. Heat a plain soufflé or cake tin. 3. Dissolve the loaf sugar in the water, bring to the boil and boil quickly, without stirring, until a deep golden brown colour. 4. Pour the caramel into the tin and turn it quickly round and round on its side until the bottom and sides are coated. Allow to cool.	

Name	Ingredients		Method	
			5. Prepare the custard and strain into the tin. Allow to stand so that any air bubbles may rise and burst. 6. Cover with greased paper and steam with the water at simmering point only until firm (45–55 minutes). 7. Allow to stand on a board for a few minutes. 8. Turn out on to a hot dish, and serve at once, or if to be served cold (Caramel Cream), allow to stand in the tin until quite cold (preferably until the next day). The caramel will be quite soft and the cream turn out much more readily than when hot.	
Queen of Puddings— Plain	3 ozs breadcrumbs 1/2 oz butter 1 teasp vanilla essence Rind of 1/2 lemon 2 tbs warm jam *Meringue* 1 egg white 1 1/2 ozs sugar	1–2 egg yolks 3/4 pint milk 1/2 oz sugar	1. Heat the milk and butter, add the essence, lemon rind and 1/2 oz sugar. 2. Pour over the breadcrumbs and soak for 20–30 minutes until swollen. 3. Add the egg yolks and pour into a pie dish (1 1/2 pint size). 4. Bake in a very moderate oven (325° F) until set (20 minutes). 5. Spread thinly with warm jam. 6. Make the meringue with the egg white and sugar, beating until firm and close in texture (see the making of meringue in the chapter on cakes). 7. Pile the mixture on top of the pudding and return to a slow oven (250° F) until the meringue is firm to the touch.	
Queen of Puddings— Chocolate	As above plus 1/2 oz breakfast chocolate powder	As above	As above, adding the chocolate to the milk.	
Queen of Puddings— Coconut	As above plus 1 oz desiccated coconut	As above	As above, adding the coconut to the breadcrumbs.	
Viennoise	2 1/2 ozs bread 1/2 oz peel 1 1/2 ozs sultanas Rind of 1/2 lemon grated 1 tbs sherry 1 tbs cream *Caramel* 1 oz loaf sugar 1 teasp water	2 eggs 1 1/2 pt milk 1 1/2 ozs castor sugar	1. Grease a mould and prepare a steamer. 2. Put the loaf sugar and the water in a pan, dissolve and then boil briskly until a dark golden colour. 3. Add the milk and allow to cool. 4. Mix the egg, slightly beaten, cream, sherry and flavoured milk. 5. Cut the bread into small dice, add the peel, sultanas and rind. 6. Strain the custard over the bread etc. Soak for 30 minutes. 7. Put the mixture into the prepared mould, cover with greased paper. 8. Steam very gently for 30–40 minutes until the mixture is firm to the touch.	Cup Custard Sauce flavoured with sherry

In all custards, a richer flavour is obtained if the proportion of yolks is high.   An extra yolk also helps to produce a smooth even texture, but such a custard when steamed will often split when turned out.

Preparation
1. Break the eggs separately to make sure that all are fresh.
2. Add the sugar and flavouring and mix well together until the white is no longer ropy.   Avoid beating as this would introduce more air, which would spoil the smoothness of the custard.
3. Heat the milk to blood heat and pour over the eggs, stirring well all the time.
4. Strain the mixture through a pointed strainer into the utensil used for cooking.   In this way any lumpiness left by inadequate mixing of the egg is retained in the strainer.

Cooking Custards

Cup or Pouring Custard

1. Strain into a well-rinsed saucepan and cook over a gentle heat, stirring all the time until the mixture thickens.   If 2 or 3 eggs are used to 1 pint of milk the result will be a thin pouring sauce.
2. As soon as the mixture is cooked, pour into a cold wet dish or basin to prevent further cooking, which would cause curdling.
3. If the mixture should show signs of curdling in cooking, remove from the pan at once and beat with a fork or egg whisk.

Baked Custard

1. Strain into a greased pie dish.   Grate a little nutmeg on the top.
2. Allow the custard to stand before cooking to let air bubbles rise to the surface and burst.
3. Cook in a slow to moderate oven (325° F) until firm to the touch (20–30 minutes).
4. To make quite sure that the heat is maintained at a slow steady temperature, the pie dish should stand in water in a deep tin such as is used for baking meat.   If the water is put in the tin when the custard is put into the oven, the water becomes the same temperature as the custard, and will not slow down the cooking.   So, after the custard has been cooking for 10 mins, 1 inch of cold water should be poured into the tin to prevent the albumen becoming overheated.

Steamed Custard

1. Strain into a greased mould or basin. Stand the basin aside to allow air bubbles to rise and burst.
2. Cover with greased paper.
3. Put in a steamer and cook over a pan of water which remains at *simmering point* only throughout the cooking.
    Cook for 30–40 minutes.
4. If the mixture is cooked in individual moulds, the cooking time will be 10–15 minutes.
5. Place the basin on a wooden board for a few minutes before turning out.
6. If there is no steamer available, the mould may be cooked in a pan of water, the water reaching halfway up the mould which stands on a cloth folded to 4 thicknesses, and put on the bottom of the pan. If this method is used the water should bubble *slowly at one side only* of the pan.

OMELETS

The main ingredient of any type of omelet is eggs, which are at their best for this purpose when new laid, 2–3 days old. There are two main types, namely, French or Plain Omelets, and Puffed Omelets, often known as " Omelettes Soufflées ". The many variations are produced by adding flavourings to the egg mixture or enclosing in the fold of the omelet a filling or farce.

A special pan is needed for omelets, preferably one which is used for nothing else. It should be made of heavy aluminium, stainless steel, or copper, and should be curved at the sides. It must be heavy to give an even heat and curved to prevent egg mixture from sticking in the sharp edge at the bottom of the pan. A 6–7″ diameter pan will cook a 2–3 egg omelet.

The pan should *never be washed*; only by avoiding water in cleaning can the pan be kept in such condition that the omelet does not stick.

Preparation of the Pan

For the treatment of a new pan, see chapter on Care of Kitchen Utensils. For a pan in regular use, put a handful of coarse salt in the pan, and heat until the salt browns. Rub well with paper and tip out the salt.

Then heat a little *unsalted* butter until it smokes and rub the pan again. Wipe out with a clean cloth.

After making an omelet, the pan should be rubbed with soft paper and wiped with a clean cloth.

Plain Omelets

The success of these depends upon even cooking at a steady, fairly quick heat, during which time the egg mixture must be kept moving with a fork or spoon to ensure even cooking. This action is one of moving the fork across the bottom of the pan to get the characteristic flaky consistency of a Plain Omelet, *not stirring round*, which would give the consistency of scrambled egg.

Basic Recipe for Plain Omelets

To each egg — $\frac{1}{4}$ oz butter
1 teasp water
$\frac{1}{8}$ teasp salt and a pinch of pepper if savoury
$\frac{1}{4}$ teasp sugar if sweet

Salad oil may be substituted for the butter and both give an excellent flavour. Clarified margarine is a fairly good substitute but does not give the correct mellow flavour to an omelet.

Method

1. Prepare the pan, have ready all the ingredients and the dish for serving.
2. Break the eggs one at a time and put into a basin with the salt and pepper or sugar, and the water.
3. Add parsley, grated onion or herbs if they are being used.
4. Mix the eggs, with a fork, until they are no longer ropy, but do not whisk; air introduced by whisking would spoil the flakiness of the finished omelet.
5. Heat the butter until it just begins to turn brown.
6. Pour in the egg mixture and as it sets move the still liquid mixture across the bottom of the pan with the fork, meanwhile keeping the pan in motion with the left hand. This allows the still liquid mixture to come in contact with the hot pan, when it sets at once. A 2 egg omelet will take 1–1$\frac{1}{2}$ minutes.
7. When the mixture is almost set and is still soft and creamy, smooth the top and loosen the edges, then tilt the pan away from you and jerk it sharply so that the part nearest the handle of the pan folds over the other half, making a half moon shape. Until this knack is perfected, assist the movement by sliding a palette knife under the top half, and helping the mixture to roll into shape.
8. Hold the pan over the heat to brown the underneath, and turn out at once on to a hot dish with the brown side uppermost. Garnish and serve immediately.
9. If a farced or filled omelet is being made, the hot filling is laid on half the omelet before folding over and shaping.

VARIATIONS OF A PLAIN OMELET

for two persons

Name	Basic Mixture	Flavouring	Farce	Method
Asparagus	3 eggs 3/4 oz butter 3 teasp water	1/2 teasp salt dash of pepper 1 teasp chopped parsley	2 tbs asparagus tips 1/2 oz butter	Add the flavourings to the egg before cooking. Heat the cooked or tinned asparagus tips in the butter. Lay on the cooked omelet before folding.
Cheese	As above	1 oz cheese salt and pepper	—	Grate the cheese and mix with the egg before cooking.
French	As above	1 teasp chopped parsley Salt and pepper	—	Add to the egg mixture before cooking.
Ham	As above	Salt and pepper; chopped parsley if liked	1 1/2 ozs cooked ham 1/2 oz butter 1/2 teasp chopped onion	Cook the onion in the butter until soft but not brown. Add the chopped ham and heat thoroughly. Lay on the cooked omelet before folding.
Kidney	As above	Salt and pepper	1 sheep's kidney 1/2 oz butter 1 teasp paprika pepper	Cut up the prepared kidney. Sauté in the butter for 15–20 minutes until tender. Just before the cooking is finished, add the paprika pepper. Lay in the centre of the omelet and fold over.
Mixed Herb (Omelette aux fines herbes)	As above	Salt and pepper 1/2 teasp chopped fresh herbs, or a pinch of dried herbs or 1 teasp chopped chives Suitable herbs are chervil, tarragon, lovage, winter savory	—	Add to the egg mixture before cooking.
Mushroom	As above	Salt and pepper	2 ozs mushrooms 1 oz butter	Prepare the mushrooms. Cut into pieces if large. Sauté in the butter. Fold into the cooked omelet.
Spanish	As above	Salt and pepper	2 sliced onions 2 tomatoes 1 tbs olive oil 1 tbs tarragon vinegar Cayenne pepper	Cook the onion and tomato in the oil until tender, but not brown. Add the cayenne to taste and the tarragon vinegar. Heat thoroughly, stirring well. Fold into the cooked omelet.
Tomato	As above	Salt and pepper	3 sliced tomatoes 1 dessertsp olive oil 1 teasp mixed fresh herbs	Skin and slice the tomatoes. Cook in the oil for 5 minutes. Add the chopped herbs. Fold into the cooked omelet.

Puffed Omelets

These are a much lighter type of egg dish, as the white of egg is whipped and added to the other ingredients. The method of cooking is different, the egg mixture being cooked over the heat only long enough to incorporate the butter with the egg mixture. Then the whole pan is put into a moderate oven (350° F) until set and a light biscuit colour (8–12 minutes).

Basic Recipe for a Sweet Omelet

2 eggs	2 teasp melted butter
$\frac{1}{2}$ teasp vanilla essence	2 teasp castor sugar

Method

1. Prepare a 6″–7″ diameter omelet pan, also the oven.
2. Separate the eggs.
3. Beat the yolks and sugar in a basin over a pan of hot water until the eggs have gone paler in colour, and are the consistency of cream. Stir in the flavouring.
4. Whisk the egg whites until they are so stiff that they stand up in peaks.
5. Fold the egg whites into the yolks very lightly.
6. Heat the melted butter but do not allow to colour. The fat will do little more than grease the pan.
7. Pour the omelet mixture into the pan.
8. Hold the pan over the heat and stir two or three times.
9. Then put into the oven, just above halfway up, at 350° F and leave for 8 minutes without opening the oven door.
10. When firm to the touch (from 8–12 minutes) take from the oven and turn out on to a sugared paper.
11. Spread one half with the chosen filling (which should be warm). Using a palette knife, turn the other half of the omelet over.
12. Serve at once.

Suggested fillings

1. 1 tbs warm jam.
2. 1 tbs warm sweet fruit purée such as apricot, raspberry.
3. 2 tbs fresh pineapple cut into dice and heated in a syrup made from 2 tbs water, 2 teasp sugar and the juice of $\frac{1}{2}$ lemon and 1 teasp rum.
4. 4 ozs chopped crystallised fruit plus 1 teasp rum, heated together in a basin standing in hot water.

Omelette Soufflée

2 egg yolks plus 3 whites   1 teasp flour
2 teasp melted butter   2 teasp castor sugar
1 teasp vanilla essence

Method

Make as for a Sweet Omelet, folding the flour into the egg and sugar mixture just before the beaten egg whites.

The mixture will take a few minutes longer to set. It will be much lighter and bulkier than a sweet omelet.   Fill with any of the fillings suggested for a sweet omelet.

CHAPTER XV

BATTERS

A BATTER is a mixture of flour, milk or milk and water, and generally egg. The mixture is beaten well, as the name implies, and in the process air is incorporated in the mixture. This air expands when the mixture is heated during cooking, making the mixture light.

Types of Batter

1. Coating or Thick batters (see chapter on frying).
2. Yorkshire pudding or Pancake or Thin batter.

Except for the simplest of the coating batters, no raising agent other than egg and air is used. For the simple coating batter, baking powder is used instead of egg for motives of economy. For all other batters, plain flour is used as enough air to make a light mixture is introduced by beating, and retained in the batter by the egg. Once the air has been beaten in, the mixture should be used as soon as possible as, if left to stand, air bubbles would rise to the surface and burst (see notes on making custards when the mixture stands for a few minutes *in order to* allow any enclosed air to escape). Another reason for cooking a batter as soon as it has been mixed is that harmful bacteria from the air might be absorbed by the mixture which, being made from eggs and milk, would form an excellent breeding ground. If a batter has to be made before it is needed, it should stand covered in a cool place, preferably a refrigerator.

Thin Batter

Basic Recipe	Richer Recipe
1 egg	1 egg and 1 yolk
½ pt milk	½ pt milk
¼ lb flour	¼ lb flour
¼ teasp salt	¼ teasp salt
	1 tbs oil or melted butter

Method

1. Sieve the flour and salt into a deep basin.
2. Make a hole in the centre and drop in the egg.

VARIATIONS OF THE BASIC RECIPE

Type	Additions to Basic Recipe	Method of Cooking	Accompaniments
Baked Batter Pudding	None	As for Yorkshire Pudding.	Serve as a sweet with jam, syrup or butter and sugar.
Black Cap Pudding	2–3 ozs currants	1. Grease a basin. 2. Sprinkle the cleaned currants over the bottom. 3. Pour over the batter. 4. Cover with greased paper. 5. Steam over simmering water for 1 hour.	Serve with syrup sauce.
Fruit in Batter	$1/2$ lb fresh fruit or 3 ozs dried fruit such as dates, raisins or sultanas	1. Prepare the fruit according to kind. 2. Stir the fruit into the batter. 3. Bake as for Yorkshire pudding or steam as for Black Cap pudding.	Serve with custard sauce.
Pancakes	Lemon juice and sugar for dishing	1. " Prove " a frying pan (see chapter on omelets). 2. Heat sufficient lard in the pan just to cover the bottom. Pour off any surplus fat. 3. Pour in enough batter to make a thin layer over the base of the pan. 4. Cook (about $1/2$ min) until lightly brown. 5. Turn over either with a fish slice or by tossing. 6. Cook the second side until brown. 7. Turn on to sugared paper, dredge with sugar and sprinkle with lemon juice. Roll up.	Garnish with pieces of lemon or orange and serve at once.
Savoury Pudding	1 tbs sage 3 onions cooked and chopped $1/8$ teasp pepper an extra $1/4$ teasp salt 4 heaped tablesp breadcrumbs, to replace 1 oz of the flour	1. Mix the crumbs, sage, seasoning and chopped onion (which should be well drained) in a basin. 2. Pour over the batter made from 3 ozs flour, $1/2$ pt milk, 1 egg and $1/4$ teasp. salt. 3. Bake as for Yorkshire Pudding.	Serve as an accompaniment to roast pork, goose or duck, or serve with gravy as a supper dish.
Toad-in-the-Hole	1 lb sausage	1. Prick the sausages, put into a baking tin (12" × 14") and cook in a moderate oven 375° F for 10 mins or until there is sufficient fat to cook the batter. 2. Pour the batter over the sausages and proceed as for Yorkshire Pudding, allowing the full time (35 mins) to cook the batter.	Serve with vegetables and a good gravy.

3. Add just enough milk (about 4 tablespoons) to incorporate all the flour.
4. Stir round and round until quite smooth. Add oil if used.
5. Add the remainder of the liquid gradually, stirring all the time.
6. Beat well until the surface of the batter is covered with tiny air bubbles. To do this, tip the basin slightly and, holding the spoon bowl upwards, lift the portion of the batter and allow it to drop back with a gentle " plop ". Or the mixture may be whisked with an egg whisk.

Cooking

Baking as for Yorkshire Pudding

1. Melt $1\frac{1}{2}$ ozs dripping in a tin $10'' \times 12''$ in size. This will give about $\frac{1}{8}''$ liquid fat which must be at hazing point.
2. Stir the batter mixture and pour into the fat. The depth of the batter should be $\frac{1}{4}$ inch.
3. Cook in the middle of a moderately hot oven 375° F for 15–20 minutes or until the liquid batter is set. Then raise the tin to the top of the oven and continue to cook until the mixture is well risen and brown (35 minutes in all).
4. Cut into suitably sized pieces, six to eight in number, and serve at once.

This is the traditional accompaniment to roast beef. It should be crisp underneath; that is why it is cooked fairly low in the oven to begin with. Many housewives using a Yorkshire Range start their puddings on the bottom of the oven to get this crispness underneath. It is necessary to cook a batter in a *tin* in order to get the characteristic texture. Cooked in a pie dish or in fireproof ware, a batter becomes soggy.

When joints of meat were cooked on a spit in front of the fire, the Yorkshire Pudding was allowed to cook under the joint so that the meat dripped into the batter. The drips carried a delicious " meaty " flavour and the centre part of the pudding which caught the drips was considered the choicest piece. The pudding was finished off in the oven.

To prevent pancakes from sticking

A special pan should be kept for pancakes if sticking is to be avoided completely. This, like an omelet pan, should not be washed, but be cleaned by rubbing with absorbent paper and salt if necessary.

If the pan has a firm base and straight sides, the pancake can be tossed easily.

When pancakes are cooked in a pan used for other purposes, very

RECORD OF LONG DISTANCE CALL

(DATE) _____ (TIME) _____

TO (PLACE) _____

NUMBER _____

PERSON _____

_____

ADDRESS _____

_____

FROM (EXTENSION) _____

PERSON _____

REMARKS

thorough proving is necessary. If the pan is cleaned with salt, and butter or oil is heated after the salt is rubbed away, the thinnest of pancakes should not stick. (See p. 207, " Preparation of the Pan "). Cooking of pancakes cannot be done successfully in a thin or buckled pan.

CHAPTER XVI

RÉCHAUFFÉS OR REHEATING OF FOOD

It is inevitable that there will be food left over from many meals, and the use of the scraps is an important part of economical house-keeping. Sometimes this takes the form of re-dishing or re-dressing the remains of a dish to make it attractive and appetising, sometimes using the scraps to turn them into a completely different dish.

Immediately after a meal the following attention is necessary to keep the food fresh and wholesome:—

1. Put left-over food into clean containers and protect from dust and flies.
2. Cool the food as quickly as possible and put into a refrigerator if possible. Do not put hot food into the refrigerator.
3. Some foods are best reheated when divided into small portions, and such foods as potatoes and fish are more easily divided when hot, so if left-over potatoes are to be used up sieved or riced, do this before putting them away. Similarly flake fish and remove it from the skin and bone.
4. Gravy can often be used to help to moisten a réchauffé, but care must be taken to do so before there is any trace of taint. Thickened gravies become tainted very quickly. All gravies should be used the day they are made.
5. Cut bread or bread and butter should be wrapped in grease-proof paper or cellophane and, if to be kept overnight, covered with a damp cloth.
6. Left-over cake can be used up in puddings in place of bread-crumbs.

Stale yeast buns may be dipped in warm water or milk and water and freshened up in a moderate oven.

If carefully stored in clean airtight tins, cakes and buns will keep for several days. The tins should be lined with greaseproof paper, and the paper kept free from crumbs. It is often the careless storage of cakes which makes them look unpalatable so that they need to be used up in other dishes.

Points to remember in reheating :—

1. Foods which are already cooked need only reheating, especially
meat and fish. Recooking would toughen the protein and
make the food indigestible; it is essential therefore to avoid
overheating.
2. Skin, gristle and excessive fat must be removed from meat, and
skin and bone from fish.
3. Cold meat and fish lack moisture, so gravy or sauce is used to
replace the original moisture. These must be carefully
seasoned and flavoured. Many dishes are improved by serving a good sauce as an accompaniment. Reference to the
chapter on sauces will give suggestions for variation. Experi-
menting with a variety of sauces is strongly recommended.
4. Cooked meat and fish have less nourishment and flavour than
fresh, so both flavour and further food value must be added in
reheating.

   It is easier to add to flavour if the meat or fish is divided finely,
but flavourings must be cooked before being added, as the
quick reheating would not allow for cooking any raw ingredients. It is in the adding of flavourings that the skill of
the cook is most important. A few suggestions are :—

   (a) For dark meats : chopped freshly cooked onion, tomato,
mushrooms, parsley, freshly gathered herbs such as
winter savory, lovage (which has a celery flavour) or a
mixture of mint, thyme and sage.
   (b) For white meats : lemon rind or juice, parsley, herbs,
spices such as mace or nutmeg.
   (c) For all meats : accompaniments such as fried apple or
pineapple slices, fried parsley, sliced fresh tomato
soaked in a marinade of oil and herb vinegar.
   (d) Dishes such as mince, hash, blanquette or fricassée made
of cold meat or fish should be served with toast triangles or fried sippets of bread to make a contrast in
texture.

5. When making croquette mixture a thick binding sauce (panada)
is necessary to hold the various ingredients together. This
must be very well cooked before the other ingredients are
added, as the process of reheating will not cook the panada.
If it is not well cooked, the finished dish will have a raw flavour.
(See chapter on sauces for the method of making the panada.)
6. In order merely to reheat the food, a coating must be used to
protect from great heat such as is used in frying or baking.
Frying is a favourite method of reheating as it produces an

appetising appearance and a succulent flavour. Four varieties of coating are:—

(*a*) Covering with creamed potato, as in shepherd's pie or potato balls.

(*b*) Dipping in batter, as in Kromeskies.

(*c*) Coating with egg and breadcrumbs or milk and flour, as in croquette mixtures.

(*d*) Covering with pastry.

7. When cold meats, fish, vegetables or hard-boiled eggs are served as hash, mince, fricassée or curry, the appropriate sauce should be well cooked and the food added for just as long as is required to heat it through.

8. Reheated dishes should be served hot, as soon as they are ready, and care should be taken to serve neatly and to garnish carefully. Modern fireproof earthenware and glass help to make the dish attractive.

Method for Making Croquettes and Cutlets

1. Mince or chop finely the main ingredients.

2. Make the panada or thick sauce and cook thoroughly, adding the main ingredients and the flavourings. Season and taste. It is most important to taste the mixture at this stage, to make sure that it is palatable and really interesting in flavour.

3. Turn the mixture on to a plate to cool. Spread it evenly so that it can be divided into even sized portions. Cover with a greased paper to prevent hardening of the surface.

4. When cool, shape as required. To do this, roll each portion into a ball, using a little flour on the hands to prevent sticking. The balls should be free from cracks. Then shape, using a palette knife and the hand:—

(*a*) Croquettes into cork shapes, keeping the ends flat.

(*b*) Cutlets into a cutlet shape: flatten out the ball into a triangle with a rounded end and then, using the thumb of the left hand to make an indentation, about halfway up the triangle, shape to represent a cutlet.

Avoid having too much flour on the board as this would spoil the flavour and possibly cause cracking.

5. Coat with egg and breadcrumbs.

6. Insert a piece of macaroni in the narrow end of the cutlet to represent the bone.

7. It is best to fry croquettes and cutlets in deep fat to retain the shape. The necessary turning in shallow frying tends to break them.

CROQUETTES

	Main Ingredient	Panada	Additional Flavourings	Accompaniments	No. of Croquettes
Chicken and Ham	6 ozs cold chicken 2 ozs cooked ham	1 oz flour 1 oz fat ¼ pt milk ¼ teasp salt	Grated rind of ½ lemon or pinch of herbs	Tomato, Hollandaise or Tartare sauce	6
Fish	8 ozs cold fish preferably a mixture of white and smoked fish	As above	1 teasp chopped parsley plus 1 teasp lemon juice or 2 teasp anchovy essence or ¼ teasp ground mace	Parsley or Hard-boiled egg or Hollandaise, Tartare or Tomato sauce or Fried parsley	6
Egg	2 hard boiled eggs chopped finely	As above	1 dessertsp chopped mushroom or 1 oz chopped ham or 1 oz grated cheese plus ⅛ teasp cayenne pepper	As above	4
Macaroni Cheese	1½ ozs cooked macaroni 1½ ozs grated cheese	As above	½ cooked onion, finely chopped ⅛ teasp cayenne	As above	4
Meat	8 ozs cooked meat of one type or a mixture	As above	1 tbs chopped cooked onion plus ketchup or pinch herbs	Any good brown sauce or tomato sauce plus fried parsley	6
Potato	½ lb cooked potatoes 1 teasp salt	1 egg yolk	½ oz butter plus 1 teasp chopped parsley or 1 tbs grated cheese	Fried parsley	8

RÉCHAUFFÉS

Dish	Main Ingredient	Preparation	Sauce	Accompaniments	Serving
Curry (a) Cold Meat	¾ lb cooked meat, poultry, rabbit or game	1. Remove bone, skin and gristle. 2. Cut into neat cubes. 3. Reheat in the sauce.	1 pint curry sauce (see page 66)	6 ozs Patna rice Pieces of fresh lemon Variety of Chutneys and see page 244	Serve the curry in a casserole, and the accompaniments in separate dishes.
(b) Egg	5 hard-boiled	Cut the eggs into halves lengthwise.	¾ pt curry sauce	As above	As above
(c) Fish	¾ lb cooked white fish	Divide the cold fish into pieces about 2 inches in length and of a thickness according to the fish.	1 pt curry sauce	As above	As above
(d) Vegetables	1½ lbs mixed root vegetables and pulses	Cut the vegetables into neat blocks about 2 inches in length and width, and about 2″ thick, celery into 2 inch lengths. Steam and use at once. Cook the pulses in a pressure cooker or boil (see page 477 or 179).	1 pt curry sauce	As above	As above
Fricassée	¾ lb cold white meat, or poultry or rabbit	Prepare as for curry.	1 pint white sauce made with ½ milk and ½ stock from the meat bones	Bacon rolls Sippets of fried bread and toast Lemon butterflies Chopped parsley	In a shallow casserole, with the garnish suitably arranged.
Hash	¾ lb cold dark meat and pieces of freshly cooked root vegetables	1. Cut the meat in thin slices as if it were to be served cold. 2. Cut the vegetables in large dice.	1 pint good brown sauce or 1 pint tomato sauce	3 ozs Patna rice or 3 ozs macaroni or other pasta Chopped parsley	Serve on a hot dish, surrounded with a border of the starchy food, sprinkled with parsley.

| Mince | ¾ lb cooked meat | Pass through a mincer or chop finely, discarding skin and gristle and any excess fat. | ¾ pt good brown sauce or gravy | Mashed potato of tomato Cooked halves of tomato Triangles of toast | Surround the meat and sauce with a border of mashed potato. Garnish with tomato and pieces of toast. |

Method for Making Meat or Fish Cakes

1. Mince the meat, discarding skin, fat and gristle. Flake the fish.
2. Mash the potatoes, put in a pan with the milk. Heat well and beat until smooth and creamy.
3. Add the meat or fish and the additional flavourings. Season carefully and taste.
4. Put on a plate to cool, keep covered.
5. Roll into a long sausage shape until free from cracks. Cut into 4 or 6 pieces of even thickness.
6. Shape each piece into a flat cake about 2–2½" in diameter and 1" thick. Use a palette knife for patting.
7. Flour the board to prevent sticking.
8. Coat evenly with the coating chosen.
9. Fry, drain and serve at once.

	Main Ingredients	Binding	Flavourings	Coating	Cooking	Accompaniments
Fish Cakes	½ lb cooked white fish or mixture of white and smoked fish ½ lb mashed potato 1 oz butter 2 tbs milk Salt and pepper	1 beaten egg	1 teasp chopped parsley or 2 teasp anchovy essence or ¼ teasp ground mace	Egg and flour batter or Egg and bread-crumbs	Deep or shallow frying or baking in a greased tin in a hot oven for 20 minutes.	Parsley, Caper, Tomato or Brown sauce Fried parsley or pieces of lemons
Meat Cakes	½ lb cooked meat ½ lb mashed potato 1 oz butter 2 tbs milk Salt and pepper	1 beaten egg	1 freshly cooked onion finely chopped 1 teasp chopped parsley or 2 teasp well flavoured sauce or ¼ teasp ground herbs	Any coating as on page 218	As above	Tomato or Brown sauce Baked tomato Green or root vegetables

Additional Recipes
Cold Meat Mould

½ lb cooked minced meat, pre-
    ferably a mixture of meats or
    meat and poultry
1 oz fine breadcrumbs
½ oz crumbled cornflakes
¼ small cooked onion

1 gill stock or gravy
½ teasp chopped rosemary or a
    mixture of fresh herbs
1 egg
Seasoning

Method

1. Grease a 5″ cake or 1 lb loaf tin very thickly. Coat with sieved raspings.
2. Mix the minced meat, herbs, bread and flake crumbs with the seasonings.
3. Beat up the egg and add to the mixture with the stock. The mixture will be slack enough to drop easily from the spoon.
4. Taste, and if there is not enough flavour add tomato or mushroom ketchup as required.
5. Turn into the prepared tin. Cover with greased paper.
6. Bake in the middle of a moderate oven (350°–375° F) for ¾–1 hr.
7. Turn out on to a hot dish and serve with a good gravy or sauce.

If the mould is made with cold pork and ham in it, serve apple sauce instead of gravy.

Kromeskies

(A small entrée for 4 persons or a supper dish for 2)

3 ozs cooked white meat
1 oz cooked ham or tongue
Dessertsp chopped mushrooms
½ teasp grated lemon rind
Slices of fat bacon cut thin

½ gill milk ⎫
½ oz butter ⎬ Panada (see p. 59)
½ oz flour ⎭
Fritter batter (see chapter on
    frying)

Method

1. Make the panada and stir in the minced meat, mushrooms and lemon rind. Season well. This should be soft yet firm enough to divide into pieces.
2. Shape each piece into a cork shape and wrap in a piece of thin fat bacon. (If the bacon is thick it will not cook in the time it takes the batter to brown and crisp.)
3. Make the fritter batter.
4. Dip the rolls in the batter and fry in deep fat brought to a faint haze.

5. Drain well and serve at once, garnished with lemon and parsley.
6. If used for a supper dish, serve with thick slices of wholemeal bread and butter.

Potato Casserole and Mince

cold meat mince prepared as   2 teasp salt
   on page 221 $\frac{1}{8}$ teasp pepper
1 lb potatoes   baked halves of tomato
1 oz butter   parsley
$\frac{1}{2}$ egg or 1 egg yolk

Method

1. Scrub the potatoes and steam them in their jackets 25–35 mins.
2. Skin *while hot*, mash well with seasoning, butter and egg.
3. Grease a 7-inch cake tin with a loose base very thickly and dredge with crumbs.
4. Press the potato mixture into the sides and bottom of the tin. Make this lining $\frac{1}{2}''-\frac{3}{4}''$ thick and keep the top edge neat.
5. With the egg left in the basin and a little added milk brush over the inside of the potato mixture.
6. Bake in the top third of a hot oven (420° F) until crisp and brown (20–30 mins).
7. Turn out on to a hot dish, fill up with hot mince.
8. Garnish with tomatoes and parsley.

Rissoles

Filling

2 ozs cooked meat minced $\frac{1}{8}$ teasp cayenne pepper   or
2 tbs thick white sauce   ground mace
$\frac{1}{2}$ small cooked onion chopped   ketchup or chutney if liked
salt and pepper to taste

Pastry case

   2 ozs flour   approx 2 teasp water
   1 oz fat

Garnish

   Triangles or crescents of fried bread
   Mushrooms and slices of gherkin

Method

1. Mix the ingredients for the filling and taste carefully.
2. Make the pastry, roll it out very thinly and cut out with a 4-inch cutter.   (5 or 6 circles according to thickness.)

3. Put 1 tbs of the mixture on each circle of pastry, laying it on one half.
4. Wet the edges of the pastry, fold over the spare pastry and press the edges together.
5. Press the half circle to make a crescent shape.
6. Coat with eggs and breadcrumbs and fry in deep fat brought to a faint haze.
7. Garnish with fried mushrooms, slices of gherkin heated in a little vinegar, and fried bread.

Scalloped Fish

¼ lb cooked fish flaked coarsely	salt and pepper
½ pt good white sauce	⅛ teasp ground mace or 1 des-
½ lb cooked sieved potato	sertsp lemon juice
½ oz butter	1 tbs melted butter
2 tbs milk	1 dessertsp fresh breadcrumbs

Method

1. Grease 4 scallop shells or 4 individual earthenware or ovenware dishes.
2. Mix the fish with half the sauce, season and flavour and taste carefully.
3. Divide this mixture between the four cases while still very hot.
4. Cover with the remainder of the sauce.
   Dredge with fresh crumbs and sprinkle on melted butter.
5. Mix the potato, butter and milk in a pan, making the mixture thoroughly hot.
6. Put in the forcing bag with a vegetable forcing nozzle and pipe round the edges of the fish mixture (or simply arrange in a border round the fish mixture).
7. Brown under the grill.
8. Garnish with parsley.

Fish Pie

Double the Scalloped Fish recipe, put all the fish mixture into a greased pie dish (1½ pint size) and cover with the potato mixture, either by smoothing it firmly with a knife or by piping it on the top.

If the mixture is left smooth brush over with milk. Bake in the top of a hot oven (400° F) until well heated and brown (20 mins).

The mixture can be varied by adding one or more of the following:

(*a*) 1 tbs chopped parsley
(*b*) 1–2 hard-boiled eggs, sliced
(*c*) 1 tbs chopped capers or gherkins

(*d*) 1 tbs anchovy essence
(*e*) 2 sliced skinned tomatoes
(*f*) 1 tbs chopped sauté shallot
(*g*) 1 sliced scalded green pepper

Vary the top by sprinkling on a mixture of raspings and cheese or fried crumbs as for game, or thinly sliced potatoes instead of mashed.

Shepherd's Pie

½ lb cooked meat minced
1 freshly cooked onion
1 freshly cooked carrot or 1 tomato chopped
2 teasp chopped parsley or ¼ teasp herbs
1 tbs ketchup
sufficient stock or well flavoured gravy to moisten well
½ lb cooked mashed potato
2 tbs milk
½ oz butter
seasoning

Method

1. Mash the potatoes while hot, add the butter and milk and 1 teasp salt. Taste.
2. Mix the meat, vegetables and the flavourings and stock. Taste and season as required.
3. Put the meat mixture into a greased pie dish (1½ pt size).
4. Cover with the potato mixture. Smooth it tidily with a knife, brush with milk.
5. Bake in the top of a hot oven (400° F) until well heated and brown.
6. Serve with a good gravy.

H

CHAPTER XVII

SUPPER, LUNCH OR HIGH TEA DISHES
including Savoury, Egg, Cheese and Vegetarian Dishes

MOST families have one meal in the day which is more substantial than the others. This may be taken at midday or in the evening according to the circumstances of the family, but housewives with little or no domestic help find they must produce a second meal which can be prepared well in advance, or very quickly at the time of the meal. The domestic budget often makes it necessary to plan an economical meal which, however, must be appetising, satisfying and nourishing. It is an opportunity for using left-over foods such as are described in the chapter on reheating, and also for utilising any uncooked perishable food not required for the main meal, especially fruit or vegetables which, if kept, would deteriorate. These can often be used as a garnish. Sometimes the factor in the choice of a supper meal is that there shall be very little washing up afterwards because the evening is a young mother's only time for relaxation.

When the second meal is taken as High Tea, a meal which is particularly suitable when there are school children in the family, one dish supplying the protein or body-building requirements is supplemented with bread and butter and jam, scones and cake, and a hot drink and snack taken at bedtime. Because there is a considerable time between this meal and bedtime, the main dish can be substantial, but when the meal is taken as supper, possibly rather late in the evening, the food must be light and easily digested.

Probably most of the day's protein will have been eaten between breakfast and the main meal, but some protein should be eaten at the second meal. This is the time to serve protein foods which are cheaper than meat, such as cheese, pulses, nuts and eggs. Meat and fish will find a place in this meal, particularly cold meats and oily fish (such as herrings and pilchards) to be served with salads.

The choice of the main ingredient depends upon what is served at other meals in the day. Variety is needed in the day's meals, and the cost of ingredients and the season of the year must be considered.

Supposing this meal is high tea or supper and the housewife wants to prepare as much as possible while she is cooking the luncheon, the following jobs can be done without spoiling the appearance, flavour or nutritional value of the meal :—

1. Dishes made from reheated fish or meat can be prepared so that they are ready to fry or bake, unless they are to be coated with batter.
2. Fresh fish can be prepared and coated ready for cooking.
3. Sauces can be made up to the point at which they are ready for the last boiling.
4. Root vegetables can be prepared and left in cold water, but fresh fruit, green vegetables and salads should be prepared just before use in order to retain their Vitamin C.

Vegetarian or Meatless Cooking

From time to time most housewives need to prepare a meatless meal. This may be because, for health reasons, a diet without meat has been recommended or it may be that someone has humanitarian reasons for not eating foods which necessitate the slaughtering of animals, birds and fish. If a person is a very strict vegetarian or food reformer, more detailed information than can be given here will be needed, but certain general principles must be observed whether it is for one meal or for a long period :—

1. A balanced diet must be planned i.e. the right proportion of body building, protective and energy foods must be provided (see chapter on " Meal Planning ").
2. Most normal diets derive a high proportion of body-builders from meat, fish and poultry. If these are not taken, body-building material must be obtained from milk, cheese, eggs, nuts and pulse vegetables such as peas, beans and lentils.

    If butter and lard are not taken, vegetable fats, oils and certain margarines can be substituted.

    Similarly, vegetable extracts can replace meat extracts. They are strong in flavour and rich in yeast extracts and make excellent substitutes for meat stock.
3. There is no difficulty in providing energy foods for meatless meals, in fact one of the main problems is to avoid undue amounts of starchy foods and to prevent the meal from becoming too bulky. Some cereals, however, contain a certain amount of protein (macaroni, all pastas and semolina) so that although they are bulky, they provide more nutrients than those which have little or no protein (flour, cornflour).

    Vegetables absorb water in cooking, therefore raw vegetable

salads are preferable to cooked vegetables, if palatable when served in this way.

4. Great care must be taken in flavouring and seasoning, as vegetarian foods tend to be tasteless. Accompaniments and garnishes are of great importance.

Many of the following recipes contain no protein from slaughtered animals and are therefore suitable for meatless or vegetarian meals.

Cooking with Cheese

Cheese is one of the products of milk, a very concentrated food because much of the water content of the milk is removed during the processing. A hard cheese such as Cheddar is suitable for cooking as it grates easily and has a fairly strong flavour. Cheshire, Caerphilly and Wensleydale, having a mild flavour, do not give so well-flavoured a dish. Stilton and other blue-veined cheeses are not suitable for cooking—neither are soft cheeses such as Brie and Coulommier. Gruyère and processed cheeses, though more difficult to grate, are good for cooking.

It is probable that Cheddar cheese will be found to be the most economical.

Cheese is rich in both protein and fat and is a very valuable source of calcium. It is therefore excellent for growing children who need calcium for the growth of their bones and teeth. It is, however, not readily digested by everyone, and many people find cooked cheese more difficult to digest than raw cheese.

To make cooked cheese digestible:—

1. Grate very finely and avoid overcooking, which makes the casein (one of the proteins) very tough and indigestible.
2. Combine with starchy foods, as the starch helps in the digestion of the fat content of the cheese.
3. Avoid cooked cheese late at night for those of the family who find it difficult to digest.
4. Use mustard and possibly vinegar as seasonings as these help to make the cheese digestible and if used discreetly are not distinguishable in the finished dish.

RECIPES
Bacon and Egg Tart

6 ozs shortcrust pastry	Flavouring:—
2–4 eggs	either 1 tbs chopped parsley
4 small rashers of bacon	or ¼ teasp mixed herbs
1 teasp salt	or 2 sliced tomatoes
⅛ teasp pepper	or 4 mushrooms

Method

1. Line a 7″ sandwich tin with rather more than half of the pastry.
2. Roll out the remainder as a top.
3. Spread the bacon on the bottom of the tin.
4. *Either* drop in the eggs whole *or* beat them and pour over the bacon.
5. Sprinkle on the parsley or herbs or add the tomato or mushroom.
6. Damp the edges of the pastry, cover with the lid, pressing the edges well together.
7. Pinch the edges with the thumb and forefinger of the right hand, pressing against the finger of the left hand. Brush the top with milk.
8. Bake in the centre of a hot oven, 425° F, for 10 mins, then reduce the heat to 350° for a further 30 mins.
9. Serve hot or cold.

Baked Eggs (Eggs en Cocotte)

4 eggs
2 ozs butter (margarine is not successful)
4 pinches of salt

Method

1. Divide the butter into 4 portions and put one in each of four small fireproof " cocotte " dishes.
2. Break each egg separately into a cup. Add a pinch of salt to each.
3. Slide one egg into each cocotte dish.
4. Bake in a moderate oven (325° F) for 10 mins or until the white of egg is set.
5. Serve with split toast.

Broccoli with Bacon Sauce

1 medium-sized broccoli	2 ozs chopped bacon
$\frac{1}{2}$ pt boiling water	1 oz flour
1 small onion	salt and pepper
$\frac{1}{4}$ teasp curry powder	$\frac{1}{4}$ pt milk

Method

1. Break up the broccoli into sprigs and wash well.
2. Cook in the $\frac{1}{2}$ pint of boiling salted water. Drain and keep hot.
3. Chop the onion and fry with the bacon without browning.
4. Add the curry powder and flour and cook for 2–3 mins.
5. Make up the milk to $\frac{1}{2}$ pint with the water from the broccoli.

Add this gradually to the sauce and stir till boiling. Cook 2–3 mins.

6. Pour over the broccoli and serve at once.

Cheese Eggs

4 eggs	1 tbs grated cheese
½ pt cheese sauce	1 tbs browned breadcrumbs

Method

1. Grease a shallow fireproof dish (1 pint capacity).
2. Drop in the raw eggs.
3. Coat with the cheese sauce.
4. Mix together the grated cheese and raspings, sprinkle over the sauce.
5. Bake in the top of a moderate oven (350°) until the top is brown, by which time the eggs will be set (15 mins.).

Cheese Flan

4 ozs cheese pastry (see page 390)	1–2 hard-boiled eggs
1–2 freshly cooked carrots	2 skinned tomatoes
2 tbs cooked peas	½ pt cheese sauce (see page 61)
	½ oz grated cheese

Method

1. Roll out the pastry and line a well-greased flan ring or sand-wich tin, size 7″ diameter.
2. Prick the base, cover the base with greaseproof paper and fill up with baking beans or crusts of bread.
3. Bake in the centre of the oven (420° F) for 10 mins, then reduce to 375° for 15–20 mins. Just before the pastry is cooked remove the crusts and paper and allow the flan case to dry off. Cool.
4. Slice the carrot, tomatoes and egg and arrange in the flan case with the peas in layers. Between each layer of vegetables pour some sauce, making the last layer of sauce.
5. Sprinkle the grated cheese over the sauce.
6. Bake in the top of a moderately hot oven (375° F) until the cheese is browned (20 mins) *or* if the vegetables and sauce are hot when put into the flan case, it may be put under a grill to brown (5 mins).

Cheese Potatoes

4 large potatoes	4 tbs milk
2 ozs grated cheese	2 teasp salt
1 oz butter	parsley

Method

1. Scrub the potatoes; prick with a fork and bake in their jackets until soft (oven 375°—time 1-1½ hours).
2. Remove a large oval from the top of each potato. Scoop out the inside.
3. Mash the potato with the butter, milk and 1½ ozs cheese and salt.
4. Refill the potato cases, piling a little of the mixture above the opening.
5. Sprinkle with the remaining ½ oz of cheese.
6. Bake or grill until brown.

Cheese Pudding

2 ozs breadcrumbs	½ pt milk
2½ ozs grated cheese	¼ teasp made mustard
1-2 eggs	1 teasp salt

2 teasp coarsely chopped parsley

Method

1. Grease a pie dish or fireproof dish (1 pint size).
2. Separate the yolks and whites of the eggs.
3. Beat the egg yolks, add the warmed milk, cheese and seasonings.
4. Pour over the breadcrumbs.   Allow to cool.
5. Beat the egg whites until stiff enough to peak.
6. Fold them into the breadcrumb mixture and pour into the dish.
7. Bake for 30 mins in the top of a hot oven (400° F).

Cheese Soufflé

½ oz butter	1½ ozs grated cheese (parmesan
¼ oz flour	if possible)
⅛ pt milk	⅛ teasp cayenne pepper
2 egg whites	1 teasp salt
1½ egg yolks	

Method

1. Grease a fireproof dish, 1½ pint size.
2. Make a panada with the butter, flour and milk.
3. Add the salt and pepper and allow to cool slightly.
4. Beat in the egg yolks.
5. Add the cheese, reserving a little to sprinkle over the soufflé.
6. Check the seasoning.
7. Beat the egg whites stiffly and fold lightly into the mixture.

8. Turn into the greased dish. Sprinkle very lightly with the remainder of the grated cheese.
9. Bake in the middle of an oven preheated to 350° F for 15–20 mins.
10. Serve at once.

Chestnut Croquettes

2 lbs fresh chestnuts or 1 lb dried nuts soaked overnight.
1 onion finely chopped and fried
1 egg
seasonings
a little milk if necessary
beaten egg and breadcrumbs to coat (see frying, page 193)
deep fat for frying (see frying, page 193)

Method

1. Heat the fresh chestnuts in a moderate oven until the outer skin bursts and the inner fine skin can be rubbed off.
2. Cook until tender in boiling water.
3. Rub through wire sieve; add onion previously fried, beaten egg, and seasonings. If the mixture is too stiff add a very little milk.
4. Turn on to a floured board; form into a long cork shape.
5. Divide into even sized cork-shaped pieces about 3″ long and 1″ diameter.
6. Coat with egg and breadcrumbs.
7. Fry in deep fat.
8. Drain thoroughly; serve immediately. Garnish with fried parsley.

Cornish Pasties

4 ozs raw meat freshly minced   1 teasp salt
2 large raw potatoes $\frac{1}{8}$ teasp pepper
6 ozs shortcrust pastry

Method

1. Prepare the pastry, divide into 4 and roll out to $\frac{1}{4}$″ thickness, keeping a good round shape.
2. Divide the meat, well seasoned, between the 4 rounds of pastry.
3. Cover with very coarsely grated potato.
4. Wet the edges of the pastry and draw up the sides so that the edges meet in the centre.
5. Press the edges well together. Flute with the fingers.
6. Brush over with egg and milk.

7. Bake in the centre of a hot oven (425° F) for 10 mins, then reduce the heat to 350° F and cook for a further 45–50 mins.
8. Serve with a good gravy.

Egg Cutlets

See recipe in réchauffé dishes, page 219 (Egg Croquettes).

Kedgeree

2 ozs rice	1 oz butter
½ lb cooked fish, preferably a mixture of white fish and smoked haddock	1 teasp chopped parsley
	1 hard-boiled egg
	approximately 2 teasp salt
1 egg or 2 tbs good white sauce	¼ teasp pepper

Method

1. Cook the rice until tender in 2 pints boiling water with 1 teasp salt. Boil rapidly with the lid off the pan (10–15 mins). This keeps the grains separate and prevents them from sticking to the pan. Strain through a wire strainer. If the quantity of water used has been sufficient, there is no need to rinse the rice under cold water to separate the grains. If the grains do stick together, the rice can be rinsed under the cold tap, but it must be reheated before serving.
2. Flake the fish.
3. Melt the butter in a saucepan.
4. Add the fish and rice to the melted butter.
5. Stir in the beaten raw egg or the sauce.
6. Add the chopped egg white. Heat thoroughly.
7. Pile on a hot dish, garnish with hard-boiled egg yolk rubbed through a wire strainer, and chopped parsley.
8. Serve with pieces of lemon and wholemeal bread and butter or toast.

PASTAS

Pasta, made from huskless wheat grindings, is made into a number of shapes and thicknesses each having its particular name. Of the 150 or so varieties the following are easily obtained in England.

Macaroni.	Hollow tubes up to ¼" diameter.
Spaghetti.	Hollow tubes up to ⅛" diameter.
Vermicelli.	A very fine tube approximately the thickness of darning wool.
Noodles.	Flat strips about ¼" wide.
Lasagne.	Flat strips 1"–2" wide.
Ravioli paste.	Flat squares 1"–2".

Shaped pasta in the form of shells, stars, animals, initials.

These pastas have very little flavour of their own, but are used as a base for strongly flavoured sauces, and meat or fish mixtures. They are boiled in salted water until cooked to the correct texture and appearance, that is firm and yet tender and creamy and opaque. Overcooked pasta is sticky and floury. The length of time of cooking depends upon the thickness of the pasta. The thick varieties such as **lasagne** and **ravioli** must be cooked in large quantities of water, at least 4 quarts per ½ lb of pasta. Add the pasta slowly as the water boils rapidly so that the temperature is not reduced. Add salt in the proportion of 2 teasp to 4 ozs of pasta.

Boil for 15–20 mins, stirring occasionally to separate the strips or squares.

Rinse in hot water and separate the pieces to drain. The long strips can be hung over the edges of the colander.

Macaroni, Spaghetti and Noodles

Use 1½ pts boiling water and 2 teasp salt to every 4 ozs pasta. Add the pasta slowly to keep the water at boiling point. Boil rapidly for 2 minutes, stirring all the time. Withdraw the pan from the heat, put on a very tight lid, and leave for 10 minutes. The pasta will then be firm but chewy, that is, of " al dente " texture, and can be strained.

After draining, put back into the pan in which a lump of butter has been heated. Toss the pasta in the butter, season with salt and freshly ground pepper. Serve immediately.

The pasta may be combined with a sauce and grated cheese. A mixture of parmesan and gruyère is best. Most of the pasta dishes take their name from the sauce accompanying them, and all should be served with additional grated cheese.

SAUCES TO SERVE WITH PASTA
Bolognese Sauce

1 onion	½ lb peeled tomatoes or 8 oz tin
2 tbs olive oil	tomatoes
1 oz butter	2 tbs Marsala or Sherry
1 clove garlic	½ pt stock or stock and tomato
bouquet garni	juice
½ oz flour	1 teasp salt
2 tbs tomato paste	freshly ground black pepper
4 ozs minced raw beef or liver	

Method

1. Heat the oil and butter and fry the finely chopped **onion** slowly until it begins to colour.

2. Add the minced beef or liver and fry quickly for 3 mins.
3. Sprinkle on the flour, mix well.
4. Add the stock and bring to the boil, stirring all the time.
5. Add the bouquet garni, the garlic finely chopped, tomato paste and the peeled tomatoes.   Season.
6. Simmer for 30 mins, stirring occasionally.   Keep the lid on the pan to prevent evaporation of the liquid.
7. Remove the bouquet garni and add the wine.   Heat but do not boil.

Tomato Sauce for Pasta

2 lbs tomatoes or 1 large tin
1 stick celery
1 clove garlic crushed with salt ($\frac{1}{2}$ teasp)
$\frac{1}{2}$ bay leaf, sprig of lemon thyme, marjoram and parsley
$\frac{1}{2}$ oz butter
freshly ground black pepper

Method

1. Melt the butter and fry the crushed garlic for 2 mins.
2. Cut up the tomatoes and add to the garlic.
3. Add the herbs and seasoning.
4. Cook *slowly* for $1\frac{1}{4}$ hrs.
5. Sieve the sauce or pass through a mouli.
6. Reheat the purée, which should be thick and dark red.

Milanese Sauce

$\frac{1}{4}$ pt tomato sauce for pasta
1 oz mushrooms, sliced
$1\frac{1}{2}$ ozs cooked ham
$1\frac{1}{2}$ ozs cooked tongue

$1\frac{1}{2}$ ozs butter
1 oz parmesan cheese
seasoning

Method

1. Melt the butter, add the mushrooms and cook for 2–3 mins.
2. Add the ham and tongue cut into thin strips, and the tomato sauce.   Correct the seasoning.
3. Add the grated cheese and serve at once.

Mornay Sauce

See page 62.

Macaroni Cheese

2 ozs macaroni
4 ozs grated cheese
$\frac{3}{4}$ oz butter
$\frac{3}{4}$ oz flour
$\frac{1}{2}$ teasp made mustard

$\frac{1}{2}$ pt milk or milk and macaroni
   water
2 teasp salt
$\frac{1}{8}$ teasp pepper
sippets of toast or fried bread

Method

1. Break the macaroni into small pieces and cook in 2 pints (approximately) boiling water with 1 teasp salt (20–30 mins).
2. Make the sauce from the fat, flour and milk and add 3 ozs grated cheese, the made mustard, 1 teasp salt and the pepper. Taste and reseason if necessary.
3. Stir in the macaroni.
4. Turn into a greased pie dish (1½ pint), sprinkle on the remainder of the cheese and brown under the grill.
   If made previously, bake in the top of a moderate oven (375°) for 40–45 mins or until the mixture is brown on the top.
5. Decorate with triangles or half-moons of toast or fried bread.
6. Serve with grilled or baked tomatoes, water-cress or endive.

Macaroni Cheese Cutlets

See chapter on réchauffés (pp. 218–19).

Nut Cutlets

4 ozs minced nuts (walnuts, pine kernels or mixed nuts)
2 ozs breadcrumbs
2 tbs chopped cooked onion *or* 2 teasp finely grated raw onion
½ raw egg
½ teasp chopped parsley
¼ teasp mixed herbs *or* ¼ teasp ground mace
1 teasp lemon juice
1 oz butter ⎫
1 oz flour ⎬ panada
¼ pt milk   ⎭

Method

1. Make a panada of the butter, flour and milk, add the grated raw onion (if used) and cook thoroughly.
2. Stir in the nuts, breadcrumbs, seasonings and egg. If cooked onion is used, add at this stage.
3. Turn on to a plate. Mark into 8 portions. Cool.
4. Shape into cutlets, round flat cakes or croquettes, coat in egg and breadcrumbs and fry in deep fat.
5. Serve hot with a good sauce such as Tomato, Piquante or Espagnole, or serve with tomatoes sliced and soaked in French dressing (marinated tomatoes) or a mixed salad.
6. Serve cold with marinated tomato, potato mayonnaise or mixed salad.

Quiche Lorraine

4 ozs shortcrust pastry, used to line a 7-inch sandwich tin and
" baked blind " (see instructions for lining a flan ring, page 265)

Filling

2 ozs bacon rashers cut into
small pieces
1 egg and 1 yolk
¼ pt milk or cream
1 oz grated cheese or 1 oz
gruyère cheese in small pieces

½ oz butter
2 ozs finely chopped onion or
10 whole small spring onions
¼ teasp salt, ⅛ teasp black pepper

Method

1. Beat the egg yolks and add the cheese, milk and seasonings.
2. Melt the butter in a pan and fry the onions and bacon slowly
   until they are tender and just turning colour.
3. Add the onions etc. to the egg yolks and cheese.
4. Stiffly beat the egg whites and add to the mixture.
5. Pour into the pastry case.
6. Bake in the centre of a moderately hot oven (375° F) until the
   egg mixture is firm and lightly brown (25–30 mins).

Ratatouille

The many variations of this dish come from the differing proportions of the vegetables used, as well as the variety of ingredients. The
dish is a mixture of aubergines or courgettes or zucchini or baby
marrows or outdoor cucumbers, together with tomatoes, onions and
green peppers or potatoes. Mushrooms are sometimes used,
especially the field variety, and the whole is cooked in olive oil and
served with grated cheese.

Flavourings can be garlic, chopped herbs, ground mace or
coriander seeds.

Method

1. Slice the aubergines or other similar vegetable unpeeled, and
   sprinkle it with salt. Leave for ½-hour in a colander with a
   plate and weight over it to press out the excess liquid.
2. Slice and chop the onions.
3. Skin and slice the tomatoes and potatoes.
4. Remove the seeds from the pepper and slice thinly.
5. Fry the onion in the oil and when cooked but not brown add the
   other vegetables, and seasoning.
6. Cook slowly with a lid on the pan until all the vegetables are
   tender (about 30 mins).
7. Serve with grated cheese handed separately.

Risotto (for 2 generous portions)

2 ozs chopped cooked meat,   6 ozs rice
   game, poultry or liver   3 ozs cheese (parmesan)
2 ozs chopped mushrooms   1 pt hot stock
   or tomatoes   ⅛ teasp black pepper
2 ozs fat   2 teasp salt
3 ozs chopped onion

Method

1. Using a thick heavy frying pan, melt the fat and fry the onion slowly until tender and just turning colour.
2. Add the unwashed rice and fry for 3 mins.
3. Add ⅓ of the stock, bring to the boil and cook for 20 mins or until the rice is tender. It will be necessary to add the remainder of the stock gradually as the rice absorbs the liquid. Add liquid as it is required, and stir only when necessary.
4. Add the cooked meat and mushrooms or tomatoes (or both). Heat thoroughly. Season carefully.
5. Serve sprinkled with the grated cheese or hand the cheese separately.

Sausage, Egg and Tomato Pie

6 ozs shortcrust pastry   2 tomatoes
6 ozs sausage meat   1–2 hard-boiled eggs

Method

1. Line a 7 inch sandwich tin with ⅔ of the pastry. Damp the edges. See page 265 for the method of lining a tin.
2. Spread with the sausage meat.
3. Cover with slices of tomato and hard-boiled egg.
4. Cover with the remaining third of the pastry.
5. Press the edges well together and flute or pinch with the fingers to decorate.
6. Score the top. Brush over with milk.
7. Bake just below the centre of a hot oven (425°) for 10 mins, then reduce to 350° for 45 mins.
8. Serve hot or cold.

Sausage Rolls

A. *With closed ends*

   4 ozs rough puff or flaky pastry
   4–6 ozs sausage meat
   egg yolk and water to glaze

Method

1. Roll out the pastry into an oblong 8″ wide and 12″ long and with a thickness of $\frac{1}{8}$″.
2. Cut in half lengthways and into quarters widthways leaving 8 pieces of pastry each 4″ × 3″.
3. Divide the sausage meat into 8, roll each piece into a small sausage and put one on each piece of pastry.
4. Damp the edges of the pastry, fold over and press the edges together.
5. Knock up the edges with the back of a floured knife.   Nick them.
6. Place rolls on a baking sheet.   Brush over with the glaze.
7. Place the baking sheet just above halfway up an oven preheated to 450° F.
8. After 15 minutes reduce the heat to 370° and continue cooking for a further 15–20 minutes.
   Serve hot with vegetables and thickened gravy or cold with salad.

B. *With open ends*

4 ozs shortcrust   6–8 ozs sausage meat

Method

1. Roll out the pastry into an oblong 8″ long and 6 ″ wide.
2. Cut in half lengthways leaving 2 strips 8″ × 3″.
3. Roll the sausage meat into 2 sausages 8 inches long.
4. Turn over each piece of pastry so that the rolled side faces the pastry board and long side of the pastry lies parallel with the worker.   Damp the edge further away from the worker.
5. Put a strip of sausage meat on each piece of pastry.
6. Roll the pastry over the meat so that one edge is tucked under. Roll sufficiently to make sure that the two pieces of pastry stick together and the join lies underneath the roll.   See that the meat extends to the ends of the pastry.
7. Cut into lengths with a sharp knife.   Put on a baking sheet.
8. Brush over with the glaze.
9. Bake first in the top third of an oven preheated to 425° F for 10 minutes.
10. Reduce the heat to 350° and continue cooking for a further 15–20 minutes.

Scotch Eggs

3 hard-boiled eggs

3 sausages *or* 3 ozs veal forcemeat (3 ozs breadcrumbs) *or* 4 ozs cold meat croquette mixture (4 ozs cold meat) *or* 8 ozs potato croquette mixture

Method

1. Shell the eggs and roll in flour.
2. Skin the sausages and wrap each one round an egg, keeping the mixture even over the egg, *or* coat the floured egg with forcemeat or croquette mixture.
3. Coat with egg and breadcrumbs and fry in deep fat. If sausage or forcemeat is used, the fat should show a *very* faint haze. If cooked meat is used, a normal haze should rise from the fat when the food is put in.
4. Cut the eggs in half and serve on circles of fried bread.
5. Serve either hot, or cold with salad.

Stuffed Eggs

4 hard-boiled eggs	8 circles of fried bread or toast
2 ozs butter	fillings as below

Method

1. Cut the eggs in half (*a*) lengthways with a straight cut *or* (*b*) widthways with a vandyke cut, i.e. slip a pointed knife through the white in a series of V shapes.
2. Cut enough off the base of the egg to make it stand firmly.
3. Remove the yolks and sieve or pound with the seasonings and butter.
4. Fill up the cups made from the egg whites either by piling the mixture in with a spoon or by forcing it through a bag with a vegetable forcing pipe in the end.
5. Place on rounds of toast or fried bread and garnish with salad.

Fillings

(*a*) 4 anchovies + 1 teasp anchovy essence + $\frac{1}{4}$ teasp cayenne pepper
(*b*) 1 oz grated cheese + $\frac{1}{2}$ teasp made mustard
(*c*) 2 tbs chopped picked shrimps + 1 tbs chopped capers
(*d*) 4 small sardines + 1 teasp vinegar from gherkins + 1 tbs chopped gherkin

Stuffed Mushrooms

6 medium mushrooms	1 teasp chopped parsley
1 dessertsp chopped cold ham or chopped bacon	$\frac{1}{2}$ oz butter
1 teasp chopped onion	$\frac{1}{4}$ teasp salt, a dash of cayenne pepper
1 tbs breadcrumbs	6 croûtes of fried bread

Method

1. Skin the mushrooms.
2. Melt the butter in a small pan. Fry the onion and bacon (if used) until tender.
3. Add the chopped ham (if used), breadcrumbs, parsley and seasonings.
4. Divide the mixture into 6 portions and pile on the mushrooms.
5. Bake in a fireproof dish in a moderate oven (375° F) for 15 mins, or until soft.
6. Slip the croûtes of bread under the mushrooms and serve in the dish in which they were cooked.

Stuffed Onions

4 large onions	1 oz butter
1 tbs cold minced meat or sausage meat	$\frac{1}{2}$ teasp salt; $\frac{1}{8}$ teasp pepper
2 tbs breadcrumbs	2 ozs dripping for baking

Method

1. Partly cook the onions in boiling water.
2. Drain well and remove the centres to give a hole big enough to take $\frac{1}{4}$ of the filling.
3. Melt the butter, add the meat, crumbs, seasoning and the chopped centres of the onions.
4. Pack this mixture into the onions, piling the surplus on the top.
5. Pin a greased paper band $1\frac{1}{2}''$ deep round each onion.
6. Heat the dripping in a baking tin, put in the onions and baste well.
7. Cook in the top of a moderate oven (375° F) for $\frac{3}{4}$–1 hour until the onions are brown and tender.
8. Remove the pins and the paper band.
9. Serve with a good gravy or sauce.

Stuffed Tomatoes

4 large firm tomatoes or 6 medium (to weigh $\frac{3}{4}$ lb or more)	1 teasp chopped parsley
$\frac{1}{2}$ oz butter or bacon dripping	1 rasher of bacon chopped finely
2 tbs breadcrumbs	$\frac{1}{4}$ teasp salt
$\frac{1}{2}$ onion finely chopped	pinch of pepper, sugar and nutmeg
1 tbs grated cheese	croûtes of fried bread or toast

Method

1. Wash the tomatoes, cut off a slice at the stem end.
2. Using a small teaspoon, or the handle if more convenient, scoop out the pulp. Leave the walls of the tomato intact.

3. Rub the pulp through a wire strainer to remove the seeds.
4. Fry the bacon and onion until tender, add the crumbs, season-ings and pulp.
5. Stuff the tomatoes with this mixture, piling it above the top.
6. Sprinkle with the grated cheese.
7. Bake in a moderate oven (350° F) for 15–20 mins according to the size of the tomatoes.
8. Serve hot on croûtes of bread.

Stuffed Vegetable Marrow

1 small vegetable marrow
4 ozs cooked minced meat (dark, white or ham)
1 oz butter
2 teasp finely chopped onion
1 oz breadcrumbs

$\frac{1}{2}$ egg
4 mushrooms (optional)
2 teasp salt
$\frac{1}{8}$ teasp pepper (mixture of white and cayenne)

To coat

1 tbs browned crumbs and 2 ozs dripping

Method

1. Peel the marrow, cut lengthways and remove the seeds.
2. Steam until almost cooked; at this stage it will still be firm enough to handle without breaking. This will probably take 15–20 mins.
3. Fry the onions and the chopped mushrooms in the butter.
4. Add the breadcrumbs, cooked meat, seasoning and egg.
5. Fill the hollows in the marrow halves and put one on top of the other.
6. Heat the dripping in a baking tin. Lay in the marrow, baste and sprinkle with crumbs.
7. Bake in the middle of a hot oven (400°) for 30 mins.
8. Serve with a piquante sauce (see page 63).

Tomato, Cheese and Onion Pasties

6 ozs rough puff pastry (see p. 392)
2 large tomatoes
1 egg

1 grated onion
1 tbs breadcrumbs
2 ozs grated cheese
seasoning

Method

1. Roll out the pastry into an oblong $\frac{1}{4}''$ thick. Cut into 6 equal portions.
2. Skin the tomatoes, remove the seeds, chop the pulp.

3. Mix the tomato, onion, breadcrumbs, cheese, seasoning and beaten egg.
4. Divide the mixture evenly between the pieces of pastry, putting the mixture on one half diagonally.
5. Damp the edges of the pastry and turn over the pastry to make a triangle.
6. Knock up the edges of the pastry, make 2 nicks in the top.
7. Bake in a hot oven (425° F) for 10 mins, reduce to 375° for a further 20 mins.

Tomato Dumplings

As for stuffed tomatoes. Coat them with short crust pastry (1 oz flour + $\frac{1}{2}$ oz fat to each medium tomato). Bake in a hot oven (425° F) in the middle of the oven for 25 mins.

Tomato Jellies

2 hard-boiled eggs	$\frac{3}{4}$ oz powdered gelatine, light
2 tbs cooked peas	weight
$\frac{1}{2}$ lb tomatoes	1 teasp salt
rather less than $\frac{1}{2}$ pt stock or water	$\frac{1}{8}$ teasp pepper

Method

1. Cut up the tomatoes and onion, add the stock and seasonings and cook until tender.
2. Sieve and taste to make sure the flavour is strong. If not, add some tinned tomato purée. The quantity should measure $\frac{1}{2}$ pint.
3. Dissolve the gelatine in about 1 tbs water and add to the purée.
4. Pour into a basin previously rinsed in cold water and left wet. Allow to cool.
5. As the jelly sets, drop in slices of hard-boiled egg and peas so that they are distributed evenly throughout the mixture.
6. When quite cold turn out on to a flat dish and serve garnished with lettuce and spring onions, both tossed in French dressing.

Vegetable Hot Pot

1 large or 2 small carrots	4 tbs baked beans
3 small onions	4 medium potatoes
1 piece swede the size of a tomato	2 tbs grated cheese
	1 tbs seasoned flour
3 tomatoes	1 teasp Marmite
2 large sticks celery	$\frac{3}{4}$ pt stock
1 tbs dripping	chopped parsley to garnish

Method

1. Prepare the vegetables and cut into small rough pieces.
2. Toss all except tomatoes and potatoes and beans in the seasoned flour.
3. Grease a casserole (2 pint size) and put in the vegetables, including the beans and tomatoes.
4. Dissolve the Marmite in the stock and pour over the vegetables.
5. Cover with sliced potatoes. Dot with the dripping.
6. Put on the lid of the casserole and bake in a moderate oven (375° F) for 1½ hours.
7. Remove the casserole lid, sprinkle with grated cheese and return to the oven.
8. Raise the heat to 400° to brown the cheese (15 mins).
9. Sprinkle with chopped parsley and serve at once.

Welsh Rarebit

See p. 42.

Accompaniments to Curries

As well as rice, there is a variety of side dishes to serve with curries. Some of these can be bought ready prepared, for instance, Chapattis, Bombay duck, pappadums.

Chapattis is a sort of pancake made from a paste of wholemeal flour and water, rolled out thinly and fried.

Bombay duck is generally baked in a hot oven until crisp and brown, and served either crumbled or broken in small pieces sprinkled on top of the curry. It is generally bought in tins.

Pappadums are round biscuits looking rather like pieces of cardboard which are fried in hot oil or fat and served hot after draining well. They may also be heated under the grill.

Sambol is the name given to the accompaniments which are like dressed vegetable hors d'œuvre: cold cooked potato, hard boiled egg, sliced skinned tomato, sliced green peppers (pimiento), chopped onion or sliced cucumber, are dressed with an oil and lemon juice or vinegar dressing. These are typical examples of sambols.

In addition, gherkins, sliced bananas, green olives, shredded fresh coconut and all kinds of hot sweet chutneys are suitable.

These accompaniments should be served in small dishes grouped on a large tray, put in the middle of the table, or handed round for each person to make their own selection.

CHAPTER XVIII

PUDDINGS AND SWEETS

THERE are many varieties of hot puddings and of those that may be served hot or cold. They can be classified into the following groups :—

A. Milk puddings
B. Custards and custard puddings
C. Suet mixtures
D. Rubbed-in mixtures
E. Creamed pudding mixtures
F. Yeast mixtures
G. Batter mixtures
H. Sweets using pastries
I. Hot soufflés

A. MILK PUDDINGS

As the name suggests, milk is the main ingredient of these puddings. The importance of milk in the diet, especially of children and invalids, has been indicated in the chapter on Meal Planning.

Milk puddings can be classified according to the variety, the size, or the nature of the grain that is used to thicken the milk :—

(a) Whole grain puddings : rice, barley, tapioca, also macaroni.
(b) Crushed or small grain puddings : sago and semolina.
(c) Powdered grain puddings : ground rice, cornflour and arrow-root.

Whatever the type of pudding, it is essential that the grain be thoroughly cooked without producing a stiff unappetising result. All milk puddings should be creamy in texture, the milk being nearly all absorbed during the very slow even cooking.

General Proportions

To each pint of milk allow :—

1¾ ozs whole grain *or*
1½ ozs crushed grain *or*
1½ ozs powdered grain
1 oz sugar

Suitable Flavourings

1. Lemon rind infused with the milk.
2. Essences, such as vanilla or almond, added to the mixture.
3. Cocoa or chocolate blended with the milk.
4. Nutmeg grated on the top of whole grain puddings.

Eggs may be added to enrich the pudding but, if so, great care should be taken not to add them until the grain has been thoroughly cooked, as the prolonged cooking would make the mixture curdle. The pudding should be allowed to cool a little before the egg is beaten in, and then reheated *without boiling* for a few minutes to cook the egg.

Basic Recipe for Whole Grain Puddings

1¾ ozs rice or other grain	1 pint milk
1 oz sugar	nutmeg

Method

1. Wash the rice in cold water and drain well.
2. Soak the rice in the milk for half to one hour to soften it. This may be done in the greased pie dish in which the pudding is to be cooked.
3. Add the sugar and stir well.
4. Grate the nutmeg over the top.
5. Bake in the centre of a slow oven (300° F) for at least two hours for a pint pudding. (For a large pudding up to 4 hours).

Variations of the Basic Recipe

Type	Addition to or Alteration of the Recipe	Alteration of the Method
Rice pudding with egg	Add 1 egg	1. When the pudding has cooked for 1¾ hours, allow it to cool for 10 minutes. 2. Stir in the beaten egg. 3. Return to the oven and cook for ¼ hour.
Chocolate rice pudding	Add 1 oz cocoa and ½ oz sugar *or* 1½ ozs chocolate	Blend the cocoa with a little cold milk *or* grate the chocolate and stir it into the milk.
Barley pudding	Substitute 1¾ ozs barley for the rice	None
Tapioca pudding	Substitute 1¾ ozs tapioca for the rice	None
Macaroni pudding	Substitute 1¾ ozs macaroni for the rice. Add 1 egg if liked.	1. Break the macaroni into ½" lengths. 2. Add the egg as for the rice pudding.

Basic Recipe for Crushed Grain Puddings

1½ ozs sago or semolina   1 pint milk
1 oz sugar   nutmeg

Method

1. Warm the milk in a rinsed pan.
2. When it is moderately hot sprinkle the grain on to the milk, stirring all the time.
3. Continue stirring until the milk boils.
4. Add the sugar.
5. Reduce the heat and continue cooking gently for at least 15 minutes or until the grain appears clear. Keep the mixture stirred.
6. If liked the pudding may be poured into a greased pie dish and cooked in a very moderate oven (325° F) for a further twenty to thirty minutes. It may be sprinkled with grated nutmeg before putting it into the oven.

   If this method of cooking is used, it is necessary only to boil the grain in the milk for five minutes.

Variations of the Basic Recipe

TYPE	ADDITIONS TO OR ALTERATIONS OF THE RECIPE	ALTERATION OF THE METHOD
Sago or Semolina with Egg (1)	Add 1 egg	1. When the grain appears clear allow the pudding to cool for 10 minutes. 2. Add the beaten egg and reheat in the rinsed saucepan for 5 mins. or in the oven for 15–20 mins.
Semolina with Egg (2)	Add 1 egg	1. Separate the white and yolk. 2. Beat the yolk of egg into the mixture as for recipe (1). 3. Fold in the stiffly beaten white and pour into a greased pie dish. 4. Bake in the centre of a moderate oven (350° F) for 15–20 mins. Serve at once.
Chocolate Semolina	Add 1 oz cocoa and ½ oz sugar *or* 1½ ozs grated chocolate	Blend the cocoa with a little cold milk or stir the grated chocolate into the warm milk.
Lemon Sago or Semolina	Add the rind of ½ lemon	1. Peel the rind off very thinly and add it to the warm milk. 2. When the pudding has cooked remove the lemon rind before serving.

Basic Recipe for Powdered Grain Puddings

1½ ozs ground rice, cornflour   1 pint milk
    or arrowroot   Nutmeg (if liked)
1 oz sugar

Method

1. Heat all except ½ gill of the milk in a rinsed pan.
2. Blend the grain with the ½ gill of cold milk to form a smooth thin paste.
3. When the milk has reached boiling point pour it over the paste, stirring all the time.
4. Rinse the pan and return the pudding.
5. Add the sugar.
6. Bring to the boil, stirring all the time, and cook for 4–6 minutes until the grains appear clear.
7. Allow to cool and serve in a glass dish with fruit or fruit syrup or fruit vinegar.

Variations of the Basic Recipe

TYPE	ADDITIONS TO OR ALTERATIONS OF THE RECIPE	ALTERATION OF THE METHOD
Ground rice with egg (1)	Add 1 egg	1. Allow the pudding to cool for 10 minutes in the saucepan. 2. Add the beaten egg. 3. Reheat for 5–10 mins. without boiling.
Ground rice with egg (2)	Add 1 egg	1. Separate the yolk and white. 2. Beat in the yolk as above. 3. Fold in the stiffly beaten white and pour into a greased pie dish. 4. Cook in the centre of a moderate oven (350°) for 15–20 minutes, until well risen and pale brown.
Chocolate Corn-flour	Add 1 oz cocoa and ½ oz sugar *or* 1½ ozs grated chocolate	Blend the cocoa or chocolate with the cornflour.

Milk puddings may be served cold as moulded sweets. See section on cold sweets.

WHAT WENT WRONG—AND WHY

A whole grain pudding is too stiff

    (*a*) The wrong proportions were used.
    (*b*) The pudding was cooked too quickly and the milk has evaporated.
    (*c*) The pudding was cooked for too long.

The whole grain pudding is too thin

    (*a*) The wrong proportions were used.
    (*b*) The pudding was cooked too slowly.
    (*c*) The grain was not soaked before cooking.

The pudding has a tough dark skin

    (*a*) The pudding was cooked in too hot an oven.
    (*b*) It was placed too high up in the oven.

The pudding made from crushed or powdered grain is lumpy

    (*a*) The milk was too hot when the crushed grain was added.
    (*b*) The crushed grain was added too quickly.
    (*c*) The powdered grain was not blended smoothly with the cold milk.
    (*d*) The pudding was not stirred sufficiently throughout the making.

The pudding appears curdled

    (*a*) The milk was not fresh.
    (*b*) Lemon juice or other acid flavouring has caused the milk to curdle.
    (*c*) The egg was allowed to cook too quickly or for too long.

B. CUSTARDS AND CUSTARD PUDDINGS

See chapter on Egg Cookery.

C. SUET MIXTURES

Suet is the fat used in many puddings that require long slow cooking. The method of cooking employed is either boiling or steaming. For instructions on cooking see section on Steaming.

The type of suet suitable and the method of preparation are given under " Suet Pastry ".

Points to remember in mixing

1. As the suet is very slow in melting, the starch grains in the flour tend to burst and cook before the fat has melted, making the pudding rather close and hard. To make a suet mixture light, breadcrumbs should be substituted for part of the flour, half and half being the usual proportion.
2. Suet puddings made with ½ lb flour and a small amount of fruit should be steamed for at least 2 hours. The time varies according to the amount of dried fruit, and a mixture such as a rich Christmas pudding should cook for 8 hours.
3. When a dark-coloured pudding is wanted—e.g. Ginger or Rich Fruit, bicarbonate of soda is substituted for baking powder, as the soda makes the mixture dark in colour. The bicarbonate of soda leaves a residue of sodium carbonate (washing soda) which has an unpleasant taste; therefore it is very important not to use bicarbonate of soda unless the pudding has a fairly strong or definite flavour that will mask the taste of the soda.

   Use ¼ oz of bicarbonate of soda in place of the ½ oz baking powder.
4. The proportions of fat, sugar and eggs to flour are similar in these puddings as in cakes, but extra liquid is needed, especially when breadcrumbs are used to replace some of the flour or when the pudding is cooked by steaming.

Basic Recipe for Suet Puddings

to serve 4–6 portions

4 ozs flour	2 level teasp baking powder or 1
4 ozs breadcrumbs	level teasp bicarb. soda
3–4 ozs shredded suet	1 egg
½ level teasp salt	¼–⅓ pt milk
3–4 ozs sugar	

Method

1. Sieve the flour, salt and baking powder into a basin.
2. Add the breadcrumbs, shredded suet and sugar.
3. Beat the egg and add the milk to it.
4. Add the egg and milk to the mixture.
5. Mix with a wooden spoon until well blended. It should be a soft dropping consistency, that is, when a spoonful of mix-

ture is taken up in the spoon it drops off easily without any persuasion.

6. Two thirds fill a well-greased basin.
7. Cover with greased greaseproof paper, using two layers if the pudding is to be steamed for more than 2½ hours.
8. Steam for 2–2½ hours.
9. Turn out on to a hot dish.
10. Serve with a suitable sauce.

Variations of the Basic Recipe

Type	Amendments to the Recipe	Amendments to the Method	Sauce
Date	Use 2 ozs brown sugar only. Add 3 ozs chopped dates.	Add the dates with the sugar.	Custard
Fig	As above, using figs in place of dates.	As above.	Custard
Ginger	Use 2 ozs brown sugar only. Add 2 level teasp ground ginger, 1 teasp syrup. Omit the baking powder and use 1 level teasp bicarbonate of soda.	1. Sieve the bicarbonate of soda and ginger with the flour. 2. Add the syrup with the sugar.	Syrup
Lemon	Use 6 ozs breadcrumbs and 2 ozs flour. Add the rind of 2 lemons. Use white sugar.	Add the finely grated lemon rind with the sugar.	Lemon
Marmalade	Add 2 tbs marmalade.	Add with the sugar.	Marmalade
Plum	Use 6 ozs breadcrumbs and 2 ozs flour. Omit the baking powder and use 1 level teasp bicarbonate of soda. Add 8 ozs of mixed fruits, e.g. raisins, currants, sultanas. 1 oz mixed peel. ½ level teasp spice.	1. Chop the raisins and peel. 2. Sieve the spice and bicarb. with the flour. 3. Add the fruit and peel with the sugar. 4. Steam 3 hours.	Sweet White
Raisin (Baroness)	Add 4 ozs raisins.	Chop the raisins and add with the sugar.	Custard *or* Sweet White *or* Melted butter

Variations of the Basic Recipe *continued*

Type	Amendments to the Recipe	Amendments to the Method	Sauce
Rothesay	Omit the baking powder and use 1 level teasp bicarbonate of soda. Add 2 tbs raspberry jam, ½ teasp vinegar.	1. Sieve the bicarbonate of soda with the flour. 2. Stir in the jam with the liquid. 3. Add the vinegar last.	Raspberry jam *or* Sweet White
Snowdon	Use 4 ozs breadcrumbs 2 ozs flour 2 ozs riceflour. Add 3 ozs raisins 2 tbs marmalade the rind of 1 lemon.	1. Decorate the greased basin with the halved raisins. 2. Add the marmalade and lemon rind with sugar.	Marmalade
Syrup	Use brown sugar. Omit the baking powder and use 1 level teasp bicarbonate of soda. Add 2 tbs syrup.	1. Sieve the bicarbonate of soda with the flour. 2. Add the syrup with the sugar.	Syrup
Treacle	As for syrup but use treacle in place of syrup or half treacle and half syrup.	1. Sieve the bicarbonate of soda with the flour. 2. Add the treacle with the sugar.	Treacle

Additional Recipes Using Suet

Christmas Pudding (Plain)

No. of portions 12–16 (3 puddings)

¼ lb flour
½ level teasp salt
½ lb breadcrumbs
6 ozs suet
6 ozs brown sugar
1 level teasp baking powder
½ ,, teasp spice
6 ozs currants

6 ozs sultanas
4 ozs raisins
3 ozs peel
1 oz ground almonds
Rind 1 lemon
3 eggs
½ pint milk or ale

Method
1. Sieve the flour, salt, baking powder and spice into a basin.
2. Add the breadcrumbs, shredded suet and sugar.
3. Chop the raisins and peel and add with the cleaned currants and sultanas, the ground almonds and lemon rind.
4. Mix with the beaten eggs and milk.

5. Grease basins well; fill ¾ full.
6. Cover and steam 8 hours.
7. Serve with brandy, rum or hard sauce.

Christmas Pudding (2)
No. of portions 15–18 (3 puddings)

¼ lb flour   1 lb currants
¾ lb white breadcrumbs   ½ lb sultanas
1 teasp bicarbonate of soda   1 lb raisins
½ level teasp salt   ¾ lb mixed peel
1 lb demerara sugar   1 nutmeg
½ lb suet   5 eggs

Method

1. Sieve the flour, salt, bicarbonate of soda and grated nutmeg together.
2. Add the breadcrumbs, sugar and shredded suet.
3. Chop the raisins and peel and add with the cleaned currants and sultanas.
4. Beat the eggs and add.
5. Mix well and add a little milk if necessary.
6. Steam 8 hours.

Christmas Pudding (3)
No. of portions 15 (3 puddings)

2 ozs flour   ½ lb sultanas
¾ lb breadcrumbs   ½ lb currants
½ lb moist brown sugar   ¼ lb raisins
½ level teasp salt   ¼ lb mixed peel
6 ozs suet   Rind of 2 lemons
2 level teasp mixed spice   4 eggs
1 tbs syrup or treacle   ¼ pint milk or ale or brandy

Method

As for Christmas Pudding (2).

WHAT WENT WRONG—AND WHY

The pudding is heavy and sad

(*a*) Wrong proportions of flour and breadcrumbs were used.
(*b*) Insufficient raising agent was used.
(*c*) Too much liquid was used.
(*d*) The water was off the boil for a time so that the pudding was not steaming continuously.
(*e*) The pudding was steamed for too short a time.

The pudding has a wet sticky top

    (*a*) The paper was not secured on the basin and therefore the condensed steam dropped on to the pudding.

    (*b*) The water boiled up and seeped into the pudding.

The pudding sticks to the basin instead of turning out whole

    (*a*) The basin was insufficiently greased.

    (*b*) Insufficient time was allowed for shrinking after steaming and before turning out.   3–5 minutes should be allowed.

    (*c*) A knife was eased part way down the basin instead of tapping the basin sharply on a cloth.

D. RUBBED-IN PUDDING MIXTURES

These mixtures can either be baked or steamed, and whichever method of cooking is used, the recipe and the method of preparation are identical with those used for rubbed-in cakes.

(For details of suitable ingredients and method of making see section on Cakemaking.)

(For details on steaming see section on Steaming.)

Baked puddings are cooked in the dish in which they are to be served, heatproof china or glass being used. These do not allow the heat to penetrate readily, so that the outside crust of a pudding is softer and lighter in colour than that of a cake. The temperature of the oven and the position in the oven are the same as for large cakes.

One of the main differences between a baked pudding and a cake is the depth; a pudding is not more than 2–2½ inches deep and quite often is only 1½ inches. Because the heat penetrates more quickly through a shallow pudding covering more space, the length of time needed for cooking is reduced by about 15 minutes in each hour.

Basic Recipe for Rubbed-in Puddings
To serve 6 portions

½ lb flour	3 ozs sugar
½ level teasp salt	1 egg
2 level teasp baking powder	¼–⅓ pint milk
3 ozs butter	

Method

    1. Sieve the flour, salt and baking powder together.

    2. Rub the fat into the flour until no lumps of fat are left, and the mixture is like fine breadcrumbs.

    3. Add the sugar.

4. Beat the egg and add the milk to it.
5. Add the egg and milk mixture all at once to the flour.
6. Mix with a wooden spoon to a soft dropping consistency. The mixture should drop off the spoon without being shaken.
7. Either put into a greased 2-pint pie dish or a greased 2-pint basin.
8. Smooth off the top of the mixture.
9. *Cooking*

    (*a*) Steaming: $\frac{2}{3}$ fill the basin, cover with greaseproof paper and steam for $1\frac{1}{2}$ hours.

    (*b*) Baking: Cook in the middle of the oven preheated to 375° F for 15 mins. Reduce the temperature to 350° F for a further 20–30 minutes. The exact time depends upon the depth of the pudding.

10. *Serving*

    (*a*) Steamed: Turn out, following the instructions given for a suet pudding, and serve with a suitable sauce.

    (*b*) Baked: Serve in the dish in which the pudding is cooked and with a suitable sauce.

Variations of the Basic Recipe

Almond
Chocolate
Coconut
Coffee
Currant   For additions to the basic recipe and method
Date   see section on rubbed-in Cakes.
Date and Walnut
Fruit (Luncheon)
Lemon
Orange

Additional Recipes Using the Rubbed-in Method
Eve's Pudding
(No. of portions 6–8)

1 lb cooking apples
4 ozs sugar
$\frac{1}{2}$ lb flour etc—basic rubbed-in mixture

Method

1. Peel, core and slice the apples.
2. Put half the apples in a pie dish.
3. Add the sugar.

4. Add the remaining apples.
5. Cover with the pudding mixture.
6. Bake for ¾ to 1 hour as for other mixtures.

Other fruits may be substituted for apples, e.g. blackberries, damsons, gooseberries, plums, rhubarb.

Fruit Crumble
(No. of portions 6–8)

1 lb fruit—Apples, currants, damsons, gooseberries, plums, rhubarb, etc.
4–6 ozs sugar depending on the fruit used.
Also ½ lb flour
     4–6 ozs butter
     3–4 ozs sugar

Method
1. Prepare the fruit and put it into a greased pie dish in layers with the sugar.
2. Rub the butter into the flour.
3. Add the sugar and continue to rub in until the mixture forms very small lumps.
4. Sprinkle evenly over the fruit.
5. Press well down and level off the top.
6. Bake in a moderate oven, preheated to 375° F, for 15 minutes.
7. Reduce the temperature to 350° F and bake for a further 20–30 minutes.
8. Serve with custard sauce.

Date Crunch

4 ozs dates	1½ ozs flour
¼ pint water	3 ozs butter
4 ozs rolled oats	1½ ozs sugar

Method
1. Chop the dates and stew until soft in the ¼ pint water.
2. Allow the mixture to cool.
3. Rub the butter into the oats and flour.
4. Add the sugar and mix very well.
5. Put half the oat mixture into a greased sandwich tin. Press it down very firmly.
6. Spread the date mixture over this and cover with the second half of the oat mixture.
7. Smooth over the top and press well down.
8. Bake in a moderate oven 375° F for ¾ hour.
9. Serve with custard sauce.

WHAT WENT WRONG—AND WHY

For common faults in mixing and baking see section on cakes.

For faults in steaming see section on steaming suet pudding mixtures.

E. CREAMED PUDDING MIXTURES

These mixtures can either be baked or steamed, and whichever method of cooking is used the recipe and the method of preparation are identical with those used for creamed cake mixtures.

(For suitable ingredients, points in mixing and proportions see Creamed Cake Mixtures.)

(For details on steaming see section on Steaming.)

As with rubbed-in mixtures the baked puddings are cooked in heatproof china or glass. The depth of the pudding is similar to that for a rubbed-in mixture; therefore the length of time of cooking is 15 minutes in each hour less than for a similar quantity of cake mixture.

Basic Recipe for Creamed Pudding Mixtures

Plain Family Recipe	Richer Recipe
6 ozs flour	4 ozs flour
½ level teasp salt	¼ level teasp salt
3 ozs butter or butter and margarine	4 ozs butter or butter and margarine
3 ozs castor sugar	4 ozs castor sugar
1½–2 eggs	2 eggs
¾ level teasp baking powder	¼ level teasp baking powder
⅛ pint milk or water	1 tbs milk or water

Method

1. Cream the fat and sugar very well either with a wooden spoon or by hand. In cold weather the fat should be warmed very slightly but not oiled.
2. Beat up the egg in a basin and stand it in a bowl of warm water.
3. Add the egg gradually to the fat and sugar, beating very well between each addition.
4. When all the egg has been added scrape down the sides of the bowl and the spoon and beat again to ensure even mixing.
5. Add the liquid to the creamed mixture.
6. Sieve the flour, salt and baking powder.
7. Gradually fold in the flour with a metal spoon, adding a little at a time.

I

8. When all the flour has been added scrape down the sides of the bowl and spoon.
9. Fold lightly again, to ensure even mixing.
10. Put into the greased pie dish or basin.
11. Smooth off the top of the mixture.
12. For a baked pudding have the oven preheated to 375° F. Put in half way up the oven and reduce to 350° F immediately. Bake for ¾ to 1 hour.
13. For a steamed pudding, cover with greased paper and put in a steamer over fast-boiling water. Steam for 1½ hours.
14. Turn out a steamed pudding, leave a baked pudding in the dish in which it is cooked.
15. Serve with a suitable sauce.

Variations of the Basic Recipe

Almond
Cherry
Chocolate
Coconut
Coffee   } for additions to the basic recipe and
Currant   method see section on creamed cake
Ginger   mixtures
Lemon or Orange
Pineapple and Raisin
Sultana

Type	Amendments to the Recipe	Amendments to the Method
Beresford	Use the richer recipe and add the grated rind of 2 oranges, 1 oz breadcrumbs ⅛ pint milk	1. Add the rind and breadcrumbs with the flour. 2. Steam 1½ hours. 3. Turn out and decorate with cherry and angelica. 4. Serve with orange sauce.
Canary	Use the richer recipe and add the grated rind of 1 lemon.	1. Add the rind with the flour. 2. Grease and coat with rice flour 6–8 small dariole moulds. 3. Two-third fill each mould. 4. Steam 30–40 minutes. 5. Turn out and serve with jam sauce.
Castle	As for Canary.	1. As for Canary but bake each pudding 20–30 minutes. 2. Turn out and serve with jam sauce.

Type	Amendments to the Recipe	Amendments to the Method
Eve's	Add 1 lb apples or other fruit + 3 ozs sugar.	1. Prepare and slice the apples. 2. Half fill a pie dish with the apples and sugar in layers finishing with apples. 3. Cover with the pudding mixture. 4. Bake for ¾–1 hour.
Patriotic	Use the plain family recipe and add 2 teasp grated lemon rind, 4 tbs syrup or jam.	1. Put the jam or syrup at the bottom of the greased basin. 2. Pour over the mixture. 3. Steam for 1½–2 hours.
Upside Down	Use the plain family recipe and add slices of orange, peach or banana and 2 tbs golden syrup. Grated rind of 1 orange or 1 lemon improves the flavour of all three.	1. Line a greased 1½ pint size dish with golden syrup and arrange the sliced fruit neatly. 2. Cover with the pudding mixture. 3. Bake for ¾ to 1 hour. 4. Turn the pudding out so that the fruit is uppermost. 5. Serve with syrup sauce or custard.
Prince Albert	4 ozs fresh breadcrumbs ½ oz rice flour 3 ozs margarine or butter 3 ozs castor sugar 2 eggs Grated rind of 1 lemon ¼ lb cooked prunes (weighed before soaking)	1. Stone the prunes and line a greased basin with them, placing the skin side next to the basin. 2. Cream the fat and sugar. 3. Beat in the egg yolks. 4. Add the rice flour and breadcrumbs. 5. Fold in the stiffly beaten egg whites. 6. Two-thirds fill the lined basin. 7. Steam for 1½ hours. 8. Turn out and coat with a sauce made from the prune juice.

WHAT WENT WRONG—AND WHY

For common faults in mixing and baking, see section on cakes.

For faults in steaming see section on steaming suet pudding mixtures.

F. YEAST MIXTURES

See section on Richer Yeast Mixtures (pp. 327–335).

G. BATTER PUDDING MIXTURES

See chapter on Batters.

H. PUDDINGS USING PASTRIES

These are some of the most popular types of puddings and many of them can be eaten hot or cold. Variety can be introduced by changing the filling; e.g. in pies, flans, etc., the method of making being the same whatever filling is used.

Where a choice of pastry can give variety this will be indicated, but where a traditional dish is made, using a specific type only, this variety will be stated. This does not mean that the cook cannot vary the pastry according to circumstances and tastes.

Where the recipe gives the quantity of pastry it implies that weight of flour made into pastry. E.g., 4 ozs short pastry means 4 ozs flour made into short pastry.

For the methods of making and baking pastries see chapter on Pastry-making.

To Line a Basin With Pastry

For a basin of a pint size, use 6 ozs suet pastry.

Short pastry may be used in place of suet; if so, baking powder should be added to the flour in the proportion of $\frac{1}{2}$ oz baking powder to each pound of flour.

Method

1. Prepare the filling.
2. Roll out the pastry into a circle about $\frac{1}{8}$ inch thick and with a diameter twice the depth of the basin.
3. Cut out $\frac{1}{6}$ of the circle as a segment, retaining it to form the top.
4. Lift the remaining pastry carefully into the basin so that the centre angle, where the segment was cut, is in the centre of the bottom of the basin.
5. Without stretching the pastry, press one cut edge up to the side of the basin. The outer edge of the circle should just reach the top of the basin.
6. Gradually working round the basin, press the pastry against the sides, making certain no air bubbles are left between the basin and the pastry and no creases are made in the pastry.
7. Damp the cut edges and place them so that they overlap about $\frac{1}{8}$ inch.
8. Press the two edges together very carefully so that the join is even and very secure.
9. Fill the basin with layers of fruit and sugar starting and finishing with fruit.
10. Knead up the pastry for the top and form it into a circle.

11. Roll it out to form a round slightly larger than the top of the basin.
12. Damp the edges of the pastry round the top of the basin.
13. Lay the lid on and press the two edges of the pastry very securely together.
14. Cover with a greased paper and steam for two hours.

To Turn Out a Pudding

Remove the basin from the steamer. Carefully take off the paper cover without tearing the pastry. Lift the basin and tilt it sideways, allowing the weight of the pudding to pull it away from the side of the basin as the pastry shrinks.

Turn the basin round slowly, keeping it tilted, until the pastry has been loosened all round.

Turn the pudding out on to a dish.

Serve with custard sauce.

Suggested fillings

Apples	Gooseberries
Blackberries	Greengages
Currants	Plums
Damsons	Rhubarb

4–6 ozs sugar according to the fruit used
2–3 tbs water according to the fruit used

To Make a Layer Pudding

For a basin of a pint size, use 6 ozs suet or short pastry.

Filling

8 ozs syrup + 2 ozs breadcrumbs
(for other fillings, see below)

Method

1. Divide the pastry into 5 or 6 uneven portions. The largest piece should be $\frac{1}{4}$ of the total and the smallest just sufficient to form a circle $\frac{1}{4}''$ thick to cover the base of the basin.
2. Roll out each piece of pastry into a circle $\frac{1}{4}''$ thick, each circle being a little larger than the previous one.
3. Mix the syrup and breadcrumbs together.
4. Grease the basin thoroughly and put in the smallest circle of pastry.
5. Cover the pastry with the syrup mixture.
6. Continue with layers of pastry and syrup mixture, using a slightly larger circle of pastry each time so that it completely covers the syrup and just fits the basin.
7. Cover with the final layer of pastry.

8. Cover with greased paper.
9. Steam for 2 to 2½ hours.
10. Turn out in a similar way to that suggested for a basin lined with pastry.
11. Serve with suitable sauce.

Variation of Fillings

Syrup and breadcrumbs + ½ level teasp ginger or rind of ½ lemon finely grated

Treacle and breadcrumbs

Jam

Delaware 1 apple, finely chopped   1 oz moist brown sugar
          1 oz currants   2 ozs syrup
          ½ oz chopped peel   1 tbs water
          ½ level teasp spice

To Make a Pie

For a pint pie dish
4 ozs short, rough puff, or flaky pastry

Filling

Apples, blackberries, cherries, currants, damsons, gooseberries, greengages, plums, pumpkin, raspberries, rhubarb are suitable.
Allow 3 to 6 ozs sugar to each pound of fruit according to the sharpness of the fruit.

Method

1. Fill the pie dish with fruit and sugar, or other filling, so that the top is slightly domed. The sugar must not be on the top or it will go into the pastry and cause a sodden crust or uneven browning.
2. Knead the pastry lightly and form it into the same shape as the pie dish.
3. Roll it out to $\frac{1}{6}''$ to $\frac{1}{8}''$ thick and an inch larger than the top of the pie dish. The pastry should be kept the same shape as the pie dish throughout and the edges of the pastry kept free from cracks by light pressing with the edge of the hand or the fingertips.

To cover the pie

1. Cut off a narrow strip round the edge of the pastry about $\frac{3}{4}''$ wide. Use a sharp knife to avoid dragging the pastry.

2. Wet the lip of the pie dish and press this strip on it, easing the pastry a little as it is pressed on to the lip. Keep the cut edge of the pastry to the inside of the rim.
3. Damp this strip of pastry with cold water.
4. Lay the rolling-pin very lightly over the remaining pastry and fold it back over the pin.
5. Lift the rolling-pin with the pastry over it and cover the pie, rolling the pastry lightly off the pin over the pie dish. The pastry should be very slightly larger than the top of the pie dish.
6. With the fingers under the lip of the pie dish and the thumbs on top, press the edge of the pastry down and slightly back towards the centre of the dish, moving the hands steadily all round the dish. This method will join the two edges without stretching the pastry.
7. Holding the dish on the palm of the left hand, cut off any surplus pastry with a sharp knife, held with the blade pointing up and away from the worker. The flat side of the knife should just touch the edge of the pie dish and slope out at an angle of 60°. A sharp down-stroke should be used to keep a clean edge.

To knock up the edge

1. Place the index finger of the left hand, knuckle side down, on the top of the rim of the pastry. Press lightly.
2. Hold the knife horizontally with the back of the blade towards the pastry edges. Beginning near the rim of the dish and working up towards the finger of the left hand, flake the edges by knocking the back of the knife against the cut edges of the pastry.
   Work all round the pie crust.

To flute the edges of the pie

1. Place the thumb of the left hand on the top of the pastry and the index finger under the rim.
2. Press down lightly.
3. At the same time, move the knife, held upright in the right hand, up and in to make a small nick. The pressure of the thumb against the knife will make a flute.
4. Work from right to left.
   For sweet pies the flutes should be $\frac{1}{8}''-\frac{1}{4}''$ apart.
   For savoury pies they should be $\frac{1}{2}''-1''$ apart.

Short pastry is left unglazed, but rough puff and flaky should be glazed with milk or egg and milk.

The pie should be left to relax for at least 10 minutes before cooking. Cook in centre of oven 425° F for 10 minutes reducing heat to 350° F for 25–40 minutes according to size.

When cooked, dredge sweet pies with castor sugar if served hot— if cold with icing sugar.

Apple Balls or Dumplings

For each medium sized apple :—

$1\frac{1}{2}$ to 2 ozs short pastry
$\frac{1}{4}$ oz sugar

Method

1. Peel and core the apples. If they have to stand leave in salt water ($\frac{1}{2}$ oz salt to 1 pint water) to prevent them from turning brown.
2. Knead the pastry for each apple into a round.
3. Roll out into a circle $\frac{1}{6}''$ thick.
4. Turn the pastry over.
5. Rinse the apple in clean cold water and stand it on the pastry.
6. Fill up the hole with the sugar.
7. Draw up the pastry into four points at right angles to each other.
8. Carefully draw in the four pieces of pastry between these points, if possible without forming folds in the pastry.
9. Hold the apple in the palm of the left hand and carefully mould the pastry evenly round the apple so that it completely covers it without stretching the pastry in any one place.
10. See that the edges of the pastry are securely sealed.
11. Turn the apple upside down and place it on a greased baking tin.
12. Let the pastry relax for 10 minutes.
13. Bake for 10 minutes in an oven preheated to 425° F. Place halfway up in the oven.
14. Reduce the temperature to 350° F and bake until the apple is tender, 30–40 minutes total.
15. Dredge with castor sugar and serve on a heated dish with custard sauce.

Plate Tarts and Tartlets

To line a plate tart or a patty tin

Requirements depend on the size of the plate or tin.

For a 10″ plate use 4 ozs short, rich short, rough puff, flaky or puff pastry.

Method

1. Knead the pastry into a round.
2. Roll out, keeping the pastry in a round and the edges even, until the pastry is $\frac{1}{8}''$ thick.
3. Lay the rolling-pin lightly on top of the pastry and fold the pastry over it.
4. Lift the pin and roll the pastry off on to the plate. Use a tin plate whenever possible.
5. See that the pastry is lying centrally on the plate.
6. With the thumbs press the pastry down in the centre, moving the plate round smoothly with the fingers.
7. Gradually bring the thumbs out towards the edge of the plate.
8. When the thumbs have pressed the pastry down in the well of the plate, check to see that no air has been trapped; then press down the pastry round the lip of the plate.
9. The edge may be trimmed, flaked and fluted as for a fruit pie, or it may be trimmed and decorated.

To decorate a plate tart

1. Roll out the trimmings very thinly, cut out with a small plain or fancy cutter and arrange on the lip. The pastry should be damped first.
2. An alternative decoration may be made by trimming the edge, then cutting with short strokes at right angles to the edge about an inch apart. Damp the pastry and turn each piece over diagonally to make a " star " edge.
3. Lightly prick the pastry and bake blind or fill and bake.
4. Small patty tins can be lined with pastry that has been stamped out with a plain or fluted cutter. The cutter should be slightly larger than the patty tin. Press the pastry into the tin as in the case of the plate tart.

Note Stamp out the rounds with a firm movement of the cutter. Do not twist. Transfer carefully to the patty tin. If you get an unsuccessful result, see What Went Wrong in the section on Pastry.

Fillings

Jam, marmalade, syrup or treacle. For syrup or treacle use 1 oz fresh breadcrumbs to each $\frac{1}{4}$ lb syrup. Crushed breakfast cereals may be used in place of breadcrumbs.

Flans

To line a flan ring or sandwich tin

For a 7″ or 8″ ring:—4 ozs pastry.
For flans, use short, rich short or cheese pastry.

Method

1. Grease the ring very well and place it on a greased baking tin.
2. Knead the pastry into a round and roll it out into a circle $\frac{1}{8}''$ thick.
3. Fold the pastry lightly in half one way and over in half the other way.
4. Lift the pastry into the ring with the point exactly in the centre of the ring.   Carefully unfold it.
5. Press the pastry on to the baking tin with the thumbs, working right up to the sides of the ring.
6. When no air bubbles are left under the base of the flan, press the pastry against the sides of the ring, using the thumbs inside and the fingers on the outside of the ring.   Press with a downward stroke to shrink rather than stretch the pastry.
7. Fold the excess pastry outwards over the edge of the flan ring and roll off with the rolling pin or cut off sharply with a knife.
8. Press the sides once again and leave to relax for at least 10 minutes.   Prick the base well.
9. Bake blind and fill when cold.

To bake blind

1. Prick the pastry in the plate or flan ring and cover with greased paper.
2. Fill with crusts of bread or haricot beans.   The latter may be kept for the purpose and used over and over again.
3. Bake according to the type of pastry used until the pastry has set and is three parts cooked.
4. Remove the paper and the crusts or beans.
5. Finish baking.

Fillings

Any fresh fruit if suitable to eat raw.
Any stewed, bottled or canned fruit.
Arrange the fruit neatly in the cold flan case.
Make an arrowroot glaze by mixing 1 teasp arrowroot and $\frac{1}{4}$ pt fruit juice or water.   Boil up.   Colour and flavour if necessary. When *cool* pour over the fruit.   Decorate with whipped cream if desired.

RECIPES FOR PUDDINGS USING A FLAN BASE

Type	Variety of Pastry	Recipe for the Filling	Method of Making	Baking Instructions
Apple Apricot Flan	4 ozs rich short	1 lb peeled and sliced apples 4 ozs sugar 4 ozs sieved apricot jam	1. Fill the uncooked flan case with the apple arranged neatly in a whirl. 2. Add the sugar and lay another whirl of sliced apple on the top.	Bake for 25 mins. in a moderate oven, 375° F. When cooked, brush flan case and apple with hot apricot jam.
Banana Cream Pie	4 ozs short or rich short pastry	2 bananas 1 ¹/₂ ozs flour ³/₄ pint milk 1 lemon 2 egg yolks 1 tbs castor sugar *Meringue* 2 egg whites 2 tbs castor sugar	1. Line a deep plate or flan ring with pastry. Bake blind. 2. Make a simple sauce with the flour and milk. Add sugar and grated lemon rind. 3. Bring to the boil and cook 5 mins. 4. Cool. Add the lemon juice and then the egg yolks. Beat well. 5. Add the sliced banana. 6. Pour into the pastry case. 7. Make a meringue with the egg whites and sugar and pile on the pudding.	Bake in a cool oven, 275° F until the meringue is lightly brown, about 40 minutes.
Banana Custard Flan	4 ozs rich short pastry	1 tbs raspberry jam 2 bananas ¹/₂ pint custard sauce	1. Line a plate or flan ring with the pastry. Bake blind. 2. Spread the jam thinly over the bottom of the pastry. 3. Cover with layers of sliced bananas and custard 4. Decorate with banana, cherry and angelica *or* pile up with meringue.	Blind bake the pastry. If meringue is used bake in a very cool oven, 250° F, for 1–1¹/₂ hours, to dry out the meringue.
Bakewell Pudding	4 ozs short or rich short	1 tbs raspberry jam 4 ozs flour used for the basic recipe creaming method 2–3 drops almond essence	1. Line a plate or flan ring with the pastry. 2. Spread with the jam. 3. Make up the creamed pudding mixture and spread over the jam.	Bake halfway up, in a moderate oven, 400° F for 10 minutes. Reduce the temperature to 350° F and bake for a further 25–35 minutes.
Bakewell Tart	4 ozs puff pastry	6–8 ozs jam 4 yolks of egg 1 white of egg ¹/₂ lb sugar ¹/₂ lb melted butter 1 lemon, rind and juice	1. Line a plate or flan ring with pastry. Bake blind. 2. Spread jam over ¹/₂″ thick. 3. Mix the yolks and white with the sugar, butter and finely grated lemon rind. 4. Add the juice. 5. Pour on to the jam.	When filled bake halfway up in a cool oven, 325° F for ¹/₂ hour. Serve cold.

RECIPES FOR PUDDINGS USING A FLAN BASE *continued*

Type	Variety of Pastry	Recipe for the Filling	Method of Making	Baking Instructions
Butterscotch Tart (1)	4 ozs rich short pastry	1 gill milk 2 tbs water 1 teasp coffee essence 3 ozs moist brown sugar 1/4 oz butter 1 oz cornflour 1 teasp vanilla essence	1. Line a plate or flan ring with pastry. Bake blind. 2. Blend the cornflour and water. 3. Add to the boiling milk and cook for 5–7 minutes. 4. Add the other ingredients and reheat. 5. Allow to cool. Pour into the flan. 6. Serve cold.	—
Butterscotch Tart (2)	4 ozs rich short pastry	4 ozs moist brown sugar 1 1/2 pint milk 1 oz butter 3 ozs flour 1/2 pint water 1 teasp vanilla essence 1 egg 2 ozs castor sugar	1. Line a plate or flan ring with pastry. Bake blind. 2. Heat the milk and butter. 3. Blend the flour with the water to a smooth paste and add to the milk. 4. 5. Bring to the boil and cook for 3–4 minutes. 6. Add the essence and beat in the yolk of egg. Allow to cool. 7. Fill the pastry case. 8. Make a meringue with the white of egg and castor sugar. 9. Pile on the top.	Bake the flan with the meringue on for 1 hour halfway up in a cool oven, 275° F.
Custard Tart	4 ozs short or rich short pastry	1/2 pint egg custard (see p. 203 Baked Custard)	1. Wet a tin plate. 2. Line the plate with pastry. 3. Pour in the egg custard.	Put the tin on a very hot baking sheet. Cook halfway up in a moderate oven, 375° F for 15 mins. Reduce the temperature to 320° F. Cook until the custard has set.
Felixstowe Tart	4 ozs flour 4 ozs cornflour 3 ozs butter 1 teasp baking powder 1 yolk of egg 1 oz castor sugar 1/8 pint milk	2 lbs apples *Meringue* 1 egg white 2 ozs sugar	1. Make the pastry as for rich short and line a deep plate. 2. Bake the pastry blind. 3. Cook and sieve the apples. 4. Fill the tart with the cold sieved fruit. 5. Pile the meringue on top. 6. Decorate with cherry and angelica.	Dry off in a cool oven, 275° F, until the meringue has set (1 hour).

	Ingredients	Method	Baking
Lemon Meringue Pie	4 ozs short or rich short pastry 1 oz cornflour 1 oz sugar 1 oz butter 1 lemon 1/2 pint milk or water 1 or 2 egg yolks *Meringue* 1 or 2 egg whites 2–4 ozs castor sugar	1. Line the plate or flan ring with pastry. 2. Bake blind. 3. Blend the cornflour with a little of the liquid and make it into a thick sauce with the remaining liquid. 4. Beat in the butter. 5. Add the sugar and the grated rind and juice. 6. Beat in the egg yolks. 7. Pour into the pastry.	Bake in a moderate oven, 375° F, in the centre for 15–20 mins. Top with the meringue and dry off in a cool oven, 275° F, 30–60 minutes.
Russian Pudding	4 ozs puff pastry 2 tbs apricot jam 4 ozs castor sugar 4 ozs butter Juice of 2 lemons 4 egg yolks *Meringue* 4 egg whites 4–8 ozs castor sugar	1. Line a plate or flan ring with the pastry. 2. Bake blind. 3. Spread the jam on top of the cooked pastry. 4. Melt the fat and sugar in a pan, add the lemon juice. Cool. 5. Beat in the yolks of egg. 6. Pour the mixture on top of the jam.	Bake in the centre of a moderate oven, 350° F, until the mixture has set. Top with meringue and dry off in a very cool oven, 275° F.
Welsh Cheese Cakes	2 ozs rich short pastry 1 egg 2 ozs butter 2 ozs castor sugar 2 ozs flour 1/2 level teasp baking powder 1 tbs raspberry jam 4 drops vanilla or almond essence or grated rind of 1/2 lemon	1. Line small patty tins with very thin pastry. 2. Spread each with a little jam. 3. Make up a creamed cake mixture. 4. Flavour with lemon or almond or vanilla. 5. Put a teasp of mixture on the top of the jam.	Bake in the centre of a moderate oven, 350° F, for 20 minutes. When cool dredge with icing sugar.
West Riding Pudding	4 ozs short, rough puff or flaky pastry 2 tbs jam Creamed mixture as for Welsh Cheese Cakes, using lemon rind for flavouring	1. Line a deep plate with pastry. 2. Spread with jam. 3. Cover with the creamed mixture, flavoured with lemon rind.	Bake as above for 30 minutes.

Covered Plate Tarts

To line and cover a plate

8 ozs pastry for an 8-inch plate (short, rich short, rough puff, flaky or puff pastry may be used).

Method

1. Divide the pastry into two.
2. Knead up each piece into a round and roll out to an $\frac{1}{8}''$ thick circle.
3. Line the plate with one piece of pastry as for lining a plate— leave the edge undecorated. Put in the filling.
4. Damp the edge of the pastry.
5. Cover with the second piece of pastry.
6. Finish the edge as for a fruit pie *or* turn in any surplus pastry and pinch the edge of the pastry with the thumb and index finger of the right hand, pressing the index finger of the left hand down between them.
7. Leave the pastry to relax for 10 minutes. Bake according to the pastry used.

Fillings

Any fruit as for a fruit pie; jam, syrup or treacle; mincemeat.

Spiced Apple Tart

$1\frac{1}{2}$ lbs apples   1 teasp ground cinnamon
$\frac{1}{4}$ lb sugar $\frac{1}{8}$ pt water
$\frac{1}{2}$ lb dates or soaked prunes
$\frac{1}{2}$ lb rich short pastry made with 1 teasp cinnamon added
   to the flour

Method

1. Stew the apples in the water until soft.
2. Add the dates or prunes and cook for 5–10 minutes.
3. Mash or sieve.
4. Add the sugar and cinnamon: cool.
5. Line a plate with pastry, reserving a circle to cover the tart.
6. Fill the lined plate with the mixture.
7. Cover with the 2nd circle of pastry. Trim and decorate.
8. Bake at 400° F for 10–15 minutes, half way up the oven.
9. Reduce the temperature to 350° F and continue cooking until the *base* of the tart is cooked (approx. 1 hr. total time).

Cornish Treacle Tart

3 ozs fresh breadcrumbs   White of egg for glazing
1 lemon   A little icing sugar
½ lb syrup
     6 ozs short, rich short, rough puff or flaky pastry

Method

1. Line a Yorkshire pudding tin or square cake tin with pastry, reserving another layer for the top of the tart.
2. Mix the breadcrumbs and syrup.
3. Add the finely grated lemon rind and the juice. Put into the pastry case.
4. Cover with the 2nd layer of pastry. Trim and decorate. Glaze with white of egg.
5. Bake in the centre of a hot oven according to the type of pastry used.
6. When cold cut into squares for serving.
7. Dredge with icing sugar.

To Line the Sides of a Pie Dish

For a pint pie dish, use 2 ozs pastry—short, rich short, puff or flaky.

Method

1. Divide the pastry into two. Knead each into an oblong.
2. Roll out into two very thin strips, 2½″ to 3″ wide.
3. Make diagonal cuts about 1″ deep along one edge of each strip.
4. Lift one strip, and, with the cut edge down towards the base of the pie dish, line the sides of half the pie dish.
5. Use the 2nd piece of pastry to line the other half.
6. Cut off any overlapping pieces of pastry and press the join thoroughly so that it is no longer visible.
7. Trim the edges and decorate the lip of the dish.

Apple Amber

Filling

1 lb apples   Rind and juice ½ lemon
2–4 ozs sugar   ½ teasp ground cinnamon
1 oz butter   2 yolks of eggs

Meringue

2 whites
4 ozs castor sugar

Method

1. Stew the apples and sieve them.
2. Add the sugar and butter, lemon and cinnamon.
3. Beat in the yolks.
4. Pour the mixture into the lined pie dish.
5. Bake until the pastry is set halfway up a hot oven, 400° F. (20 min.).
6. Top with meringue and dry off (275° F for 1 hour).

Additional Recipes Using Pastry
Banbury Puffs

6 ozs rough puff or flaky pastry

Filling

1 oz butter	1 oz chopped peel
2 ozs moist brown sugar	1 yolk of egg
½ oz flour or 1 oz cake crumbs	¼ level teasp ground cinnamon
4 ozs currants	or mixed spice

Method

1. Melt the butter, add the flour or crumbs and cook for 3 minutes.
2. Cool and add the other ingredients.
3. Roll out the pastry very thinly and cut into circles 4″ to 5″ in diameter.   Turn each circle over.
4. Put a heaped teaspoonful of the mixture on each circle.
5. Damp the edges of the pastry and draw together, forming a boat shape.
6. Turn each one over and roll it out until the fruit just shows through.   Keep the boat shape.
7. Brush with lightly beaten egg white. Dredge with castor sugar and score through the pastry in a diamond pattern.
8. Place on a baking tray and allow to relax for 10 minutes.
9. Bake just above the centre of a hot oven 450° F for 15–20 minutes.   Cool on a wire tray.

Eccles Cakes

4 ozs rough puff, flaky or puff pastry

Filling

1 oz butter	1 oz chopped peel
1 oz moist brown sugar	2 ozs currants

Method

1. Melt or cream the butter.
2. Add the other ingredients.
3. Roll out the pastry very thinly.
4. Cut out with a 4″ cutter and turn each piece over.
5. Place a teaspoonful of mixture on each piece of pastry.
6. Damp the edges of the pastry and draw together.
7. Turn each one over, roll into circles until the fruit can just be seen through the pastry.
8. Brush with lightly beaten white of egg and dredge with castor sugar.
9. Score in a diamond pattern.
10. Place on a baking sheet and allow to relax for 10 minutes.
11. Bake just above the centre of a hot oven 450° F for 15 minutes.
12. Cool on a wire tray.

Puff Pastry Patties

For directions on making the patties see section on Puff Pastry.

Suitable Fillings

Fresh raw fruit e.g. raspberries, strawberries, etc.
Stewed, bottled or canned fruit.
Jam.
Decorate with fresh whipped cream or buttercream.

Cream Horns

3 ozs puff pastry or scraps from puff pastry patties.
Raspberry jam.
Whipped cream or mock cream.

Method

1. Roll out the pastry into a long strip $\frac{1}{8}$″ thick.
2. Cut into lengths $\frac{1}{2}$″ wide and damp half of each strip.
3. Grease 8 to 10 cream horn tins.
4. Carefully roll the pastry round each tin, starting at the point and overlapping by $\frac{1}{4}$″. Avoid stretching the pastry.
5. Lay the tin on a baking sheet in such a position that the end of the strip lies on the baking sheet.
6. Leave the pastry to relax for 10 to 20 minutes.
7. Bake in the top third of a hot oven, 450° F for 10 to 15 minutes.
8. Cool on a wire tray and remove the tins very carefully.
9. Put a teaspoonful of jam in each horn and pipe cream to fill up the cavity.

Mille-Feuilles

3 ozs flaky or puff pastry
jam and whipped cream

Method

1. Roll out the pastry into three circles $\frac{1}{8}''$ thick and bake according to the type of pastry used, *or* roll out 1 circle of pastry $\frac{3}{8}''$ thick, bake and split into three when cold.
2. When quite cold spread one circle with jam, place the second piece of pastry on the top.
3. Spread with whipped cream and cover with the third circle of pastry.
4. Decorate with glacé icing.

Scotch Tart

$\frac{1}{4}$ lb short pastry, i.e. 4 ozs flour 2 ozs fat.

Filling

$2\frac{1}{2}$ ozs stale cake crumbs	3 ozs castor sugar
2 ozs candied peel	3 ozs butter
2 ozs glacé cherries	1 oz cornflour
$\frac{1}{2}$ egg	1 oz flour

Method

1. Line a 7″ plate or flan ring with the pastry.
2. Mix the crumbs, cornflour and flour together.
3. Rub the butter into this mixture.
4. Add the chopped peel, cherries and sugar.
5. Add the egg and mix well.
6. Fill the pastry case and press down lightly.
7. Bake in the centre of a moderate oven, 350° F, for 25 to 30 mins.

Vanilla Slices

scraps of puff pastry
cream or mock cream
glacé icing

Method

1. Roll the pastry $\frac{1}{8}''$ thick and cut into pieces $1\frac{1}{2}'' \times 2\frac{1}{2}''$.
2. Bake in the top third of a hot oven, 450° F for 10 to 15 minutes.
3. Split each one and fill with cream and jam.
4. Ice with glacé icing.

I. HOT SOUFFLÉS

All hot soufflés have a panada base into which egg yolks are beaten and lastly stiffly beaten whites are folded in. These soufflés may be steamed or baked, and, owing to their very light texture, they should be served immediately they are cooked. In particular the cooking of baked soufflés should be so carefully timed that they are lifted out of the oven and carried straight to the table. If a baked soufflé is kept hot while the earlier courses of a meal are eaten it will have shrunk badly in the soufflé case and be less attractive in appearance and tough to eat.

General Proportions

1 oz flour ⎫	3 yolks of eggs
1 oz butter ⎬ ¼ pint panada	4 whites of eggs
¼ pint milk ⎭	

The amount of sweetening varies according to the flavour; for a sweet flavouring, e.g. vanilla, 1 oz castor sugar is sufficient. If the flavouring is sharp, e.g. orange or lemon, 2 ozs sugar will be required.

The other proportions are identical whichever method of cooking is employed.

To prepare a soufflé tin for steaming

A plain mould or cake tin may be used. The former is the more satisfactory as it is wider at the top than the base, so that the soufflé, when turned out, has a wide base on which to stand. The tin should be quite dry and clean and it should be well greased with clarified butter.

A band of greaseproof paper should be tied round the tin. This band should be made of three thicknesses of paper and should come 2½″ to 3″ above the top of the tin. It is not necessary for it to go to the base of the tin, but it should be very securely tied into position. It must be greased with the tin.

A piece of greaseproof paper may be cut to fit the base of the tin exactly. This assists in turning out, but it is not essential if the tin is well greased. A piece of paper should be greased to lie on top of the paper band during steaming to prevent the condensed steam from dropping on to the soufflé.

To prepare a soufflé case for baking

As a baked soufflé is served in the dish in which it is cooked, a fireproof, china or glass soufflé case should be used. It should be greased with clarified butter.

Points to remember in making

1. All ingredients should be prepared before beginning the actual making.
2. The fat and flour should be cooked as a roux and the milk blended in to make the panada. This should be cooked until it leaves the side of the pan.
3. The panada should be allowed to cool and the flavouring added; then the yolks should be beaten in one at a time. If the panada is left to get too cool it will be very difficult to combine the yolks smoothly.
4. When the yolks have been added the mixture should be similar in appearance and texture to choux pastry (see page 378).
5. Whisk the whites until they are stiff and peaked. Fold them in very carefully and pour the mixture into the tin or soufflé case.

Cooking a soufflé

The soufflé should be cooked as soon as it is made. This is very important. The speed of cooking should be very moderate to enable the entrapped air to expand fully before the albumen of the egg has coagulated.

A steamed soufflé should be firm to the touch when it is cooked. If it is cooked too quickly it will collapse and be tough and close in texture. It will also collapse if it is moved before it has fully set. If it is allowed to cook for too long the albumen will toughen and again cause collapse. A steamed soufflé takes about 1 hour to cook and the pan should be on the side of the source of heat so that the water is simmering at one side of the pan only.

To turn out a steamed soufflé

Allow the weight of the soufflé to pull it away from the sides of the tin, by moving the tin round very gently while it is slightly tipped. Hold a dish inverted over the top of the soufflé without actually touching it. Carefully turn the dish and the soufflé over, allowing the soufflé to fall gently on to the dish and holding the tin so that its weight does not rest on the soufflé.

A baked soufflé should be cooked half way up the oven at 350° F for 30 to 40 minutes. By this time it should have risen and browned lightly. It will start to fall immediately it begins to cool.

Basic Recipe for a Hot Soufflé

1 oz flour	1 oz castor sugar
1 oz butter	3 yolks of eggs
¼ pint milk	4 whites of eggs
flavouring	

Method

1. Prepare the soufflé case or tin.
2. Separate the eggs.
3. Prepare the flavouring.
4. Make a roux with the fat and flour.
5. Gradually blend in the milk and cook until the panada thickens and leaves the sides of the pan.
6. Add the sugar and flavouring and cool a little.
7. Beat in the yolks one at a time.
8. Whisk the whites until they are stiff.
9. Fold in very lightly until well blended.
10. Pour into the case or tin.
11. Cover with a sheet of greased paper laid on the top and put in a steamer. Steam gently for one hour,
   or put into a moderate oven preheated to 350° F. Bake 30–40 minutes.

Variations of the Basic Recipe for Hot Soufflés

Type	Additions to the Recipe	Adaptations of the Method	Method of Cooking	Suitable Sauce
Chocolate	1½–2 ozs grated chocolate 2–3 drops vanilla essence ¼–1 oz castor sugar.	Add the additional ingredients with the sugar to the panada.	Baking or steaming	Chocolate or Coffee *or* Jam
Coffee	2 tbs coffee essence	Add with the milk.	Baking or steaming	Chocolate or Coffee *or* Jam
Lemon or Orange	1 lemon or 1 orange	Grate the rind finely and squeeze the juice. Add to the panada with the sugar.	Baking or steaming	Lemon or Orange
Vanilla	2 teasp vanilla essence	Add with the milk.	Baking or steaming	Jam

Cheese Soufflé see chapter on Supper Dishes.
Fish Soufflé see chapter on Fish.

WHAT WENT WRONG—AND WHY

The soufflé is close and the mixture uneven in texture
   (*a*) The panada was too hot or too cold when the yolks were added.
   (*b*) The whites were folded in carelessly and unevenly.

The steamed soufflé rose well but collapsed when turned out

- (a) It was not cooked through.
- (b) It was cooked too slowly.
- (c) It was cooked for too long.

The baked soufflé is close and not risen

- (a) It was baked in too hot an oven.
- (b) It was baked too high up in the oven.
- (c) It was kept too hot after baking.
- (d) It was baked for too long a time.

J. ADDITIONAL RECIPES

Apple Charlotte (1)

1 lb cooking apples	Rind and juice of 1 lemon
4 ozs sugar or golden syrup	1½ ozs suet or butter
3 ozs fresh breadcrumbs	

Method

1. Peel and slice the apples thinly.
2. Mix the breadcrumbs, sugar and suet if used.
3. Add the finely shredded rind to the crumbs.
4. Add the lemon juice with the apple.
5. Put the apples and breadcrumbs into a greased pie dish in alternate layers with the breadcrumb mixture at the bottom and the top.
6. If butter is used melt it and sprinkle over the crumbs in the dish.
7. Finish with a layer of breadcrumb mixture.
8. Bake in a moderate oven 375° F for ¾ to 1 hour.

Apple Charlotte (2)

1 lb cooking apples, weighed after peeling	3 ozs clarified butter
3–4 ozs sugar	Rind and juice of ½ lemon
3–4 slices stale bread ⅜″ thick	2 yolks of eggs

Method

1. Cut a slice of bread to fit the base and top of a fireproof glass or china dish.
2. Cut the remaining bread to line the sides of the dish neatly.
3. Dip the bread in the clarified butter.
4. Cook and sieve the apples.

5. Add the lemon rind and juice, sugar and remaining butter.
6. Beat the yolks.
7. Pour this apple mixture into the lined dish.
8. Cover with the slice of bread.
9. Cover with greased paper and press with a weighted saucer.
10. Bake in the centre of a moderate oven, 375° F for 1½ hours.
11. Turn out on to a heated dish or serve in the dish in which it was baked.
    The bread should be pale brown and crisp.

Apple Sago

1 lb cooking apples   1 pt water
4 ozs sugar   a little lemon rind
2 ozs sago

Method

1. Heat the water and lemon rind.
2. Sprinkle on the sago and whisk in (see Sago Pudding).
3. Bring to the boil and cook for 15–20 minutes until the grain appears clear.
4. Stew the apples in the minimum of water.
5. Add to the sago and sweeten.
6. Allow to cool.   Whisk well and serve cold.

Austrian Cheese Cake

2 ozs butter   10 ozs curd (cream if possible)
4½ ozs castor sugar   2 ozs raisins
3 eggs   2 ozs ground almond
2 ozs semolina

Method

1. Cream the butter and sugar together until white and fluffy.
2. Beat in the sieved curd, almonds, raisins and semolina with the egg yolks.
3. Whisk the egg whites to a peak.   Fold into the mixture.
4. Pour into a well-greased 7″ sandwich tin.
5. Bake for 50–60 mins in the centre of an oven preheated to 350° F.   Serve hot or cold.

Baked Apples

3–4 large cooking apples
1 teasp sugar or syrup for each apple
1 oz dates or raisins for each apple
Juice and grated rind of 1 orange or lemon, if liked.

Method

1. Wash and core the apples.
2. Cut a circle round the apple just through the skin.
3. Stand the apples on a baking tin or in a fireproof glass or china dish.
4. Fill the holes with sugar or syrup and the fruit and rind.
5. If liked a little water and juice may be poured into the dish.
6. Bake halfway up in a moderate oven, 350° F for ½ to 1 hour, depending on the size of the apples.
7. It is very important that the apples should be cooked through —even if they tend to burst a little. Moderate heat for a longer time gives more satisfactory results than quick cooking.

Canadian Lemon Soufflé

2 ozs flour	3–4 eggs
3 ozs butter	rind and juice of 1 large lemon
6 ozs sugar	½ pint milk

Method

1. Cream the butter and sugar, add the egg yolks and lemon, and beat well.
2. Stir in the flour and the milk.
3. Whisk the whites very stiffly and fold in carefully.
4. Pour into a greased dish and bake in a moderate oven, 350° F halfway up the oven. After 15 minutes reduce the temperature to 325° F. Bake for ¾ hour total time.

    The pudding should be pale brown in colour and separated into two layers: sponge on top and lemon sauce below.

    Serve at once.

Mincemeat (1)

6 ozs suet	¼ lb chopped peel
½ lb apples	1 lemon
½ lb stoned raisins	¼ lb moist brown sugar
½ lb currants	1 oz chopped nuts
½ lb sultanas	⅛ pt brandy or sherry
½ teasp mixed spice if liked	

Method

1. Wash and dry the fruit.
2. Chop or mince the suet, apples, fruit and peel separately.
3. Mix and rechop or mince with the nuts.
4. Add the sugar, lemon rind and juice and brandy.

5. Pack into clean and dry jam jars.
6. Tie down with parchment jam covers.

Mincemeat (2)

4 ozs suet	$\frac{1}{4}$ lb candied peel
$\frac{1}{2}$ lb raisins (stoned)	$1\frac{1}{2}$ lbs currants
1 lb apples	1 lb sultanas
1 lb sugar	

Method

1. Wash and dry the fruit.
2. Chop or mince the suet, apples, fruit and peel separately.
3. Mix and chop again or mince.
4. Add the sugar.
5. Pack into clean dry jars.
6. Tie down with parchment jam covers.

Mince Pies

4 ozs short, rich short, rough puff or flaky pastry.   4 ozs mincemeat

Method 1

1. Roll out the pastry thinly (4 ozs short pastry should provide 12 circles $2\frac{1}{4}''$ each).
2. Stamp with a cutter slightly larger than the patty tin.
3. Line each tin with a circle of pastry using the circles cut from the re-rolled pastry for the underside.
4. Put 1 heaped teasp mincemeat into each.
5. Damp the edges and cover with a circle of pastry. Press the edges together and finish as desired.
6. Three nicks across the top is a traditional finish to mince pies.
7. Bake according to the type of pastry.

Method 2.   Suitable for rough puff or flaky pastry only.

1. Roll out the pastry $\frac{1}{8}''$ thick.
2. Stamp out with a $2\frac{1}{2}''$ plain cutter.
3. Put a heaped teaspoonful of mincemeat on half the circles of pastry.
4. Damp the edges of the pastry and cover with the second circle of pastry.
5. Press the edges firmly together and finish as for a fruit pie (p. 263).
6. Glaze with egg wash and bake according to the type of pastry used.
7. Choose the circles which were cut from the first rolling for the tops of the pies. Cut the underneath pieces from the re-rolled scraps.

Pineapple Pudding
(To serve 4–6 portions)

2 ozs cornflour or custard powder

½ pt milk

½ pt pineapple juice

1 oz sugar

½ tin pineapple chunks

2 egg yolks

Meringue

2 egg whites

2–4 ozs castor sugar

Method

1. Make a thick sauce with the cornflour and milk, and after cooking add the pineapple juice.
2. Add the sugar and chopped pineapple.
3. Beat in the yolks.
4. Bake in the centre of a moderate oven 350° F for 15 minutes.
5. Make a meringue with the whites and sugar.
6. Pile up or pipe on to the pudding.
7. Dry out for 1 hour in the centre of a cool oven, 250°–275° F.

Orange Pudding

As for pineapple pudding but substitute a small tin of mandarin oranges for the pineapple cubes.

CHAPTER XIX

COLD SWEETS AND ICES

THIS branch of cookery offers wide scope to the experienced as well as the inexperienced cook.

For convenience cold sweets may be grouped thus :—

1. Fruits or fruit mixtures.
2. Custards, junkets and un-moulded milk sweets.
3. Moulded sweets, with or without cream.
4. Jellies, uncleared and cleared.
5. Cold soufflés.
6. Unclassified, e.g. trifles, meringues etc.
7. Ices.

FRUITS
Stewed Fruit (Fresh)

The aim when stewing fruit should be to retain the shape of the fruit whilst making the fruit tender and sweet.

Allow ¼ lb sugar to 1 lb fruit,
   and ¼ pt water to 1 lb fruit for soft berry fruits, rhubarb etc.
     ½ pt water to 1 lb fruit for medium hard and stone fruits,
   e.g. apples, all varieties of plums, apricots, gooseberries, peaches etc.
     ¾ pt water to 1 lb fruit if very hard, e.g. pears, quinces etc.

Preparation of Syrup

Dissolve the sugar in the water, bring to the boil and leave to evaporate, without stirring, for about five minutes, until a syrupy consistency is obtained.

Suitable flavourings are :—

Strips of lemon rind, a piece of stick cinnamon ½" long, or 1 or 2 cloves. When any of these is used, the flavouring should be added to the sugar and water, cooked in the syrup before the fruit is added, and left in with the fruit. After cooking, the fruit is removed, and the syrup is then strained so that the pieces of flavouring are extracted.

Cooking of Fruit

1. *In the saucepan.*

Add the prepared fruit and simmer *gently* until tender, with the lid on the pan.

2. *In a casserole in the oven.*

Place the prepared fruit in the casserole, pour over the syrup, and cover with a lid.

Cook in the middle of the oven preheated to 325° F until tender. This will take approximately twice as long as in a pan, but prevents the breaking down of the fruit as there is little movement of the liquid.

This method is not recommended for fruits such as apples and pears which discolour readily after preparation.

Dishing of the Fruit

Lift carefully from the container with a perforated spoon. Place in a dish and pour the syrup over. If the syrup is thin, reduce in quantity by boiling quickly in an open pan until the required consistency is obtained. When flavouring such as lemon rind is used, the syrup should be strained over the fruit.

To Stew Dried Fruit

e.g. Prunes, apricots, peaches etc.

1. Wash the fruit thoroughly in tepid water, add sufficient cold water to cover completely and leave to soak for 12 to 24 hours in order to replace the water lost during the process of drying.
2. Put the fruit and the water into a pan; bring to the boil and allow the fruit to simmer very gently until it is tender.
3. Strain off the liquid, measure it and add sugar according to the natural sweetness of the fruit. Prunes and figs require none or very little; apricots, peaches and apples require 2–4 ozs to each pint of liquid.
4. Dissolve the sugar in the liquid, boil well in an open pan until it is reduced to a syrupy consistency, and pour it over the fruit. Flavourings such as are used for fresh fruit may be added.

Fruit Fools

These consist of stewed fruit, cooked until very soft, rubbed through a sieve and the pulp combined with an equal quantity of half-whipped cream. Cup custard or evaporated milk may be used in place of cream, or a combination of these three may be used. Fruit fools should be served in individual glasses, decorated simply with a little whipped cream or finely chopped nuts, and served with savoy or sponge fingers or simple biscuits.

Banana Fool may be made by rubbing fresh ripe bananas through a sieve and proceeding as above. All fruit fools are delicate and refreshing sweets, and are very suitable to serve in hot weather.

Fruit Salad

Fruit salad may be made from fresh, canned or bottled fruit. Fresh fruit, e.g. apples, pears, bananas, oranges, pineapples, grapes should be prepared according to kind, all skins and seeds being removed (grape skins may be left on to give colour), and cut into neat pieces.

Preparation of the Syrup

1. Allow approximately ½ pt syrup to every lb fruit, prepared as for stewed fruit and flavoured with lemon juice and sherry if liked.
2. When cool, pour over the fresh fruit and allow to stand to extract the full flavour of the fruits.

When canned or bottled fruit is used, the juice should be strained off and, if not dark coloured, may be used in place of sugar syrup. Juice from canned fruit may be rather sweet and is much improved by the addition of lemon juice to sharpen the flavour.

The fruit should stand in the syrup only as long as is required to extract the flavour, so that the shape and colour of each ingredient may be kept.

Serve in individual dishes or in a suitable bowl. Show, in the form of decoration, a selection of the fruits used.

Cold Fruit Charlotte or Summer Pudding

4 or 5 slices bread (without crusts) or stale sponge cakes
1 lb fresh fruit (preferably the soft berry type e.g. raspberries, red currants etc.)
¼ lb sugar
¼ pt water

Method

1. Stew the fruit (see page 283).
2. Rinse a pudding basin with cold water and line it with fingers of stale bread or stale sponge cake cut about ¼″ thick and wedged together very tightly.
3. Fill the centre with the *hot* stewed fruit and syrup.
4. Cover with a round of stale bread or cake cut to the same thickness as the fingers of bread or cake. See that there is sufficient juice to soak all the bread or cake.
5. Put an old saucer and a weight on top and set aside until quite cold.
6. When cold turn out and serve with cold custard or whipped cream.

JUNKETS
Basic Recipe

1 pt fresh milk
1 teasp essence of rennet
½ oz castor sugar

Method

1. Heat the milk to *blood heat only* i.e. 98° F. (To test, dip in the tip of the little finger. If comfortably warm the temperature is approximately correct.)
2. Add to the milk the sugar and any flavouring to be used, and pour into a glass dish.
3. Stir in the rennet and leave undisturbed in a cool place but *not* in a draught for 1½ to 2 hours.
4. When set, grate nutmeg on the top and serve with stewed fruit, fruit salad, or with cream.

Variations of Above Recipe

FLAVOURING	ADDITIONS TO BASIC RECIPE	ADDITIONAL POINTS IN METHOD
1. Brandy .	A few drops of brandy	Stir into the milk with the sugar.
2. Chocolate .	1 oz plain chocolate 2 tbs water 1 tbs sugar 3 drops vanilla essence	Grate the chocolate, add the water and heat in a small pan very gently until the chocolate has dissolved. Add the milk, vanilla and sugar and warm to blood heat.
3. Coffee .	2 teasp coffee essence	Add to the milk with the sugar.
4. Lemon .	The rind of 1 lemon 1 or 2 drops lemon colouring	Pare the rind very thinly and infuse with the warm milk for ½ hr (do not boil the milk).
5. Orange .	The rind of 1 orange 1 or 2 drops of orange colouring	As for lemon.
6. Rum . .	A few drops of rum or rum essence	Add to the milk with the sugar.
7. Vanilla .	½ teasp vanilla essence or 1 vanilla pod	Add to the milk with the sugar. Infuse in the warm milk for ½ hour.

MOULDED SWEETS

These sweets are stiffened with a starchy food or with gelatine or isinglass.

The starchy foods are usually ground or powdered grains, e.g. ground rice or cornflour, but occasionally whole grain such as rice is used.

The sweet takes its name from the distinctive flavouring agent and from the thickening agent used.

Moulds made with Cornflour, Ground Rice, Semolina or Arrowroot

1 pt milk	strip of lemon rind
1½ ozs cornflour *or*	1 to 2 ozs sugar
1½ ozs semolina *or*	½ oz butter, if liked
1¾ ozs ground rice *or*	
1¼ ozs arrowroot	

Method

1. Blend the cereal smoothly with some of the cold milk.
2. Boil the remaining milk and whilst heating the milk add a strip of lemon rind or vanilla pod to extract flavour.
3. Strain the boiling milk on to the blended cereal, stirring well with a wooden spoon.
4. Return to the rinsed pan and heat gently, stirring well; boil for four or five minutes in order to cook the starch very thoroughly.
5. Add the butter if liked, then the sugar, and mix thoroughly. If no flavouring has been added to the milk already, one or two drops of lemon, vanilla or other essence may be added (and if desired a little colouring).
6. Pour the mixture into a mould rinsed with cold water and leave until set.
7. When set turn out and serve with stewed fruit.

Variations of the Basic Recipe

TYPE	ADDITIONS TO BASIC RECIPE	ALTERATION IN METHOD
Chocolate .	Add 1 oz cocoa and a few drops of vanilla essence. Omit the lemon rind.	Mix the cocoa with the cornflour. Add the vanilla essence after cooking and just before moulding.
Coffee . .	Add 1–2 tbs coffee essence. Omit other flavourings.	Proceed as for basic recipe.
Custard .	Substitute custard powder for cornflour.	Proceed as for basic recipe.
Orange . .	Substitute orange rind.	Proceed as for basic recipe.

Whole Rice Mould

2½ ozs rice (Carolina)   1½ ozs sugar
1 pt milk   few drops of vanilla essence

Method

1. Wash the rice, cover with cold water, bring to the boil and pour off the water. Add the milk, bring to the boil and leave to simmer one to two hours, to cook the starch in the rice thoroughly. (If possible use a double saucepan or porridge pan for this purpose.) When the rice is thoroughly cooked add the sugar and flavouring.
2. Pour into a rinsed mould.
3. When set turn out and serve with jam or stewed fruit.

JELLIES

Jellies may be classified as uncleared or cleared and may be either savoury or sweet.

The making of jellies is simplified by the use of commercial gelatine, which is purer than that which is extracted from bones and sinews by home methods, though this method must still be used to prepare home made Calves' foot jelly for invalids.

General Rules for Making Jellies

All utensils must be scrupulously clean and free from grease, otherwise the jelly does not sparkle.

Gelatine must be weighed carefully so that the correct proportion is used to give the proper consistency. A jelly should " shiver " when lightly shaken. Too much gelatine will give a tough hard mould, while too little will fail to result in setting and will cause cracking and collapse of the shape.

General Proportions for Uncleared Jellies

¾ oz gelatine to 1 pt thin liquid e.g. milk, fruit purée or flavoured water.

½ oz gelatine to 1 pt thick liquid e.g. fruit or vegetable purée.

Method

1. Add the measured quantity of cold liquid to the gelatine and allow to soak for a few minutes.
2. Dissolve very slowly, stirring all the time to prevent burning.
3. Bring to the boil; the mixture should be clear and free from lumps before boiling point is reached.

If allowed to boil the gelatine will lose its setting properties.

When using milk with gelatine, it is very important to prevent the liquid from boiling as this would cause the milk to curdle.

Fresh pineapple, if used, must be stewed before the addition of the gelatine in order to reduce its acidity, which would cause the gelatine to lose its setting properties.

The jelly should be moulded when cool though still liquid.

The moulds must be scrupulously clean and free from all blemishes. Moulds which are used for jellies, especially cleared jellies, should be kept exclusively for this purpose and must be most carefully washed and dried after use so that they do not rust. A tinned mould gives the best results though aluminium is fairly satisfactory. On no account should small dariole moulds be used for steaming or baking if jellies are to be set in them.

To turn out

A *Small Moulds*

(*a*) Have ready a deep bowl of water so hot that the hand can just bear the heat.

(*b*) Immerse the mould twice quickly. Dry well to avoid sprinkling the serving dish with water.

(*c*) Put the thumb of the right hand under the base of the mould and cover the top with the fingers.

(*d*) Holding the hand over the serving dish, shake the mould on to the fingers and slide the mould on to the wet dish. If the dish has been wetted slightly the mould can be moved into the exact centre if it has slipped to one side.

B *Large Moulds*

(*a*) Lower the mould into the hot water deep enough for the water to come level with the top of the jelly. Do not wet the jelly.

(*b*) Turn on to the palm of the right hand and slide on to the slightly wetted dish.

K

UNCLEARED JELLIES

Type	Recipe	Method	No. of Portions
Dutch Flummery	2 whole eggs or 3 yolks 1 large lemon 6 ozs sugar 1/4 pt cooking sherry 3/4 pt water 1/2 oz powdered gelatine	1. Wash the lemon, peel the rind thinly. 2. Put the lemon rind and juice, sugar, gelatine, sherry and water into a pan, heat gently until the gelatine and sugar are dissolved. Allow to infuse for 10 minutes but do not overheat. 3. Beat the eggs until all traces of ropiness have gone. 4. Pour the lemon mixture over the eggs, stirring all the time. Strain into the rinsed pan. 5. Stir over a gentle heat until the mixture thickens. 6. Cool, stirring occasionally during the cooling to prevent a skin from forming. 7. Pour into a rinsed mould, individual sundae glasses or small moulds. 8. When set, turn out and decorate with whipped cream, crystallised flowers or angelica.	3 normal 4 invalid
Egg	2 lemons 2 eggs 5-6 ozs castor sugar 1/2 oz gelatine water enough to make up the juice of the lemons to 1 pt	As for Dutch Flummery	4 normal 6 invalid
Milk	1 pt milk 1 1/2 ozs castor sugar strip lemon rind 3/4 oz gelatine	1. Put the milk, lemon rind and gelatine into a rinsed pan. 3. Heat gently until the gelatine is dissolved. DO NOT BOIL. Strain into a basin. Remove from the heat, add the sugar and stir until dissolved. 4. Stir from time to time as the mixture cools until it becomes the consistency of thick cream. This prevents the separation of the milk during the setting process. 5. Pour into wetted moulds and leave to set. 6. Do not leave overnight or the milk next to the mould will discolour. 7. Turn out and decorate with cherry and angelica.	3 normal 4 invalid
Orange	2 or 3 oranges 1/2 pt orange juice 1/2 pt water juice of 2 lemons 3 ozs sugar 3/4 oz gelatine	1. Wash the oranges and remove the rind very thinly. 2. Put the water, sugar, orange rind and gelatine into a pan and heat gently until the sugar and gelatine are dissolved. 3. When the liquid is clear, cover with a lid and infuse for 10 minutes in a warm place. This will extract the full flavour from the rind. 4. Strain into a basin and cool. 5. When cool strain in the orange and lemon juice. Mix well. 6. Pour either into one large or 6 individual moulds or in sundae glasses. 7. When set, if in glasses decorate the edge of each with stars of whipped cream and pieces of orange rind cut into attractive shapes. If in moulds, turn out in the usual way, on to a glass or a silver dish, and pipe cream round the base.	6
Tomato	3/4 pint tomato purée well flavoured with garlic, sugar and lemon juice 1/4 pt water 3/4 oz gelatine, very light weight	1. Dissolve the gelatine in the water. 2. Add the tomato purée, season and taste. 3. Pour into a mould when cool. If tinned tomato purée is used, reduce the quantity of purée to 1/2 pint and add	4

CLEARED JELLIES

Cleared jellies may be savoury or sweet and in both cases may be used with a variety of suitable ingredients set in the jelly to form a more substantial dish. They make an attractive addition to a cold table, but must be carefully prepared to make sure that the jelly is clear and sparkling while preserving the full flavour of the ingredients used. The clearing of the liquid is achieved by the addition of egg whites and shells, which, when whisked in the flavoured liquid as it comes to the boil, form a filter. This entangles all the solid matter, leaving the liquid clear. The liquid is further cleared as it passes through the jelly bag.

Choice and care of equipment for making jellies

1. *Pan* It is best to use a white lined or aluminium pan deep enough to allow the jelly to rise well during the period of clarifying, i.e. when the mixture, including the egg whites and crushed shells, is coming to the boil. The pan must be absolutely clean and free from grease, and to make sure that this is so, the pan should be filled with water and boiled for 2–3 minutes beforehand. The water is then poured away and the pan rinsed in cold water.
2. *Whisk* A balloon whisk which is long enough to reach the bottom of the pan should be used to avoid any risk of the fingers touching the liquid. This should be put in the pan with the water and so cleared of all traces of grease beforehand.
3. *Jelly bag and stand* (*a*) Flannel bags shaped like a pierrot's hat, with loops attached, and the metal stand from which the bag is suspended, may be purchased from any good hardware store.

   (*b*) A clean, closely woven linen towel may be tied by the corners to the legs of an upturned chair. If this method is used, it is more convenient if one spindle is removed from the chair to make it easier to put a basin under the steaming cloth.

   Immediately before use, pour a kettleful of boiling water through the bag. This ensures cleanliness and heats the bag, so preventing the jelly from setting in the bag.
4. *2 Basins* are necessary, both scalded and rinsed to make sure that they are scrupulously clean. These should be of a convenient size to fit in the stand or chair under the bag.
5. *Moulds* Clear tin moulds give the best outline to a jelly or gelatine sweet. They may be of any size and may be plain or shaped to give a patterned outline.

   Cleared jellies do not show to advantage unless they have

been set in moulds. Set in individual glasses the jelly does not catch the light which gives the desired sparkling brilliance. They show to best advantage if served on a silver dish.

The moulds should be kept exclusively for jellies and gelatine sweets in order that the tinned surface can be kept free from scratches and rust. They must be scalded and rinsed before use and very carefully washed and thoroughly dried after use.

BASIC RECIPES FOR CLEARED JELLIES

Savoury Jelly (Aspic)	Sweet Jellies	
	Lemon	Wine
1½ pts cold water ¼ pt cooking sherry ¼ pt vinegars (Malt, tarragon, chilli) *or* mixture of vinegar and lemon juice Rind of 1 lemon 1 carrot 1 stick celery sprig parsley Bouquet garni ½ teasp salt 2 egg whites and shells 1½ ozs gelatine	1½ pts cold water ½ pt lemon juice Rind of 2 lemons 6 ozs granulated or loaf sugar 1 or 2 cloves ½ to 1 stick cinnamon 2 egg whites and shells 1½ ozs gelatine	1¼ pts cold water ½ pt port or sherry ¼ pt lemon juice 6 ozs granulated or loaf sugar 1 or 2 cloves ½ to 1 stick cinnamon 2 egg whites and shells 1½ ozs gelatine

If the jelly is to be used for lining moulds or chopping, use 2 ozs gelatine to the pint of liquids.

Method of Making Jelly

1. Prepare the pan and whisk.
2. Put the measured liquids into the pan, add the gelatine. Leave to stand in cold water whilst preparing the remaining ingredients.
3. Wash the lemons if used and peel the rind very thinly, removing all traces of white pith as this would impart a bitter flavour to the jelly. Add to the pan.
4. Add the flavourings.
5. Wash and crush the eggshells and add with the unbeaten whites to the other ingredients.
6. Using the egg whisk, stir all the ingredients over a very gentle heat until the gelatine is dissolved, then whisk steadily over slightly greater heat until a good froth is seen covering the entire surface and the liquid has almost reached boiling point. Remove the whisk and allow the liquid to boil through

the froth for about ½ minute. The egg whites and shells help to clear the jelly. During the heating and whisking the egg whites partially coagulate and entangle insoluble particles and impurities from the sugar and other ingredients. It is necessary to stop whisking just before boiling point is reached, otherwise the partially coagulated albumen is broken up and the impurities previously entangled are released, thus preventing the clearing of the jelly.

7. When the froth on the jelly has risen in the pan, remove from the heat and cover the pan. Leave to stand in a warm place for approximately 5 minutes.

8. Scald the jelly bag.

9. Ladle the froth from the surface of the jelly into the bag and pour through it the jelly, making sure that all the eggshell is poured into the jelly bag or cloth.

10. When a small quantity of jelly has filtered through and is still running in a gentle trickle, raise the basin, put the second one in its place, and pour the filtrate (filtered liquor) through the jelly bag. The second lot of filtrate should be clearer than the first. If necessary repeat this process a third time. It is most important to avoid stirring the contents of the bag or squeezing it during the straining of the jelly; otherwise some impurities or scum will be forced through the bag and cloudiness will result.

When making Aspic Jelly, allow the mixture to stand for 20 minutes after bringing to the boil in order to extract the maximum amount of flavour from all the ingredients.

Uses of Cleared Jellies

Lemon or wine jelly may be moulded as for uncleared jellies and served with suitable decoration as a sweet.

Jellies may serve as a decoration to another dish, and for this purpose are usually chopped as a garnish.

To chop jelly, either sweet or savoury

(a) Wet a piece of greaseproof paper and lay it on a board.

(b) Turn out the required amount of jelly, preferably set in a shallow tin.

(c) Chop with a scrupulously clean wet knife held upright until the jelly is fairly small. If chopped too fine, it will lose its sparkle.

Using cleared jelly to line a mould for a cream or similar dish

(a) Scald and rinse the mould—leave wet.

(b) Have ready a shallow basin of ice.

(c) Pour a little jelly into the bottom of the mould, and keeping the mould on the ice bed turn it slowly round and round, tipping it slightly to allow the jelly to run down the sides.

(d) Add liquid jelly little by little to the sides of the mould until a smooth thin covering of jelly coats the whole inside of the mould.

   The ice will help the jelly to set quickly but it must not set so rapidly that a ridged coating of jelly results.

To decorate a mould

(a) Line the mould with jelly and, when quite firm, dip the decoration in liquid jelly, and, using 2 hatpins or fine skewers, place the decoration in position remembering that the outside of the decoration must face the mould.

(b) Hold the decoration in position with a drop of additional jelly.

(c) The decorations must be very neatly cut and placed, and must be set firmly in place before the mould is filled up with other mixture.

To set small portions of solid food in jelly

   e.g. fruit, prawns, crayfish or lobster claws, hard-boiled-egg slices, vegetables.

(a) Line a wet mould as described above and decorate the base using carefully shaped and trimmed pieces of food. The design must be clearly planned so that when the finished jelly is turned out the effect is attractive when looked at from both the top and the sides.

(b) When the decoration is firmly set, pour a depth of jelly in and allow to set firmly.

(c) Arrange a further layer of decoration on the sides of the mould and across the surface. Allow to set.

(d) Cover with the depth of jelly used in the first layer. Allow to set.

(e) Continue in this way until the mould is filled to within 1" of the top.

(f) When arranging the last layer of decoration, which will form the base of the jelly when turned out, allow sufficient solid pieces to give a bold outline to the shape.

(g) Cover with a final layer of jelly and allow to set.

(h) Turn out and decorate with chopped jelly and choice pieces of the solid food retained for the purpose.

Suggested combinations of fillings

   Lemon Jelly

   1. Mandarin oranges and black and green grapes.

2. Grapes and pears cut into fancy shapes.
3. Cherries and apples or pears cut into shapes.
4. Sliced peaches and black cherries.
5. Strawberries or raspberries with sliced almonds.

Port Wine Jelly
White fruits and grapes.

CREAMS

Creams are moulded sweets set with gelatine.

Types of cream

1. Flavoured cream.
2. Fruit purée and cream.
3. Custard and cream *or*
   Custard and fruit purée and cream. This is known as Bavaroise.

Note All or part of the cream may be replaced by evaporated milk which has been boiled in the unopened can for 20 minutes, cooled and chilled for at least 24 hours in the refrigerator. Evaporated milk thus prepared will keep for several weeks in the refrigerator if the can is unopened.

General Rules for Making Creams

1. *General Proportions*
   $\frac{1}{4}$ oz gelatine to $\frac{3}{4}$ pint total liquid.
2. The moulds kept for jellies can be used for creams as it is customary to line the mould with clear jelly before putting in the cream mixture.
3. Creams may be set in individual glasses and when set decorated with chopped jelly and piped cream.
4. The gelatine must be weighed carefully, soaked and dissolved as for making jellies.
5. The cream should be " double cream " in order to make sure that it will whip.
   Cream or evaporated milk should be half whipped, that is, it should leave a trail when taken across its own surface. If both are used, they should be whisked separately and combined when both are the correct consistency. This gives lightness and sponginess to the texture of the cream. If the cream is overwhipped, it may turn to butter on the addition of other ingredients, thus causing a close heavy result.

6. Custard and fruit purées should be prepared in the usual way (page 284) and used cold. The consistency should be that of half-whipped cream.
7. The prepared cream should be well mixed in a china basin with any custard, purée and flavouring used.
8. The dissolved gelatine, which should be completely dissolved and warm when tested with the little finger, is poured into the cream mixture, stirring all the time. The gelatine should be poured in a thin stream from a height.
9. If the gelatine is too cool when added to the cream mixture it will set before it is evenly distributed throughout the mixture and either the cream will not set evenly, which will affect the turning out, or strings of gelatine will appear in the mixture, giving a ropy appearance. This can be corrected if the bowl is placed in another bowl containing moderately hot water. The heat will remove the strings of gelatine but air is lost from the whipped cream and a close texture results. Bulk is also lost and the finished dish appears much smaller.
10. If the gelatine is too hot when added to the cream mixture, some of the fat in the cream is melted, giving a close texture. The heat of the gelatine may also cause loss of air, causing a close texture and loss of bulk.

Honeycomb Mould

1 pint milk	$\frac{1}{8}$ pt water
2 large or 3 small eggs	1–2 teasp vanilla or almond
2 ozs sugar	essence
$\frac{1}{2}$ oz gelatine	

Method

1. Dissolve the gelatine in the water.
2. Make a custard with the milk and egg yolk, sweeten and flavour. (See Cup Custard page 206.)
3. Add the gelatine while still warm and quite liquid to the custard, which should be the same temperature. Cool thoroughly.
4. Beat the egg whites stiffly, whisk into the custard mixture.
5. Mould when beginning to set.

If after the egg whites have been added, the mixture is brought to boiling point and then moulded, the jelly will rise to the top of the mould, and when turned out will give definite layers, egg mixture at the top and jelly at the base.

This is known as **Bavarian Cream.**

Name	Ingredients	Method	No. of Portions
Velvet Cream	*Filling:* 1/2 pt cream; 1 1/2 ozs castor sugar; 1/8 pt sherry; 1/8 pt water; Lemon juice to flavour (about 1/2 teasp); 1/4 oz gelatine. *Decoration:* Lemon jelly; cherry and angelica or pistachio nuts	1. Put the gelatine to soak in the water. 2. Line a mould or the base of a mould with jelly. Decorate. 3. Half whip the cream, add the flavourings including the lemon juice. 4. Add the warm gelatine to the cream mixture, pouring in a thin stream and stirring all the time. 5. Taste and correct the flavour if necessary. 6. Stir until the mixture begins to thicken and then pour into the prepared mould. 7. When set, turn out and surround with chopped jelly.	4
Rum Cream	*Filling:* Substitute rum for sherry	As for Velvet Cream.	
Charlotte Russe	*Filling:* 1/2 pt cream; 1/4 pt milk; 1/2 oz castor sugar; 1/2 teasp vanilla essence; 1/2 teasp lemon juice; 1/8 pt water; 1/2 oz gelatine. *Decoration:* Lemon jelly, cherry and angelica or violets; 7–9 savoy finger biscuits	1. Cover the base of a plain charlotte mould (like a cake tin with slightly sloping side) and decorate. Cover with 1/4 inch jelly. Allow to set very firm. 2. Trim the savoy fingers and arrange them round the sides of the tin so that they fit very tightly. 3. Make the filling as for a Velvet Cream, adding the milk to the whipped cream. 4. When the mixture begins to thicken, pour into the lined mould. 5. Turn out when set—tie a ribbon round the base of the russe to hold the biscuits firmly in place. 6. Decorate with chopped jelly.	3–4

FRUIT CREAMS

Name	Ingredients	Method	No. of Portions
Apricot Cream	*Filling:* 1/4 pt cream; 1/4 pt apricot purée; 1/8 pt fruit juice; 1/8 pt water; 1 oz castor sugar; 1 teasp lemon juice; 1/4 oz gelatine colouring. *Decoration:* Lemon jelly, pieces of apricot, angelica	1. Line the mould or the base only with jelly. Decorate with choice pieces of fruit and angelica for stalks and leaves. Allow to cool. 2. Prepare the fruit purée, allow to cool. 3. Half whip the cream, add the fruit purée, juice and flavouring. 4. Colour as necessary. 5. Add the dissolved gelatine while warm. Stir all the time. 6. Mould when it begins to thicken. 7. Turn out and decorate with chopped jelly and pieces of fruit.	4
Gooseberry Orange Raspberry Strawberry	Substitute gooseberry purée for apricot; " orange purée for apricot; " raspberry purée for apricot; " strawberry purée for apricot	As for Apricot Cream.	4
Pineapple	Substitute 2 ozs chopped pineapple for the purée	As for Apricot Cream, except that the chopped fruit is added after the gelatine, when the mixture shows signs of thickening. Stir until the mixture is thick enough to hold the pieces of pineapple in suspension. Continue as for Apricot Cream.	4

CUSTARD CREAMS

Name	Ingredients	Method	No. of Portions
Vanilla Cream	*Filling:* ¼ pt cream ¼ pt custard 1 oz castor sugar ½ tsp vanilla essence 3 tbs water ¼ oz gelatine (light weight) *Decoration:* Jelly, cherries and angelica	1. Decorate a mould lined with jelly. Allow to set. 2. Make the custard and allow to cool. 3. Half whip the cream, add the custard and flavourings. 4. Stir in the warm dissolved gelatine. 5. Mould when it begins to thicken. 6. When set, turn out and decorate with jelly.	3
Coffee	Substitute 1–2 tbs good coffee essence for the vanilla	As for Vanilla Cream.	3–4
Chocolate	Add 1 oz chocolate to the milk and when dissolved, use it for making the custard	As for Vanilla Cream.	3–4
Fruit, e.g. Apricot Gooseberry Raspberry Strawberry	*Filling:* ¼ pt cream ¼ pt custard ¼ pt fruit purée ⅛ pt water sugar to taste 1 teasp lemon juice ¼ oz gelatine colouring *Decoration:* Lemon or raspberry jelly pistachio nuts	1. Line and decorate a mould with the jelly and nuts. 2. Make the custard and cool. 3. Half whip the cream and add the custard, purée and flavourings. 4. Taste carefully and adjust the flavour. 5. Add the gelatine dissolved in the water. 6. Stir until it thickens and mould. 7. When set, turn out and decorate with chopped jelly.	4
Orange	Substitute ¼ pt orange juice for the purée	As for Fruit Cream.	3–4
Trifle Eugénie	*Filling:* ¼ pt custard ¼ pt cream ½ oz castor sugar ½ teasp vanilla essence or 1 teasp cooking sherry ¼ oz gelatine 2 tbs water *Base:* Sponge cake 1 tbs jam *Decoration:* lemon jelly, cherries, angelica and blanched almonds ⅛ pt thick cream 1–2 teasp castor sugar 3 drops vanilla essence	1. Line a border mould with jelly and decorate with cherries, angelica and blanched almonds. 2. Make a cream as for a custard cream. 3. When thickening pour into the border mould and allow to set. 4. When set turn into a glass dish. 5. Spread the sponge cake with jam and soak in the fruit juice and sherry. 6. Fill up the centre of the mould with the soaked sponge cake. 7. Whip the ⅛ pt of thick cream, sweeten and flavour and pipe over the sponge cake. 8. Decorate with cherries and angelica.	4–5

Burnt Cream

1 pt cream
4 egg yolks
1 oz castor sugar

1 vanilla pod or ½ teasp
essence
additional castor sugar

Method

1. Heat the cream with the vanilla pod in a double saucepan.
2. When thoroughly hot but not boiling, remove the vanilla pod. If essence is used, add at this stage.
3. Pour on to the beaten yolks and sugar, return to the pan and cook until thick as for an egg custard. Do not overheat.
4. Strain into a shallow dish and stand overnight in a cool place.
5. Sprinkle the surface with castor sugar so that there is an even coating approximately ¼″ thick.
6. Put under a very hot grill and watch carefully as the sugar melts and turns to a caramel.
7. Remove from the heat when the sugar is golden brown and allow to set.
8. Serve very cold.

Caramel Rice

(A " family " variation of the burnt cream)

2 ozs Carolina rice
1 pt milk
vanilla pod or lemon rind
1 oz castor sugar
2 egg yolks

juice of 1 orange
2 ozs chopped citron peel
⅛ pt cream
4 ozs (approx) moist brown
sugar

Method

1. Stew the rice and vanilla pod or lemon rind in the milk in a double saucepan until the rice has absorbed the milk, but the mixture is still creamy in consistency.
2. Add the castor sugar and egg yolks, and continue cooking until the yolks are absorbed.
3. Add the orange juice and the chopped peel, and turn into a shallow pie dish.
4. Cool and then chill in the refrigerator.
5. Cover the surface with the moist brown sugar (the pale brown variety) to about ¼″ thick.
6. Grill under a hot grill until the sugar turns to caramel. Watch carefully and move the dish as necessary so that the whole surface becomes like toffee.
7. Serve very cold.

Pear Trifle

4 or 6 small sponge cakes	2 to 3 tbs castor sugar
2 tbs raspberry jam	2 or 3 drops vanilla essence
1 tin pears	2 or 3 drops pink colouring
½ pt thick custard	small pieces of angelica; a few
½ pt thick cream	cloves

3 tbs cooking sherry made up to ¼ pt with syrup from the can of pears

Method

1. Split the sponge cakes and spread them with jam. Cut and place neatly in a glass dish.
2. Soak the cake with pear juice and sherry.
3. Coat with custard whilst it is hot and leave until cold.
4. When cold arrange the pears evenly on top of the custard, placing the rounded side of each half pear uppermost.
5. Put the cream into a basin, add the castor sugar, vanilla essence and a very little pink colouring. Whip the cream until it is thick enough to coat the pears and coat each half pear with it.
6. Whip the remaining cream until it is thick enough to pipe. Then pipe it between each pear and in the centre of the dish.
7. Place a small piece of angelica to represent a stalk at the tip of each half pear and a clove at the base of each pear.

Strawberry Gâteau

1 lb fresh or frozen strawberries
1 piece genoese pastry 1½″ thick and approximately 6″ across, *or* 6 circles of genoese cut with a 2″ cutter
¼ pt sherry
¼ pt fruit juice
⅛ pt whipped and sweetened cream, suitably flavoured
strips of browned almonds

Method

1. Hollow out the centre of the genoese.
2. Place on a silver or glass dish. Soak with sherry and fruit juice.
3. Pile the fruit into the hollow in the cake, keeping the best for the top. Arrange with the point of the fruit uppermost.
4. Pipe round the fruit and along the edge of the cake with the cream.
5. Decorate with strips of browned almonds.

Any fresh, tinned or frozen fruit may be used in this way. Red fruits are best decorated with browned almonds, black fruits with blanched almonds, and yellow fruits with pistachio nuts.

Trifle

4 sponge cakes or pieces of stale sponge cake or cake trimmings
1 tbs apricot jam
1 tbs raspberry jam
$\frac{1}{4}$ pt fruit juice or cooking sherry
1 oz almonds or cashew nuts

2 ozs ratafia biscuits or small macaroons
$\frac{1}{2}$ pt thick custard
$\frac{1}{2}$ pt thick cream
cherry and angelica for decoration

Method

1. Split the sponge cake and spread with jams, using apricot and raspberry in alternate layers.
2. Cut into neat pieces; place in a glass dish and pour over them the fruit syrup and/or sherry.   Leave to soak for about $\frac{1}{2}$ hour.
3. Blanch the almonds and chop roughly; break or crush half the ratafia biscuits and place both the nuts and the biscuits on top of the sponge cake.
4. Pour the custard whilst hot over these and leave until cold.
5. Whip up the cream; add a little castor sugar and four or five drops of vanilla essence.   Whip the cream until it adheres to the whisk.
6. Put into a forcing bag with a small vegetable forcer at the end; pipe the cream so that it completely covers the custard.
7. Decorate with the rest of the ratafia biscuits and neatly cut cherries and angelica.

WHAT WENT WRONG—AND WHY

A mould is lumpy

(a) Insufficient stirring while the mixture was coming to the boil.
(b) The mixture was allowed to stand before moulding until a skin was formed and the skin stirred into the mixture.

A mould does not set

Incorrect proportions.   The gelatine has " roped ".

A mould, jelly or cream does not turn out well

(a) The mould was not sufficiently wetted.
(b) The mould was not scrupulously clean before wetting.
    Moulds for setting cold sweets should be kept exclusively for this purpose, in order that the surface may be kept absolutely smooth and unblemished.

A cream does not set

  (a) Incorrect proportions.

  (b) The gelatine was boiled.

  (c) The gelatine was added too cold causing " roping ".

A honeycomb mould separates out

The beaten egg whites were added when the mixture was too hot.

A cream is close in texture

  (a) Cream was insufficiently whipped.

  (b)   „   „   overwhipped.

  (c) Gelatine was added when too hot.

  (d) Over-stirring after the addition of the gelatine.

COLD SOUFFLÉS

These are a mixture of eggs, sugar, cream or evaporated milk, gelatine and flavourings. The method of making is similar to the making of a sweet omelet with the addition of cream and gelatine.

Soufflés are served in china or glass dishes or paper cases of a characteristic design, that is, a deep circular dish with straight sides, fluted on the outside.

Preparation of the Soufflé Dish

Tie round the dish a double band of greaseproof paper ($3\frac{1}{2}$″ deep) keeping the fold uppermost. The band should stand 2 inches above the rim of the dish and about $1\frac{1}{2}$ inches below the rim. The paper must fit tightly round the top edge of the dish as the mixture comes above the rim and would run out between the dish and paper if the fit were poor.

Basic Recipe

2 eggs	$\frac{1}{4}$ oz gelatine
2 ozs fine castor sugar	$\frac{1}{4}$ gill water

$\frac{1}{4}$ pt cream or evaporated milk or mixture of the two (see *Note* page 295).

Method

  1. Prepare the soufflé case.

  2. Separate the egg whites from the yolks.

  3. Dissolve the gelatine in the water and let it stand in a warm place.

  4. Put the yolks, sugar and flavouring (except almond rock as in praline soufflé) into a basin and whisk them together over a pan of hot water until pale and thick (see whisking of eggs for sponges).

  When the mixture is thick, remove the basin from the hot water and continue whisking until the mixture is cool.

5. Half whip the cream or evaporated milk.
6. Whisk the whites of eggs until they " peak ".
7. Using a metal spoon, fold the gelatine into the egg yolk mixture, pouring the gelatine in a thin stream. Pour from a height to keep the stream thin.
8. Fold in the whipped cream and last of all the egg whites.
9. Fold lightly, only until the mixture is thoroughly blended.
10. Pour the mixture into the prepared soufflé case, smooth the top with a palette knife and set aside to cool.
11. When set, remove the paper band. The soufflé will stand 1" above the rim of the dish.

To remove the band

Untie the string, place the edge of a sharp knife held straight against the outside of the band, and, holding the knife lightly but firmly against the dish, pull the paper away from the soufflé.

To decorate the soufflé

As there is a high proportion of cream in the mixture, only a little whipped cream is piped as a decoration. The sides of the soufflé should be lightly coated with chopped pistachio nuts or chopped browned almonds. Crushed ratafia biscuits or crystallised violets make attractive alternatives.

VARIATIONS OF BASIC RECIPE FOR SOUFFLÉ

Type	Addition to Recipe	Addition to Method of Making
Chocolate .	1½ ozs sweetened chocolate 2–3 drops vanilla essence 2 tbs water	Grate the chocolate and melt with the water in a basin over hot water. Add to the yolks, sugar, etc. Decorate with chopped walnuts.
Coffee .	3 teasps coffee essence	Add to the yolks and sugar. Decorate with chopped nuts and coffee-flavoured cream.
Milanaise .	The rind and juice of 1 lemon	Add to the yolks and sugar. Decorate with chopped pistachio nuts and piped cream.
Praliné .	2 ozs almond rock (see next page).	Pound the rock and sieve. Add to the yolks and sugar after beating. Decorate with sieved almond rock and piped cream.

Almond Rock

4 ozs granulated sugar
$\frac{1}{8}$ pt cold water
1$\frac{1}{2}$ ozs almonds

$\frac{1}{8}$ teasp cream of tartar dissolved
in tbs water

Method

1. Blanch and skin the almonds.   Place on a baking sheet covered with paper and toast in a moderately hot oven until golden brown.
2. Put the almonds on to a clean tin previously brushed with a little oil or clarified margarine.
3. Heat the sugar and water over very gentle heat, stirring until all the crystals are dissolved.
4. Bring to the boil, add the dissolved cream of tartar and continue to boil *without stirring* until the syrup begins to change colour, i.e. begins to brown, or caramel.
5. When the syrup is a good golden brown colour pour it over the almonds and leave it to set.
6. When set, pound well and keep it in a covered tin until required for use.

WHAT WENT WRONG—AND WHY

A cold soufflé is close in texture

(a) The egg yolks and sugar were overheated during beating.
(b) The egg and sugar mixture was allowed to stand for too long over the hot water, thus cooking the part of the mixture nearest the heat.
(c) The whites of egg were insufficiently whisked.
(d) The egg whites were folded in carelessly.

White flecks appear in the finished mixture

(a) Over-whisking of the egg whites—this prevented the even blending of the whites with the other ingredients.
(b) There was insufficient folding in of whites.

A layer of jelly appears at the bottom of the soufflé

(a) The gelatine was too hot when added.
(b) The egg yolk mixture was too hot when the dissolved gelatine was added.

The texture is ropy or lumpy

The gelatine was too cool when added to the rest of the ingredients.

MOUSSES

A mousse is a light whipped sweet or savoury mixture.

When it is a cold sweet it consists of fruit purée and whipped cream blended together. Stiffly beaten white of egg is folded in to open and lighten the texture. The richer varieties have yolk of egg whipped with the purée to enrich the mixture. The traditional mousse is " set " by freezing, but if this is not practicable, gelatine may be added to maintain the open texture.

The following fruits are suitable to use for the purée: apricot, banana, loganberry, peach, pineapple, raspberry, and strawberry.

Basic Recipe for the Rich Iced Varieties

¼ pt fruit purée
½–1 oz castor sugar according to the sharpness of the fruit
¼ pt double cream or evaporated milk or a mixture of the two
4 egg yolks
2 egg whites
a few drops of lemon juice according to the flavour of the fruit
a little colouring according to the colour of the fruit

Method

1. Put the egg yolks, sugar and purée into a basin and whisk over a pan of hot water until thick. (See section on sponges.)
2. Remove from the heat and continue whisking until the mixture is cold.
3. Half whip the cream or evaporated milk, add to the purée mixture, folding in lightly.
4. Add the sugar and lemon juice to taste.
5. Colour as required.
6. Fold in the stiffly whisked egg whites.
7. Pour into an ice mould.
8. Seal with lard and wrap in greaseproof paper.
9. Bury in ice and salt and leave two to three hours.
10. Remove the greaseproof paper and lard, dip into cold water, pass a clean cloth over the base of the mould to absorb any moisture.
11. Turn out and keep in a refrigerator until required or serve immediately.

Variations

Coffee   3 teasp coffee essence and ¼ teasp vanilla essence in place of ¼ pint purée.

Chocolate   1½ ozs sweetened chocolate dissolved in 2 tbs water and 2–3 drops vanilla essence in place of ¼ pint purée.

Vanilla   1 dessertspoon vanilla essence and 1 teasp brandy in place of ¼ pint purée.

Basic Recipe for Plainer Iced Varieties

¼ pt fruit purée
½–1 oz castor sugar according to the sharpness of the fruit
¼ pt double cream or evaporated milk or a mixture of the two
2 egg whites
juice of ½ lemon
colouring as required

Method

1. Put the purée and lemon juice and sugar into a basin.
2. Half whip the cream or evaporated milk.
3. Whisk the whites very stiffly.
4. Fold the cream into the purée mixture.
5. Colour if necessary.
6. Add the stiffly beaten whites and fold in.
7. Put the mixture into an ice mould or the freezing trays of a refrigerator.
8. Freeze lightly.
9. Serve in individual glasses which have been previously chilled.

Basic Recipe for Mousses Set with Gelatine

¼ pt fruit purée
½ –1 oz castor sugar
¼ pt cream or evaporated milk or a mixture of the two
½ oz gelatine
2 tbs fruit juice or water
2 whites of egg
a few drops of lemon juice
colouring as required

Method

1. Put the purée, lemon juice and sugar into a basin.
2. Dissolve the gelatine in the fruit juice or water.
3. Half whip the cream or evaporated milk.
4. Whisk the whites very stiffly.
5. Add the gelatine to the purée.
6. Fold in the cream and colour to taste.
7. Fold in the stiffly beaten whites.

8. Pour into a soufflé case or glass dish or individual dishes.
9. Leave to set.
10. Decorate with whipped cream if desired.

Chocolate Mousse, without cream

4 ozs plain chocolate	2 teasp brandy or orange
1 teasp powdered coffee	liqueur
1 tbs orange juice	3 eggs

Method

1. Put the grated chocolate in a large basin over hot water and leave until soft.
2. Add the coffee, orange juice and egg yolks and beat with a flat whisk until the mixture thickens slightly. Do not allow the basin to touch the hot water.
3. Remove from the heat and beat until cool.
4. Add the brandy.
5. Beat the egg whites until stiff and fold into the chocolate mixture.
6. Pour into one large or 4 small glass dishes and chill in the refrigerator before serving.

MERINGUES

Many housewives feel that the making of meringues is too difficult to attempt, but this is not really the case, as the actual making is very simple. Two factors influence the success or failure; firstly the careful addition of the sugar to the egg whites and secondly the careful drying of the " shells ".

Meringues are made of egg white and castor sugar. If the meringue is to decorate a pudding, e.g. Queen of Puddings or Lemon Meringue Pie, the proportion is 1–1½ ozs of castor sugar to each egg white. If the meringue is to be dried out in small shells and used as a cake, the proportion is 2–3 ozs castor sugar to each egg white.

A. Suitable ingredients

1. The eggs should be 2–3 days old before they are separated and the whites should be " stale ". That is, they should be allowed to stand for 24 hours after separating (see chapter on Egg Cookery).
2. Only fine castor sugar should be used. The coarse crystals of granulated sugar would break down the distended albumen.

B. Points to remember in making

1. The egg whites must be whisked in a wide earthenware or china basin until they are stiff and will stand in peaks (see Egg Cookery for whisking).
2. The castor sugar should be added a third at a time. The 1st third should be sprinkled over the egg whites and whisked in until the mixture is stiff and will peak again.
3. The second addition should be well whisked in so that the meringue will continue to stand in peaks. This whisking will change the whites from a rather open " cotton wool " texture to a fine smooth close texture that is firm and in no way syrupy.
4. The last third should be whisked in only until the sugar has been blended evenly. Whisking should stop as soon as this has been done, and over-whisking should be avoided as it will cause syrupyness.
5. As soon as the meringue is made, it should be piped out or piled upon the pudding. It should not be allowed to stand, otherwise it will become watery.

C. To shape meringue " shells "

1. Prepare an old wooden board or a thick baking tin. Wood, being a bad conductor of heat, is preferable as it prevents browning of the base of the shell.
2. Cover with one or two layers of greaseproof paper (two if tins are used).
3. Brush the paper with olive oil very sparingly.
4. To pipe the shells; $\frac{2}{3}$ fill a forcing bag which has a plain or a large star pipe in it. The plain pipe should be $\frac{1}{2}''-\frac{5}{8}''$ in diameter. Pipe out in cone shapes with three distinct pushes to give a ridged effect; if a star is used pipe into bars or fancy shapes.
5. To shape the shells by the use of spoons; wet two dessert spoons, take a spoonful of meringue, smooth off the excess and scoop out with the second spoon and ease on to the baking sheet.
6. Dredge the shells with castor sugar.

D. Drying the meringues

1. Meringue on the top of a pudding which will be served at once may be dried for about 20–30 minutes in a cool oven, 300° F, placed below halfway in the oven. The outside crust will then be crisp and the peaks slightly browned. The centre of the meringue will be soft.
2. If the pudding is to be served cold the meringue should be

dried out in a very cool oven, 250°–275° F with the door not quite shut to allow any steam to escape. The time to dry will be 1–1½ hours. The meringue will then be crisp all through and not lose its shape on cooling.

3. Meringue shells should be put into a very cool oven, 250°F and allowed to *dry* without browning at all for about 2 hours, or until quite firm on the outside. Each shell should then be lifted carefully off the paper and pressed on the base with the thumb to make a slight hollow. This allows the heat to penetrate and dry the inside. It also gives space for the cream for filling. The shells should then be put back on the paper upside down and allowed to dry for a further 1–1½ hours. This second stage may be done in a warm cupboard or on the rack of the stove for a longer time. It is imperative that the centre of the shell be completely dry or it will soften and collapse when cool.

E. To test if the meringue is dry

1. A pudding meringue should be lightly tapped on the top. It should be quite firm and sound hollow.
2. A meringue shell should be pressed with the thumb into the hollow. It should be quite firm and appear dry in the centre. It too should sound hollow when tapped.

F. To store meringue shells

1. As soon as they are dry the shells should be put into a lined airtight tin and stored in a dry place.
2. The shells should be kept in the tin until they are required—they will keep several weeks.
3. They should be filled with cream and decorated with chopped nuts, grated chocolate or " hundreds and thousands " *immediately* before they are required. Once filled the shell will absorb moisture from the cream and soften.

G. To make meringues from egg white substitutes

There are several varieties of substitute on the market. Some are dried albumen and are usually sold as powder. Others are synthetic substances which are of a viscous nature and are capable of holding air. These may be in powder or liquid form. The powders usually need to be soaked before use.

In every case the directions given should be carefully followed. Once the meringue mixture has been whipped it should be treated exactly like egg white—using the same proportions of castor sugar and the same method of drying.

Basic Recipe for Meringue

2 egg whites
2–4 ozs castor sugar
colouring (optional)

Method

1. Separate the egg whites into a china basin. Leave overnight in a cool place.
2. Whisk until very stiff and dry.
3. Add $\frac{1}{3}$ of the sugar. Whisk again until it peaks.
4. Add another third and repeat.
5. Add the last third and whisk until the sugar is evenly distributed.
6. Pile on the pudding or pipe out on a board covered with oiled greaseproof paper.
7. Dry off in a cool oven, 250° F, for 3–4 hours.

RECIPES WITH A MERINGUE BASIS

Variety	Recipe	Method of Making	Baking Temperature and Time	Method of Finishing
Coconut Pyramids	2 whites of eggs 4 ozs castor sugar 1 level teasp rice flour 3 ozs desiccated coconut Colouring (optional)	1. Make the meringue. 2. Fold in the rice flour and coconut. 3. Shape into pyramids. 4. Put on to rice paper.	200° F for 1 hour.	None.
Cream Cheese Cake	3 whites of eggs 3 ozs castor sugar 2 ozs hazel-nuts or almond nibs	1. Blanch the nuts if necessary. 2. Roast till pale brown. 3. Chop. 4. Make the meringue. 5. Fold in the nuts. 6. Divide the mixture evenly between 3 lined and oiled sandwich tins (6″ diameter).	200° F until crisp—1–1½ hours.	Remove the paper at once and cool. When cold sandwich together with butter cream and sprinkle with powdered nuts.
Japanese Cakes	3 whites of eggs 6 ozs castor sugar 6 ozs ground almonds	1. Make the meringue. 2. Fold in the almonds. 3. Spread in a shallow tin which has been lined and oiled.	(1) 200° F until firm on the top, about ¾ hr. (2) When marked, bake 275° F until crisp, about 1 hour.	Mark with a circular cutter 1¼–1½″ diameter; return to oven. Remove the paper and stamp out the circles. Dry off the trimmings and crush. Coat the cakes with coffee butter cream, roll in the sieved trimmings. Decorate with glacé icing, either pale pink or pale cream.
Mushroom Cakes	3 whites of eggs 6 ozs castor sugar 2 ozs grated chocolate 2 ozs chocolate butter cream Almond paste	1. Make the meringue. 2. Shape into mushroom sized cones. 3. Sprinkle with chocolate.	Dry off as for meringues.	Spread the underside with chocolate butter cream and mark with a fork to imitate the underside of a mushroom. Make a stalk with almond paste. Set into the butter cream and allow to harden.
Nut Meringues	2 whites of eggs 3 ozs castor sugar 2 ozs chopped nuts	1. Make the meringue. 2. Fold in the nuts. 3. Shape into shells or pipe out.	250° F for 2–3 hours as for basic recipe.	Fill with butter cream and sandwich together. Dredge with icing sugar and sprinkle with nuts.

WHAT WENT WRONG—AND WHY

Egg white did not whip up stiffly

- (*a*) There was grease on the whisk or basin.
- (*b*) Egg whites were too stale and watery.
- (*c*) Some yolk of egg was included.
- (*d*) Preserved eggs were used.

The meringue mixture was sticky and not stiff before drying off

- (*a*) The whites were not whisked until firm and peaking.
- (*b*) Sugar was added too quickly.
- (*c*) After the sugar had been added, the mixture was over-whisked.

The meringue is tough and leathery

- (*a*) Sugar was not whisked in sufficiently.
- (*b*) The meringue was dried off in too hot an oven too quickly.
- (*c*) The meringue was not dried sufficiently.

The meringue shells soften on storage

- (*a*) The shells were not fully dried out.
- (*b*) They were stored in a damp place.
- (*c*) They were stored with cream between.

ICES

The making of ices is usually associated with the use of an old-fashioned freezer or ice cream machine. Today, however, in many homes, ices are made in the ice drawers of the refrigerator.

They may be classified thus:—

- (*a*) *Cream ices*, which usually consist of equal quantities of cream and fruit purée.
- (*b*) *Custard cream ices*, which usually consist of $\frac{2}{3}$ custard and $\frac{1}{3}$ cream. It is customary to serve with these a hot sauce, e.g. chocolate, butterscotch or jam sauce.
- (*c*) *Water ices* consist of well-flavoured clarified syrup plus fruit juice or purée in equal quantities; except lemon, when $\frac{2}{3}$ syrup and $\frac{1}{3}$ lemon juice are used.

Important Points to Remember when Making Ices

1. Use thick double cream and half whip this before adding other ingredients. Evaporated milk can replace part or all of the cream. It should be boiled in the tin, chilled and used as for soufflés.

2. Add sugar carefully, remembering that too much sugar prevents the mixture from freezing and if too little sugar is added the frozen mixture will be rough in texture.

3. Use any form of alcohol for flavouring sparingly, as too much alcohol prevents a mixture from freezing.

To Prepare an Ice Cream Freezer for Use

A freezer consists of two main parts:—

(*a*) The metal pot, usually of tin. This should be kept dry when not in use and it should be scalded thoroughly after use.

(*b*) The wooden tub. The tub should be filled with cold water for several hours before use to prevent warping and leaking.

To Charge the Machine

1. Have ready a good supply of crushed ice and coarse salt.

2. Put the pot into its correct position in the tub and see that the crank is working smoothly.

3. Pack the space between the pot and the tub with a mixture of crushed ice and salt, using two parts ice to 1 part of salt; be sure to pack tightly, ending with a layer of ice. When ice and salt are mixed the ice melts, extracting heat from the surrounding substances. The metal of which the pot is made is a good conductor of heat, and the tub is made of wood, which is a bad conductor of heat. Hence, when the tub is packed with ice and salt, heat is drawn from the mixture inside the metal pot more than from the outside air, resulting eventually in the production of a frozen mixture inside the pot.

4. After charging the machine any surplus salt must be wiped off the handle and the lid before the cream mixture is put in the tub.

5. As the ice melts during the freezing process the water should be run off and the tub filled up with the ice and salt mixture.

When Freezing Ices in a Cream Freezer

1. Dry the freezing pot before putting in the mixture to be frozen.

2. Fill only $\frac{1}{3}$ of the pot, because the mixture increases in bulk during the freezing process.

3. Use the mixtures to be frozen only when they are cold.

4. When the mixture is in the pot, replace the lid and turn the handle steadily and evenly. During the freezing process remove the lid from time to time and scrape with a wooden spatula to prevent the mixture from becoming uneven.

5. When the mixture is required for serving in glasses or on ice

plates, i.e. unmoulded, it is necessary to freeze the mixture very stiffly.

6. If the mixture is needed for moulding, pack smoothly into the moulds.

To Make Ices in a Refrigerator

In order to obtain a creamy consistency of the ice, it is necessary to incorporate air during the freezing. When using a freezer this is done during the stirring and churning.

1. Prepare the mixture, omitting the cream, and egg whites if these are given in the recipe.
2. Put the flavoured custard into the ice drawers and leave until firm.
3. About 1 hour before it is required for serving remove the mixture into a large basin and allow it to melt partially but remain chilled.
4. Whip the cream and whisk the egg whites stiffly.
5. When the custard is soft, beat it until it is smooth; then add the cream and whisk all together until the mixture is quite smooth. Then fold in the stiffly whisked egg whites.
6. Return the mixture to the ice drawers and leave until required

The refrigerator must be adjusted to its coldest setting before using.

To Mould Ices

1. Use special ice moulds; these are usually made of pewter and can be bought in various shapes and sizes.
2. Rinse the moulds with cold water before using them.
3. Have ready a deep clean pail and a supply of crushed ice and coarse salt as for a freezer.
4. Have ready greaseproof paper and a little lard.
5. Pack the ice in the rinsed mould and put on the lid. Seal the lid with a thick coating of lard; then wrap the mould in a double sheet of greaseproof paper. Bury this in the pail containing the freezing mixture and leave from three to four hours according to the size of the mould.
6. When ready remove the paper; dip the mould into cold water; remove the lard and remove the top and bottom of the mould.
7. Turn the moulded ice on to a piece of genoese pastry and serve immediately; or leave in a refrigerator until required.

RECIPES FOR ICES

Type	Recipe	Method
Vanilla or Plain Ice	$\frac{1}{2}$ pt cold unsweetened custard (1 egg and 1 yolk to $\frac{1}{2}$ pt milk) $\frac{1}{4}$ pt cream or evaporated milk $1\frac{1}{2}$ ozs castor sugar $\frac{1}{2}$ teasp vanilla essence	1. Half whip the cream or evaporated milk. If a mixture of the two is used, whip separately and combine. 2. Add the cold custard, stirring very gently. 3. Add sugar and flavouring. 4. Freeze.
Chocolate	$\frac{1}{2}$ pt custard as above $\frac{1}{4}$ pt cream 1 oz sugar 2 drops vanilla essence 2 ozs grated chocolate (sweetened)	1. Dissolve the chocolate in the milk used for making the custard. 2. Continue as for vanilla ice.
Coffee	$\frac{1}{2}$ pt custard as above $\frac{1}{4}$ pt cream $1\frac{1}{2}$ ozs sugar 2–3 teasp coffee essence	As for vanilla ice.
Fruit Ices, e.g. Apricot, Pear, Peach, Raspberry, Strawberry	$\frac{1}{2}$ pt cream $\frac{1}{2}$ pt fruit purée or $\frac{1}{4}$ pt purée + 1 tbs appropriate jam 2 ozs sugar	1. Sieve the fruit to make the purée. Sieve the jam if used. 2. Half whip the cream. 3. Add the purée and the jam if used to the cream. 4. Sweeten, taste carefully and add more sugar if necessary. 5. Freeze.
Ginger	$\frac{1}{2}$ pt custard as above $\frac{1}{4}$ pt cream $1\frac{1}{2}$ ozs sugar $\frac{1}{2}$ teasp ground ginger $1\frac{1}{2}$ ozs chopped preserved ginger	As for vanilla ice.

Additional Recipes

Neapolitan Ice

Have ready: Chocolate Ice Mixture
Vanilla Ice Mixture
Either Strawberry or Raspberry Ice Mixture
A quantity of freezing mixture and greaseproof paper.

Method

1. Line a small oblong box with greaseproof paper.
2. Put into the box enough chocolate ice to fill one third of the box. Leave on ice until firm.

3. Add another third vanilla ice and leave to become firm.
4. Add the raspberry or strawberry ice.
5. Put the lid on the box; seal the edges with lard; wrap in greaseproof paper and bury in ice and salt; leave from 1 to 2 hours until quite firm.
6. Remove from the pail; remove the paper, scrape away lard; turn out and cut into slices.

Peach Melba

4 half peaches drained from the syrup
½ pt vanilla ice cream
¼ pt thick raspberry jam sauce (thickened with arrowroot)
carmine
⅛ pt thick cream
1 to 2 teasps castor sugar
little vanilla essence
ice wafers

Method

1. Dry the peaches with a piece of muslin and place them on a wire cake rack.
2. Have ready the jam sauce of a coating consistency. Improve the colour by adding a little carmine if necessary.
3. Glaze each half peach with the jam sauce.
4. Place ⅛ pint cream in each of four stem glasses.
5. Place a glazed peach on top of each ice.
6. Whip the cream and add castor sugar and vanilla essence.
7. Decorate with the prepared cream, using a small star tube.
8. Serve with ice wafers.

Ice Pudding

1 pt custard
½ pt double cream, or
¼ pt double cream and ¼ pt evaporated milk
2 egg whites
1 oz crystallised ginger
3 ozs glacé cherries and French fruits
½ oz chopped almonds if desired
1 oz castor sugar
1 to 2 teaspoonfuls of vanilla essence or lemon juice *or* brandy
a round of genoese cake
⅛ pt whipped cream flavoured and sweetened

Method

1. Cut the fruits into small pieces and leave to soak in the brandy or other flavouring.
2. Chop the nuts finely.
3. Put the custard into the freezer and turn the handle until it is partially frozen.
4. Add the remaining ingredients and lastly the egg whites stiffly whisked.
5. Continue to turn all the ingredients in the freezer until the mixture is the correct consistency for moulding.
6. Pack into a prepared mould and mould according to instructions.
7. Leave for 3 to 4 hours buried in a bucket containing freezing mixture.
8. Unmould and serve on a piece of prepared genoese cake.
9. Decorate with whipped cream flavoured and sweetened.

To prepare the genoese cake

Cut a round of cake slightly larger than the base of the ice pudding mould.   Brush the edge of the cake with warm sieved jam and roll it in very finely chopped pistachio nuts or in finely chopped browned almonds or coconut.

Omelette Soufflée en Surprise (Surprise Omelet)

piece of sponge cake or genoese cake	1½ ozs icing sugar or 2 ozs castor sugar
½ pt stiffly frozen ice cream	3 egg whites
1 egg yolk	½ oz castor sugar
	vanilla essence

Method

1. Prepare the soufflé mixture thus:—

    (*a*) Cream together the egg yolks and icing sugar, adding a few drops vanilla essence.
    (*b*) Fold into the above the stiffly whisked egg whites.

2. Hollow the centre of the cake and place it on a fireproof dish.
3. Fill the hollow with stiffly frozen ice.
4. Spread or pipe the soufflé mixture over the ice.
5. Dredge with castor sugar.   Decorate with a little cherry and angelica.
6. Place in a very hot oven *until the top is pale brown and very crisp.*

Water Ices or Sorbets

Clarified Syrup

½ lb granulated sugar	rind 1 lemon
1 pt water	juice of ½ large lemon

Method for syrup

1. Put the sugar, lemon rind and water into a clean pan, stir over gentle heat until the crystals are dissolved.
2. Bring to boiling point and boil briskly for about ten minutes, without stirring.
3. Remove any scum from the surface; strain through muslin; leave until cold; add the strained lemon juice.

Any fruit purée and/or fruit juice may be combined with the prepared syrup, using equal quantities of the prepared syrup and fruit juice or purée.

Exception—Lemon water ice.   Use ⅔ clarified syrup and ⅓ strained lemon juice.

Method for ices

1. Mix the fruit juice and/or purée with the clarified syrup; add suitable colouring, e.g. green for pear water ice, orange for orange water ice, lemon for lemon ice or pineapple, red for redcurrant or a mixture of gooseberry purée and red currant juice.   Remember that when the mixture is frozen the colour will be paler.
2. Freeze and use as required.

Fruit Coupe (or Coupe Glacée)

Mixture of fruits, e.g. finely chopped pineapple

,,   grapes

pears cut small

orange cut into small pieces

Water ice, e.g. pineapple or lemon or pear or orange

whipped cream

ice wafers

Method

1. Put the mixture of fruits into suitable glasses.
2. Pile water ice on top.
3. Decorate with whipped cream, flavoured and sweetened.
4. Serve with ice wafers.

CHAPTER XX

BAKING

GENERAL INFORMATION

A. Flours

WHATEVER type of bread, bun, pudding or cake is made, some finely-ground cereal forms part of the basic ingredients. Of all cereals, wheat is the most widely used in this country.

There are several types of wheat flour on the market and the quality and property of the flour depends on the quality of wheat used, the skill of the milling and the length of extraction. The purpose of milling is the separation of the endosperm of the wheat from the bran and the germ. The wheat grain consists of approximately 83·3% endosperm : 2·2% germ : 14·5% bran.

Various types of wheat grain vary slightly in composition; the percentage of water and the gluten content are not always the same. Gluten is the chief protein constituent of flour and the amount present varies according to the grain and the method of milling.

The gluten content is very important in bread and cake-making as, when moist, it is an elastic substance which is capable of holding a gas. When heated, it hardens and forms the framework of the cooked dough. Gluten absorbs water during the mixing, so that more liquid will be absorbed by a strong flour than a weak one, and slightly larger bulk will be produced. This should be noted, as when a soft flour is used, a little less liquid will be needed. Flour with a high gluten content is called a hard, or strong, flour, and when the gluten content is low it is called a soft or weak flour. For this reason, millers blend varieties of grain to give different degrees of hardness of flour.

There are three *types* of flour:—

1. Strong flour milled from a mixture of wheats in which spring wheat predominates. Canadian wheats contain a high proportion of strong gluten and therefore a high proportion of such wheat is found in " strong " flours for breadmaking. They provide the strong elastic gluten necessary for good bread.
2. Medium or general-purpose flour which is generally a blend of strong and weak wheats.

319

3. Soft flour made from soft winter wheats which contain a weaker quality of gluten in less quantity.

There are several *grades* of flour, the grade being determined by the proportion of bran and germ extracted during milling. When the whole wheat is milled, with nothing extracted at all, a wholewheat flour is obtained. This is often stoneground and has poor keeping qualities because of the presence of the fat and enzymes in the germ.

If there is about 90% of the whole grain (the very coarse gritty bran having been removed) the flour is known as wheatmeal. The term " flour ", when used unqualified, refers to white wheaten flour of which there are three grades:

(*a*) " First Patents ", the one with almost nothing in it except endosperm. It is a very white flour, as it is the first stream from the roller-mills.

(*b*) " Second Patents ", being the second stream.

(*c*) " Straight Run ", the next stream which comes on the market as a general-purpose flour.

Self-raising flour is a mixture of soft white flour made from English " Winters " or Australian or French wheats. Sometimes a proportion of strong flour is added to increase the proportion of gluten.

The flour is milled rather dry, so that lumps do not form, nor does carbon dioxide. The amount of raising agent put in is fairly low, so that it is suitable for some forms of baking, such as plain cakes and puddings. For rich cakes with a high egg content, there will be too much raising agent, and for scones not enough. For most pastries and yeast mixtures it should not be used, because of the low gluten content.

Other types of cereals used are rice flour, oatmeal, cornflour (obtained from the maize grain), and occasionally barleymeal. All lack gluten and are sometimes mixed with wheat flour to give variety in texture and flavour, but are rarely used alone owing to this low gluten content.

Rye contains gluten, but is not often used in this country. In Germany it is used for black bread.

B. Raising Agents

As already explained, the gluten content of flour is very important as it is the substance that is capable of holding air or a gas. When moist it is elastic, so that it stretches. When cooked, it hardens and sets in the raised or " blown up " state.

Eggs have a substance called albumen which is also capable of holding gases, expanding, and setting on heating. One or other or both aid a mixture by being " blown up ".

Mixtures that rely on the gluten content to hold the gas are usually plain cakes and scones—the texture of these is fairly open.

Where the albumen content is high, i.e. a comparatively large number of eggs have been used, the texture is usually finer and the holes smaller and more even. The higher the proportion of eggs used, the less baking powder or its equivalent is required, as there is more air to blow up the mixture. The fewer eggs used, the larger the amount of baking powder required, and therefore the " blowing up " is done by carbon dioxide from the baking powder.

Air is incorporated by some mechanical means—beating of a batter, whisking of whole eggs or only the white; creaming of fat, sugar and egg for rich cakes and puddings—whisking of eggs and sugar for sponge cakes.

Carbon dioxide is used as the gas in many mixtures—it is produced by a chemical action which takes place when the mixture is made.

Baking powder is the substance most widely used to produce the action. It is made from bicarbonate of soda and a mild acid, usually cream of tartar. When moist and warm, these chemicals react and give off carbon dioxide. A starchy substance is added to prevent the two chemicals from becoming damp.* Bicarbonate of soda alone will give off carbon dioxide when wet and warm, but it leaves sodium carbonate (washing soda) as a residue which tastes unpleasant and gives the mixture a yellowish brown coloration.

Bicarbonate of soda can be mixed with cream of tartar by the cook—there should be one part of soda to two of cream of tartar to give satisfactory results. They should be sieved together before use.

Bicarbonate of soda may be mixed with tartaric acid, in which case equal parts are sieved together.

All these are known strengths of acid and alkali, so the chemical action can be controlled by the proportion of each. Lemon juice, sour milk and vinegar are all acids which are used with bicarbonate of soda to produce carbon dioxide, but the strength of the acid is not constant, so they are not so reliable as the pure chemicals. Also, as they are liquids, they must not be mixed until they are actually in the cake or pudding mixture. Syrup and treacle are used with bicarbonate of soda, not because of their acid content, but because they disguise the brown colour and the strong flavour of the soda which is left when the mixture is cooked.

Yeast is another raising agent used; it consists of minute fungi capable of fermenting a sugar solution, producing carbon dioxide and alcohol. The yeast plant consists of a single cell, round or oval in shape and of microscopic dimensions. It multiplies by budding in suitable conditions, and the process of fermentation which takes

* *Recipe for Baking Powder*: ¼ lb bicarbonate of soda, ½ lb cream of tartar and ¼ lb rice flour.

L

place when a dough is "rising" depends upon changes brought about by the action of enzymes either in the flour or in the yeast.

Diastase is an enzyme present in both yeast and flour: it converts soluble starch into maltose and dextrin.

Invertase in yeast converts sucrose (cane sugar) into dextrose and glucose. All flour contains some sucrose.

Maltase in yeast converts maltose to glucose.

Zymase in yeast converts the simple sugar glucose into alcohol and carbon dioxide. Thus the gas which aerates the dough is produced. The action takes place in the presence of moisture and at a temperature between 74° F (cool to the touch) and 90° F (comfortably hot to the touch). The best results are obtained when the dough is kept between 80° and 85° F.

During the baking the activity of the yeast increases as the temperature of the dough rises. When the centre of the loaf reaches 120° F, activity slows down and ceases when the temperature reaches 140° F.

During baking the alcohol is driven off but during the process the CO_2 expands and the dough rises further, the gluten in the bread becomes set and the crust keeps to shape on cooling, giving a well risen loaf. This last rising is known as "oven spring".

Yeast is marketed either compressed or dried. Compressed yeast is composed chiefly of moist living cells pressed into a cake form with a small amount of starch as a binder. It is perishable, and will remain fresh only for a few days. It should be pale fawn in colour, moist but not slimy and should crumble to the touch. Dark brown bits or a slimy condition indicate that the yeast is old and has lost some of its effectiveness and good flavour.

Dried yeast is made from an active strain of yeast, dried in fine granular form and packed in sealed tins or packets. It will keep for about 6 months in a cool dry place. Most makes have the date of packing on the container. After the tin has been opened, the contents should be used within 3 weeks.

To use dried yeast

One tablespoon of dried yeast is equivalent to 1 oz fresh yeast. Reconstitute by taking $\frac{1}{4}$ pint of the warm liquid required for the chosen recipe, add $\frac{1}{2}$ teaspoon sugar or honey and sprinkle 1 tbs dried yeast on the top of the liquid. Leave until frothy (about 10 mins). Whisk with a fork and use in place of 1 oz fresh yeast.

YEAST MIXTURES

As already explained, yeast is used as a raising agent in the making of bread and to produce the gas that aerates the dough, the yeast must have warmth, moisture and food. The utensils and ingredients must be kept warm—approximately at a temperature 80°–85° F throughout the process.

The flour should be hard or strong, that is one which has a high proportion of gluten. This is tough and harsh at the beginning of the breadmaking process, but during fermentation it is softened and stretched. Kneading and handling divides the strands of gluten and spreads them evenly through the mixture. There are other substances such as lactic acid produced during fermentation which help to ripen the gluten, and these together with natural mineral matter contained in flour produce a dough with the distinctive flavours which are associated with a good bread. These mineral salts help to nourish the yeast cells. Other ingredients used in yeast mixtures also affect both fermentation and flavour:

Salt gives flavour to the bread and helps the structure of the bread by preventing the yeast from working too fast and so producing a coarse crumb. When salt is mixed directly with the yeast it draws moisture from the yeast and so kills it, but mixed with the flour and liquid in proper proportion, salt improves the appearance of the crust as well as the flavour and texture of the crumb.

Sugar is necessary in fermentation and a little added to the yeast and warm liquid helps to start the process. Some recipes recommend blending the yeast with some sugar to cream it, but this is now considered to be too drastic and to kill some of the yeast cells.

Fat is added to rich doughs either by rubbing it into the flour before the addition of the yeast or by adding it in small pieces or melted during the kneading process. Fat slows the action of the yeast; therefore when it is used in a recipe, an increase either in the proportion of yeast or in the length of time for rising must be allowed.

Liquid is necessary in all yeast mixtures. It can be water, milk or a mixture of both. It must be at the correct temperature, i.e. lukewarm. This can be arrived at by adding $\frac{1}{3}$ boiling liquid to $\frac{2}{3}$ cold.

Eggs, fruit and flavourings are added to vary the doughs.

One of three methods may be used during mixing:—

(a) *The quick method.* For this, the dough is mixed, kneaded and put straight into the tins to rise. Then, when risen to twice its size, it is put into a hot oven. The advantage of this method is speed, but the texture is often uneven with large holes and close patches, owing to uneven distribution of the yeast.

(b) *Usual method.* Here the dough is mixed well, beaten and left to rise in a basin until double its size, then turned on to a floured board and well kneaded until the dough is smooth with no large holes in it. It is then divided and shaped into loaves and put in the tins and allowed to rise or " prove " the second time until double its size, then baked as above.

(c) *The slow method.* For this, the yeast is whisked with the tepid water and added to the flour as for the start of the two previous methods (see basic recipe), but instead of beating in the flour, a little is sprinkled on the top of the liquid and the mixture allowed to stand in a warm place for ½ hour. During this time the yeast ferments and the liquid froths up, a process which is known as " sponging ". Then the mixture is beaten, and the basic recipe followed. The advantage of this method is that the yeast has a better chance of developing in the liquid than in the heavier dough, so the mixture is lighter, but a disadvantage is the longer time taken.

The proportion of yeast to allow is ½ oz in quantities up to 1 lb flour, 1 oz up to 3 lbs flour, 2 ozs up to 7 lbs flour.

The proportion of water to allow is about ½ pint for each lb of flour used. If whole wheatmeal is used, a little more water may be required owing to the husk in the flour which absorbs more water. 12 ozs flour produces approximately 1 lb dough.

Bread should be put into a hot oven, preheated to 450° F, and after 5 mins the heat should be reduced. This ensures that the yeast plants are killed quickly, and therefore there is no over-proving, but a good " oven-spring " occurs.

Basic recipe for Bread

3 lbs flour	2 level teasp sugar *or* honey
1 oz yeast	*or* syrup
1 oz salt (4 level teasp)	1½ pt water

Method

1. Sieve the flour and salt into a warm bowl, stand in a warm place.
2. Heat ⅓ of the water to boiling point.
3. Add this to the ⅔ to form tepid water.
4. Whisk the yeast in the liquid with the sugar, honey or syrup.
5. Make a well in the centre of the warm flour, pour in the yeast mixture.
6. Mix together with a wooden spoon or by hand, and form into a soft dough.
7. Knead the dough by drawing the outside to the centre, turning the bowl round, until the dough is smooth, velvety and even in texture, and leaves the side of the bowl and the fingertips.
8. Cover with a wet cloth or fasten a polythene bag round the bowl. Allow to rise in a warm place for ½ hr, a cool room for 1 hr, a cold larder for 3–4 hrs or a refrigerator for 12 hrs.

9. When the dough has doubled its size, turn it on to a floured board and knead well until it is even in texture and contains no large holes when cut in half.

10. Shape into 5 even oblong rolls and put into well-greased bread tins. (1 lb size.)

11. Press down firmly with the back of the hand to make the dough take the shape of the tin. It should half fill the loaf tin.

12. Put to " prove " in a warm place until the dough reaches the top of the tin and has doubled its size. Keep covered.

13. Put half way up the oven, 450° F. Leave for 10 mins.

14. Reduce the heat of the oven to 375° F and bake 45–60 mins in all. If liked, the loaves may be removed from the tins after 30 mins and finished on a baking sheet to crisp the sides and base.

15. To test for readiness, tap the sides and base of the loaf. It should sound hollow.

Variations of the Basic Bread Recipe

KIND OF BREAD	INGREDIENTS	ADDITIONAL INSTRUCTIONS
1. Brown bread	Use ⅔ wholemeal flour ⅓ white flour	—
2. Whole wheatmeal bread	Use all wholemeal flour	Allow the yeast, sugar and water to ferment for 15 mins. When mixed and lightly kneaded put straight into the tins. Put to prove until well risen; allow ¾ to 1 hour. Bake as basic recipe.
3. Dinner Rolls	1 lb flour 2 teasp salt 1 teasp sugar ½ oz yeast 2 ozs butter ½ pt milk	1. Rub the fat into the flour and salt. 2. Follow basic recipe until second kneading has been done. 3. Divide into 16 even sized pieces, approximately 1½ ozs each. Shape into small round buns. 4. Put to prove on a greased tray until double their size (approx. 15 mins). 5. Put in the oven ⅔ way up. 6. Bake at 450° F for 5 mins, then at 375° F for 10 mins. 7. Glaze with milk or an egg and milk wash. 8. Return to the oven to dry off for 1 min.

Variations of the Basic Bread Recipe *continued*

KIND OF BREAD	INGREDIENTS	ADDITIONAL INSTRUCTIONS
4. Sally Lunn	1 lb flour 2 teasp salt 1 teasp sugar ½ oz yeast 2 eggs 2 ozs butter 1½ gills milk	1. Melt the butter in a saucepan, add the milk and make it tepid. 2. Beat the eggs and add the milk mixture and the yeast. 3. Add the flour and mix thoroughly. Put into 2 very well-greased tins 5″ in diameter. Set to rise until the dough fills the tins, about ¾ to 1 hour. Bake half way up the oven pre-heated to 450° F. Cook for 15–20 mins. Glaze with sugar and water.
5. Vienna Bread	1 lb flour 1 oz butter 2 teasp salt 1 teasp sugar ½ oz yeast 1 egg Use ½ pt milk instead of ½ pt water	Melt the fat in the milk and mix with the egg, add the yeast and continue as basic recipe. Shape dough into rolls, plaits and fancy twists.
6. Bridge Rolls	As above	Shape the dough into buns, then roll into finger shapes, set in a tin almost touching. Prove and bake as for dinner rolls.
7. Yeast dumplings	As dinner rolls Jam, treacle or butter and brown sugar	1. Make up the dough and allow to rise. 2. Divide into small portions about ½ oz weight. Roll into small balls. 3. Drop into a pan of fast boiling salted water, cook for 7–8 mins, turning constantly. 4. Serve at once with the jam or treacle or butter and sugar.

WHAT WENT WRONG—AND WHY

The dough is heavy and close with little or no increase in bulk after first rising

The liquid used was too hot and the yeast was killed.

The dough is heavy and close with little or no increase in bulk after second proving

There was too much heat during the first rising.

The dough rises slowly

(*a*) The yeast was stale or had been stored in too cool a place.
(*b*) The mixture was too dry.

The loaf or roll is well risen but the surface is wrinkled and there is a heavy layer just below the surface

(*a*) The dough was over-proved, causing the gluten to overstretch and collapse.
(*b*) Too cool an oven was used for initial cooking.

The dough is well risen but has large uneven holes

(*a*) There was a lack of kneading after the first rising, and therefore the yeast and gas were not evenly distributed.   This often occurs in brown bread made by the quick method.
(*b*) The oven was too cool when the bread was put in.

The loaf is badly risen and has a close texture

(*a*) The dough was too dry.
(*b*) Insufficient time was allowed for proving.

Dinner Rolls crack round the base, with a heavy layer underneath

The place for proving was too hot so the yeast was killed near the base and a skin formed over the roll which cracked when put in the oven.

Bread has a sour unpleasant flavour

(*a*) The rising and proving process was too slow, allowing acids to develop.
(*b*) The yeast was stale.
(*c*) Too much yeast was used giving a strong flavour.

RICHER YEAST MIXTURES

The principles underlying the making of bread apply to all mixtures where yeast is used as the raising agent.   But in some buns and cakes, more sugar, eggs and fruit are used, and these delay the action of the yeast plants and slow down the fermentation.   The greater the proportion of these ingredients, the slower the fermentation.

Because of this, the yeast and liquid are often added to a pro-portion of the flour, beaten to form a smooth batter and allowed to ferment first. This " ferment " is then beaten into the remaining ingredients and allowed to rise. The advantage of this method is that the yeast plants are allowed to grow and multiply in ideal conditions in the first dough. This makes the whole process quicker than when all the ingredients are added at the beginning of the mixing. The texture of the finished buns and cakes is light and spongy.

The proportion of yeast to flour is slightly increased, allowing 1 oz up to 2 lbs of flour, and 2 ozs up to 4 lbs flour.

The average proportion of fat is 3–4 ozs to 1 lb flour.

The average proportion of eggs is 1–2 to 1 lb flour, and usually the liquid is made up to $\frac{1}{2}$ pt with the egg to 1 lb of flour.

Basic Recipe for Richer Yeast Mixtures

Ferment

$\frac{1}{2}$ lb flour	1 teasp sugar
1 teasp salt	$\frac{3}{4}$ pt milk
1 oz yeast	

Second Mixture

$1\frac{1}{4}$ lbs flour	$\frac{1}{4}$ lb sugar
$\frac{1}{4}$ lb butter	2 eggs

Method

1. Sieve the flour for the ferment into a warm bowl with the salt. Put to warm.
2. Bring 1 gill of milk to the boil and add $\frac{1}{2}$ pt cold milk.
3. Whisk the yeast and sugar in the warm liquid.
4. Add this liquid to the flour, gradually beating with a wooden spoon to form a batter.
5. Put to rise in a warm place, covered with a wet cloth, for $\frac{1}{2}$ hour until well risen. If left too long it will collapse.
6. Rub the fat into the $1\frac{1}{4}$ lbs flour, add the sugar.
7. Beat the eggs lightly.
8. Add the ferment and the eggs to this mixture and stir with a wooden spoon.
9. Beat by hand until the mixture is smooth, velvety and even in texture. It should spring away from the hand and the sides of the bowl.
10. Cover with a wet cloth and set it to rise for one hour or until it has doubled its size.
11. Shape it into buns etc. or into loaves.

12. Put them to prove on a greased tray for 15 mins or until they have doubled their size. Loaves should fill the tin when proved.
13. Bake in a hot oven, 450° F, for 5 mins ¾ way up the oven. Reduce the heat to 400° F or, if solid fuel is used, put on to the floor of the oven for 15 mins. Bake loaves in the centre of the oven.
14. Glaze them with a sugar glaze, 2 ozs sugar to ½ gill water. Dissolve the sugar and boil. Use the glaze while very hot.
15. The buns may be returned to the oven for about ½ min to dry off if liked.

Variations of Basic Recipe for Richer Yeast Mixture

Type	Additional Ingredients	Additional Instructions in the Method
1. Currant Buns	6 ozs currants 2 ozs mixed peel	Add the fruit and peel to the second mixture. Shape into buns.
2. Currant Bread	As above	Shape the dough into loaves, prove in tins. Bake as for bread.
3. Hot Cross Buns	6 ozs currants 2 teasp mixed spice short crust pastry	Shape into buns and when proved, put a cross of thin strips of pastry on each bun.
4. Yorkshire Tea-cakes	6 ozs currants 2 ozs mixed peel	Shape the dough into flat cakes, approximately 6–8 inch. in diameter and 1 inch thick. Prove and bake as for buns.
5. Swiss Buns	Glacé icing flavoured with lemon	Shape the dough as for bridge rolls. When baked, coat with glacé icing while still in a batch.
6. Chelsea Buns	3 ozs dried fruit 1 oz peel 2 ozs brown sugar 2 ozs melted butter	1. Roll the dough into an oblong about ¼ inch thick. 2. Brush with the butter, sprinkle with sugar, fruit and peel. 3. Roll up like a Swiss roll. 4. Cut into slices 1 inch thick. 5. Put to prove almost touching each other, cut side up. The buns must touch the sides of the tin. 6. Prove ½–¾ hour. 7. Bake as basic recipe for 20–30 mins.
7. Bath Buns	2 ozs candied peel	Shape into buns. When cooked, brush with egg and milk glaze and sprinkle with sugar nibs.

Variations of Basic Recipe for Richer Yeast Mixture *continued*

TYPE	ADDITIONAL INGREDIENTS	ADDITIONAL INSTRUCTIONS IN THE METHOD
8. Danish Pastry	$\frac{1}{2}$ lb fat, preferably $\frac{1}{2}$ lard and $\frac{1}{2}$ butter	1. Roll the dough into an oblong. 2. Divide the fat into 3 and incorporate in the dough in the same way as the fat is incorporated in flaky pastry. Allow the dough to relax for 15 mins after the third addition of fat. 3. Roll and fold again and allow to relax for 10 mins. 4. Roll out to a thickness of $\frac{1}{3}$ inch, cut into the required shapes. 5. Place on a baking sheet allowing enough space for the mixture to rise and expand while proving. 6. Allow to prove for 5–10 mins. 7. Brush over with beaten egg and if liked dredge with castor sugar and chopped almonds. 8. Bake as for the basic mixture. These shapes may be baked without a glaze and iced with glacé icing when cold. The mixture may be rolled and cut like chelsea buns, using almond paste as a filling in place of dried fruit.

Additional Recipes Using Yeast
Bara Brith

6 ozs sultanas
6 ozs currants
6 ozs raisins
6 ozs sugar
6 ozs lard
1 pt milk and water mixture

2 lbs plain flour
1 oz candied peel
$\frac{1}{4}$ oz mixed spice
$\frac{1}{4}$ teaspoon grated nutmeg
$\frac{1}{2}$ oz yeast
2 eggs

Method

1. Whisk the yeast in the lukewarm liquid.
2. Mix into the flour. Knead well.
3. Allow to rise for 30 minutes or until nearly double its size.
4. Melt the lard and beat into the dough, gradually adding fruit and spices during the process.
5. Beat in the eggs.
6. Divide into two, knead each piece into an oblong roll and press into a loaf-tin. The tin should be $\frac{2}{3}$ full.
7. Prove until the loaf reaches the top of the tin.

8. Bake in the centre of an oven preheated to 450° F for 10 minutes, reduce the heat to 350° F and continue cooking for another hour or until the loaf is thoroughly cooked.

Christmas Spice Bread

(An old Yorkshire recipe)

3 lbs flour	5 ozs peel
3 teasp salt	1 lb valencias
$\frac{1}{2}$ lb lard	1 lb sultanas
3 ozs yeast	$\frac{1}{2}$ oz cinnamon and allspice
$1\frac{1}{2}$ lbs sugar	4 eggs
$\frac{3}{4}$ lb currants	$1\frac{1}{3}$–$1\frac{1}{2}$ pts milk

Method

1. Sieve the flour, spice and salt together.
2. Rub the fat into the flour.
3. Whisk the yeast and a teasp sugar with the milk.
4. Beat the eggs and add to the liquid.
5. Mix the dough.
6. Scatter in the fruit and sugar during kneading, also mix in the eggs.
7. Shape into 4 loaves.
8. Put each into a 2 lb loaf tin.   The tins should be $\frac{2}{3}$ full.
9. Set to rise in a cool place overnight.   When the mixture has risen just to the top of the tins it is ready to bake.   This dough will take 24 hours to rise if kept cool.
10. Bake in a moderate oven (350° F) for $1\frac{1}{2}$–2 hours.
11. When baked and cool, wrap in a clean towel and store in a tin for at least 3 weeks before using.   The loaf will be hard and heavy when first cooked, but will be soft when ready for use.   Serve cut in thin slices and buttered.

Doughnuts

1 lb flour	$\frac{1}{2}$ pt milk
2 teasp salt	1 oz butter
1 oz yeast	a little red jam
4 teasp sugar	

Method

1. Sieve the flour and salt and put to warm.
2. Whisk the yeast in half the milk and add the sugar.
3. Melt the butter and add the remainder of the milk.
4. Mix the two liquids and add to the flour.
5. Beat the dough well.

6. Set to rise until double its size.
7. Roll out the dough ¼ inch thick.
8. *Either* cut out with 1½ inch cutter, put a little jam on 1 circle, damp the edges and put another circle on the top, joining the edges very well; *or* cut out with a 2 inch cutter, put a little jam in the centre, damp the edges and draw up to cover the jam, and shape carefully into a bun, pressing out all creases.
9. Put either shape to prove for a quarter of an hour. Fry in deep fat. (See Section on frying.)
10. Dredge well with castor sugar.

Malt Loaf

8 ozs flour	½ oz yeast
1 teasp salt	1 oz dried fruit
1 teasp sugar	¼ pt tepid milk
1 dessertsp malt extract or cod liver oil and malt	

Method

1. Whisk the yeast in the milk. Add the sugar.
2. Sieve the salt and flour together.
3. Add the fruit.
4. Add the malt, yeast and tepid milk to the flour.
5. Mix thoroughly, leave to rise in a warm place for 1 hour.
6. Knead and shape into a loaf.
7. Put into a well greased 1 lb bread tin.
8. Leave to prove for 20 mins or until it has filled the tin.
9. Bake in a hot oven, 450° F, for 10 mins, then reduce to 375° F and cook for a further 25 mins.

Orange Bread

1 lb plain flour	1 teasp honey or syrup
1 teasp salt	1 egg
1 oz sugar	1 whole orange, minced or
1 oz fresh yeast or ½ oz dried yeast	finely chopped
	¼ pt warm water

Method

1. Mix the water and honey in a jug and sprinkle the yeast on the top. Leave until frothy (about 10 minutes).
2. Sieve the flour, salt and sugar into a warm bowl.
3. Add the yeast, the minced orange peel and juice and the beaten egg.
4. Mix to a soft dough. Sometimes extra warm water is needed. Knead well.

5. Allow the dough to rise in the usual way for about an hour or until it is 1½ times the original size.
6. Turn on to a floured board, and knead lightly.
7. Shape into 2 loaves, put to rise again in well-greased 1-lb bread tins for about 40 minutes.   Cover.
8. Bake in an oven preheated to 400° F for 30–35 minutes.
9. Cook in the middle of the oven.
10. Glaze with melted butter, when taken from the oven.

Princess Bun

½ lb flour	½ teasp castor sugar
½ teasp salt	⅛ pt milk
2 ozs butter	2 eggs
¼ oz yeast	

Filling

2 ozs ground almonds made into paste (see page 381)

Decoration

½ lb icing sugar made into glacé icing (see page 382)
½ oz shredded browned almonds

Method

1. Sieve the flour and salt into a warm basin.
2. Rub in the fat.
3. Whisk the yeast in the warm milk and sugar.
4. Beat the eggs, add the warmed milk mixture and pour into the centre of the flour.
5. Beat until the dough is elastic and smooth.
6. Allow to rise ¾–1 hour until double the size.
7. Make the almond paste and roll into a sausage shape 10″ long.
8. Turn the risen dough on to a board, knead lightly and roll into a strip 12″ long.
9. Lay the roll of almond paste on the dough.   Roll up.
10. Place on a warm greased baking sheet, and shape into a horseshoe.
11. Prove for 20 minutes in a warm place.
12. Bake in the centre of a hot oven 450° F for 5–10 minutes, reduce the heat to 400° F for 20–30 minutes.
13. Cool on a wire tray.
14. When cold, coat with glacé icing and sprinkle with browned almonds.
15. Cut into slices to serve.

Savarin

4 ozs flour	1½ ozs butter
¼ oz yeast	¾ gill milk
1 level teasp sugar	pinch of salt
1 egg	

Method

1. Warm the flour and salt.
2. Whisk the yeast and sugar with the milk.
3. Melt the butter.
4. Add all the liquid to the yeast and pour into the flour.
5. Set to sponge for 30 mins.
6. Gradually beat in the flour and beaten egg until it is a smooth " batter " dough.
7. Pour into a border mould which has been previously greased and dusted with rice flour. Only fill half full.
8. Set to rise until it has filled the tin.
9. Bake in a hot oven, 450° F, for ¼ hour, reduce the heat to 375° F and bake for a further ¼ hour.
10. Turn out on to a plate or dish.
11. The savarin may be soaked in syrup flavoured with sherry, rum or brandy, or with a fruit syrup.
12. Decorate with chopped nuts, pieces of stewed or canned fruits or whipped cream. It may be served hot or cold.

Baba

As for savarin, but add ½ oz currants to the dough. Pour the dough into plain border moulds or dariole moulds prepared as for savarin and with a few currants in the bottom. Finish as for savarin. When baked, soak with a sugar and water syrup flavoured with rum.

Soul Cakes

(from a very old Shropshire recipe)

3 lbs flour	2 eggs
¼ lb butter	¼ teasp allspice
½ lb sugar	1¼ pts milk
2 ozs yeast	

Method

1. Rub the fat into the flour.
2. Whisk the yeast and 1 teasp sugar with the milk.

3. Beat the eggs and add with the liquid to the flour.
4. Beat to a smooth dough.
5. Put to rise for half an hour.
6. Add the sugar and spice.
7. Shape into flat buns.
8. Bake in a hot oven, 425° F, for 10–15 mins. Place $\frac{2}{3}$ of the way up the oven.

SCONE-MAKING

When scones are made the mixture is " blown up " by a chemical action and the texture is fairly open (see Section on Baking). The chemical action is produced by the use of baking powder or bicarbonate of soda and cream of tartar (1 part to 2 parts) or bicarbonate of soda and cream of tartar in equal quantities, and the scone mixed with sour milk or buttermilk. The proportion of baking powder is 1 oz (8 *level* teasp) to each pound of flour. As most baking powder has $\frac{1}{4}$ starchy substance (p. 321) allow $\frac{1}{4}$ oz bicarbonate of soda and $\frac{1}{2}$ oz of cream of tartar, if using them separately, and sieve with the flour three times to ensure that there are no lumps of soda which would give brown patches to the scone. If sour milk or buttermilk is used halve the quantity of cream of tartar, but still sieve with the flour three times.

It may save time to prepare scone flour by sieving a large quantity of the flour and raising agent together and storing them in an airtight tin until required.

If self-raising flour is used put half the quantity of baking powder or its equivalent into the flour.

Scones are fairly plain, so that the fat content in the mixture is low—2–3 ozs to each pound of flour. If the scones are eaten on the day they are made, the smaller amount of fat may be used, but if they are to be left until the next day 3 ozs of fat to each lb flour should be used.

The scone dough should be springy and elastic. The proportion of liquid is $\frac{1}{2}$ pint to each pound of flour. The liquid should be added all at once and the dough mixed with a round-ended knife until it forms large lumps. It should be turned on to a floured board and kneaded with the fingertips *very* lightly—not with the knuckles as in yeast mixtures.

Most scones should be $\frac{3}{4}''$ thick before cooking and $1\frac{1}{4}''$ thick when cooked. The dough should be lightly rolled to this thickness.

Scones should be baked in a hot oven, 450° F, and placed in the top third of the oven. They require 10–15 mins, depending on the size of the scone.

Plain Scones

½ lb flour	½ teasp salt
½ oz baking powder (4 level teasp)	1½ oz butter
	¼ pt milk

Method

1. Sieve the flour, baking powder and salt together.
2. Rub in the fat.
3. Add the milk all at once.
4. Mix with a round-ended knife until a dough is formed.
5. Knead very lightly with the fingertips on a lightly floured board until the dough is smooth.
6. Roll out into a circle ¾″ thick.
7. Either cut into small scones or bake in 4 large scones.
8. Brush with milk.
9. Put into a hot oven pre-heated to 450° F; place ¾ way up the oven.
10. Bake 10 mins for small scones, 15 mins for large ones.

Variations of the Basic Recipe

KIND OF SCONE	ADDITION TO RECIPE	ADDITION TO METHOD

1. Afternoon Tea Scones	1 oz sugar
	1 oz dried fruit
	  or cherries
	  or chopped walnuts
		1. Add the ingredients to the flour and fat.
		2. Roll out dough.
		3. Cut with a 1¼″ cutter.
		4. When cool split and butter.

2. Brown Scones	Use—
	  5 ozs wholemeal flour
	  3 ozs white flour
	(instead of 8 ozs flour)
	1 oz sugar (optional)
		One extra tbs of milk will be required in the mixing.

3. Cheese Scones	2–3 ozs grated cheese Cayenne pepper	Add to basic recipe, method as basic recipe.

4. Oatmeal Scones	Use—
	  4 ozs fine oatmeal
	  4 ozs flour
	(instead of 8 ozs flour)
	1 oz sugar
		As basic recipe.

5. Potato Scones	Use—
	  4 ozs sieved cooked potato
	  4 ozs flour
	(instead of 8 ozs flour)
		As basic recipe using ⅛ pt milk only to mix.

6. Treacle Scones	½ level teasp ground ginger ½ level teasp spice 1 tbs treacle	Warm the treacle, mix with the milk. Add all dry ingredients and mix with treacle and milk.

Additional Scone Recipes
Soda Bread

1 lb flour	¼ oz bicarbonate of soda
2 level teasp salt	(2 level teasp)
1 oz lard, margarine or drip-	¼ oz cream of tartar
ping	(2 level teasp)
	½ pt sour milk

Method

1. Sieve the flour, salt and raising agent together.
2. Rub in the fat.
3. Mix with milk to a soft dough.
4. Knead very lightly on a floured board.
5. Form into 2 loaves and bake on a greased tin.
6. Bake in a hot oven, 425° F, for 30–40 mins two-thirds way up the oven.

Dropped Scones

½ lb flour	1 dessertsp golden syrup
1 level teasp salt	1 dessertsp sugar
¼ oz cream of tartar (2 level	1 egg
teasp)	1–1½ gills milk
⅛ oz bicarbonate of soda (1	
level teasp)	

Method

1. Sieve the flour, salt and raising agent together.
2. Add the sugar, syrup and beaten egg.
3. Mix to a very thick batter with the milk.
4. Heat a greased girdle or a very thick frying pan. A solid top electric hot plate is excellent. It should be hot enough for warmth to be felt when the hand is held 1″ away.
5. Drop the mixture into small rounds from the end of a dessert-spoon held point downwards.
6. When bubbles start to burst, and the under side is light brown, turn over with a palette knife.
7. Cook the second side until light brown and the scone when split is dried through.
8. Allow approx. 3 mins for first side and 2 mins for the second.
9. Place inside a clean folded towel laid over a cake cooling rack.
10. When cool, butter and serve.

Girdle Scones

8 ozs flour	$\frac{1}{2}$ oz lard, margarine or bacon
1 level teasp bicarbonate of	fat
soda	$\frac{1}{2}$ oz sugar (optional)
2 level teasp cream of tartar	$\frac{1}{4}$ pt milk
1 ,, salt	

Method

1. Sieve the flour, salt and raising agent.
2. Rub in the fat and add the sugar.
3. Mix to a soft dough with the milk.
4. Prepare a girdle, frying pan or electric hot plate as for dropped scones.
5. Divide the dough into two. Roll into two circles $\frac{1}{4}$ inch thick and divide each into 6 to form triangular portions.
6. Cook on the girdle until evenly brown on one side.
7. Turn and cook on the other side. Allow 5 mins for each side.
8. When cool split and butter.

Welsh Cakes

6 ozs flour	2 ozs fruit (currants or sul-
$\frac{1}{2}$ level teasp salt	tanas)
$\frac{1}{4}$ oz baking powder	$\frac{1}{4}$ teasp grated nutmeg
2 ozs butter	1 egg
2 ozs sugar	$\frac{1}{2}$ gill milk

Method

1. Sieve the flour and salt.
2. Rub in the fat.
3. Add the dry ingredients.
4. Beat up the egg and milk and mix to a soft dough.
5. Roll out to $\frac{1}{4}''$ thickness.
6. Cut out with a 2″ plain cutter.
7. Cook on a girdle as for girdle scones.
8. Allow 6–7 mins for each side.
9. May be eaten hot or cold, and should be split and buttered.

WHAT WENT WRONG—AND WHY

The scone is heavy and badly risen

(*a*) Insufficient raising agent was used.
(*b*) The handling was heavy, especially whilst kneading.
(*c*) Insufficient liquid was used.

(*d*) It was allowed to stand in a warm kitchen for too long before baking.

(*e*) The oven was too cool or the position for baking was too low in the oven.

The cooked scone has a strong flavour of soda and brown speckled marks

(*a*) The flour and raising agents were not sieved sufficiently. This is especially noticeable if bicarbonate of soda is used, plus an acid, in preference to baking powder. The soda is usually very lumpy and, unless well sieved, leaves small pieces of soda which do not unite with the acid.

(*b*) The proportion of soda and acid was incorrect. If equal parts of soda and cream of tartar are used, plus sour or butter milk, this may occur. It is due to insufficient acid in the liquid to compensate for the smaller amount of cream of tartar used.

Scone is rather heavy with a very white dough and an acid flavour when cooked

There was too much acid in the mixture which may be due to:
(*a*) incorrect proportions being used.
(*b*) too strong an acidity in the liquid (this rarely happens).

Scones spread and lose their shape

(*a*) This may be due to a slack dough through too much liquid being used.

(*b*) Too much raising agent was used.

(*c*) The tin was greased too heavily; the fat melts on heating in the oven and pulls out the soft dough before it has set.

(*d*) The kneading was badly done, especially of the scraps for the second rolling, also twisting the cutter round as the scones are stamped out. Such scones are oval instead of round when cooked.

Scones have risen unevenly

This is due to bad kneading and/or rolling so that the dough is stretched more in one part than another or is of uneven thickness after rolling owing to uneven pressure of the hands on the rolling pin.

Scones have a very rough surface when cooked

(*a*) The kneading was insufficient or badly done.

(*b*) When the scone was transferred from the board to the baking tray, it was badly handled.

Scones are undercooked on top and black underneath

This occurs if the baking tray is too large for the oven and does not allow circulation of hot air. The heat hits the tray and is deflected down, hence over-cooking of the bottom of the scones and insufficient cooking of the top. There should be a gap of at least 2 inches between the sides of the shelf and the baking tray, especially over the gas flame.

Scones cooked on a girdle

The scones appear cooked but are raw inside

The cooking was too quick; the girdle must not be too hot or the outside will cook too quickly and the inside will still be underdone.

The scone was cooked unevenly

(*a*) The girdle was heated over a gas flame and the centre became much hotter than the sides. An asbestos simmering mat should be placed over the flame first so that the heat is spread more evenly.

(*b*) A frying pan with a thin uneven base was used and caused uneven cooking.

The dropped scones spread on the girdle

The batter was too thin. The batter should be thick and only just pour from the spoon.

The dropped scones stuck on the girdle

The girdle was insufficiently greased, or was dirty. The girdle should be proved by rubbing it with salt while it is heating. Then it should be greased by rubbing it with a small lump of raw suet tied up in a piece of muslin. This is better than brushing it with melted fat.

Flour Test for Oven Temperature

To test oven temperature when no thermometer is available, sprinkle a little flour on to a baking sheet, put it into the oven and shut the door. The flour will gradually change colour.

Open the door after three minutes, compare the colour of the flour to the following:—

COLOUR	DESCRIPTION OF OVEN HEAT	OVEN TEMPERATURE
Light cream	Cool	200° to 250° F
Deep cream	Moderate	250° to 350° F
Light brown	Hot	375° to 450° F
Dark brown	Very hot	450° to 500° F

CHAPTER XXI

CAKES AND BISCUITS

CAKES are usually classified according to the proportion of fat and sugar to flour. A plain cake is one with half or less than half fat to flour. A rich cake is one with more than half fat to flour. Sponges, which technically contain no fat, form a separate group. The question of fruit or flavouring does not determine the type of cake; a " plain cake " may contain a high proportion of fruit and a " rich cake " such as Madeira contain none.

The method of incorporating the fat and sugar with the flour generally distinguishes the type of cake. Fat may be rubbed in, creamed first with the sugar or melted and then added to the flour.

RUBBED-IN CAKE MIXTURES

Cakes made by rubbing the fat into the flour are the plain variety, as it is not practical to rub in more than half the weight of fat to flour. The mixture would become sticky and unmanageable.

The proportions for rubbed-in mixtures are $\frac{1}{4}$ to $\frac{1}{2}$ the weight of the flour in fat and sugar, also dried fruit if it is used. From two to six eggs may be used to each pound of flour, and the additional raising agent used is baking powder, allowing $\frac{1}{2}$ oz, that is 4 level teaspoons, for each pound of flour. As this is the average proportion of chemical raising agent used in self-raising flour, those who prefer may use the latter quite satisfactorily.

Margarine is the fat most commonly used, although butter, lard and clarified dripping may be substituted. Butter or a mixture of butter with some other fat gives a much better flavour, even $\frac{1}{4}$ butter and $\frac{3}{4}$ other fat.

Granulated sugar gives satisfactory results and is cheaper than castor sugar. For cakes with a high proportion of dried fruit, or spice cakes, brown sugar may be used. Moist brown sugar is better than demerara as the latter is in large crystals.

The flavouring of these cakes can vary very widely. Any dry powdery ingredients such as spice or cocoa should be sieved with the flour, but any ingredient which would leave lumps in the flour should not be added until the fat has been rubbed in. It is important

341

to be able to feel if there are any lumps of fat left after rubbing in; if it is not well rubbed in the texture of the cake will be uneven with large holes and sticky or heavy patches.

These rubbed-in mixtures will need some liquid in addition to the egg. Milk is often used, although water can be substituted and may give a lighter result but has less nutritive value. The exact quantity of liquid depends on the type of cake or bun to be made. Those which are baked on a tray as small buns, for example Rock Cakes, require less liquid than the buns cooked in patty tins, or the larger cakes baked in a cake tin.

The Rock Cake variety should be of a soft, slightly sticky dough which is stiff enough to support the fork with which it is mixed when stood up in the mixture. Those cooked in patty tins or in a larger cake tin should be of a soft dropping consistency, that is, the mixture should just drop off the spoon without the spoon being shaken.

The tins or trays should be greased with lard or clarified margarine and may be dusted with flour if liked. This is not essential, and it is very important that no excess flour should be left in the tin. Lining a tin is not necessary for cakes made by the rubbing-in method.

If dried fruit is used in the mixture it should be cleaned first. This can be done by rubbing it in flour and then sieving all excess flour off again, or it can be washed. If it is washed it must be dried in a tea towel and then allowed to finish drying overnight in a warm place. On no account should it be used wet as it will be heavy and tend to sink to the bottom. It will also spoil the consistency of the mixture. Glacé cherries, which are preserved in a thick syrup, should be washed in *hot* water, dried in a cloth and lightly dusted with a little of the *weighed* flour.

A variety of flavouring essences may be used, and should be added with the liquid so as to blend evenly in the mixture. The quantity to use depends on the strength of the essences; some are very strong indeed and one or two drops will be sufficient. Most varieties sold by the grocer or chemist are not so strong as this and about 2 teaspoonfuls to each pound of flour will flavour successfully. It is advisable to use an unknown strength very carefully until it has been tested. A blending of two or more essences together gives a much better flavour.

To test if Cakes are cooked

Small cakes should be evenly brown and the underneath should be firm to the touch when lightly pressed with a finger. There should be no sound of bubbling.

Large cakes should be evenly brown, they should have shrunk a little away from the side of the tin, and should be firm when touched with a finger.

Testing with a hot steel skewer or knitting needle is not always a sure guide, as if fruit has been used in the cake it may have a slightly greasy appearance which can be confused with undercooking.

Type	Oven temperature and cooking instructions	Position in Oven
Small Cakes	Preheat to 400° F. Cook for 20–25 minutes. The oven door should not be opened during the first 10 minutes. If two trays are in use, reverse the positions after 10 minutes, putting the underneath one on the top.	2/3rds way up.
Large Cakes	Preheat oven to 375° F. After 10–15 minutes or when the cake has risen, reduce the heat to 350° F.	Just below half way.

Cooling Cakes

Plain cakes can be removed easily from the tin after 1–2 minutes' cooling. A light tap on the base of the tin may help. The cake should stand on a wire tray or sieve until cold, to prevent steam going back into the cake and making it " sad ". While cooling, the cake should stand out of draughts.

Storing of Plain Cakes

Plain cakes should not be stored for more than 2–3 days, as they have a low percentage of fat and so dry easily. When quite cold, they should be put in a tin which is lined with greaseproof paper. The tin should have a tight-fitting lid.

Basic Recipe for Small Buns

½ lb flour   2½ ozs sugar
½ level teasp salt   1 egg made up to ¼ pint with
2   „   baking powder   milk
2½ ozs butter

Method

1. Sieve the flour, salt and baking powder together.
2. Rub the fat into the flour until no lumps of fat are left and the mixture is of breadcrumb consistency.
3. Add the sugar.
4. Beat up the egg and add the required amount of milk to make up the quantity given.
5. Add the egg and milk mixture, all at once, to the flour.
6. Mix with a fork until a soft, slightly sticky dough is formed. The mixture should be stiff enough for the fork to stand up in it.

7. Divide into small portions and put them on a greased tray, allowing at least an inch space all round each one.
8. Rough up each bun with the fork.
9. Put ⅔rds of the way up the oven, which has been preheated to 400° F. Bake for 15–20 minutes.
10. Cool the buns on a wire tray.

This mixture should make 12 average sized buns.

Variations of the Basic Recipe

Variety	Additions to the Recipe	Adaptation of the Method
Almond	Either 1 teasp almond essence and 2 drops vanilla essence, or 2 ozs ground almonds	Add the essence to the milk or the ground almonds to the sugar.
Cherry	2–3 ozs glacé cherries	Prepare the cherries and add with the sugar.
Chocolate	Use 7 ozs flour and 1 oz cocoa instead of 8 ozs flour ½ teasp vanilla essence	Sieve the flour and cocoa together. Add the essence to the liquid.
Coconut	2 ozs desiccated coconut	Add the coconut with the sugar.
Coffee	1 tbs coffee essence plus 2 ozs chopped walnuts (optional)	Add the coffee to the liquid. Add the walnuts with the sugar.
Ginger	1 teasp ground ginger 1 oz preserved ginger (optional)	Add the ground ginger to the flour and the preserved ginger with the sugar.
Lemon or Orange	The rind of one lemon or orange	Grate the rind very finely and add with the sugar.
Raspberry	About 1 tbs raspberry jam	Shape each bun into a round and make a small hole in the top. Fill the hole with ⅛ teasp jam.
Rock Cakes	2½–4 ozs dried fruit (currants and/or dates, sultanas, peel) ¼ teasp grated nutmeg	Add the fruit with the sugar. Add the nutmeg with the flour.
Seed	1 teasp carraway seeds	Add the seeds with the sugar.
Spice	1 teasp mixed spice or ½ teasp cinnamon plus ½ teasp nutmeg	Sieve in with the flour.
Lemon Jumbles	Substitute 1 level teasp bicarbonate of soda and 1 level teasp cream of tartar for the baking powder The rind and juice of one lemon	Sieve the raising agents with the flour three times. Add the rind and juice with the liquid, keeping to the stated quantity (¼ pint to ½ lb flour). Divide into 12 portions. Roll each into a sausage shape and twist into a flat coil.

Basic Recipe for Large Cakes

½ lb flour
½ level teasp salt
2 level teasp baking powder
3 ozs butter

3 ozs sugar
1 egg
¼ pint milk

Method

1. Sieve the flour, salt and baking powder together.
2. Rub the fat into the flour until no lumps of fat are left, and the mixture is like fine breadcrumbs.
3. Add the sugar.
4. Beat the egg and add the milk to it.
5. Add the egg and milk mixture all at once to the flour.
6. Mix with a wooden spoon to a soft dropping consistency. The mixture should just drop off the spoon without the spoon's being shaken.
7. Put into a greased 6″ cake tin.
8. Level off the top of the mixture.
9. Have the oven preheated to 375° F.
10. Put halfway up the oven.
11. Bake for 15 minutes. Reduce the temperature to 350° F and bake a further ¾ to 1 hour.
12. Cool on a wire tray.

Variations of the Basic Recipe

VARIETY	ADDITIONS TO THE RECIPE	ADAPTATION OF THE METHOD
Almond	1 teasp almond essence plus 2 drops vanilla essence or 2 ozs ground almonds	Add the essence to the liquid or the ground almonds to the sugar.
Chocolate	Use 1 oz of cocoa, 1 oz rice flour or semolina and 6 ozs flour ¼ teasp vanilla essence	Sieve the flour, cocoa, and rice flour together. Add the essence to the liquid.
Coconut	2 ozs desiccated coconut	Add with the sugar.
Coffee	1–2 tbs coffee essence	Add with the liquid.
Countess	Substitute ¼ lb cornflour for ¼ lb flour 2 ozs raisins 2 ozs currants ½ teasp ground ginger ¼ teasp ground nutmeg ¼ teasp ground cinnamon *Either* the eggs as basic recipe or ½ teasp bicarbonate of soda and 1 dessertsp vinegar	Add the spices and bicarbonate of soda to the flour plus cornflour. Add the fruit with the sugar.

Variations of the Basic Recipe *continued*

VARIETY	ADDITIONS TO THE RECIPE	ADAPTATION OF THE METHOD
Currant	3–4 ozs currants	Add with the sugar.
Date	2–3 ozs dates ($\frac{1}{2}$ oz less sugar can be used if liked)	Chop the dates finely and add with the sugar.
Date and Walnut	2–3 oz dates 1 oz walnuts	Chop both finely and add with the sugar.
Housekeeper or Luncheon	3–4 ozs dried fruit $\frac{1}{2}$–1 oz chopped peel (optional) 1 teasp treacle 1 teasp spice	Add with the sugar.
Lemon or Orange	The rind of one lemon or orange	Add with the sugar.
Sultana	3–4 ozs sultanas	Add with the sugar.
Vinegar	Use 1 level teasp of bicarbonate of soda and 1 dessertsp vinegar in place of the baking powder 3 ozs sultanas $\frac{1}{2}$ oz chopped peel $\frac{1}{2}$ level teasp nutmeg cinnamon or mixed spice (eggs may be omitted)	Sieve the spices and bicarbonate with the flour. Add the fruit and peel with the sugar. Add the vinegar last of all when the cake has been mixed. Mix again very quickly and bake at once.
Walnut	2 ozs chopped walnuts 2 ozs raisins (optional) $\frac{1}{2}$ level teasp vanilla essence	Add the walnuts with the sugar and the essence with the liquid.

WHAT WENT WRONG—AND WHY

The texture is heavy and close

(*a*) Insufficient baking powder was used.

(*b*) Too much flour was used.

(*c*) Too much fat was used or the fat was oiled while it was rubbed in.

(*d*) Too much liquid was used.

(*e*) Over-mixing when the liquid was added.

(*f*) The oven was too slow.

(*g*) There was insufficient cooking.

The texture is coarse and open

(*a*) Too much baking powder was used.

(*b*) There was insufficient mixing of the flour etc. with the liquid.

(*c*) Too hot an oven was used for baking.

(*d*) A poor quality of fat was used.

The texture is uneven, with large holes in the cake

(a) Insufficient rubbing in of the fat. This left small lumps which melted and left a hole and a close texture.
(b) Over-mixing after the liquid had been added.
(c) The mixture was put into the tin in small spoonfuls, so large bubbles of air were entrapped.

The cake is very dry

(a) Insufficient eggs in the mixture; the plainer the cake the sooner it will dry out.
(b) Insufficient liquid was used.
(c) Too much baking powder was used.
(d) It was baked for too long.

The small buns have spread on the tin

(a) Too much liquid was used.
(b) The tin was greased too heavily. The fat melted and pulled out the soft mixture before it had set.
(c) The oven was too cool.

The small buns are pale on top and the base is overcooked

(a) The buns were cooked too low down in the oven.
(b) Too large a baking tray was used, or it was put in the wrong way round so that the tray was over the flame and so prevented the heat from getting to the top of the oven.

A cake has risen unevenly

(a) The oven had not been preheated to the correct temperature and consequently the heat was rising instead of remaining steady or falling.
(b) The cake was placed on one side of the oven so that the heat was uneven.
(c) Too much baking powder was used.

A cake has risen to a peak in the centre

(a) The cake was put into too hot an oven but the heat was turned down fairly quickly.
(b) The cake was put too high up in the oven.

A cake has cracked badly and the mixture boiled out through the crack

(a) The cake was put into too hot an oven and the temperature was not reduced. The surface of the cake formed a crust too quickly and the mixture underneath pushed through it as it cooked.

(b) The cake was put too high up in the oven and the oven was too hot.

A cake has sunk in the middle

(a) Too much baking powder and too much liquid were used.

(b) The oven door was opened too soon and/or the cake moved before it had set.

(c) The oven door was slammed.

(d) The cake was cooked in too slow an oven.

(e) The cake was removed before it had cooked.

The fruit has sunk in the cake

(a) Too much liquid was used.

(b) The fruit was washed but not dried.

(c) Cherries were not washed—the thick syrup causes them to be very heavy and so sink.

(d) The cake was cooked in too slow an oven; the fat and sugar liquefied but the gluten was not cooked, so the mixture did not set quickly enough to hold up the fruit.

A cake has a hard sugary crust

(a) Too much sugar was used.

(b) The cake was cooked too long in too slow an oven.

(c) Sugar was used to coat the greased tin before the mixture was put in. It is better to use half sugar and half rice flour if anything at all.

CREAMED CAKE MIXTURES

Cakes which have the fat and sugar creamed together first are the richer type, where the weight of the fat and the sugar is equal to, or more than, the weight of flour. The proportions are $\frac{1}{2}$ to equal weight of fat to flour, the same weight of sugar as fat and 4–12 eggs to each pound of flour. As the proportion of egg increases the amount of liquid is decreased, and so is the amount of baking powder. When the weights of fat, sugar and flour are all equal and also equal the weight of egg (each egg weighing approximately 2 ozs), no additional liquid or raising agent is required. The egg itself is capable of holding sufficient air to make the mixture light (see chapter on Egg Cookery).

A. Suitable ingredients

1. Margarine is often used for these mixtures, but with the larger quantity of eggs, which are comparatively expensive, at least

a proportion of butter should be used. The flavour of butter is so much better than that of any other fat that the increased cost is justified. For ordinary use, ¼ of the fat should be butter. This makes little difference to the cost and improves the flavour very much indeed. In cakes where there is little flavouring added, all butter should be used whenever possible. For cakes with a large quantity of fruit or spices margarine can be used without a marked loss of flavour.

2. Castor or moist brown sugar gives the best results, as the larger crystals of granulated or demerara do not blend with the fat.

3. Hen, duck or goose eggs may be used. If either of the latter the number must be decreased (see chapter on Egg Cookery). The proportions given all refer to hen eggs.

4. As in rubbed-in mixtures, the flavourings used are numerous. The dry powdery ones are sieved with the flour but those which are in " lumps ", such as dried fruit, should be added either immediately before the flour or with it. (For preparation of dried fruit see Rubbed-in Mixtures). Liquid flavourings such as essences should be added with the eggs or additional liquid if used. (For quantities see Rubbed-in Mixtures.)

B. *Points to remember in mixing*

1. The fat and sugar should be creamed very well until they are light and fluffy and white in colour. This creaming incorporates some air and breaks down the sugar crystals by friction.

2. The eggs should be broken into a basin, beaten and stood in a bowl of warm water (about 70° F) for ten minutes so that they are approximately the same temperature as the creamed fat and sugar. They should be added a little at a time and the mixture very well beaten before any further addition. If the eggs are warm and there is sufficient beating, as many as 12 eggs may be added to one pound of fat without the mixture curdling. Curdling is due to the fat, cooled by the cold egg liquid, separating out from the sugar and eggs. A curdled mixture will hold less air than one which has not curdled. If the mixture shows signs of curdling, warming the bowl in warm water will help to restore it to the creamy consistency.

3. The flour should be added to the mixture gradually and should be folded in with a metal spoon so as to keep as much air in the mixture as possible. Stirring in with a wooden spoon will break down the egg and release the air (see chapter on Egg Cookery). The minimum of folding in should be done, just sufficient to incorporate the flour evenly.

4. The consistency of a creamed mixture should remain very much the same as when the fat and sugar have been creamed

together before the addition of any further ingredients.   The
mixture should just drop off the spoon when a very slight flick
is given.   It is a little stiffer than the consistency for large cakes
made by the rubbing-in method, as the mixture slackens very
much during the initial cooking, because the fat and sugar
content is higher.

C. Preparation of the tins for baking

1. Because of the high fat and sugar content, creamed mixtures
   brown or burn readily while cooking.   To ensure even baking
   it is advisable to use a thick cake tin.
2. The tin should be well greased and lined with greaseproof
   paper on the bottom and the sides.   Use a double layer of
   paper for large cakes.
3. Christmas cakes and those with a high proportion of dried
   fruit need longer baking, so, in addition, a layer of brown paper
   can be tied round the outside of the tin.   This reduces the
   penetration of heat to the cake, as paper is a bad conductor
   of heat.   It therefore prevents a thick crust from forming on
   the sides and base of the cake.
4. For sandwich cakes the tins may be greased and lined as above,
   or greased and then dusted with equal quantities of castor
   sugar and rice flour as an alternative to lining.   This method
   gives a thin sugary crust to the cakes.   No excess flour or
   sugar must be left in the tin after dusting.   The tin should be
   turned upside down and tapped gently.

D. Cooking the cakes

Type	Oven temperature and cooking instructions	Position in Oven
Small Cakes	375° F for 20–25 mins. until firm to the touch.	⅔ of the way up, i.e. in the top third of the oven.
Large cakes with little or no fruit	375° F; reduce to 350° F *at once* and cook for 1½ hours. If the cake requires longer than 1½ hours reduce to 325° F for the remainder of the time.	½ way up or one rung below.
Fruit cakes (high proportion of fruit)	350° F for 30 mins. or until set. 325° F until the cake has been in the oven for 1½ hours. Any further cooking at 300° F.	One rung below the middle of the oven.

For all creamed mixtures the oven should be preheated for at
least 20 mins., so that the heat is steady and uniform.   Cakes should
be cooked in a falling heat, so in all cases the heat is gradually

reduced during cooking. The same position in the oven should be used as that given for small and large cakes using the rubbed-in mixture, but creamed mixtures are cooked at a slightly lower temperature.

E. To test if the cakes are cooked

The same tests can be used as given for rubbed-in mixtures. When large cakes are taken out of the oven and held close to the ear there should be no " hissing " sound, as this denotes steam in the cake which has not fully dried out. Experience is needed, especially with large very rich fruit cakes where the fruit and fat may cause a slight bubbling which must not be confused with the " hissing ".

F. Cooling the cakes

Sandwich cakes should be put on a damp cloth for about half a minute; this will cause them to shrink and come out of the tin easily. A slight tap of the tin on the cloth may help.

Cakes which have had a greaseproof paper lining can be lifted out with the paper. Those containing little or no fruit should have the paper carefully removed at once. Cakes with a high proportion of fruit such as Christmas cake may be left in the tin to cool. This helps to keep the crust soft. In any case the paper should be left on till they are ready for using or icing.

G. Storing of rich cakes

These cakes can be kept for several days and in some cases even months. When cold they should be put in airtight tins lined with greaseproof paper. If they are to be kept for some weeks rich fruit cakes are greatly improved if they have the surface skewered and a little brandy, rum, sherry, or light wine brushed over them when they are quite cold. Then they should be wrapped in greaseproof paper before being put in the airtight tin. The tin may be sealed with adhesive strapping.

Basic Recipe for Creamed Mixtures

Plain	Family	Rich
$\frac{1}{2}$ lb flour	$\frac{1}{2}$ lb flour	$\frac{1}{2}$ lb flour
$\frac{1}{2}$ teasp salt	$\frac{1}{2}$ teasp salt	$\frac{1}{2}$ teasp salt
4 ozs butter	6 ozs butter	8 ozs butter
4 ozs sugar	6 ozs sugar	8 ozs sugar
2 eggs	4 eggs	6 eggs
1 teasp baking powder	$\frac{1}{2}$ teasp baking powder	
$\frac{1}{8}$ pt milk	1 tbs milk	

352 BETTER COOKERY

Method

1. Cream the fat and sugar very well either with a wooden spoon or by hand. The fat should be warmed very slightly but not oiled.
2. Beat up the eggs in a basin and stand it in a bowl of warm water.
3. Add the egg gradually, beating very well between each addition.
4. When all the egg has been added, scrape down the sides of the bowl and the spoon and beat again to ensure even mixing.
5. Add the liquid if required to the creamed mixture.
6. Sieve the flour, salt and baking powder (if used).
7. Gradually fold in the flour with a metal spoon, adding a little at a time.
8. When all the flour has been added scrape down the sides of the bowl and the spoon.
9. Fold lightly again, to ensure even mixing.
10. Put into the tin or tins, make a hole in the centre of the mixture, in a large cake, to prevent the mixture from rising to a peak in the centre. For a cake which contains a high proportion of fruit and which is to be iced, make a deep hole.

Variations of the Basic Recipe

VARIETY	ADDITIONS TO THE RECIPE	ADAPTATION OF THE METHOD
1. Almond	3–4 ozs ground almonds ¼ teasp ratafia or vanilla essence	Add the almonds with the flour, and the essence with the egg and milk.
2. Cherry	3–4 ozs glacé cherries	Add the prepared cherries with the flour.
3. Chocolate	Substitute 1 oz cocoa and 1 oz rice flour for 2 ozs flour. Add ½ teasp vanilla essence	Sieve the cocoa and rice flour with the flour. Add the essence with the liquid.
4. Christmas	Use equal quantities of fat, brown sugar and eggs 6 ozs sultanas 6 ozs currants 6 ozs raisins 4 ozs glacé cherries 1½ ozs mixed peel 1½ ozs preserved ginger 3 ozs almonds or walnuts	Add the fruit, peel, ginger and nuts immediately before the flour or when ⅓ of the flour has been added.
5. Coconut	3–4 ozs desiccated coconut	Add with the flour.

Variations of the Basic Recipe *continued*

VARIETY	ADDITIONS TO THE RECIPE	ADAPTATION OF THE METHOD
6. Coffee	1–2 tbs coffee essence 2 ozs chopped walnuts	Add the essence immediately after the eggs and the nuts with the flour.
7. Cornflour or Ground Rice	Substitute 4 ozs of cornflour or ground rice for 4 ozs flour + 1 teasp vanilla essence	Sieve the cornflour with the flour. Add the essence with the eggs or liquid.
8. Currant	4–6 ozs currants 1 teasp grated lemon rind	Add immediately before the flour.
9. Dundee	1–2 ozs ground almonds 3–4 ozs sultanas 3–4 ozs currants 3–4 ozs raisins 1½–2 ozs candied peel Rind of lemon 1–2 ozs split almonds	As for Christmas Cake. When the centre of the cake has filled in and the surface is nearly set put on the split almonds carefully.
10. Genoa	½ lb sultanas (or ¼ lb currants, ¼ lb sultanas) 2 ozs glacé cherries 2 ozs peel, citron if possible Rind of ½ lemon 2 ozs almonds (chopped) 1 oz split almonds	As above.
11. Ginger	3–4 ozs chopped preserved ginger ¼ teasp ground ginger (optional)	Add the chopped ginger with the flour. Sieve the ground ginger with the flour.
12. Lemon or orange	Rind of 1–2 lemons or oranges	Add with the flour.
13. Madeira	Use the family recipe Rind of 1 lemon Slices of citron peel	Add the rind with the flour. When the hole has filled in lay the peel on the top.
14. Pineapple	3 ozs crystallised pineapple 3 ozs raisins (optional)	Add with the flour.
15. Plum (plain)	2 ozs raisins 2 ozs currants 1 oz peel	Add with the flour.
16. Plum (rich)	¼ lb currants ¼ lb raisins ¼ lb sultanas 2 ozs peel 2 ozs ground almonds Rind ½ lemon ½ level teasp nutmeg ½ ,, ground ginger	As for Christmas cake.

M

Variations of the Basic Recipe *continued*

Variety	Additions to the Recipe	Adaptation of the Method
17. Queen	3–4 ozs currants or sultanas	Add with the flour—bake in paper cases or small cake tins.
18. Seed	2 level teasp carraway seeds	Add with the flour.
19. Simnel	As for Dundee or Christmas Cake ½ lb almond paste	Put half the mixture in the tin. Cover with a layer of almond paste. Put the 2nd half of the mixture on top.
20. Sultana	4–6 ozs sultanas Rind of ½ lemon or ½ teasp vanilla	Add with the flour.
21. Tennis	3 ozs sultanas 3 ozs currants 2 ozs glacé cherries 1 oz peel 1 oz chopped almonds Rind ½ lemon Rind ½ orange	As Christmas cake.
22. Victoria Sandwich	4 ozs flour ¼ level teasp salt 4 ozs butter 4 ozs castor sugar 2 eggs ½ level teasp baking powder raspberry jam for filling	Divide the mixture into 2 sandwich tins (7″). Cook at 350° for 30 mins. When cooked and cold put together with raspberry jam between. Sprinkle with castor sugar.
23. Walnut	1–2 ozs chopped walnuts ¼ teasp ratafia or vanilla essence	Add the nuts with the flour and essence with the liquid.

WHAT WENT WRONG—AND WHY

The cake has a heavy close texture

(a) The fat and sugar were insufficiently creamed. A fairly large quantity of air may be beaten in during this initial stage.

(b) Insufficient beating while the eggs were added. Most of the air is beaten in during this process.

(c) The mixture curdled owing to too rapid addition of the egg or to the eggs being too cool.

(d) Insufficient baking powder was used.

(e) Too much liquid was used.

(f) Cooked in too slow an oven, so that the air did not expand to its fullest extent before the gluten and albumen set.

(g) Cooked in too quick an oven, so that the mixture formed a hard crust on the top before the air had expanded.

(h) It was insufficiently cooked.

The texture is coarse and open

  (*a*) The fat, sugar and eggs were insufficiently creamed.
  (*b*) Too much baking powder was used.
  (*c*) Too low a proportion of fat and sugar and too high a proportion of flour and liquid were used.
  (*d*) It was baked in too hot an oven.

The texture is uneven, with large holes in the cake

  (*a*) The flour was stirred into the fat, sugar and egg for too long and too heavily. The flour should be lightly folded in.
  (*b*) Insufficient mixing so that the flour was unevenly distributed.
  (*c*) The cake mixture was put into the tins a little at a time, so air pockets formed.

The texture is very dry and crumbly

  (*a*) Too much baking powder was used.
  (*b*) The cake was baked for too long in a cool oven.
  (*c*) The fat, sugar and egg were curdled.
  (*d*) Bad storage.

Cakes have streaks on the crust and in the crumb

  (*a*) The scraping down of the sides of the bowl after creaming the fat and sugar or after beating in the eggs was badly done.
  (*b*) The flour was insufficiently folded in. Streaks of fat and sugar with little or no flour mixed in cause these marks.

A cake has risen unevenly

  (*a*) The oven was not correctly preheated.
  (*b*) The oven shelf was not level.
  (*c*) The cake was not placed in the centre of the shelf.

A cake has risen to a peak in the centre and cracked badly

  (*a*) The cake was cooked in too hot an oven.
  (*b*) The cake was placed too high up in the oven.

A cake has sunk in the middle

  (*a*) Over-creaming of the fat, sugar and egg and/or the use of too much baking powder caused the mixture to rise and over-stretch the gluten and albumen. These collapsed and so the cake sank in the centre.
  (*b*) Too much liquid was used.
  (*c*) Wet fruit was used.

(d) The oven door was opened and/or the cake moved before it had set.

(e) The oven door was slammed.

(f) The cake was cooked in too slow an oven.

(g) The cake was removed before it had cooked.

The fruit has sunk in the cake

See Rubbed-in Mixtures.

MELTED FAT MIXTURES

The third method of incorporating the fat with the flour is by melting it, usually with the sugar and/or syrup or treacle. It is added to the flour in liquid form. This is the method employed for gingerbread, parkin, malt bread and similar mixtures, giving a texture which is fairly coarse and open.

The average proportions are ⅓ fat to flour, ⅓ sugar to flour plus ⅓–⅔ syrup or treacle to flour. Eggs are used in the richer mixtures but many recipes do not include any. The raising agent is bicarbonate of soda alone or baking powder. The average proportion is 1 level teasp bicarbonate of soda or 2 level teasps of baking powder to a pound of flour. Milk and/or water are used, allowing ½ pint of liquid to the pound of flour. This includes the egg when used. 2 level teasp ground ginger or spices may be added to each pound of flour.

A. Suitable ingredients

1. Lard, margarine or clarified dripping can be used; a pure fat with no water content is preferable, e.g. lard or good dripping.

2. Moist brown or demerara sugar is preferable to white as it helps to give a rich dark colour. Whether syrup, treacle or a mixture of the two is chosen depends entirely on the flavour required. Black treacle only gives a rather strong bitter taste. The loose treacle (if obtainable) or the " Liverpool refined " syrup, which are about half way between golden syrup and black treacle, give excellent flavour and colour. In malt breads, half the syrup is replaced by malt extract; cod-liver oil and malt may be substituted for pure malt extract, as, 24 hours after baking, little or no cod-liver oil flavour can be detected.

3. When bicarbonate of soda is used alone, it makes the mixture dark in colour. This is advantageous for ginger mixtures, where a brown colour is traditional. When the bicarbonate of soda is heated, gas is given off and a residue of sodium carbonate is left; this acts on the starch, making it dark in colour.

The flavour of sodium carbonate (washing soda) is disguised by the ginger and/or the spices used.   The gas is given off by bicarbonate of soda alone at a much slower rate than from baking powder, and this too is an advantage, as the mixture is heavy because of the syrup used.   The idea that syrup or treacle acts as the acid with bicarbonate of soda is false; the very slight acidity of treacle would not prove sufficient to make an appreciable difference and the syrup is even less acid.

4. Dried fruit, walnuts and crystallised ginger all give additional flavour and variety to these cakes.

5. The Parkin mixtures have oatmeal or rolled oats added in place of some of the flour.

B. Points to remember in mixing

1. The bicarbonate of soda and the spices should be sieved with the flour and the salt.

2. The fat, sugar and syrup, malt or treacle should be warmed gently in a saucepan, without overheating, as this would result in a toffee-like substance being formed.

3. Any additional liquid should be added to the flour with the fat mixture.

4. The cake should be mixed with a metal spoon as the sharp edge blends the sticky liquid quickly with the flour and so prevents a tough shiny crust to the cake.

C. Preparation of the tins for baking

1. A square, oblong or loaf-shaped tin is traditional for ginger-breads, but a round tin can be used.

2. The tin should be greased and lined with greaseproof paper and the paper greased, as the syrup sticks and burns readily.

D. Cooking the cakes

1. These mixtures should be put into a moderate oven preheated to 350° F, and after 20 mins. the temperature should be reduced to 325° F.

2. They should be put half way up the oven.   Owing to the high percentage of sugar and syrup these cakes easily burn, so careful cooking is necessary.

E. To test if the cakes are cooked

1. The cakes should be evenly brown and should have shrunk a little from the sides of the tin.

2. They should be firm when lightly pressed with a finger.

3. There should be no sound of bubbling.

F. Cooling the cakes

1. The cake should be removed from the tin and the paper removed while it is still hot. The slight stickiness of the syrup will cause the paper to pull some of the cake away if it is left until it is cold.
2. The cake should stand on a wire tray until cold.

G. Storing of gingerbread etc

At least 24 hours should elapse before the cakes are cut. When first cold the outside is crisp and rather hard. During storage this crispness will disappear and the cake will become soft and slightly moist.

The cakes should be stored in tins (see creamed cake mixtures).

Gingerbreads, Parkin and Malt loaves

Method

1. Sieve the flour, salt, ginger, bicarbonate of soda and spices together.
2. Heat the fat, sugar and treacle or syrup in a pan until the fat has melted and the mixture is *warm*.
3. Add this mixture to the flour, with the additional liquid including the egg.
4. Stir well until fully mixed, but do not beat.
5. Pour into a lined and greased tin.
6. Put $\frac{1}{2}$ way up the oven, preheated to 350° **F.**
7. Bake 1–3 hours according to the size.

(see *Cooking the Cakes*).

Gingerbread Recipes

Plain Gingerbread

$\frac{1}{2}$ lb flour	2 ozs lard
$\frac{1}{2}$ level teasp salt	2 ozs brown sugar
2 level teasp ground ginger	4 ozs treacle
$\frac{1}{2}$ level teasp bicarbonate of soda	$\frac{1}{4}$ pt milk

Size of tin 6 inches square

Richer Gingerbread

6 ozs flour	4 ozs treacle (or syrup)
$\frac{1}{2}$ level teasp salt	1 oz lard
2 level teasp ground ginger	1 oz brown sugar
$\frac{1}{2}$ level teasp bicarbonate of soda	1 egg
$\frac{1}{2}$ level teasp mixed spice	$\frac{1}{8}$ pt boiling water
$\frac{1}{2}$ oz candied peel	

Size of tin 6 inches square

Fruit Gingerbread

6 ozs flour
½ level teasp salt
1 level teasp ground ginger
½ level teasp bicarbonate of soda
2 ozs lard
2 ozs brown sugar

1½ ozs sultanas
1½ ozs preserved ginger
½ oz candied peel
2 tablesp syrup or treacle
⅛ pt milk

Size of tin 6 inches square

Thick Gingerbread

1½ lbs flour
1½ level teasp salt
4 teasp ground ginger
2 teasp allspice
2 level teasp bicarbonate of soda

1 lb golden syrup
¼ lb lard or margarine
¼ lb brown sugar
2 eggs
¼ pt warm water

Size of tin 8 inches square

Spice Gingerbread

1 lb flour
1 teasp salt
2 teasp ground ginger
2 teasp cinnamon
2 teasp mixed spice
1 teasp ground cloves
1 teasp bicarbonate of soda

½ lb lard
½ lb brown sugar
½ lb treacle
¼ lb raisins
¼ lb chopped almonds
¼ lb preserved ginger
2–4 eggs
⅛ pt milk if 2 eggs are used

Size of tin 7 inches square

Gingerbread with Nuts

10 ozs flour
½ level teasp salt
3 level teasp ground ginger
1 level teasp bicarbonate of soda
3 level teasp ground cinnamon
2 eggs

6 ozs margarine or lard
6 ozs brown sugar
¼ lb treacle
¼ lb sultanas
2 ozs almonds or walnuts
⅛ pt warm milk

Size of tin 6 inches square

Coburg Cakes

8 ozs flour
4 ozs moist brown sugar
3½ ozs margarine or lard
¼ level teasp grated nutmeg
1 egg
almonds

1 level teasp cinnamon
2 teasp treacle
2 teasp syrup
1 level teasp bicarbonate of
  soda

Method
1. Make as for Gingerbread.
2. Grease 16 small bun tins and place 1 or 2 pieces of split almond on the bottom of each.
3. Divide the mixture between the tins.
4. Bake in a moderate oven 350° F for 20 mins.

Parkin

10 ozs medium oatmeal
6 ozs flour
1 level teasp salt
5 ozs margarine or lard
2 level teasp ground ginger
1 level teasp bicarbonate of soda

4 ozs black treacle
4 ozs golden syrup
2 ozs brown sugar
⅓ pt milk
1 egg

Bake in a tin 7″ square or round.

Cake Bread

8 ozs flour
2 ozs soft brown sugar
4 ozs treacle
¼ pt milk
1½ ozs lard

½ teasp salt
1 level teasp bicarbonate of soda
1 level teasp mixed spice
½ teasp cinnamon

Method
1. Sieve the dry ingredients.
2. Warm the syrup, milk, lard and sugar until the lard is melted.
3. Add to the dry ingredients.   Stir well but do not beat.
4. Bake in the centre of an oven preheated to 350° F for 1¼ hours approximately.
5. Use a 6″ cake tin lined with greased paper, or greased and floured.
6. Serve cut in slices and buttered.

Date Bread

8 ozs plain flour
3 level teasp baking powder
¾ level teasp salt
⅛ level teasp soda bicarbonate
2 ozs Barbados sugar

3 ozs chopped dates
2 ozs black treacle
1½ ozs chopped walnuts
1 oz lard
⅜ pt milk

Method
1. Grease and line a 2-lb loaf tin.
2. Sieve flour, salt, baking powder and bicarbonate of soda.

3. Add chopped dates and nuts.
4. Warm lard, treacle, sugar and milk. Avoid overheating.
5. Pour over the dry ingredients and mix without heating to a stiff batter consistency.
6. Pour into the lined tin. Bake at 350° F for 1¼ hours.

WHAT WENT WRONG—AND WHY

The mixture rose and then sank in the middle

(a) Too much raising agent was used.
(b) Too much syrup or treacle was used.
(c) The oven was too hot.
(d) The oven door was opened too soon.

The cake is too dark and hard on the outside

(a) Too much syrup was used.
(b) The cake was cooked for too long.
(c) The oven was too hot.

The cake is overcooked at the side and doughy in the centre

(a) Too much syrup was used.
(b) Too much liquid was used.
(c) The oven was too hot.
(d) The tin was too thin.

The cake has risen and cracked

(a) There was too much flour or oatmeal.
(b) Insufficient liquid was used.
(c) Too much raising agent was used.
(d) The cake was cooked too high up in the oven.

The cake is shiny on top and close in texture

The mixture was beaten after the addition of liquid. Beating would free the gluten in the flour and this, being a sticky substance, prevents the mixture from rising and gives a shiny appearance after baking.

SPONGES

Unlike other cake mixtures, true sponges have no fat in them. They are made by whisking eggs and sugar and incorporating flour. The whisking gives the characteristic texture to a sponge: a fairly open, even sized, cell-like structure. This is owing to the even distribution of air during the whisking and the even distribution of flour during the folding-in process. The lightness of the sponge depends upon the amount of air incorporated.

Compared with other cake mixtures, the proportion of eggs is high, and the quantity of flour very low; for each egg allow 1 oz castor sugar and ¾-1 oz of flour. If three or more eggs are used a little hot water may be added. This helps to give a light sponge. Allow 1 tablespoon of water for every 3 eggs.

A. Suitable ingredients

1. Eggs should be fresh (2–7 days old) as these whisk up much more readily than older eggs (see Egg Cookery). It is very important that no grease should be present while whisking, and it is advisable to use a basin of china, earthenware or glass.
2. The fine crystals of castor sugar give a smoother, more even texture than granulated sugar.
3. The flour should be dry and, if possible, a " soft " flour. Cornflour or rice flour may be mixed with the flour to give a lower gluten content, 2 parts wheat flour and 1 part corn or rice flour being a satisfactory mixture. This will make ordinary household flour " soft ".
4. Flavourings are rarely used in the mixture. If they are liquid, the essences must be fairly concentrated as too much of them will make the mixture wet, and consequently heavy. Dry ingredients such as spices may be added with the flour. When cocoa is used the flour should be less by the same amount. Any heavy ingredient such as fruit will sink in such a light mixture, and should be avoided.

B. Points to remember in mixing

1. The whole egg may be broken into a basin or it may be separated and the yolks put with the sugar, and the whites whisked until stiff and incorporated later. (For whisking see Egg Cookery.)
2. The basin of eggs should stand over a pan of hot water without touching the water. The mixture should be lightly whisked. Then after the sugar has been added, it should be whisked again. Use a flat whisk and turn the basin round so that it is heated evenly. Continue until the eggs become paler in colour and the mixture leaves a trail when taken across its own surface. The warmth helps to thicken the egg, but care should be taken not to overheat it and so cause coagulation, as coagulated egg will not hold air.
3. Remove the basin from the water and whisk until cool. More air will be incorporated and the egg will thicken a little more.

4. Have the flour dry and warmed to the same temperature as the egg mixture. If the flour is too cool it will chill the egg and some of the distended albumen will be broken down, releasing air and making the mixture heavy.

5. Sieve the flour evenly and gradually over the surface, and, at the same time, begin to fold it in with a large metal spoon. *Careful folding is most important.* The spoon is held so that the sharp edge cuts through the frothy mixture and is then turned, carrying some of the egg mixture across the flour so that the flour is literally folded inside. This action must be light and smooth so that the minimum of entrapped air is lost.

6. If the eggs have been separated and only the yolks whisked with the sugar over the hot water, the whites should be whisked until very stiff and folded in when the yolks and sugar are thick. The method as above is then followed.

C. Preparation of the tins for baking

For details see Creamed Mixtures.

It is traditional to have a sugary crust, which is obtained by dredging with castor sugar and rice flour.

Swiss rolls and slab genoese should be put into lined and greased shallow tins with straight sides.

D. Cooking the cakes

1. Sponges should be put half-way up in the oven which has been preheated to 375° F.

2. The temperature should be reduced at once to 350° F and after 20 mins to 325° F.

3. A two-egg sandwich cake will take about 20 minutes, a three-egg one 30 mins.

4. A swiss roll cooked in a tin 6″ × 10″ (using 2 eggs) should be cooked $\frac{2}{3}$ way up the oven. The temperature should be 425° F and it should be cooked for 7–8 minutes.

The deeper the cake the longer time it will need to be cooked, and it is important to allow the air to expand fully before the egg coagulates. As egg coagulates at a low temperature the oven must be very moderate.

E. To test if a cake is cooked

1. Slight pressure of the finger should leave no impression on the surface.

2. The sides of the cake should shrink a little from the tin.

3. There should be no sound of bubbling.

VARIATIONS OF THE BASIC RECIPE

Variety	Additions to the Recipe	Adaptation of the Method	Size of Tin	Baking Instructions	Method of Finishing
Swiss Roll	None	None	6 × 10 inches	425° F for 7 minutes, 2/3rds up the oven	Turn on to a sheet of greaseproof paper, dredged with castor sugar, over a damp cloth. Spread with hot jam. Roll up tightly. Dredge with sugar.
Swiss Roll with cream filling	None	None	As above	As above	Turn out as above. Cover with greaseproof paper and roll up with the paper inside. When cold unroll carefully, spread with buttercream. Re-roll and dredge with sugar.
Chocolate Swiss Roll	Use 1½ ozs flour and ½ oz cocoa 2–3 drops vanilla essence	Sieve the cocoa with the flour. Add the essence with the egg	As above	As above	Use either of above finishes. The buttercream may be flavoured with cocoa.
Sponge Sandwich	None	None	Use two 6-inch sandwich tins	As basic recipe; cook 15 minutes	When cold spread the base of one cake with jam (usually raspberry) and place the base of the second cake on top. Dredge the top with icing sugar.
Layer Cake	None	None	One 6-inch cake tin	As basic recipe	Cut the cake in half or into three. Sandwich together with buttercream, flavoured with orange, lemon or chopped walnuts. Coat the cake with glacé icing and decorate.
Sponge Fingers	None	None	Approximately 1 dozen sponge finger tins	As basic recipe for 10–15 minutes	As basic recipe.
Mocha Cake	Use 2 ozs flour and 2 ozs cornflour 4 ozs castor sugar 4 eggs	Sieve the cornflour with the flour. Separate the eggs. Whisk the yolks and sugar together. Whisk the whites very stiffly and add to the yolks. Fold in the flour	7" square tin	As basic recipe	Split into two or three layers; spread coffee buttercream between. Coat the sides with the coffee buttercream and chopped walnuts. Coat the top with coffee glacé icing. Decorate with piped cream and walnuts.

F. Cooling the cakes

1. Sponges should stand for about half a minute on a damp cloth. This helps in removing them from the tin.
2. They should be turned upside down on a wire tray and the tin lifted carefully.
3. Another wire tray should be rested on the cake and the two trays carefully inverted so that the top of the cake is uppermost. No pressure must be used or the impression of the wire tray will be seen.
4. The cakes should be cooled away from draughts as a sudden change of temperature will cause a slight shrivelling.

G. Storing the cakes

1. Ideally, the fatless sponge should be used the same day. It should not be kept longer than 2–3 days at the most, as it will become very dry.
2. Genoese may be kept 3–7 days, stored as for creamed mixtures.

Basic Recipe for Fatless Sponge

2 eggs
2 ozs castor sugar
2 ozs flour

Method

1. Prepare the tin.
2. Put the flour to warm and dry.
3. Break the eggs into a basin and whisk lightly.
4. Add the sugar and whisk over hot water until the mixture is thick and creamy (10–15 mins).
5. Remove the basin from the heat and whisk until cool and the mixture leaves a trail.
6. Fold in the flour very lightly with a large metal spoon.
7. Pour into the prepared tin.
8. Put into a moderate oven preheated to 375° F. Turn down at once to 350° F.
9. Bake 20 mins.

Size of tin: either a 7 inch sandwich tin or a 6 inch cake tin.

Genoese Pastry

If it is necessary to keep a sponge cake, or to cut it up for small iced fancies, some fat may be used. The addition of fat gives a more moist and slightly closer texture which will crumble less when cut. This is known as Genoese pastry. The proportions are 1 oz castor sugar, ¾ oz fat and ¾ oz flour to each egg.

Basic Recipe for Genoese Pastry

3 eggs

3 ozs castor sugar

2¼ ozs flour

2¼ ozs butter or margarine

Method

1. Sieve the flour and put to warm to blood heat.
2. Clarify the butter or margarine as any curd would cause an uneven heavy texture.
3. Whisk the eggs lightly and add the sugar.
4. Whisk over hot water until thick and creamy (see page 362).
5. Remove the basin from the heat and continue whisking until blood heat.
6. Warm the margarine to the same temperature as the egg mixture. The fat will be liquid.
7. Sieve half the flour on to the eggs.
8. Add half the butter gently, pouring in a thin stream.
9. Fold in very lightly as the stream of fat falls.
10. Add the remaining flour and butter in the same manner.
11. Fold in carefully with as few movements of the spoon as possible, as each movement of the spoon tends to rupture the albumen cells thus dispelling air.
12. Pour into a lined and greased tin.
13. Bake as for a sponge cake for at least 35 mins (see page 363).

This cake may be baked as a slab and cut up for small iced fancies or may be used for layer cakes. Size of tin 6″ × 10″.

Battenberg Cake

Pieces of Genoese of different colours.

Almond paste, 4 to 5 ozs per cake.

Method

1. Cut 4 strips of Genoese of different colours, of approximately 1″ × 1″ × 10″ in size. Use two colours, e.g. pink and white or chocolate and white.
2. Brush with hot sieved jam and stick together to make a block 2″ × 2″ × 10″, alternating the colours.
3. Leave until firm.
4. Roll out the paste to a rectangle, approximately 4½″ × 10″. Brush with jam.
5. Wrap around the cake, leaving the ends uncovered.
6. Score the top in a diamond pattern with a knife.
7. Pinch the two top edges to form a simple border.

WHAT WENT WRONG—AND WHY

The texture is close and heavy

(a) The eggs and sugar were insufficiently beaten.
(b) The eggs and sugar were overheated while whisking.
(c) The flour was carelessly folded in. If the flour is beaten or stirred in, the albumen will be broken down and the air released.
(d) The flour was added too quickly. The heavy flour crushed out the air.
(e) Too much flour was used.
(f) The oven was too hot. The air had not expanded before the gluten and albumen set.

The crumb is moist and heavy or " sad "

(a) Too much sugar was used.
(b) Insufficient cooking. The cake was removed from the oven too soon.
(c) The oven door was opened and/or the cake moved before it had set.
(d) The oven was too hot. The air expanded too quickly and the gluten and albumen collapsed.
(e) Too cool an oven. Insufficient heat to expand the air.

There are hard lumps in the crumb

The flour was not evenly folded into the mixture. This may be caused by:

(a) adding too much flour at a time.
(b) insufficient folding in of the flour.

A swiss roll cracks badly when rolled

(a) The texture was too close.
(b) Overcooking.
(c) The tin was not lined with greaseproof paper so the edges became hard.
(d) It was not rolled on top of a damp cloth.
(e) It was not rolled quickly enough.

A sponge has sunk in the centre

(a) The oven was too hot. The air had been over-expanded and the gluten was not able to hold it so the cake collapsed.
(b) The cake was moved too soon.
(c) The oven door was slammed.
(d) Insufficient cooking.

Genoese has a heavy layer at the base

(*a*) The fat was not the same temperature as the other ingredients.
(*b*) Too much fat was added at one time.
(*c*) The fat and flour were insufficiently folded in.

BISCUITS

Biscuits may be classified according to the method of making, in the same was as cakes are grouped, i.e. rubbing in, creaming etc. The actual method of mixing each group is similar to its counterpart in cakemaking. The main differences lie in the amount of moisture added to the mixture and in the baking. Biscuits are dried out rather then baked. They should be the same texture all the way through when broken. Most biscuits should *snap* as they break.

A. Suitable ingredients

When possible a soft flour, that is one with a low gluten content, should be used. Rice flour or cornflour is mixed with wheat flour to reduce the gluten content.

Margarine is generally used for biscuits, but whenever possible butter should be substituted as it gives a much better flavour. $\frac{1}{3}$ butter $+ \frac{2}{3}$ margarine is very satisfactory. Where syrup, treacle, spice and/or ginger are used, lard gives satisfactory results, especially when the melted fat method is employed.

The type of sugar depends upon the type of biscuit. Broadly speaking castor sugar gives better results than granulated as the coarser crystals tend to give a speckled appearance when cooked. Moist brown sugar is preferable to demerara for the same reasons.

The flavourings employed are very varied. The methods of incorporating them are similar to those used for cakemaking.

B. Points to remember in mixing

The initial mixing of the ingredients depends on the type of biscuit. The points are similar to those used for the same method in cakemaking. (See rubbed-in mixtures, creamed cake mixtures etc.)

A stiff dough is the consistency required for most biscuits. In some cases no liquid is required, the fat being in a high enough proportion to bind the flour and sugar together. When additional liquid is used it may be water, milk, whole egg or yolk of egg. In almost all cases just sufficient is used to bind the dry ingredients together so that the dough may be shaped or rolled out and cut without crumbling. It is important that the dough should be well and lightly kneaded in order to get it smooth and even.

C. Preparation of tins for baking

Biscuits with a low fat and sugar content may be baked on lightly greased baking tins.

Those with a high fat and sugar content are better baked on a baking sheet covered with greaseproof paper, as the paper, being a bad conductor of heat, prevents too strong a bottom heat and helps even drying out.

Rich mixtures, especially those with a meringue or marzipan base, are often baked on rice paper.

D. Cooking of the biscuits

For all biscuits the oven should be preheated for at least 20 minutes so that the heat is uniform and steady. The temperature is lower than for cakes of a similar size and consequently the time for baking is much longer. This slow, very moderate heat allows the moisture to be driven off slowly and the biscuit to become crisp and dry without over-browning. Biscuits should be cooked about halfway up the oven or one rung below halfway. They should be pale brown or barely coloured when cooked.

E. Cooling the biscuits

Most biscuits are soft when they are taken out of the oven. They should be put on to a wire cooling tray to allow the steam to escape and for them to become crisp and firm. In some instances the mixture is very soft when cooked and, to prevent spoiling the shape, it is advisable to allow it to cool on the baking tray for a few moments before moving.

F. Storage

It is important that all biscuits should be stored in really airtight tins, as they absorb moisture from the air and easily lose their crispness.

Different varieties are better stored in separate tins as some are moister than others, and if stored together some may go soft. Also the flavour of the plainer biscuits may be impaired by stronger flavours of others. On no account should biscuits be stored in the same tin as cake.

G. Finishing biscuits

Some biscuits require jam, cream etc. sandwiched between two or between a biscuit and a ring. It is advisable to sandwich the undersides together as this allows them to fit more closely and gives a smarter appearance. If the tops of ring biscuits require dredging with castor or icing sugar this should be done before they are sandwiched together.

Filling tends to soften the biscuit, so cream or jam fillings should be put on immediately before serving.

Date Torte

3 ozs flour
¼ teasp baking powder
¼ teasp salt
2 eggs

½ lb moist brown sugar
½ lb chopped dates
6 ozs chopped walnuts

Method

1. Line a 6″ square tin with paper. Grease well.
2. Beat the eggs and sugar until light and frothy.
3. Sift the flour, salt and baking powder on to the egg mixture.
4. Add the chopped nuts and dates and fold all in together.
5. Put the mixture, which should just drop from the spoon, into the lined tin.
6. Bake at 350° F for 40–45 minutes until it is brown and firm to the touch.

Nutty Balls

10 ozs flour
7 ozs butter
½ teasp vanilla essence

2½ ozs sugar
3½ ozs almond nibs

Method

1. Rub the fat into the flour.
2. Add the rest of the ingredients.
3. Knead together until the mixture forms large lumps.
4. Break into pieces the size of a walnut and shape into balls.
5. Place on a lightly greased tin and bake in the centre of a moderate oven, 325° F, for 15 mins.
6. Toss in castor sugar whilst still hot.

BISCUITS MADE BY RUBBING-IN METHOD

Type	Recipe	Method	Baking Instructions	Method of Finishing
Almond Slices	1/2 lb flour 1/4 lb butter or margarine 2 ozs castor sugar 1 level teasp baking powder 1 yolk of egg 1 tbs apricot jam *Icing* 1 white of egg 3 ozs almond nibs 3 ozs icing sugar	1. Rub the fat into the sieved flour and baking powder. 2. Add the castor sugar. 3. Bind to a stiff paste with yolk of egg. 4. Knead well. 5. Roll into a strip 1/4" thick and 2 1/2–3" wide. 6. Prick well. 7. Pinch the sides to decorate. 8. Brush the centre with sieved jam. 9. Beat the white of egg until frothy. 10. Stir in the icing sugar and spread over the jam. 11. Sprinkle with the nuts.	Bake on a papered tin. Oven heat 350° F. Time of baking—40–45 mins.	Cut into slices about 3/4 to 1 inch wide while still warm.
Chocolate	6 ozs flour 1/2 level teasp baking powder 4 ozs butter or margarine 1 oz castor sugar 1 yolk of egg 1 tbs water	1. Rub the fat into the sieved flour and baking powder. 2. Add the sugar. 3. Mix to a stiff paste with egg yolk and water. Knead well. 4. Roll out 1/8 inch thick. 5. Prick well. 6. Cut out with 1 1/2 inch cutter.	Bake on a papered tin. Oven heat 350° F. Time of baking 10 mins.	When cold sandwich together with chocolate butter-cream (see icings). Coat with chocolate glacé icing (see icings).
Cinnamon	6 ozs flour 1/2 level teasp baking powder 4 ozs butter or margarine 4 ozs castor sugar 1 teasp cinnamon 1 egg 1 tbs jam	1. Sieve the flour, cinnamon and baking powder together. 2. Rub in the fat. 3. Add the sugar. 4. Bind with beaten egg to a stiff paste. Knead well. 5. Roll out 1/8" thick. 6. Prick well. 7. Cut out with a 1 1/2 inch cutter.	Bake on a papered tin. Oven heat 350° F. Time of baking 10 mins.	When cold— 1. Sandwich together with jam between. 2. Dredge with icing sugar.

BISCUITS MADE BY RUBBING-IN METHOD *continued*

Type	Recipe	Method	Baking Instructions	Method of Finishing
Coconut	6 ozs flour 2 ozs coconut 3 ozs butter or margarine 1¹/₂ ozs castor sugar 1 egg 1 tbs raspberry jam	1. Rub the fat into the flour. 2. Add the sugar and coconut. 3. Bind with the yolk of the egg. 4. Knead well. 5. Roll out into two strips, ¹/₈ inch thick and about 3 inches wide. 6. Prick and spread one with sieved jam. 7. Cover with the other strip. 8. Brush with white of egg and sprinkle with coconut.	Bake on a papered tin. Oven heat 350° F. Time of baking 20 minutes.	Cut into fingers about ³/₄ to 1 inch wide while still warm. Trim neatly.
Grasmere Gingerbread	8 ozs flour 4 ozs moist brown sugar 4 ozs butter 2 teasp ground ginger 2 ozs chopped peel ¹/₂ teasp salt	1. Rub fat into flour and salt. 2. Add sugar and ginger. 3. Reserve 1 tbs of these crumbs. 4. Add peel. 5. Knead well. 6. Press into a greased 7″ sandwich tin.	Bake at 350° F for 50 mins. Sprinkle with the extra crumbs. Continue cooking for a further 10 mins or until firm when pressed.	Cool in the tin and cut into portions while still warm.
Napoleon	8 ozs flour 6 ozs butter or margarine 2 ozs ground almonds 3 ozs castor sugar 1 egg 2 tbs raspberry jam	1. Rub the fat into the flour. 2. Add the sugar and almonds. 3. Bind with beaten egg; a little milk may be required. 4. Knead well. 5. Roll out to ¹/₈ inch thick. Cut ¹/₂ the mixture into 1¹/₂″ rounds and the other half into 1¹/₂″ rounds with the centre cut out with a ³/₄″ cutter. These are known as "rings".	Bake on a papered tin. Oven temp. 325–350° F. Time of baking 10–15 minutes.	When cold brush the underside of the rounds with sieved jam. Cover with the rings previously dredged with icing sugar.
Oatmeal	¹/₄ lb medium oatmeal 3–4 ozs flour 3–4 ozs butter, margarine ¹/₂ level teasp baking powder ¹/₂ ″ teasp salt 1 teasp sugar ¹/₂ egg Water	1. Rub the fat into the flour and salt. 2. Add the oatmeal, sugar, and baking powder. 3. Mix to a stiff paste with beaten egg and water. 4. Knead well. 5. Roll out ¹/₄″ thick. Prick well. 6. Cut with a 1¹/₂–2 inch cutter, or cut into fingers 1″ × 2¹/₂″.	Bake on a greased tin. Oven temp. 350° F. Time of baking 15–20 minutes.	Cool on a wire tray.

Rice Method I	6 ozs flour 2 ozs rice flour 1 level teasp baking powder 3 ozs butter or margarine 3 ozs castor sugar 1 egg 2-3 drops vanilla	1. Rub the fat into the flour, rice flour and baking powder. 2. Add the sugar. 3. Mix to a stiff paste with the beaten egg to which the vanilla has been added. 4. Knead well. 5. Roll out to ¹/₄ inch and cut with a 2-inch cutter	Bake on a greased tin. Oven temp. 350° F. Time of baking 10-15 minutes.	Cool on a wire tray.
Shortbread Method I	4 ozs flour 2 ozs rice flour 4 ozs butter 2 ozs castor sugar	1. Rub the butter into the other ingredients. 2. Continue until the mixture forms large lumps. 3. Knead well and form into a round cake ¹/₃ inch thick. 4. Pinch the edges and prick the centre.	Bake on a papered tin. Oven temperature 325° F. Time of baking 40-45 mins.	Cut into wedge shaped pieces while still warm, and dredge with castor sugar.
Spice	As for cinnamon but substitute 1 teasp mixed spice for 1 teasp cinnamon or use ¹/₂ level teasp cloves cinnamon 1 „ „ nutmeg	As for cinnamon biscuits.	As for cinnamon biscuits.	Cool on a wire tray.

BISCUITS MADE BY THE CREAMING METHOD

Type	Recipe	Method	Baking Instructions	Method of Finishing
Almond ring	4 ozs flour 4 ozs margarine and butter 1 oz castor sugar 1 yolk of egg *Filling* 1 egg white 3 ozs castor sugar 2½ ozs ground almonds Raspberry jam	1. Cream the fat and sugar. 2. Beat in the yolk of egg and fold in the flour. 3. Form into a ball and knead well. Roll out to ⅛ inch thick. Prick and cut out with a 1½ inch cutter. 5. Beat the egg white until frothy. 6. Stir in the sugar and almonds. 7. Put into a forcing bag with an open star pipe. Pipe a circle of filling round each biscuit.	Bake on a papered tin. Oven temperature 350° F. Time 15 mins.	Cool on a wire tray. When cold put a little red jam in the centre of each biscuit.
Bourbon	4 ozs flour 2 ozs butter or margarine 2 ozs castor sugar 1 tbs syrup or honey ½ level teasp bicarb. soda ½ oz cocoa *Filling* 1½ ozs margarine or butter 3 ozs icing sugar 1 teasp coffee essence ¼ oz cocoa	1. Cream fat and sugar. 2. Add syrup or honey. 3. Sieve flour, cocoa, and bicarb. together and stir into the fat and sugar. 4. Form into a stiff paste. Knead well. 5. Roll out to ⅛ inch thick. Cut into fingers 2½ inch × ¾ inch.	Bake on a papered tin. Oven temp. 325° F. Time 15–20 mins.	Cool on a wire tray. When cold sandwich together with the butter cream made with ingredients given for the filling.
Coffee cream	As for Shrewsbury biscuits but substitute 1 teasp coffee essence for the lemon rind	As for Shrewsbury biscuits. Cut with a 1½ inch cutter into rounds and rings.	As for Shrewsbury biscuits.	Spread the base of the rounds with coffee butter icing and cover with the rings previously dredged with icing sugar.
Easter	As for Shrewsbury biscuits but add 1 level teasp mixed spice or cinnamon and 2 ozs currants	As for Shrewsbury biscuits. Cut out with a 2 inch cutter.	As for Shrewsbury biscuits.	Dredge with castor sugar while still warm.
Grantham Gingerbread	6 ozs flour 6 ozs castor sugar 3 ozs margarine or butter 2 teasp ground ginger 1 teasp ammonium carbonate ½ egg	1. Sieve the flour, ginger and ammonium carbonate together. 2. Cream the fat and sugar. 3. Beat in the egg. 4. Fold in the flour etc. 5. Knead well. 6. Shape the mixture into small balls the size of a walnut.	Bake on a greased tin. Oven temp. 325° F. Time 20–25 minutes.	Cool on a wire tray.

Name	Ingredients	Method	Baking	Finishing
Orange creams	As for Shrewsbury biscuits but substitute the rind of 1 orange for the lemon	As for Shrewsbury biscuits Cut out into rounds and rings, using a 1 1/2 inch cutter.	As for Shrewsbury biscuits.	Spread the underside of the rounds with orange butter cream and cover with the rings, previously dredged with icing sugar.
Priory	3 ozs flour 3 ozs porage oats 3 ozs sugar 2 ozs margarine or butter 2 ozs syrup 1 teasp ginger 1/2 teasp soda bicarbonate 1/2 egg	1. Cream the fat and sugar. 2. Beat in the syrup and egg. 3. Add the ginger and bicarb. soda to the flour and sieve into the mixture. Add the oats. 4. Work to a stiff paste with a knife. 5. Roll out thinly and cut into rounds using a 2" cutter.	Bake as for ginger nuts.	Leave to cool on the tin for a few minutes, then transfer to a wire tray.
Shortbread Method II	4 ozs flour 2 ozs rice flour 4 ozs butter 2 ozs castor sugar	1. Cream the butter and sugar 2. Gradually work in the flour and rice flour. 3. Roll out into one or two circles about 1/2 inch thick. Pinch the edges. Prick well.	Bake on a papered tin. Oven temperature 323° F. Time for baking 40-45 mins.	Cut into wedge shaped pieces while still hot, and dredge with castor sugar.
Shortbread biscuits	As above—a little beaten egg may be added	1. As above. 2. Roll out to 1/4 inch thick. 3. Cut out with 1 1/2-2 inch cutter.	Bake as above. Time 15–20 mins.	Dredge with castor sugar while still warm.
Shrewsbury	8 ozs flour or { 6 ozs flour 2 ozs rice flour 4 ozs butter 4 ozs castor sugar 1 egg yolk Rind of lemon	1. Cream the fat and sugar together. 2. Beat in the egg. 3. Add the lemon rind and flour. 4. Knead well until smooth. 5. Roll out to 1/4 inch thick. Prick well. 6. Cut into rounds. The original Shrewsbury biscuits are 5" in diameter.	Bake on a papered tin. Oven temperature 350° F. Time 15–20 mins.	Dredge with castor sugar while still warm.
Viennese biscuits	6 ozs flour 6 ozs butter 2 ozs castor or icing sugar 1/4 teasp vanilla essence or 1 teasp coffee essence	1. Cream the fat and sugar and work in the flour. 2. Put into a forcing bag with a star pipe. 3. Pipe into paper cases or on to tins in star or bar shapes.	Bake on greased tins. Oven temperature 350° F. Time for baking 15–20 mins.	Before baking decorate with cherry and angelica. or when cold pipe with butter cream. or sandwich two together with butter cream. or decorate with red jam. Dredge with icing sugar.

BISCUITS MADE BY MELTED FAT METHOD

Type	Recipe	Method	Baking Instructions	Method of Finishing
Brandy snap	3 ozs syrup (2 tbs) 2 ozs flour 2 ozs moist brown sugar 2 ozs butter, margarine or lard 1/2 teasp lemon rind 1 ,, lemon juice 1 level teasp ground ginger	1. Melt the fat and add the sugar and syrup. 2. Warm. 3. Stir in the flour, ginger and lemon. 4. Drop in small teasp on to a baking sheet well apart to allow for spreading. Not more than 6 on a tin, size 8 × 10 inches.	Bake on a greased baking tin. Size approx. 8 × 10''. Oven temperature 325° F. Time 8–10 mins.	Allow to cool on the tin a moment or two. Lift with a palette knife and roll loosely round the greased handle of a wooden spoon. Allow to cool. If liked fill with cream.
Flapjack	4 ozs rolled oats 2 ozs butter, margarine or lard 4 ozs syrup 2 ozs moist brown sugar	1. Melt the fat in a pan. 2. Add the sugar and syrup. 3. Warm. 4. Stir in the oats. 5. Press into a Yorkshire pudding tin forming a layer 1/4 inch thick.	Bake in a greased Yorkshire pudding tin. Oven temperature 325° F. Time 30 mins.	Cut into fingers or squares while hot. Leave in the tin until cold. Divide up when cold.
Florentines	2 ozs butter 2 ozs sugar 1 dessertsp syrup or honey 2 ozs candied peel 1 oz glacé cherries 1 oz blanched almonds 2 ozs flour 2 ozs plain chocolate to cover	1. Melt the butter and add the sugar, syrup and chopped fruit and nuts. 2. Bring to the boil and add the flour. 3. Drop teaspoonfuls of the mixture on to a tin lined with waxed paper.	Bake at 350° F for 8–10 mins. Cool on the paper.	When cold, spread the underside with melted chocolate.
Ginger Nuts	8 ozs flour 2 1/2 ozs moist brown sugar 2 1/2 ozs butter or margarine 1 teasp ground ginger 5 ozs syrup or treacle	1. Sieve the flour and ginger together. 2. Melt the fat and add the sugar and syrup. 3. Stir into the flour. 4. Leave to stand for 1/2 hour. 5. Knead well. 6. Roll out to 1/4'' thick. 7. Cut out with 2' cutter.	Bake on a greased tin. Oven temp. 350° F. Time 15 minutes	Leave on the tin for a minute or two to cool, then lift carefully on to a wire tray.

Oatcakes	4 ozs medium or fine oatmeal 1/2 level teasp salt 1/4 ,, bicarbonate of soda 2 ozs lard, dripping or bacon fat Boiling water	1. Melt the fat and stir it into the oatmeal, salt and bicarbonate. 2. Add sufficient boiling water to form into a stiff paste. 3. Knead well. 4. Roll out to a thin cake about 1/8–1/4" thick. Cut into 6–8 wedge shaped pieces.	Bake on a greased girdle or a greased tin in the oven. Dry off slowly until crisp and quite dry—about 1 hour. Oven temp. 300° F.	Cool on a wire tray.
Parkin Biscuits	4 ozs flour 4 ozs fine oatmeal 1/2 level teasp salt 2 ozs butter, margarine or lard 3 ozs moist brown sugar 1 1/2 level teasp bicarb. soda 1 ,, ground ginger 1 ,, mixed spice or cinnamon 3 ozs syrup 1/2 oz split almonds	1. Melt the fat and stir into the dry ingredients. 2. Mix with the syrup to a stiff paste. 3. Divide into small round portions, about 1/2 oz weight each. 4. Place on a baking sheet. 5. Flatten slightly and place a split almond on each.	Bake on a greased tin. Oven temp. 325° F. Time 20–30 minutes.	Cool on a wire tray.

BISCUITS MADE BY THE WHISKED METHOD

Type	Recipe	Method	Baking Instructions	Method of Finishing
Rice Method II	2 eggs 1 1/2 ozs castor sugar 1 1/2 ,, flour 1/4 ,, rice flour 1/2 level teasp baking powder	1. Beat the yolks and sugar until thick and creamy. 2. Beat the whites, add to the yolks and beat again. 3. Fold in the dry ingredients. 4. Drop in teaspoonfuls on a greased tray.	Bake on a greased tray. Rice paper may be used if liked. Oven temperature 350° F. Time 10–15 mins.	Cool on a wire tray.
Sponge fingers	2 eggs 2 ozs castor sugar 1 3/4 ozs flour 1/4 oz rice flour	1. Beat eggs and sugar over hot water till thick and creamy. 2. Fold in the flour and rice flour. 3. Half fill sponge finger tins.	Bake in greased tins dusted with rice flour and sugar. Oven temperature 325° F. Time 10 mins.	Cool on a damp cloth for 1/2 minute. Lift out carefully and cool on a wire tray.

CHOUX PASTRY

Proportions: To each egg allow:—

1¼ ozs flour
1 oz butter
½ gill water
¼ teasp salt
1 teasp sugar

This pastry is similar to hot water crust pastry in that the flour, salt and sugar are beaten into the boiling fat and water: there the similarity ends. The flour is cooked in the liquid over gentle heat until the very thick " panada " leaves the sides of the pan. To this thick mixture the egg is added and the mixture is beaten until it is smooth and elastic. This beating is very important as the lightness of the paste depends entirely on the incorporation of air at this stage. The paste is much softer than in any other pastry and when the wooden spoon is drawn up out of the mixture the paste adhering to it can be pulled out into a thin semi-transparent ribbon. The easier it is to pull out this very thin film the better is the pastry.

This paste is put into a forcing bag and piped through a plain meringue pipe into éclairs or puffs.

To shape éclairs

1. Have ready a greased baking tray.
2. Use a ½″ meringue pipe unless small buffet sized éclairs are required, when ¼″ or ⅜″ pipe can be used.
3. Holding the bag so that the pipe is about ⅛″ from the baking tray and is lying nearly parallel to it, force the paste out slowly. Draw the pipe across the tray diagonally until 2½″ to 3″ of paste has been forced out.
4. Stop pressing the paste out and draw the pipe up and back over the paste in a quick jerk. This will break off the paste and the last bit of the paste, which will stick up on the top, can be flicked off leaving a neat edge.
5. An alternative method is to cut the paste off with a wet knife against the edge of the pipe.
6. Repeat this for each éclair, leaving 1″ between each one to allow even cooking.

To shape puffs

1. Have ready a greased baking tray
2. Use a ½″ pipe as for éclairs.

3. Hold the bag so that the pipe is about ¼″ away from the tin and at an angle of 45° from the tin.
4. Force the paste out without moving the pipe at all until a small round has been formed about 1½″ to 2″ in diameter.
5. Stop pressing and break off the paste with a sharp flick down and up again.
6. If a large puff is desired a small quantity of " vol " or ammonium carbonate may be put on the tray and the paste piped on it. Use about two drops of liquid or a very tiny pinch of powder. This helps to blow up the paste.
7. 2″ to 3″ should be left round each puff and a tin may be placed over each one for part of the cooking. This makes the paste crack across and form the cabbage-like top from which the paste gets its name.

To bake choux pastry

1. The oven should be preheated to 400° F and the trays placed halfway up the oven.
2. Éclairs require 20–30 mins according to their size. It is very important that the pastry should be dried right through and be crisp and a pale golden brown.
3. Puffs cooked uncovered can be baked like éclairs. They require 25–35 minutes.
4. Puffs covered with a tin should be baked for 15 to 20 minutes with the tins over them until the paste has blown up and set. The tins should then be removed to allow the puffs to brown a little and the cooking continued until they are golden brown and quite crisp.

To test for readiness

Either tap the base (it should sound hollow), or split one open. There should be no damp dough inside and the " shell " should be fairly crisp.

If the centre is damp return the remainder to the oven and continue cooking.

Puffs and éclairs that are not dry will quickly go soft and very tough.

Many recipes for choux pastry state that the éclair or puff must be split and the damp centre scooped out and the pastry dried off. If the given recipe is used, the mixture dries off satisfactorily without being split and a neater finish is obtained.

The cakes may be stored unfilled in airtight tins for 3–4 days.

FINISHING ÉCLAIRS AND PUFFS

Variety	Adaptation to Recipe or Method	Method of Filling	Method of Finishing
Coffee éclairs	None	Use fresh whipped cream or coffee butter cream or mock cream.	Coat or dip in coffee glacé icing.
Chocolate éclairs	None	As above using vanilla-flavoured butter cream.	Coat or dip in chocolate icing.
Cream Puffs	None	As above.	Dredge with icing sugar.
Savoury éclairs	Omit sugar from the recipe. Using a ⅜" pipe force them out 1½–2" long.	Any filling suitable for patties (see section on meat or fish).	Finish with a meat glaze (see section on meat).

WHAT WENT WRONG—AND WHY

The paste is too thin

(*a*) The proportions were incorrect.
(*b*) Insufficient cooking of the flour and liquid.

The paste is too thick

(*a*) The proportions were incorrect.
(*b*) The liquid was boiled for too long before the flour was added.

The paste will not pull up into a thin film

(*a*) The consistency was too thick or too thin.
(*b*) The flour was insufficiently cooked.
(*c*) Insufficient beating.

The éclairs or puffs are close and heavy

(*a*) Insufficient beating
(*b*) The paste was cooked in too hot an oven; therefore the outside set before the air had expanded.
(*c*) The paste was put in too cool an oven, allowing the air to escape before the mixture had set.

The éclairs have cracked badly

Too hot an oven was used and the outside of the éclair set before the air inside had expanded. When expansion took place the surface crust burst.

ICINGS AND FILLINGS

Almond Paste (1)

1 lb ground almonds
1 lb icing sugar
3 eggs

flavouring of lemon juice, vanilla, ratafia and maraschino

Method

1. Whisk eggs and sugar over hot water till thick and creamy.
2. Add the almonds and mix well.
3. Work in the flavourings and knead until smooth.

Almond Paste (2)

8 ozs ground almonds
8 oz icing sugar
   or
4 ozs icing sugar and 4 ozs
  castor sugar
1 teasp vanilla essence

1 teasp orange-flower water
2 teasp lemon juice
a few drops of brandy
one drop of ratafia essence
one to two egg whites

Mix the almonds and the sifted sugar, flavourings, and enough slightly beaten white of egg to mix to a firm consistency.

Butter Icing (Butter Cream)

2 ozs butter
2–3 ozs icing sugar
flavouring and colouring

Method

1. Cream the butter.
2. Gradually add the sugar and cream together.
3. Beat until white and very creamy.
4. Flavour and colour.

Suggested Flavourings	*Suggested Colours*
1. $\frac{1}{2}$ teasp vanilla essence	Leave white or colour pink or yellow

2. $\left\{\begin{array}{l}\frac{1}{4}\text{ teasp almond essence}\\\frac{1}{4}\text{ ,, ratafia essence}\end{array}\right\}$ Leave white

3. Very finely grated orange   Colour orange
   rind, plus 1 teasp orange
   juice

4. As above but one lemon   Colour pale yellow

5. 2 teasp coffee essence

6. 2 ,, cocoa, plus $\frac{1}{2}$ teasp
   vanilla essence or 1 oz
   melted chocolate

7. Chopped walnuts

Confectioner's Custard

2 ozs butter	1 yolk of egg
1½ ozs flour	1 oz sugar
1½ gills milk	1 tbs evaporated milk

2–3 drops vanilla essence

Method

1. Make a roux with the butter and flour.
2. Add the milk and make a thick sauce.
3. Cool and beat in the yolk and sugar.
4. Cook over a gentle heat until thick.
5. Beat in the evaporated milk and flavouring.
6. Use when cool.

Mock Cream

¼ pt milk	1½ oz butter
½ oz cornflour	1 oz sugar

2–3 drops vanilla essence

Method

1. Blend the cornflour with a little milk.
2. Heat the remaining milk and pour over the cornflour.
3. Return it to the pan and cook for 3 minutes. Cool.
4. Cream the butter and sugar.
5. Beat in the cooled cornflour, a teaspoonful at a time.
6. Beat very well and flavour with vanilla essence.

Glacé Icing

½ lb icing sugar	flavouring and colouring
2 tbs warm water	

Method

1. Sieve the icing sugar into a basin.
2. Add the water.

3. Stir until fully mixed and smooth.
4. Flavour and colour.
5. Use at once.

Royal Icing

1 teasp blued sugar (see below)
½ lb icing sugar
1 white of egg
1 teasp lemon juice

(N.B. If required to keep the icing soft add 1 teasp glycerine to 1 lb sugar).

Method

1. Sieve the icing sugar and the blued sugar together.
2. Put the white of egg and lemon juice in a bowl.
3. Beat slightly with a wooden spoon.
4. Add 1 tbs sieved sugar and beat for 10 minutes.
5. Add the remainder of the sugar gradually, stirring well until the icing is of the correct consistency. Add the glycerine during the mixing.

To prepare Blued Sugar

½ level teasp Painters Lime Blue, or Reckitts Paris blue
¾ lb icing sugar
Sieve 3 times using a fine sieve.
Store in an airtight tin. It will keep indefinitely in a dry place.

American Frosting

1 lb granulated sugar
¼ pt + 1 teasp water
the whites of two eggs
2 or 3 drops of vanilla or ratafia essence

Method

1. Heat the water and dissolve the sugar slowly.
2. Brush down the side of the pan with a brush dipped in cold water to prevent the formation of crystals.
3. Bring to the boil and raise to 240° F. Be careful not to over-boil or the icing will be too hard.
4. Whisk the egg whites stiffly in a large earthenware bowl.
5. Pour the syrup on to the egg steadily from a height, whisking all the time. The syrup will cool a little on falling.
6. Whisk steadily until the icing thickens and becomes like cotton wool.

7. Spread quickly over the cake. It will harden very rapidly at this stage.
8. Rough up with a heated palette knife.

Transparent Icing

1 lb granulated sugar
juice of $\frac{1}{4}$ lemon
$\frac{1}{2}$ pt water

Method

1. Put the sugar and water into a clean pan. Dissolve carefully without boiling.
2. Brush down the sides of the pan with a brush dipped in cold water.
3. Boil to 229° F.
4. Brush down as required.
5. Put the lemon juice in a clean bowl and pour on the syrup, stirring gently all the time until it turns cloudy. Pour at once over the cake.

CHAPTER XXII

PASTRY-MAKING

PASTRY is a mixture of flour, fat and water; in some cases egg, sugar or cheese may be added, but the first three are the essential ingredients. It is the proportion and the method of incorporating these three that determine the variety and texture of the finished pastry.

When possible, a soft or weak flour should be used, as the low gluten content gives a better texture. This is particularly important with the plainer pastries. The richer ones, e.g. flaky and puff, can be made with a stronger flour as the additional gluten gives the elasticity required. Plain flour should be used whenever half or more than half fat to flour is used. When baking powder is added the pastry should be used quickly as it becomes stale and dry readily. Self-raising flour is not recommended for any except suet or very plain short pastry.

The nature of the fat and the proportions used influence the finished result. Fat may be incorporated by the following methods:

(1) Shredding finely or chopping as in suet pastry.
(2) Rubbing in as in short pastry.
(3) Adding in lumps to the flour as in rough puff.
(4) Putting on in lumps over the paste as in flaky.
(5) Folding inside the paste as in puff.
(6) Adding melted with the boiling liquid as in hot water crust.

SUET PASTRY

Proportions

$\frac{1}{4}$ to $\frac{1}{2}$ fat to flour
$\frac{1}{4}$ to $\frac{1}{3}$ pt water to each lb flour (approx)
4 teasp baking powder to each lb flour
$\frac{1}{4}$ oz salt to each lb flour (2 teasp)

Beef or mutton suet may be used. Beef suet is softer than mutton and is generally considered to have a better flavour. A pale, well-clarified dripping may be used as a substitute for suet. The suet

N

surrounding kidneys is considered the finest as it has little skin and connective tissue round it.

As suet is too hard to rub in, it should be finely shredded or chopped. At the same time the skin and connective tissue can be removed.

Suet melts slowly during cooking and there is a possibility that the starch grains will be cooked before the fat has melted, giving a hard pastry. To avoid this, baking powder should be used even with half fat to flour: the baking powder helps to give an open, light texture. Suet pastry should be eaten hot because it hardens when it cools.

Owing to the slow melting of the suet a moist method of cooking gives the best results, as the dry heat of the oven hardens the dough. Steaming gives light, palatable results and by this method it is almost impossible to overcook the pastry.

Packet suet can be bought already shredded. This saves time in preparation and the slightly higher cost is negligible. It must be remembered that this suet has a proportion of starch mixed with it to prevent its clogging during storage, thus reducing the proportion of fat. Packet suet may be kept in a cool place for some time without difficulty, but if it is allowed to become warm it will go rancid. Butcher's suet should be bought as required, as it goes rancid or sour quickly.

Recipe for Suet Pastry

1 lb plain flour
$\frac{1}{2}$ oz baking powder (4 teasp)
$\frac{1}{4}$ oz salt (2 teasp)

4–8 ozs suet
$\frac{1}{4}$–$\frac{1}{3}$ pint water

Method

1. Sieve the flour, salt and baking powder together.
2. Shred the suet finely, removing all skin and connective tissue. A little of the flour sprinkled on the suet during chopping will prevent the fat from sticking to the knife.
3. Add the suet to the flour.
4. Add the water all at once, sprinkling well over the surface.
5. Mix with a round-bladed knife until large lumps are formed.
6. Draw together with the fingertips to form one lump.
7. Knead lightly with the fingertips on a lightly floured board until the dough is even in texture and smooth on the side against the board.
8. Turn the smooth side of the ball uppermost. Roll out to the shape required and about $\frac{1}{4}$ inch in thickness.

Uses for Suet Pastry

Meat and Vegetable Pudding ⎱
Steak and Kidney Pudding ⎰ see section on meat.

Steamed Fruit Pudding ⎫
Syrup Layer Pudding   ⎬ see section on hot puddings.
Jam Layer Pudding   ⎪
Delaware Pudding   ⎭

WHAT WENT WRONG—AND WHY

Small lumps of undissolved suet appear in the cooked pastry

(*a*) The suet was not chopped or shredded sufficiently finely.
(*b*) The pastry was cooked too quickly and suet had not melted.

The pastry is hard and tough

(*a*) Insufficient baking powder was used.
(*b*) The pastry was cooked too quickly.
(*c*) The pastry was baked instead of steamed.

The pastry is sad and very solid

(*a*) Too little or no baking powder was used.
(*b*) The pastry was inadequately protected from condensed steam or water and became wet during cooking.

SHORT PASTRY

Proportions

$\frac{1}{2}$ fat to flour
2–3 ozs (approx $\frac{1}{8}$ pt) water to each pound of flour
$\frac{1}{4}$ oz salt to each pound of flour

Butter, margarine, lard or vegetable fats may be used. A mixture of fats is the most satisfactory, and the inclusion of a little butter gives a very superior flavour.

Dripping or bacon fat can be used, but care must be taken or the flavour will be too strong, especially for sweet dishes. Lard, being a pure fat, gives a " short " crisp texture, but also, being soft, tends to melt while being rubbed in and so makes the pastry tough. For this reason a mixture of fats is more generally used.

The short crispness of this pastry depends very largely on how it is handled. Coolness and very light fingertip handling are essential. The fat is rubbed in until no lumps remain and it is of fine bread-crumb-like texture. The hands should be lifted up well above the bowl so that air is incorporated into the mixture during the rubbing in. If the fat is hard this may take several minutes.

The addition of the liquid is very important; it should be sprinkled over the surface and added all at once. Gradual addition gives an uneven texture and this is often the cause of blisters in the pastry when it is cooked. For small amounts of pastry, a safe way is to use one teaspoonful of water to each ounce of flour. Too much water will give a tough pastry, as the flour will not absorb the fat, but exact quantities cannot be given because of the variations in the extraction of flour.

Once the liquid has been added, the mixture should be cut with a round-ended knife to distribute the liquid as evenly as possible and to draw the crumbs together. When large lumps are formed they should be drawn together with the fingertips to form a ball.

The kneading of the dough is important too. This must in no way be confused with the kneading of bread. In the case of pastry, it is done with the fingertips only, drawing up the edges into the centre very lightly to give a smooth even dough. When a batch of pastry is made, of which only a portion is cut off for a particular dish, the *cut* side of the pastry should be placed uppermost and the pastry rekneaded into the shape that will be required when finished. This will allow the pastry to be rolled evenly and easily.

The rolling is very important. Poor rolling can be the cause of toughness and blistering. The dough should be rolled with short sharp strokes straight forward. The minimum of flour should be sprinkled over the board and rolling pin: excess of it upsets the proportion of fat to flour. To maintain the shape required, the pastry should be turned round, not rolled sideways. It must never be turned over as this leads to toughness.

When the pastry has been rolled to the shape and size required, it must be allowed to stand in a cool place, for at least ten minutes before it is cooked. This allows the gluten, which has been stretched during the mixing and rolling, to relax. If the gluten is not allowed time for the " relaxation " the pastry will shrink badly while cooking.

Short pastry should be put into a hot oven, 425° F, about half way up the oven or slightly above. At this temperature the fat is melted and the starch grains burst and absorb the fat. As soon as the pastry has set, the temperature should be reduced to 375° F or the dish lowered in the oven. Sufficient time must be allowed to drive off the moisture which is now in the form of steam. The smaller the dish the higher it can be placed in the oven and the shorter the time required for cooking.

The only satisfactory method of cooking other than baking is frying. This is done only for small dishes such as small savouries. The pastry should be rolled very thinly so that the quick cooking will not harden it on the outside before the inside is cooked.

Short pastry may be eaten hot or cold. It will keep for three or four days; hence baking may be done in a batch. If the pastry is to be kept it should be allowed to cool away from any draught and stored in a cool dry place.

Recipe for Short Pastry

1 lb flour
½ lb fat, butter, margarine, lard or cooking fat, or a mixture of any of these
¼ oz salt (2 level teasp)
⅛ pt cold water

Method

1. Sieve the flour and salt together.
2. Add the fat cut up into lumps.
3. Cover the fat with flour before beginning to rub in.
4. Rub in until no lumps of fat are left, incorporating as much air as possible while rubbing in.
5. Add the water, sprinkling over the surface of the flour.
6. Mix with a round-ended knife until large lumps are formed.
7. Draw together with the fingertips.
8. Knead on a lightly floured board until the dough is smooth, using fingertips only.
9. Form into the shapes required when finished.
10. Roll out, turning the pastry round so as to maintain the shape.

Some uses for short pastry

Pies, Pasties, Tarts, Apple balls, Rissoles, Pastry shells.

RICH SHORT PASTRY

This pastry is made exactly like short pastry; rather more than ½ fat to flour, e.g. 5 ozs fat to 8 ozs flour, may be used, and it is enriched with yolk of egg in the proportion of 2 egg yolks to each pound of flour. Rather less liquid is used because of the increase in fat. The total amount of liquid *including* the egg yolk is approximately 4 tbs to each lb flour.

The yolk of egg, being rich in fat, gives added shortness and crispness to the pastry. It is particularly suitable for flans, custard tarts etc., where the filling may cause ordinary short pastry to become hard and tough.

This pastry may be made plain or it may be sweetened with castor sugar. Allow 1–2 ounces of sugar to each pound of flour: more will make the pastry heavy. Fine grain castor sugar should be used as a coarse-grained sugar will cause a brown speckled appearance when cooked owing to caramelisation of the sugar during baking.

Owing to its similarity to plain biscuits this pastry is sometimes called biscuit crust. It should be baked more slowly than short pastry, starting it at 375 F. It is important to see that it is not baked too quickly, especially if " blind " baking for flans. " Blind " baking is the term used when pastry is baked in a tin or flan ring before the filling is added. The pastry is kept in shape by covering with greaseproof paper and then haricot beans or bread crusts are used as a temporary filling.

Recipe for Rich Short Crust

8 ozs flour	1 oz castor sugar
1 teasp salt	1 egg yolk
5 ozs fat	1–2 tbs water

CHEESE PASTRY

Proportions

$\frac{1}{2}$ to equal quantities fat to flour
$\frac{1}{2}$ to equal quantities cheese to flour
2–4 yolks of eggs to each pound of flour
Water to make up to $\frac{1}{8}$ pint with the egg to each pound of flour
$\frac{1}{8}$ teasp cayenne pepper to each pound of flour
$\frac{1}{4}$ oz salt to each pound of flour (2 level teasp)

This pastry is similar to rich short pastry with cheese added. The cheese should be very finely grated and added to the fat and flour after they have been rubbed in. If equal quantities of fat and flour are used great care must be taken not to rub in excessively, as this will make the mixture cohere before the addition of the liquid and so cause an uneven over-moist dough. The cheese should be as dry as possible so that it blends evenly and does not form lumps. Too much moisture in the cheese will give too wet a dough if the full amount of liquid is added. As in all cheese dishes, the addition of cayenne pepper greatly improves the flavour of the pastry, especially if it is to be used for cocktail or after-dinner savouries, which require to be " hot " and piquant in flavour.

Cheese pastry should be baked moderately slowly, 325–350° F, in the centre of the oven. Like biscuits it needs to be dried out rather than baked, especially if cut into small biscuits or straws.

Recipe for Cheese Pastry

8 ozs flour	1–2 tbs water
5 ozs fat	1 egg yolk
4–5 ozs grated cheese	$\frac{1}{8}$ teasp cayenne
1 teasp salt	

Uses for cheese pastry

As a covering for savoury pies and pasties.
For savoury flans.
As biscuits forming the basis for canapés.
As straws or twists.

WHAT WENT WRONG—AND WHY

The pastry is too short and crumbly

(*a*) Wrong proportions were used, probably too much fat.
(*b*) Too little water was added.

The pastry is tough and hard

(*a*) The wrong blending of fats was used.
(*b*) The fat was melted during the rubbing in process.
(*c*) Too much water was added.
(*d*) The pastry was badly or over-kneaded.
(*e*) The pastry was rolled heavily.
(*f*) The pastry was turned over and rolled on both sides.
(*g*) Too much flour was used in rolling out.
(*h*) The pastry was cooked too slowly.

The pastry is rough or flaky in appearance

(*a*) The fat was insufficiently rubbed in and left in lumps.
(*b*) The water was unevenly mixed in.
(*c*) Too much flour was used when rolling out.

The pastry is blistered

(*a*) The fat was insufficiently rubbed in.
(*b*) The water was added unevenly or too gradually.
(*c*) The pastry was insufficiently kneaded.
(*d*) The pastry was re-rolled.
(*e*) The pastry was cooked too near the top of the oven.

The pastry has shrunk when cooked

(*a*) The pastry was stretched when rolled out.
(*b*) The pastry was stretched when being shaped.
(*c*) Insufficient time was allowed for relaxation of the pastry.

Rich short pastry has a speckled appearance

(*a*) Too much sugar was used.
(*b*) Sugar was coarse-grained.
(*c*) The pastry was baked in too hot an oven.

Cheese pastry has a rough appearance

(a) The cheese was coarsely grated.

(b) The cheese was not mixed coolly with the flour mixture.

(c) The pastry was put into too hot an oven, causing the cheese to melt and bubble out before the starch grain was cooked.

ROUGH PUFF PASTRY

Proportions

$\frac{1}{2}$–$\frac{3}{4}$ fat to flour

$\frac{1}{3}$ pt cold water to each pound of flour (approx)

$\frac{1}{2}$ teasp lemon juice to each pound of flour

$\frac{1}{4}$ oz salt to each lb of flour (2 level teasp)

Fats similar to those given for short pastry may be used. As with short pastry, a little butter greatly improves the flavour and colour of the finished pastry. If two or more fats are mixed and are of unlike texture they should be creamed together first, and the creamed fats formed into small lumps the size of a walnut. If the fat has become rather soft it should be allowed to cool in a refrigerator or larder before being added to the flour.

The fat is added to the flour in lumps and is not rubbed in. The water and lemon juice are added straight away and the flour mixed with a round-ended knife until a slightly soft dough is formed. The fat should be left in lumps rather than cut up during the mixing. The lemon juice is added to give greater elasticity to the gluten and to counteract the fattiness of the pastry.

The dough should be drawn together very lightly with the finger-tips but should not be kneaded. It should then be formed into a rectangular shape and rolled out into a long thin strip, care being taken not to force the fat to break the surface of the dough. This would make the dough difficult to handle and spoil the pastry. It is very important that the ends of the pastry should be kept straight and the corners square so that when the dough is folded it is of even thickness. The dough should then be folded into three, envelope-wise, and given a half turn on the board. The rolling and folding should then be repeated three or four times until there are no lumps of fat in the pastry. This rolling and folding distributes the fat, forming slightly uneven layers of fat between the flour and water paste. When the pastry is cooked the starch grains absorb the melted fat and the pastry rises in rough flakes. If the rolling and folding is uneven the pastry will rise unevenly, and a tough pastry will result.

In order that the starch grains may absorb the fat before it runs out this pastry should be put into a hot oven, 450° F, halfway or a little above halfway up in the oven. After the pastry has " set " the heat should be reduced to 375° F.

Recipe for Rough Puff Pastry

½ lb flour
1 level teasp salt
4–6 ozs fat (lard, margarine or butter)

6–8 tbs water
¼ teasp lemon juice

Method

1. Sieve the flour and salt together.
2. Cream the fat until it is even in texture, then form it into lumps about the size of a walnut.
3. If the fat is soft cool until it becomes firmer.
4. Add the fat in lumps. Do not mix.
5. Add the water and lemon juice.
6. Mix with a round-ended knife until large lumps are formed.
7. Draw together with the fingertips.
8. Put on to a lightly floured board, shape into a rectangle.
9. Roll out into a long strip, being very careful to keep the ends straight and the corners square. Size approx. 18″ × 6″.
10. Fold into three, envelope style; check the corners carefully to see that they are square and even.
11. Half turn on the board.
12. Re-roll and refold 4 times; leave to " relax " for 20 minutes.

This pastry is then ready for use. It may be kept for at least 24 hours if it is wrapped in waxed or greaseproof paper or a plastic bag, and stored in a cool place. For use the pastry should be rolled to ¼–⅜ inch thick depending on the type of dish being made. After the pastry has been shaped or cut out for use it should be allowed to relax the second time, for at least ten minutes, immediately before baking.

Some uses for Rough Puff Pastry

Steak and kidney pie
Meat and vegetable pie
Sausage rolls
Savoury pasties
Mince pies
Eccles cakes
Banbury puffs
For What Went Wrong see Flaky Pastry.

FLAKY PASTRY

Proportions

$\frac{2}{3}$ to $\frac{3}{4}$ fat to flour

$\frac{1}{3}$ pt cold water to each pound of flour (approx)

$\frac{1}{2}$ teasp lemon juice to each pound of flour

$\frac{1}{4}$ oz salt to each pound of flour (2 level teasp)

Half butter, half margarine gives the most satisfactory mixture for this pastry, taking into account cost as well as the flavour and texture of the finished pastry. The fats should be well creamed together to obtain an even texture; they should then be allowed to cool and harden.

A quarter of the fat may be rubbed into the flour or a dough may be made with the flour, water and lemon juice only. The latter method often gives the better results because this dough may then be kneaded very well on a lightly floured board. The kneading should be done as for a bread dough, not the fingertip kneading that is used for short crust pastry. This helps to develop the gluten. If the gluten is well developed, with the help of the lemon juice it will become very elastic. This means that it will stretch and form thin even layers.

When the dough has been kneaded until it is smooth and even in texture it should be rolled out into an oblong and one third of the fat put on to two thirds of the dough. The fat is put on in small knobs evenly over the two thirds. The dough which is free of fat is then folded over the middle third and the last third is folded down envelope style. This means that there are three layers of dough with two layers of fat sandwiched between and interspersed between the fat is cold air.

The edges of the dough should be sealed by pressing with the rolling-pin so that this air is entrapped. The dough is given a half turn and then pressed in ridges with the rolling-pin two or three times to distribute the air evenly before re-rolling. The process is repeated twice to incorporate all the fat. During the rolling, great care must be taken not to force out the air by rolling over the edge, and also to prevent the fat pushing through the dough. The edges should be kept straight and the corners square to ensure even thickness when folding. When all the fat has been incorporated the pastry should be allowed to relax for at least ten minutes in a cool place.

The pastry is then rolled and folded twice more and allowed to relax again. This pastry is then ready for use and can be rolled to the required shape and thickness.

Even rolling, straight sides, and square corners as well as careful folding are essential so that the layers are regular, giving even rising and flaking. To help the rising in the oven the folded edges of the pastry should be trimmed off with a sharp knife.

The method of baking flaky pastry is the same as for Rough Puff. During the baking the starch must absorb the fat and the air that has been incorporated during rolling will expand and cause the pastry to rise. The flakes of the pastry should be even. It is essential to allow sufficient time for the pastry to cook through and for the outside to become crisp and evenly brown. Once the pastry has set the oven temperature should be lowered to prevent over-browning.

If the pastry is not required immediately it may be prepared ready for the final rolling and shaping, then wrapped in greaseproof paper and stored in a cool place for 24–48 hours. It must be well protected so that moisture cannot escape, causing the outside to harden. It must be kept cool.

Recipe for Flaky Pastry

8 ozs flour
1 level teasp salt
6 ozs fat (butter and margarine)

6–8 tbs water
$\frac{1}{4}$ teasp lemon juice

Method

1. Sieve the flour and salt together.
2. Cream the fats until they are even in texture, and shape the mixture into a block. Allow to cool.
3. Add the water and lemon juice to the flour and mix with a round-ended knife into a dough.
4. Knead the dough on a floured board until smooth and even in texture.
5. Roll out into an oblong strip. Size 18" × 6".
6. Cut $\frac{1}{3}$ of the fat into small knobs and put evenly over $\frac{2}{3}$ of the dough.
7. Fold the fatless $\frac{1}{3}$ over the middle $\frac{1}{3}$ and the top third down envelope style.
8. Press the edges with the rolling pin to seal. Half turn the dough on the board. Press in 2 or 3 places to distribute the air.
9. Re-roll and add the second $\frac{1}{3}$ of the fat, fold and seal. Repeat to incorporate the final $\frac{1}{3}$ of the fat.
10. Let the pastry relax for at least ten minutes.
11. Roll and fold twice more. Allow to relax; the pastry is then ready for use.
12. When shaped, and before putting into the oven, the pastry should relax for the third time.

Some uses for flaky pastry

Steak and kidney pie	Mince pies.
Veal and ham pie.	Eccles cakes.
Meat and vegetable pie.	Banbury puffs.
Sausage rolls.	Vanilla slices.
Sweet and savoury patties.	

WHAT WENT WRONG—AND WHY

The pastry is too smooth and lacking in flakiness

(a) The pastry was not kept cool.

(b) The fat was too warm and blended with the flour instead of remaining in layers.

(c) The fats were not blended evenly before being added and so the softer fat was blended in the paste before the harder one was rolled in.

The pastry is hard and tough

(a) The fat and dough were rolled too long.

(b) The pastry was not kept cool.

(c) Too much water was added.

(d) Too much flour was used in rolling out.

(e) In flaky pastry the flour dough was badly kneaded.

(f) The oven was too cool and the fat ran out before the starch grains burst.

The pastry is hard outside and gluey inside

(a) Too hot an oven was used and the pastry was cooked only on the outside.

(b) The pastry was cooked too high up in the oven.

(c) The pastry was cooked for too short a time.

The pastry is unevenly risen

(a) The fat was unevenly distributed.

(b) Rolling was uneven.

(c) Owing to uneven shaping and folding of the pastry, the shape of the dough after each folding was not rectangular.

(d) The half turn after each folding was not made in the same direction each time.

(e) The edges were not cut off before using the pastry.

(f) Owing to insufficient relaxation of the pastry either between the rollings or before baking, the gluten was overstretched.

The pastry shrinks badly during cooking

(a) Owing to poor rolling and folding the dough was overstretched.
(b) There was insufficient relaxation between rollings.
(c) There was insufficient relaxation before cooking.
(d) The pastry was allowed to relax in too warm a place.
(e) The pastry was allowed to relax in a draught.
(f) The heat in the oven was uneven owing to being nearer the source of heat on one side, or the oven was not thoroughly preheated.

PUFF PASTRY

Proportions

Equal quantities of fat and flour
$\frac{1}{3}$–$\frac{1}{2}$ pt cold water to each pound of flour
$\frac{1}{2}$ teasp lemon juice to each pound of flour
$\frac{1}{4}$ oz salt to each pound of flour (2 level teasp)

Owing to the high proportion of fat, puff pastry is more difficult to manipulate than other kinds of pastry and more often gives indifferent results. Butter gives the best pastry, but, for economy, half margarine may be substituted. If a mixture of fats is used they should be creamed together to get an even texture before the pastry is made. Butter has a comparatively high water and salt content, both of which are detrimental to the texture and flavour of the pastry. In order to remove the salt, the butter should be cut into small pieces and washed in ice-cold water. It should then be put into a floured cloth and squeezed, to dry it. If the butter is kept cool the cloth will absorb the moisture and not the fat. The butter should be formed into a block about $\frac{3}{4}''$ thick and be allowed to cool.

There are several methods of making puff pastry, and in each case the object is to form even layers of flour dough, cold air and fat so that when the pastry is put into a hot oven the flour dough will absorb the fat and the air will expand and cause the pastry to rise.

The most widely known method of making puff pastry is to make a dough of flour, water, salt and lemon juice and knead it very well in exactly the same way as flaky pastry. When smooth and elastic, the dough should be rolled out to twice the length of the block of butter plus an inch each way. The fat is then placed on one end of the strip of dough half an inch from the edge, and the other half of the dough folded down to cover the fat. The dough should be half turned so that the two shorter open ends lie facing the worker, and rolled into a long strip. The dough is then folded in three, envelope style, and put into a cool place to relax for at least twenty minutes. The half turning, rolling and folding are repeated six times, allowing the pastry to relax for twenty minutes between alternate rollings. The pastry should then be left for at least thirty minutes before it is used.

This method is rather slow and the relatively large amount of handling does not improve the pastry. For these reasons the dough can be rolled a little longer, once the block of fat has been added, and " double folded " instead of using the envelope fold. A double fold is made by folding each end to the centre, then folding one half on to the other, thus giving four layers instead of three as in the envelope fold. By this means, the number of rolls and folds may be reduced from seven to four, but at least thirty minutes should be allowed between alternate rollings.

A third method of making puff pastry is to divide the flour into $\frac{1}{3}$ and $\frac{2}{3}$. The fat is rubbed into the $\frac{1}{3}$ of the flour and formed into a " shortbread paste ". This should be cooled. The $\frac{2}{3}$ of the flour plus the salt and lemon juice is made into a dough with $\frac{1}{3}$ pint cold water instead of the $\frac{1}{2}$ pint as in other methods. This dough is well kneaded until smooth and elastic. The consistency of both the fat paste and the dough should be alike. This is very important. The *fat paste* is then rolled out carefully into a strip and the flour dough into a block slightly less than half that size. The flour dough is placed on top of the fat paste and the latter folded over in half. This is a reverse of the process used in the two previous methods and is only satisfactory if the fat paste is kept cool. The mixture is then half turned and rolled into a long strip and double folded. It is then allowed to relax for twenty minutes. The rolling and double folding are repeated twice, after which the pastry is allowed to relax a second time. The rolling and folding are repeated once more and the pastry is then ready for use. This last method is quicker than the two former and gives excellent results if the fat paste is kept cool. It is not advisable to use this method on a very hot day.

When the pastry is made, it can be used as soon as convenient after thirty minutes of relaxation, but if preferred it can be wrapped in greaseproof paper and a cloth and kept cool for 24–48 hours.

In each method it is essential to keep the sides straight and the corners square so that the pastry will rise evenly. The results of carelessness in shaping are especially noticeable in puff pastry, as the paste rises more than in flaky pastry. Puff pastry should rise 6–8 times its height during cooking. As when making flaky pastry, the edges should be cut with a sharp knife which has been dipped in very hot water so that the dough is not dragged during this cutting process. If patties or vol-au-vents are cut using round or oval cutters, the cutters should be dipped in very hot water before they are used to stamp through the pastry. On no account must the cutter be twisted or dragged as this will spoil the even rising of the pastry.

When the patties or vol-au-vents have been stamped out they should be turned upside down and placed on a baking tray which has been wetted with cold water. The reason for turning the pastry upside down to cook is that the side which has been uppermost in the rolling shrinks more than the side against the table. Turning the patties upside down keeps their shape even.

All puff pastry should be cooked on baking sheets that have been wetted with cold water, as the very high fat content causes the pastry to burn underneath very readily.

The pastry should be allowed to relax for at least 30 minutes in a cool place after it has been cut to shape, and it is important that it is kept in a cool place out of any draughts. A draught may be the cause of the pastry rising unevenly or sliding over on its side.

Puff pastry should be baked in a hot oven preheated for at least 30 minutes to 475° F. When the pastry is put in the oven the temperature should be reduced to 450° F. The pastry should be cooked half way up the oven. Small pastry cases etc. take 10–15 minutes but larger patty cases or vol-au-vents require longer—up to thirty minutes. After the first 15 minutes the temperature should be reduced to 375° F.

Patty and vol-au-vent cases must be scooped out to remove any soft semi-cooked dough as soon as they are out of the oven.

Uses for Puff Pastry

Vol-au-vent cases
Patties, sweet and savoury
Vanilla slices

Mille Feuilles
Palmiers
Cornucopia

WHAT WENT WRONG—AND WHY

The pastry is hard and tough

(a) A poor quality fat was used.
(b) The rolling in of the fat was too heavy and too lengthy.
(c) The pastry was not kept cool during mixing or rolling.
(d) Too much water was added to the flour dough.
(e) The flour dough was badly kneaded.
(f) Too much flour was used during rolling and was not brushed off before folding.
(g) The oven was too cool and the fat ran out before the starch grains burst.

The pastry is badly risen

    (*a*) The flour dough was too stiff, insufficient water being used.

    (*b*) Lemon juice was omitted.

    (*c*) The flour dough was badly kneaded.

    (*d*) The fat was unevenly distributed.

    (*e*) The fat was too warm.

    (*f*) The rolling in of the fat was too heavy or too lengthy.

    (*g*) Sufficient relaxation of the pastry between rollings was not allowed.

    (*h*) Sufficient relaxation in a cool place was not allowed.

    (*i*) The pastry was cooked in too cool an oven.

The pastry is unevenly risen

    (*a*) The pastry was unevenly rolled.

    (*b*) The pastry was unevenly folded.

    (*c*) The sides were not kept straight.

    (*d*) The corners were not kept square.

    (*e*) The pastry was put to relax in a draught.

    (*f*) The pastry on the hotter side of the oven rose more quickly than that on the other, and tipping over resulted.

Patty or vol-au-vent cases are out of shape

    (*a*) The pastry was not turned over before cooking.

    (*b*) The pastry was not allowed to relax sufficiently after shaping.

    (*c*) The cutter was twisted instead of stamped straight down.

    (*d*) The cutter was not wet or not hot enough.

    (*e*) The oven heat was uneven.

HOT WATER CRUST PASTRY

Proportions

    To each pound of plain flour:—

        5–6 ozs lard
        2 level teasp salt
        1½ gills milk and water
        1 egg yolk (optional)

Method

    All pastries mentioned previously require coolness during mixing. This pastry, as the name suggests, requires entirely the opposite condition, for warmth is essential. All utensils should be warmed before use and the sieved flour and salt should be warmed in the mixing bowl.

    If home-rendered lard is used five ounces will be sufficient for every lb flour, but commercial lard or cooking fats require a larger amount as they contain a small quantity of water.

The fat and water should be heated gently until the fat has melted and then allowed to boil until a crackle is heard. Immediately this crackle is heard the liquid should be poured into a well in the centre of the flour, and mixed quickly with a wooden spoon. The heat of the liquid partially cooks the starch grains, forming a glutinous dough. When the dough has formed into lumps and has cooled sufficiently to handle, it should be kneaded well, first in the warm bowl, then on a board. The dough should be kneaded until smooth. If yolk of egg is used it should be poured into the well in the flour after the hot liquid. Pastry made with the egg is more palatable and keeps longer than when the egg is omitted, but it will crack more readily. The dough will be soft and pliable but rather rough in appearance, and should be kneaded until it is quite smooth and free from cracks. The kneading action is similar to that used for the flour dough of puff or flaky pastry. It is softer than other pastry doughs and feels greasy in comparison with the other varieties.

The pastry should be raised or moulded while tepid but still pliable. A part of the dough must be kept back for the lid and it should be kept in the bowl covered with a cloth.

To Raise a Pie

A. Over a jar

1. Grease and flour an upturned jar with straight sides.
2. Roll out the pastry to $\frac{1}{4}''$ thick, leaving a small portion (approx $\frac{1}{6}$) for the lid.
3. Lay the pastry on the base of the jar, keeping the rolled side uppermost. See that the pastry is evenly placed over the base of the jar.
4. Press the pastry to the sides of the jar without stretching.
5. Keeping the thumbs on the top, mould the sides with the fingers while turning the jar round. Press the pastry so that it gradually works down the sides of the jar to the required depth. It is important to keep the thickness of the pastry even both on the base and sides of the jar.
6. The finished pastry should be $\frac{3}{16}''$ thick and should be of even depth down the sides of the jar with no additional thickness where the base and sides meet.
7. Leave to set until quite cold.
8. When cold, turn the jar, open end upwards, and hold about $\frac{1}{2}''$ away from the pastry board.
9. Using a round-ended knife, ease the pastry away from the jar, allowing its weight to pull it away from the base of the jar.

10. Pack tightly with the chosen filling, making sure to keep the shape of the pie. A firm row of filling should be packed at the point at which the sides and base meet.
11. Roll out the pastry for the lid to $\frac{3}{16}''$ thickness.
12. Damp the edges of the pastry of both the pie and the lid.
13. Cover the filling with the lid and press the two edges of pastry together.
14. Trim off any surplus edge with a pair of scissors and use the trimmings to make leaves for decoration.
15. Flute the edges of the pie.
16. Make a hole in the centre of the lid and arrange leaves of pastry round.

B. In a cake-tin or raised pie-tin

1. Grease the tin heavily.
2. Roll out the pastry to $\frac{1}{4}''$ thickness, reserving about $\frac{1}{8}$ for the lid.
3. Fold over lightly in $\frac{1}{2}$ and then in $\frac{1}{4}$, leaving as a wedge shape.
4. Drop the point of the pastry into the centre of the mould.
5. Shape carefully to the sides, pressing away from the centre to get rid of air pockets.
6. When the base is covered, mould the side of the pastry to the tin, keeping the four fingers of both hands in the tin and moving the tin round with the thumbs, which are on the outside.
7. Pack in the filling as before.
8. Roll the lid to $\frac{3}{16}''$—damp the edges of both the pie and the lid.
9. Cover the filling with the lid, press the two edges of pastry together. Trim and decorate the edges.
10. Make a hole in the centre of the lid and arrange the pastry leaves round it.

Baking Hot Water Crust Pastry

1. Pin a " collar " of double thickness greaseproof paper round the pie or the tin. The paper should be greased if no tin is used. The collar should be $1''$–$2''$ deeper than the pie to protect the edges of the pastry.
2. Place in the centre of the oven preheated to 425°. After 20 minutes reduce the heat to 350° and cook for 2–2½ hours or until the meat is tender.
3. When the pastry is well set, i.e. after about 1½ hours, unpin the collar or remove the pie from the tin and brush over with yolk of egg and water.

4. Return to the oven to finish baking.

   If the pastry becomes too dark in colour, cover with paper during the last stages of cooking.

Uses of Hot Water Crust Pastry

Pork Pie, Game, Rabbit, Steak & Kidney and Veal & Ham Pie. See section on Meat for fillings.

WHAT WENT WRONG—AND WHY

The pastry is dry and brittle and will not mould

(*a*) Insufficient fat was used.

(*b*) The fat and water were too cool when added to the flour.

(*c*) The dough has cooled before being kneaded.

The pastry sticks to the jar or tin

(*a*) The jar was insufficiently greased *and* floured.

(*b*) The tin was insufficiently greased.

The pie crust collapses when removed from the jar

(*a*) The pastry was too warm.

(*b*) The pastry was too thin.

The pie bursts after it has been filled or during cooking

(*a*) The crust was unevenly moulded and too thin in parts.

(*b*) The meat was pushed through the crust during the filling.

The lid of the pie separates from the sides during cooking

(*a*) The two edges were insufficiently damped before joining.

(*b*) The two edges were not moulded together sufficiently.

CHAPTER XXIII

INVALID COOKERY

A STUDY of diets required for special diseases is quite beyond the scope of this book; it is, in fact a highly specialised subject, needing a long training in Dietetics. But every household has, from time to time, someone who is not able to take the normal meals provided for the rest of the family.

If a doctor has been consulted, it is essential that his instructions are carried out carefully. Often, however, the doctor orders " liquids " or " no solids " or " a light diet " without giving further details. In many cases of slight indisposition, the doctor is not consulted at all, but it is obvious that the sick person cannot take normal food.

Broadly speaking, whenever there is any sign of fever, that is, when the temperature is above normal, a liquid diet should be followed. This should consist of diluted fruit juices such as orange-ade or lemonade, apple water, diluted blackcurrant juice and milk. These drinks should be sweetened with glucose, which can be absorbed directly into the blood stream and so provide nourishment without requiring digestion. Honey is almost as easily digested as glucose, and, if the flavour is palatable to the invalid, provides a variety.

The fruit juices supply Vitamin C which is necessary to help to clear the blood stream of the effects of the illness. If there is sickness or stomach disorder, the fruit juices should be strained to remove all pulp, which may irritate the lining of the stomach. The fruit juices may be varied with strained broths, either meat or vegetable, with drinks made from meat or vegetable extracts and with weak tea.

Unless the doctor indicates otherwise, milky drinks may be given in moderation to a patient with a temperature, but often the patient prefers the flavour of fruit drinks or broths as these are more thirst-quenching and refreshing.

During the period of fever, a patient should drink at least five pints of liquid each day, and in order to make sure that this amount is taken, a variety of drinks should be provided. A covered jug of cold liquid should be within easy reach of the patient, but, when the drink is hot, any that is not used at once should be removed.

This is because a drink allowed to become cold looks unappetising, and warm liquid, particularly broth, left uncovered would make a good breeding ground for germs. Consequently any left-over food removed from a sick room should be disposed of at once.

During a period of illness, there is some loss of strength in the body, and as soon as possible this must be restored. It is done by providing easily digested body-building foods such as milk, eggs, white fish or poultry. These foods also supply mineral elements, notably calcium, which are beneficial during convalescence. The most easily digested body-builder is milk; consequently the first food to introduce is milk which can be varied by flavourings such as cocoa or chocolate, malted milk and meat or vegetable extracts. People who do not like milk to drink will often take it if thin split toast or toast fingers or semi-sweet biscuits are served with the drink. If these are nibbled slowly they are readily digested.

Milk puddings, junket and moulds make a welcome change from liquid milk. Eggs, if lightly cooked, are readily assimilated, but should be cooked without fat as fat takes a long time to digest and most people in bed find greasy food unappetising. Most patients, unless forbidden eggs, enjoy an " Egg Nog " (see p. 408) which is the most easily digested of all egg dishes.

When the patient is able to digest solid food white fish or poultry is the next food to introduce, and again a method of cooking without fat should be chosen, such as steaming or baking in milk. Oily fish such as herrings or salmon, though more nourishing than white fish, are too difficult for a person in bed to digest. The strong flavour and smell, too, are unacceptable.

The best cuts of meat are the most tender and are therefore most readily absorbed by the body and may be introduced gradually into the convalescent's diet if cooked so that they are easily digested. Steamed or grilled chops and steaks, simple non-greasy stews and mince are acceptable.

The appetite of a sick person is usually capricious and care must be taken to provide a variety of attractive meals so that there is no occasion for peevish appetite. Meal times assume great importance to the person in bed, probably because there is little else to think about. As food must be taken in very small quantities, a desire for frequent small meals is characteristic. Therefore, small portions of food or drink should be served frequently, and as attractively as possible. The meals should be dished carefully, china, glass and linen being scrupulously clean and put on to a tray which is large enough to make eating easy. If condiments are permitted, they should be on the tray and small enough not to look out of place. Coloured fireproof dishes are useful for invalids; covered marmite pots for serving soup or broth; cocottes, soufflé dishes, or the small sized earthenware entrée dishes being useful for individual helpings. Served complete in this way, the invalid's meal looks much neater and more attractive than if the portion is taken from a large dish and put on the plate. It is much easier to garnish a complete dish than a single portion, and the garnish is particularly important when serving meals to a patient in bed.

When a patient has reached the late stage of convalescence, meals must be carefully balanced. All the necessary food constituents must be provided, but they must be chosen from the more readily digested foods, and a method of cooking chosen to preserve the nourishment. Fruit and vegetables are important as they provide roughage to keep the alimentary tract working satisfactorily, but the more fibrous vegetables should be sieved or avoided altogether until convalescence is well advanced, in order to avoid irritation of the tract. In cases of diarrhoea, all fibrous matter must be avoided until the condition is cured.

Suggestions for Invalid and Convalescent Meals

	Invalids	*Convalescents*
Soups . .	Broths, strained if necessary. Consommés.	Cream soups; unstrained broths.
Fish . .	Steamed white fish, filleted, no sauce.	Steamed or baked steaks or fillets of white fish served with parsley, egg or melted butter sauce.
Meat . .	Beef tea. Fresh meat (minced). Steamed or boiled chicken or rabbit. Stewed sweetbreads or tripe.	Steamed or grilled chop or steak. Stewed or minced liver. Fresh mince, steamed, baked or roast chicken or rabbit. Tripe. Sweetbread stewed or braised.
Eggs . .	Baked, scrambled, coddled.	In any form except fried or hard-boiled.
Vegetables .	Creamed potato, sieved spinach, sprouts or carrots.	Creamed potato, sieved vegetable, tomatoes without skin or pips. Whole boiled potatoes gradually introduced, cauliflower, fresh green peas, asparagus.
˙s . .	Fruit purées, jellies, milk puddings and moulds, custards, ice cream, lemon soufflé, honeycomb mould.	Fruit fool, trifles, fruit creams, all puddings with a custard base.
ˉead	Toast, split or melba toast. Semi-sweet biscuits. Sponge fingers.	Sponge sandwich, madeira cakes. Home made biscuits such as Shrewsbury or shortbread.

Recipes for Invalid Dishes
Apple Water

2 red apples
½ pint water
1 oz sugar
Strip of lemon rind or the juice of ½ lemon

Method

1. Wash the apples; cut up into pieces including the peel, pulp and core.
2. Put into a jug with the lemon peel and sugar.
3. Add the boiling water. Stir well.
4. When cold add the lemon juice and strain.

Barley Water

1 oz pearl barley	Flavouring
1 pint water	Rind of 1 lemon or rind and
Sugar to taste	juice of 1 lemon

Method

1. Wash the barley. Put into the pan with the water and, if permitted, the very thinly peeled rind of the lemon.
2. Bring to the boil.
3. If required as a cooling drink, strain at once over the sugar and lemon juice. Serve hot or cold.
4. If required as a soothing drink for complaints of the digestive tract, stew for 1 hour, strain and sweeten.

Barley water keeps for a few hours only.

Beef Tea

1 lb lean juicy meat
1 pint cold water
Seasoning to taste if permitted

Method

1. Remove any fat, skin or gristle.
2. Using a sharp small knife, scrape the meat until it is all in fine shreds, or mince finely, taking care to collect all the juice.
3. Soak the shreds and juice for 1 hour in an earthenware jug or basin, keeping the jug covered to protect from dust.
4. Put the jug in a pan with sufficient water to come ½ way up.
5. Boil the water for 2–3 hours, stirring the contents of the jug occasionally.

6. Strain the beef tea, season and allow to cool.
7. When cold, remove any traces of fat and reheat before serving. *Do not reboil.*
8. Serve as it is or with melba toast or fingers of toasted bread.

This liquid may be used to make a custard, following the recipe for steamed custard (p. 203) using the beef tea in place of milk, and omitting the sugar.

Egg Flip

1 egg
½ pint milk
1 teasp sugar

Flavouring such as nutmeg,
vanilla or sherry

Method

1. Separate the yolk of the egg from the white.
2. Mix the yolk of egg with the sugar.
3. Heat the milk and pour over the egg. Strain and flavour.
4. Whip up the white until it froths but is not stiff.
5. Stir into the warm custard and serve at once.

Egg Nog

1 egg
¼ pint milk
1 teasp sugar
Sherry, brandy, vanilla essence or nutmeg

Method

1. Beat the egg and sugar with a little of the milk until all traces of ropiness are gone.
2. Heat the remainder of the milk to blood heat. Pour over the egg.
3. Strain into a tumbler and flavour as liked.

Invalid Fruit Tart (1)

¼ pint egg custard made from the yolk of the egg
1 piece sponge cake approx 3″ × 1½″

1 baked apple
2 tbs sugar

Cherries and angelica to decorate

Method

1. While the apple is hot, sieve to remove the skin and core.
2. Crumble the sponge cake in the bottom of 2 sundae glasses.
3. Cover with the custard while it is still warm. Allow to cool.

4. Make a meringue with the egg white and sugar.
5. Fold in the sieved apple pulp and pile on the sponge cake and custard.
6. Decorate with cherry and angelica.

Invalid Fruit Tart (2)

1 baked apple sieved   1 tbs sugar
⅓ pint milk   2 sponge cakes (3″ × 1½″)
1 egg

Method

1. Crumble the sponge cake in the bottom of a small pie dish.
2. Cover with sieved apple pulp.
3. Beat up the egg and sugar, pour over the warm milk.
4. Strain over the apple pulp.
5. Allow to stand to expel any air bubbles.
6. Bake in a slow oven as for a baked custard (325° F) until set and lightly brown (40 mins).
7. Serve hot.

Lemonade and Orangeade

1 lemon or 1 orange
½ pt water
1 oz sugar

Method

1. Remove the rind thinly from the fruit.   Take care to leave the white pith on the fruit.
2. Put the rind and sugar in a jug.
3. Pour over the boiling water.   Stir well and leave to cool.
4. Add the juice of the fruit.
5. Strain through muslin or a fine strainer.

Melba or Split Toast

Cut slices of stale bread very thinly.
Bake in a cool oven until pale golden brown and crisp.
Store in an airtight tin when cold.

Sweetbread Stewed

1 sweetbread (calf's or lamb)   1 tbs cream
½ pint white stock or milk   Lemon juice
¾ oz cornflour   Seasoning

Sweetbreads very soon lose their freshness so they should be used at once.

Method

1. Wash and soak for 1 hour in cold water to which salt (1 teasp to each pint of water) has been added.
2. Drain and rinse thoroughly, remove any membrane but do not break the sweetbread.
3. Simmer in the milk or stock for 45–50 mins.
4. Remove the sweetbread and keep hot on a small dish.
5. Make a sauce with the cornflour and stock, cook thoroughly and then add the cream.   Reheat but do not reboil after adding the cream.
6. Season with salt and lemon juice and pour over the sweetbread.
7. Garnish with lemon butterflies and a leaf of parsley.
8. Serve at once.

If the patient is convalescent, a little onion or a bouquet garni may be added to the liquor in which the sweetbread is stewed.   They should be removed before making the sauce.   Mushrooms may be stewed in the liquor and served as a garnish to the finished dish. After draining, the sweetbread may be broken into pieces, tossed in egg and fresh white breadcrumbs and fried in deep fat or tossed in seasoned flour and fried in butter.

These last two suggestions, though producing delicious dishes, are suited only to convalescents who are up and about; fried food is indigestible to people who can take no exercise.

Stewed Tripe (2–3 **portions**)

½ lb dressed tripe	½ pt milk
½ oz butter	seasoning and sippets of toast
½ oz flour or cornflour	

Method

1. Make a white sauce using the butter, flour and milk.
2. Cut the tripe into neat pieces and add to the sauce;   season if seasoning is allowed.
3. Simmer very gently for 30–40 mins.
4. Serve on a hot dish and garnish with triangular sippets of toast and a leaf of washed parsley.

If required for a convalescent a boiled onion may be chopped finely and added to the sauce as well as the pieces of tripe.   This improves the flavour but it would not be suitable for an invalid.

Fish or Tripe in Custard (2 portions)

1 egg
½ pt milk
¼ lb dressed tripe or 2 small
   fillets of fish

2 slices bread and butter
Seasoning

Method

1. Cut the bread and butter into squares and cut the tripe or fish into small pieces.
2. Grease a suitable dish; arrange the squares of tripe or fish and bread and butter in alternate layers, finishing with a layer of bread and butter.
3. Beat the egg and milk as for a custard.
4. Strain the custard over the tripe and bake in the middle of a moderate oven (325° F) until set (see Custards, pp. 206–7).

Fish, Veal or Chicken Cream

4 ozs white fish (haddock or
   whiting), minced veal or
   minced chicken
½ oz butter
½ oz fresh breadcrumbs
⅛ pt milk or veal or chicken
   stock

little lemon juice
1 egg white
Seasoning
1 tablespoon cream or un-
   sweetened evaporated milk

Method

1. Wipe and shred the fish *or* mince the chicken or veal.
2. Melt the butter, add the breadcrumbs and milk and cook until the mixture thickens.
3. Add the prepared fish or chicken or veal.
4. Pound well and rub through a sieve.   Season carefully.
5. Add the cream or evaporated milk and fold into the mixture the stiffly whisked egg white.
6. Pour the mixture into a greased basin or mould, cover with greased paper and steam fish cream gently from 20–30 mins; one hour if a chicken or veal cream.
7. When firm, turn on to a hot dish and coat with a good white sauce.
8. Garnish with lemon and parsley.

CHAPTER XXIV

FORCEMEATS, STUFFINGS AND MISCELLANEOUS RECIPES

FORCEMEATS AND STUFFINGS

Almond Stuffing for Chicken

4 ozs rice, cooked
2 ozs stoned raisins
1 oz almonds, blanched and pounded
1 small onion, finely chopped
1 tbs chopped parsley

the liver of the chicken, chopped
1 oz butter
sprig of basil, chopped
1 egg

Method

1. Mix all together, working the butter into the other ingredients.
2. Season well, and mix with beaten egg until it holds together.
3. Fill the body cavity with stuffing.

Almond, Apricot and Rice Stuffing

1 oz blanched and browned almonds, chopped
4 ozs rice, preferably long-grain
1 medium onion, chopped finely
2 ozs dried apricots, soaked for 1 hour in a very little water

1 oz stoned raisins
2 teasp chopped parsley
2 or 3 leaves of tarragon, chopped finely
$\frac{1}{8}$ teasp ground garlic
1 tbs olive oil
salt and black pepper to taste

Method

1. Cook the rice, strain and keep the grains separate.
2. Chop the apricots coarsely: there should be no surplus liquid.
3. Mix all the ingredients together, season carefully, using freshly-ground pepper if possible.
4. If used for chicken, the mashed raw liver can be added to the stuffing.
5. Fill the body of the bird with the stuffing, reserving enough to put into the crop end to make the bird a good shape.

412

Apple and Prune Stuffing

12 prunes, soaked, stewed and
  stoned
2 large apples, chopped roughly
2 ozs cashew nuts, chopped
6 ozs breadcrumbs

grated rind and juice of ½ a
  lemon
2 ozs melted butter
1 egg
seasoning

Method

1. Chop the prunes coarsely.
2. Blend all together to form a mixture which can be handled.

   Use for rabbit, pork or poultry.

Apricot Stuffing

2 ozs dried apricots
¼ pt water
1 oz butter or dripping
1 small onion, chopped
½ pt cubes of dry bread
1 teasp chopped parsley

⅛ teasp chopped tarragon
⅛ teasp chopped thyme
⅛ teasp grated lemon rind
½ teasp salt
⅛ teasp pepper
2–4 teasp apricot juice

Method

1. Soak the apricots in water overnight; simmer till tender.
2. Drain and save the juice.   Cut up the fruit.
3. Sauté the onion in the butter until tender but not brown.   Add
   the bread cubes and other ingredients and enough juice from
   the apricots to make the whole stick together.

   Use for poultry or pork or ham.

Chestnut Forcemeat

¼ lb chestnuts
2 ozs beef suet
¼ lb breadcrumbs

¼ lb sausage meat
2 teasp finely chopped thyme
½ teasp salt
¼ teasp pepper

Method

1. Score the chestnuts with a sharp knife.
2. Cook in boiling water for approximately 10 minutes *or* heat
   them in a frying pan with ½ oz fat for 4 to 5 minutes.
3. Remove the skins and peel.   Then pass nuts through a
   mincing machine and add to the other ingredients.
4. If dried chestnuts are used, soak 2 ozs overnight, boil for
   20 mins, drain and mince.
5. Season the mixture well and mix all together.

Pickled Walnut and Sage and Onion Stuffing

½ lb cooked, chopped onions, well drained
12 sage leaves, scalded and chopped
1 large apple, chopped coarsely
4 ozs breadcrumbs
6 pickled walnuts, cut into rough pieces
1 teasp lemon juice
1 oz melted dripping
1 egg, or cider to mix
1 teasp salt

Mix all together and use for goose, duck, pork or rabbit.

Sage and Onion Stuffing

4 large onions
¼ lb breadcrumbs
2 teasp powdered sage
1½ ozs butter or other fat
½ teasp salt
¼ teasp pepper
little beaten egg to bind

Method

1. Parboil the onions and chop finely.
2. Mix the ingredients well together and check the seasoning.
3. Use to stuff meat or bake in a well-greased shallow tin until it is firm and golden brown in colour.
4. Cut into squares and serve as required.

Sausage-meat Stuffing

1 lb sausage meat
½ pt breadcrumbs
1 teasp powdered thyme
1 teasp mixed herbs
2 teasp chopped parsley
¼ teasp salt
⅛ teasp pepper
little cayenne
1 egg

Method

Mix all the ingredients together and season well.

Stuffing for Tomatoes or Peppers

½ lb minced beef
2 ozs rice
¼ pt stock
2 tbs chopped dill or savory
1 oz dripping
2 tbs red wine
1 finely-chopped onion
¼ teasp pepper
1 teasp chopped parsley

Method

1. Melt the dripping and fry the onion until brown and cooked.
2. Add the rice and fry lightly.
3. Add the stock and cook until the rice is soft and the stock absorbed (10–12 minutes).

4. Add the remainder of the ingredients and knead into a firm ball. Test the seasoning.

Veal Forcemeat

¼ lb fresh breadcrumbs	⅛ teasp pepper
2 ozs finely shredded suet	little cayenne pepper if liked
1 tbs finely chopped parsley	little beaten egg or egg and
rind of ½ lemon, grated	milk
¼ teasp salt	

Method

1. Mix all the dry ingredients.
2. Moisten with a little egg or egg and milk and mix with a fork.
3. Using the tips of the fingers press the forcemeat together until it forms a ball.

Note When a forcemeat is required for fish, use butter or other soft fat instead of suet: the latter will not be cooked by the time the fish is ready.

Avoid making any forcemeat too moist.

MISCELLANEOUS RECIPES

Coffee

A good cup of coffee depends on the quality and freshness of the coffee and on the method of making. Whenever possible use the best quality coffee available. Buy freshly roasted and ground coffee beans or coffee that has been packed in vacuum-sealed tins. Good coffee cannot be made from poor quality beans or stale ground coffee. It is advisable to buy ground coffee in small quantities or in small-sized tins so that it does not stay in the store cupboard more than a few days.

The method of making coffee depends upon the equipment used. There are a number of types of special equipment or percolators on the market that make excellent coffee. If a special coffee maker is used the directions given should be followed carefully.

If no special equipment is used, coffee can be made using a china or glazed earthenware jug. A medium ground coffee should be purchased.

For each pint of finished coffee allow:—

1½–2 ozs of fresh ground coffee
1¼ pints water
⅛ level teaspoon salt

The coffee grounds will absorb the extra water.

Method

1. Heat the jug and put the measured quantity of water to heat.
2. Put the coffee and salt into the hot jug.
3. Pour over the boiling water and stand the jug in a warm place or in a pan of hot water.
4. Stir well and leave for 5 mins covered.
5. Pass a spoon through the surface crust and the grounds will fall.
6. Pour through a fine mesh strainer into a heated jug.
7. Keep everything hot to prevent the need to reheat: this spoils the flavour.
8. Avoid the use of aluminium or tin when making coffee: these spoil colour and flavour.

To serve white coffee

Heat an equal quantity of milk until the surface of the liquid is covered with small bubbles, but has not reached boiling point.

Serve the milk at once, as milk which has been kept hot for any length of time develops an unpleasant flavour. Boiled milk will also spoil the flavour of coffee.

To render fat for dripping

2 to 3 lbs trimmings of fat
½ pt (approx) cold water

Method A

1. Cut the fat into small even-sized pieces, removing all skin and any traces of lean meat left on the fat.
2. Put the fat into a strong deep pan and cover with cold water.
3. Bring to the boil and allow to boil rapidly, removing any scum as it rises to the surface.
4. Boil until the fat is soft and creamy and all the water is evaporated.
5. Reduce the heat, and continue cooking gently until the bits of skin are crisp and begin to sink to the bottom of the pan, and the surface of the fat is " still ".
6. Cool and strain through a clean kitchen towel or double muslin.
7. Leave to solidify.

Method B

1. Prepare the fat as for method A.
2. Put the fat into a roasting tin.
3. Put into the bottom half of a moderate oven, 350° F, or into an oven which has been used for roasting or baking and is

cooling, in the cool oven of a solid fuel cooker or on the cool hotplate of the same.
4. Cook until the fat has melted and the bits of skin are crisp and light brown.
5. Strain off the fat carefully. Leave to solidify.

This method gives a darker dripping than method A, but some people prefer the flavour.

To clarify dripping

1. Cut the dripping into pieces and put into a strong pan.
2. Cover with cold water.
3. Heat gently, whisking the contents thoroughly.
4. Allow to boil for 5 minutes. Whisk again. The whisking washes any impurities out of the fat.
5. Strain into a basin and allow to cool.
6. When cold remove the " cake " of fat, scrape the underside free of any sediment and put into a strong pan.
7. Heat gently until all bubbling ceases and the fat is almost at hazing point.
8. Pour into a warm basin or stone jar and allow to cool. This can be covered with tied-down parchment and stored in a cool dry place.

To clarify margarine or butter

1. Put the margarine into a pan.
2. Heat gently until it has melted. Continue heating gently until the salt has settled to the bottom of the pan and the margarine appears like clear oil above the precipitated salt. It should not be allowed to haze or discolour.
3. Strain through muslin into a basin.

Raspings

Trimming from bread, surplus pieces of cut bread or toast may be used.

1. Put the bread on to a baking tray and put into a cool oven until quite crisp.
2. Turn on to a dry board and crush with a heavy rolling pin *or* pass through a mincer.
3. Sieve the crumbs and store in an airtight tin.

Porridge (1)

2 ozs medium oatmeal   1 level teasp salt
1 pt water

o

Method

1. Heat the water in a strong pan or double saucepan. Add the salt.
2. Sprinkle in the oatmeal and stir very well.
3. Bring to the boil and stir well until it starts to thicken.
4. Put on the lid and simmer for $\frac{1}{2}$–1 hour. Stir frequently.
5. Add more boiling water if required to obtain a pouring consistency.
6. Serve with hot milk and salt or moist brown sugar.

Porridge (2)

2 ozs rolled oats   1 level teasp salt
1 pt water

Method

1. Put the water into a saucepan and add the salt.
2. Sprinkle in the rolled oats and stir very well.
3. Bring to the boil, stirring all the time.
4. Boil 5–10 minutes.
5. Serve with hot milk and salt or moist brown sugar.

Cooking Rice

The average home is unlikely to stock more than three of the many different kinds of rice, but it is worth while choosing the most suitable rice for the dish to be made. Use the long-grained Patna for the dishes where the rice is served as an accompaniment as with curries. This grain does not absorb much liquid and can be cooked so that every grain is separate. It can be used for pilaffs.

Italian rice is thick grained and is very absorbent. It is used for risottos and pilaffs and all dishes where the rice is cooked in stock.

Sweet dishes are made from the short blunt grain which comes from Carolina. It is absorbent and very white.

When cooked, rice almost trebles its bulk and $1\frac{1}{2}$–2 ozs per portion is an average allowance as an accompaniment to curry or as a basis for risotto.

There are many ways of producing well-cooked rice with dry separate grains: the following are reliable.

To Boil Rice

1. Wash the rice grains in several changes of cold water to remove surface starch.
2. Use a large pan with plenty of water, at least 2 pints to every 2 ozs rice.

3. When the water is boiling quickly, sprinkle in the washed rice and add 1 teasp salt to every 2 ozs rice.

4. Cook quickly without the lid for 5–15 mins according to the kind of rice used.

   This keeps the grains moving during the cooking and prevents their sticking to the pan.

5. Cook only until the grains are tender. To test, remove a grain of rice and split it between the finger and thumb. If soft all through, the rice is cooked. If uncooked a white speck will show in the centre of the grain.

6. Strain through a wire sieve or strainer. Stand in a warm place to dry. Serve hot.

If the quantity of water has been sufficient, there is no need to rinse the rice under cold water to separate the grains. If the grains do stick together, the rice may be rinsed by passing cold water through, but it must be reheated in the sieve, covered with a cloth, before serving.

Alternative Method

1. Measure the rice in cups. Allow 2¼ cups water to each cup of rice.

2. Boil the water, add salt and sprinkle in the washed rice.

3. Bring back to the boil, put the lid on the pan and *simmer* for 12–15 mins until the grains are tender.

4. Withdraw the pan from the heat, place a folded tea towel between the pan and the lid and leave in a warm place for a further 12–15 mins. By this time all the liquid will be absorbed and the grains separate and dry.

   For pilaff or stuffing use stock instead of water.

SANDWICH FILLINGS

The spreads for canapés given in the section on Hors d'œuvres and Savouries may be used for sandwich fillings. The following recipes are additional.

A. Savoury

Cheese Spread

2 ozs grated cheese
2 tbs milk
salt, pepper and cayenne

Method

1. **Heat** the milk to boiling point and remove the pan from the stove.

2. Add the cheese and stir rapidly until a creamy spread is obtained.
3. Season well and pour into a basin or jar.

Variations To the above mixture add one or more of the following:—

1. 1 tbs sieved sardine
2. 1 tbs chutney
3. 2 teasp chopped chives
4. 2 teasp chopped parsley
5. A clove of garlic crushed and infused with the milk
6. 2 teasp chopped celery

Cream Cheese and Nut Filling

4 tbs finely grated cheese
1 or 2 tbs finely chopped walnuts
a little finely shredded celery
salt, pepper and cayenne
1–2 tbs cream from the top of the milk or evaporated milk

Method

1. Mix the prepared nuts and celery with the cream cheese.
2. Add seasonings and sufficient cream or evaporated milk to make it a spreading consistency.   Use as required.

Egg, Water-cress and Lemon

2 hard-boiled eggs   juice of $\frac{1}{2}$ lemon
1 bunch water-cress   salt and pepper

Method

1. Chop the egg finely.
2. Wash the water-cress and pick off the leaves.
3. Chop very finely.
4. Mix all the ingredients together and season well.

Gherkin and Sardine Filling

3 or 4 sardines skinned and boned
2 hard-boiled egg yolks
1 oz butter
1 to 2 tbs mayonnaise
a little mixed mustard
      „   cayenne
      „   salt if required
1 or 2 tbs finely chopped gherkins

Method

1. Pound together the prepared sardines, egg yolks, mustard, mayonnaise and seasonings. Then rub the mixture through a fine sieve.
2. Cream the butter and add to the sieved mixture: test for seasoning.
3. Spread on to thinly cut slices of white bread; sprinkle the chopped gherkins over this and cover with thin slices of brown bread and butter.
4. Press well, trim if necessary, cut as required.

Madras Filling

3 hard-boiled yolks of eggs
1½ to 2 ozs butter
2 teasp anchovy essence or paste
a little cayenne pepper
a little chutney

Method

1. Pound together the egg yolks, chutney and anchovy flavouring, then rub through a sieve.
2. Cream the butter and add the sieved mixture.
3. Season well with cayenne and add a little salt if required.

Tomato Madras Filling

Omit the anchovy flavouring and the chutney and instead of these add 1 to 2 tablespoonfuls tomato ketchup. Add extra salt because of the absence of anchovy which is very salty.

Salmon and Cucumber

3 ozs cooked salmon   1–2 tbs mayonnaise
few sprigs water-cress   seasoning
small piece cucumber

Method

1. Remove skin and bone from salmon and flake it finely.
2. Chop the cress and cucumber finely and mix with the salmon, adding sufficient mayonnaise to produce a spreading consistency. Season well.

B. Sweet

Almond and Walnut

2 tbs finely chopped walnuts   1 teasp vanilla essence
2 to 3 tbs ground almonds   3 tbs apricot jam

Method

1. Rub the jam through a hair sieve.
2. Add the remaining ingredients and use for spreading on brown bread and butter.

Apple and Chocolate

1 dessert apple
1 oz sweetened chocolate

Method

1. Grate both finely and mix together.
2. Add a few drops of lemon juice if liked.

1 oz chopped dates *or*
1 oz chopped raisins *or* } may be substituted for the chocolate.
1 oz chopped walnuts

Ginger and Cream

2 to 3 ozs preserved ginger
2 to 3 tbs syrup from the ginger
approximately ⅛ pt cream

Method

1. Chop the ginger finely and moisten with a little syrup.
2. Spread this on to slices of bread and butter; then add a little whipped cream before covering with another slice of bread.

Nut, Raisin and Lemon Juice

2 ozs nuts
2 ozs stoned raisins
lemon juice to taste

Method

Chop the nuts and the raisins finely; add sufficient lemon juice to flavour well and to moisten the fruit and nuts sufficiently for spreading.

Pineapple and Nut

2 to 3 ozs canned pineapple drained of syrup
1 to 2 ozs pine kernels or other nuts
1 to 2 tbs whipped cream or cottage cheese
little castor sugar if liked

Method

1. Chop the pineapple and the nuts.
2. Add cream to moisten sufficiently for spreading. Sweeten as required.

Prune

½ lb well stewed prunes, drained of the syrup
¼ lb ground almonds
little vanilla essence or 1 tbs port wine
2 or 3 tbs whipped cream

Method

1. Remove the flesh from the stones of the prunes.
2. Chop them finely.
3. Add ground almonds and flavouring; then sufficient cream to moisten to a spreading consistency. Use as required.

CHAPTER XXV

PRESERVATION

Aim

In the preservation of food, the main points to be considered are safety for health, nutritive value and appetising appearance. To achieve this the housewife must consider the conditions that make fruit deteriorate and decay. Organisms that develop in fruit are not usually dangerous, as they are mainly moulds and yeasts. Vegetables and meats, however, are non-acid, and may be poisonous even after preparation if not carefully treated. The nutritive value varies according to the type of food and its condition when preserved, i.e. the nutritive value is at its height when the fruit is fully ripe. The appearance of the preserved food and the flavour are most important, and an attractive bright colour often indicates that the correct method has been used.

Causes of spoilage

Fruit and vegetables will decay if left to become over-ripe. For this reason they should be preserved in their prime condition before decay has set in. Sound fruit should be used and any parts damaged by bruising or birds or insects should be discarded. Decay may also be due to the development of micro-organisms; these are yeasts, moulds or bacteria. These, being living cells, require certain conditions for growth and, to preserve food, this growth must be prevented.

Yeasts are plant cells which float about in the air and grow best on sweet juicy foods, producing the flavour associated with fermentation. In warm conditions they will grow rapidly but are readily destroyed by heat above 120°–140° F. They develop very slowly or remain dormant below 70° F.

Moulds are tiny plants which feed on many foods; their spores float in the air and so the moulds are spread. To grow, they must have a moist condition, and although they are not so sensitive to heat as yeasts, they are killed by temperatures above 140°–160° F. Bacteria, which are the other harmful organisms, will cause food spoilage, especially of non-acid foods. They may produce poisonous substances, and for this reason it is very important that they should be destroyed. *Some can withstand fairly high temperatures, so that non-acid vegetables, meat etc., should not be preserved by bottling or canning unless a pressure cooker is used.*

BOTTLING FRUIT

The aim is to heat the jars of fruit sufficiently to kill the spoilage-organisms and to seal the jar with an airtight seal before it has cooled, thus preventing access of air to the food. There are several methods that can be employed, and the choice depends on the equipment available, the type of fruit, and the time at the disposal of the housewife.

Choice of fruit

This should be sound and in most cases just ripe.

The best fruit should be kept for bottling and the less perfect used for pulp, jam, jelly etc.

Gooseberries are best if green and firm.

Raspberries, strawberries and loganberries should be fresh, dry and free from maggots.

Plums should be ripe, but still firm and even in size; large varieties may be halved.

Windfall apples and thinnings may be bottled; also, the varieties that do not keep well can be solid-packed or pulped.

Pears should be fully ripe before bottling. Unripe pears should be stewed first and are always poorer in flavour.

Tomatoes should be bright red and firm.

Preparation of fruit

In most cases the fruit should be prepared as if for stewing. All stalks, leaves etc. should be removed and the fruit peeled if necessary.

All damaged fruit should be put aside, and where possible the fruit should be graded according to size.

Special points

Gooseberries should have a small slice cut off as they are " topped and tailed " to allow the sugar syrup to penetrate and to prevent the berry from shrivelling or splitting.

Stone fruit can be halved and the stones removed to get more in the jars.

Light-coloured fruit, e.g. apples and pears, will go brown very quickly when cut, so they should be peeled into cold water to which salt has been added ($\frac{1}{4}$ oz to each pint) or one Campden tablet dissolved in each pint of water.

Sliced apples may be plunged into boiling water for 1–2 mins. until just pliable but not pulpy, and then tightly packed into the jars. This " solid pack " allows more fruit to be packed into the jar.

" Solid pack " tomatoes should be plunged into boiling water for about 5 seconds, then peeled and packed whole, or halved or quartered, according to size. If cut, the cuts should be made where the faint marks appear on the skin. This will keep the seeds in, as the marks on the skin coincide with the divisions inside the fruit.

Sugar syrup

The sugar should be dissolved in water, using $\frac{1}{2}$–$\frac{3}{4}$ lb to each pint to give an average syrup. Apples require less sugar, $\frac{1}{4}$ lb to 1 pint being sufficient.

For tomatoes, allow 1–2 teaspoons salt and 1 teaspoon sugar to each 2 lbs tomatoes. With " solid pack " no water is required.

Bottles

These vary in size and type. The most usual are those with a glass lid and a screw metal band or with a metal top and a spring clip. Both have a rubber band which acts as a cushion for the top to fit on, to prevent the jar from leaking. The jar and the glass lid should be free from cracks and chips. The lids, whether glass or metal, should fit evenly on the jars. The rubber rings should be elastic, of the correct size, and free from holes. They should be boiled for 15 minutes before use.

The metal band and clip should hold the lid firmly in position. The bottles should be clean and well drained but need not be dry. Snap vacuum tops to use with 1 lb or 2 lb jam jars are treated like the preserving jars with metal tops and lids.

Packing

The fruit should be packed as tightly as possible without bruising or crushing it. It should be packed to the top of the jar before the liquid is added. Large pieces of fruit can be wedged down with a small wooden spoon. When the jar is filled with the liquid it should be tapped gently on a wooden board to release any air bubbles.

Fruit Grouped for Bottling

Group 1
  Soft fruit (normal pack)
  Gooseberries⎱
  Rhubarb   ⎰ for pies
  Apples, sliced

Group 2
  Soft fruit, tight pack
  Gooseberries⎱
  Rhubarb   ⎰ for dessert
  Stone fruit, whole
  Citrus fruits

Group 3
  Apples, solid pack
  Nectarines
  Peaches, halved
  Strawberries, soaked

Group 4
  Pears
  Tomatoes

Group 5
  Tomatoes, solid pack

Methods of Bottling

A. Quick Water Bath Method

Equipment required: a large saucepan with a false base of wood, cloth or paper, sufficiently deep to allow the jar to be covered with water. A fish kettle, bucket, or zinc bath may be substituted.

Method

1. Pack the jars with fruit.
2. Cover with hot liquid.
3. Fit on the rubber ring, top and screw band or clip.
4. Undo the screw $\frac{1}{8}$ turn.
5. Place the jars on the false base, not touching each other, and cover with warm water.
6. Raise the temperature of the water to approx 190° F in 25–30 minutes. There should be a slight movement on the surface of the water with no bubbles bursting.
7. Maintain at this temperature according to the chart.

Fruit				Time to maintain (*minutes*)
Group 1	.	.	.	2
„ 2	.	.	.	10
„ 3	.	.	.	20
„ 4	.	.	.	40
„ 5	.	.	.	50

B. Moderate Oven Method

Equipment needed: an asbestos mat, or a pad of newspaper or wooden rack, to put on the oven shelf.

Method

1. Heat the oven to 300° F and maintain for at least 15 minutes before use.
2. Warm the jars and pack with the fruit.
3. Fill with boiling liquid, put on the rubber rings and the tops, but not the screw bands or the clips.
4. Put the jars in the oven on the rack, allowing 2″ space round each jar.
5. Cook according to the number of jars in the oven and the time given below.
6. Remove one at a time and screw down or clip down.

Fruit				*Quantity in the Oven (minutes)*	
				(*a*) *1–4 lbs*	(*b*) *5–10 lbs*
Group 1	.	.	.	30–40	45–60
„ 2	.	.	.	40–50	55–70
„ 3	.	.	.	50–60	65–80
„ 4	.	.	.	60–70	75–90
„ 5	.	.	.	70–80	85–100

Cooling the jars

The jars should be removed carefully from the water bath or oven, the screw bands should be tightened and the jars left to cool on a wooden board, if possible without moving, for 24 hours. They should be kept away from draughts.

Testing the jars

The next day the jars may be tested for adequate sealing by removing the clip or screw band and lifting the jar carefully by the lid. If the jar is sealed the lid will hold the weight of the jar. If the lid comes off the sealing must be faulty. This may be due to :—

(1) A poor rubber ring.
(2) Uneven glass round the rim of the jar or top.
(3) Insufficient heat in processing.
(4) Insufficient time for processing.
(5) A cracked jar or glass top or chipped edge.

The jar must be re-processed or the fruit used up as stewed fruit. If the jar itself proves to be faulty do not use it for re-processing.

Labelling

The jars should be wiped and labelled with the type of fruit, whether in water or syrup and the date or year.

Storing bottled fruit

The jars when labelled should be kept in a dry cool place; if possible in the dark, as the fruit will fade if kept in the light.

The screw bands should be wiped clean and lightly greased and replaced, but not screwed too tightly.

The clips should be stored separately.

The jars should be inspected at regular intervals for mould or faulty sealing. In particular, this should be done during the first month of storage, as, if the jar has been under-processed, moulds or yeasts may develop.

The contents of such jars must be discarded.

VEGETABLE BOTTLING

The aim is to heat the jars of vegetables sufficiently to kill the spoilage organisms and to seal the jar with an airtight seal before it has cooled. Vegetables are non-acid, and some spoilage organisms are able to withstand comparatively high temperatures, so that a pressure cooker must be used or the vegetables must be processed for at least 6 hours at boiling point.

Choice of vegetables

As this is a somewhat expensive method of storing vegetables, it is best to choose those that have a short season and cannot be kept by simpler methods of storage, such as: Peas of the sugary type e.g. Lincoln, Thomas Laxton or Petits Pois. Broad beans, only special varieties—" Triple Whites ", " Threefold Whites " or " White Flowering Long Pod ". Other varieties will turn brown. Young carrots, beetroot and fresh or runner beans may be bottled if liked.

Preparation of vegetables

The vegetables should be sound and free from bruises. They should be well washed and prepared as for cooking, but carrots need not be scraped.

The vegetables should be put into boiling water in small quantities so that the water returns to boiling point within one minute. Allow 6 pints water to 1 lb vegetables. The same water may be used for six successive scaldings. This scalding removes the flavour of earth, sets the colour and prevents undue loss of Vitamin C.

The length of time for scalding depends on the vegetables used (see p. 431).

After scalding, the vegetables should be dipped at once into cold water, to stop the cooking and ease the handling.

The skins of carrots can now be rubbed off. The vegetables should be graded, cut into rings or diced as required.

Brine

Use 1 oz salt to each 2½ pints water.

Use block not table salt.

For peas, add 1 oz sugar to each 2 pints liquid used. Vegetable colouring can be added to peas and runner beans if liked as they lose colour in processing.

Bottles

These must be recognised preserving jars; jam jars will not stand the pressure. They must be sound, free from flaws as well as chips and cracks.

They should be washed, drained and left wet inside.

1 lb jars should be used when possible; if larger ones are used a longer time should be allowed for processing, 5 minutes extra for each additional lb.

Packing

Too close packing should be avoided, as the vegetables should be loose in the jar.

Method of bottling

A pressure cooker with a dial or control for *10 lbs pressure* is required.

1. Allow 1″ water in the cooker *above the trivet*. Put to heat.
2. Fill the packed jars with boiling brine, adjust the seal and turn the screw band ⅛″ back or use two clips at right angles to each other. Put the jars in the cooker.
3. Put on the lid of the cooker but leave the vent open.
4. Heat until steam issues from the vent and continue steaming for 7–10 minutes.
5. Close the valve and bring the pressure up to 10 lbs.
6. Process according to the chart. *Keep the pressure steady.*
7. Turn the heat down and cool the cooker *very slowly,* allowing at least 20 minutes to return to zero before opening the valve. Avoid overcooling, which causes a vacuum in the cooker.
8. Take out the jars carefully and stand on a wooden board. Screw tightly. Do not touch the clips.
9. Avoid draughts and leave to cool, if possible for 24 hours before moving.

Vegetable	Scalding Time (minutes)	Time for processing (minutes)
Asparagus . . .	2–3	30
Broad Beans . .	2–3	35
French, Runner Beans .	3 (simmering)	35
Carrots . . .	10–15	35
Peas	1–2	40

Testing the jars

In the same way as for bottled fruit.

Labelling and storing

In the same way as for bottled fruit.

If when opened there is any unpleasant smell or any sign of deterioration, the contents should be destroyed without tasting and should not be used for animal feeding.

JAM-MAKING

The aim when making jam is to produce a good colour, good flavour, a firm set and a jam which will keep.

Yeasts will cause fermentation, so their growth must be prevented. This is done by providing a high sugar content: 60% of the finished weight of the preserve should consist of the added sugar and only 40% of the finished weight should be fruit pulp.

Because evaporation takes place during the boiling of the fruit pulp and the sugar, the amount of fruit pulp left just before the addition of sugar is more than the equivalent of 40% of the finished weight. The amount of fruit pulp used when making 5 to 10 lbs of jam is 40% of the finished weight + ½ lb pulp e.g.

4½ lbs pulp + 6 lbs sugar = 10 lbs finished jam
2½ lbs pulp + 3 lbs sugar = 5 lbs finished jam

The amount of fruit and water required to produce the pulp varies according to the kind of fruit used and this is accurately shown in the recipes given.

The most satisfactory results are obtained when the quantity of finished jam is between 5 and 10 lbs.

Jam made in this way may be tied down with parchment or cellulose tissue covers.

If the sugar content of the jam is less than 60%, the jam must be stored in preserving jars and sealed like bottled fruit. Moulds will grow on the surface of the jam if there is condensation between the cover and the jam. To avoid this, cover the pots when very hot or when quite cold, *never* when warm.

Jam must be stored in a dry place.

Setting quality of jam

Pectin, which is found in most fruits, influences the set. Acid and sugar also play an important part, and there must be a balance in the ratio of acid, pectin and sugar. The higher the pectin content the more sugar can be used. Fruits with low content of pectin should have less sugar added. In over-ripe fruit the pectin undergoes a change and its setting value is lost.

The acid content varies but is usually high when the content of pectin is high. Fruits with a sharp flavour indicate a high acid content. The acid aids the extraction of the pectin into solution and the converting of sugar into a less crystalline form. If the acid or pectin content of the fruit is low it can be increased by the addition of lemon juice or other fruit juice rich in acid and pectin e.g. redcurrant, gooseberry, apple. Acid may be added in the form of citric or tartaric acid.

Selection of fruit

Choose fruit which has a good colour; it need not be perfect so long as the damaged parts are removed. Fruit unfit for bottling may be used. The fruit should be just ripe. It should be dry and not mouldy.

Method of making jam

1. Prepare the fruit as for stewing.
2. Allow the fruit to simmer with the water, the amount of which depends on the type of fruit: watery fruit requires very little, tougher-skinned fruit needs more.
3. Simmer until the fruit is soft and pulpy.
4. When the fruit is cooked, the sugar should be added and the mixture stirred until dissolved.
5. If whole fruit jam is desired, the sugar should be added to the fruit and the mixture allowed to stand overnight. It should be heated slowly until the sugar has dissolved.
6. The heat should then be raised to allow rapid boiling until setting point is reached.

Test for setting point

A. Weight test:

Weigh the pan before starting to make the jam.
Add the weight of the finished yield according to the recipe.

Boil down the fruit and water so that, together with sugar, it will be ½ lb heavier than the correct yield. When the sugar has been added, boil the mixture down to give the weight of the yield and the pan.

B. Thermometer test:

Heat the thermometer in water first. Boil the jam until it reaches 224° F: this is the setting point.

C. Plate test:

Put a teaspoonful of jam on a plate, cool for 1 minute. If the skin wrinkles on the surface, setting point is reached. This is a less accurate test than the other two.

Potting the jam

Pour the jam into warmed jars—if there are whole fruit or pieces of fruit in the jam, cool a little before potting to prevent the fruit from rising in the jars.

Fill the jars to the brim.

Cover with a wax circle, wipe off the edges and seal. This should either be done immediately or left until the jam is quite cold. On no account should the jam be covered while warm.

Covering the jam

(a) Cellulose tissue may be used, but it may be attacked by wasps. One side only should be damped and the damp side kept outside.

(b) Parchment paper is neat and protective, but since it is not transparent, it hides the growth of any mould that may form. It should be put on in the same way as cellulose tissue.

(c) Sticky paper tops are not recommended as they are untidy and encourage the growth of mould.

Storage

Jam must be stored in a cool, dry atmosphere, preferably in the dark as light causes loss of colour.

WHAT WENT WRONG—AND WHY

Jam is dark in colour and has little flavour

(a) It was over-boiled after the addition of the sugar.

(b) It was boiled too slowly for too long a time.

Jam is syrupy but not set

There was insufficient acid or pectin in the fruit. To correct this add lemon juice (2 tbs to every 4 lbs of fruit) and reboil the jam.

JAM RECIPES
To give 10 lbs yield

KIND	RECIPE	METHOD before sugar is added	TIME OF COOKING before sugar is added	APPROXIMATE TIME OF COOKING after sugar is added
Blackberry and Apple	4 lbs blackberries 1½ lbs prepared cooking apples ½ pt water 6 lbs sugar	Stew the blackberries in ¼ pt water till soft. Stew the apples in ¼ pt water till soft. Mix together.	Approx ½ hr Approx ¼ hr	Rapid boil 10–15 minutes
Blackcurrant	4 lbs blackcurrants 3 pts water 6 lbs sugar	Simmer gently and reduce the bulk by approximately ¼.	¾ to 1 hour	Rapid boil 2–5 minutes
Damson	4½–5 lbs damsons 1¼–2 pts water 6 lbs sugar (if fruit is wet keep water low)	Simmer gently. Remove the stones before adding the sugar.	½–¾ hour	Rapid boil 10–15 minutes
Gooseberry	4½ lbs gooseberries 1½ pts water 6 lbs sugar	Simmer gently till the skins are tender.	½–¾ hour	Rapid boil 5–10 minutes; longer gives deeper red colour
Greengage and Plum	6 lbs fruit 1 pt water 6 lbs sugar	Simmer gently till the skins are tender. Remove the stones.	½–¾ hour	Rapid boil 10–15 minutes
Loganberry and Raspberry	6 lbs fruit 6 lbs sugar	Simmer the fruit till tender.	15–20 mins	Rapid boil 5–7 minutes
Marrow	6 lbs prepared marrow Rind and juice of 4 lemons 3 ozs root ginger 6 lbs sugar	Cut the marrow into cubes. Steam until tender. Put in a bowl; add lemon and bruised ginger (tied in a muslin bag). Add the sugar and leave 24 hrs.	Steam about 20 minutes	Steady boil 1½–¾ hour until the marrow is transparent and the syrup is thick. No real set is obtained. Remove ginger before potting
Rhubarb	6 lbs rhubarb Juice of 6 lemons 2 ozs root ginger 6 lbs sugar	Cut the rhubarb into chunks. Sprinkle in the sugar and lemon juice. Stand 24 hours. Place in the pan plus ginger (tied in a muslin bag).	Nil	Boil rapidly 15–20 minutes. Remove ginger before potting
Strawberry (whole fruit)	7 lbs strawberries Juice of 2 lemons 6 lbs sugar	Put the fruit, lemon juice and sugar in a pan, heat slowly until sugar has dissolved.	Nil	10–15 minutes. Cool 3 minutes before potting

In blackcurrant jam the fruit is too hard

The fruit was not simmered with the water for long enough to soften the tough skins.

Fruit has risen to the top of the jars leaving jelly at the base

This tends to happen in whole-fruit jams owing to potting while the jam is too hot.

There are streaks of scum in the jam

The scum was stirred in. If a small knob of butter is added when the jam is finished it will help to disperse a little scum. Heavy scum should be skimmed off after boiling is finished.

There is mould on the top

It may be due to moisture getting between the cover and the wax circle, or to storage in a damp place or covering while warm.

The jam crystallises

There was a lack of acid in the fruit. This defect is difficult to rectify: when repeating with the same kind of fruit, add lemon juice, citric or tartaric acid.

JELLY-MAKING

The aim in making jelly is similar to that when making jam. In the absence of fruit tissue of any kind, the set of a jelly is sometimes difficult to obtain. Therefore only fruit with a good acid and pectin content should be used. Mixed fruits can be used to help the set or to improve the flavour and colour.

Selection of fruit

The fruit used should be just ripe. Damaged fruit unfit for bottling can be used if it is free from mould and decay, and is dry.

Preparation of fruit

Large stalks and leaves should be removed and the fruit washed if necessary.

Method

1. Put the fruit in a pan with sufficient water just to cover.
2. Simmer gently until the fruit is pulpy and the skins are soft.
3. Strain through a clean scalded felt jelly bag. A closely woven linen tea towel may be used as a substitute.

4. If the fruit used is one which gives a good set, the pulp may be returned to the pan after it has dripped for 20 minutes and re-stewed with half as much water as used for the first boiling. It should then be re-strained and allowed to drip for 30 minutes. Prolonged straining reduces the pectin quality in the juice.
5. The two extracts should be mixed and heated in a pan.

Addition of sugar

This is calculated to give a 60% sugar content. If the fruit used produces a good clot 1 lb sugar is allowed to each pint of juice. 6 lbs sugar + 6 pints juice should give a 10 lb yield of jelly.

Reduce the 6 pints of juice to 4 pints by boiling, add the 6 lbs sugar and boil the jelly rapidly until the weight is 10 lbs.

Skim off all the scum very carefully.

When making gooseberry or apple jelly, a deeper red colour can be produced by longer boiling with the sugar; and therefore the liquid is reduced less before the sugar is added.

Test for set

The weight test is the most reliable.

Potting

As jelly should be turned out to be served, straight-sided small jars should be used when possible. It should be potted immediately the setting point is reached, and the jelly poured slowly down the side of the heated jar to avoid air bubbles. The jars must be filled to the brim.

Covering

A wax tissue should be put on, and the jelly left to cool covered with a tea towel. It should be covered with a parchment cover when quite cold.

Labelling

The labels on the jars should indicate the type of fruit and the date, and any additional colouring used should be noted.

Storing

The jelly should be stored in a dry cupboard as for jams.

JELLY RECIPES

To give a 10-lb yield (this can only be approximate)

Kind	Recipe	Method	Time of Cooking before straining	Amount of Sugar	Approximate Time of Cooking after sugar is added
Apple or Crabapple	4 lbs prepared fruit 2–3 pts water *Flavouring* 1 oz, ginger or 10 cloves or rind of 4 lemons	Stew the fruit gently until really pulpy. Add the flavouring as desired during the stewing.	1 hour	1 lb to each pint of juice	10 minutes
Blackberry and Apple	4 lbs blackberries 2 lbs cooking apples (prepared) 2 pts water	Simmer the blackberries with 1½ pts water. Simmer apples with ½ pt water. Mix the extracts together.	1 hour ½ hour	1 lb to each pint of juice	10 minutes
Blackcurrant	4 lbs ripe blackcurrants 2½ pts water	Simmer the fruit in 1½ pts water, mash well. Strain for 10 minutes. Put the pulp back into the pan, add 1 pt water. Simmer ½ hour. Mix the extracts.	¾ hour ½ hour	¾ to 1 lb to each pint juice when both extracts have been mixed	2–5 minutes
Gooseberry	4 lbs green gooseberries 2–3 pts water	As for blackcurrant jelly.	¾ hour	As for blackcurrant	5 minutes
Loganberry	8 lbs fruit 2 pts water	Simmer until the fruit is tender.	¾ hour	1 lb to each pint of juice	10 minutes
Raspberry	8 lbs fruit	Simmer carefully until tender.	½ hour	1 lb to each pint of juice	10 minutes
Redcurrant and see page 465	6 lbs fruit 2 pts water	Simmer until the fruit is tender, using 1½ pts water. Strain for 10 minutes. Add ½ pt water to the pulp and simmer again. Re-strain. Mix the extracts.	¾ hour	1–1¼ lbs to each pint of juice when extracts have been mixed	1–2 minutes

WHAT WENT WRONG—AND WHY

The jelly is dull and cloudy

    (a) The sugar was dirty.
    (b) The jelly was squeezed through the jelly bag, instead of dripping gently.
    (c) A dirty jelly bag was used.
    (d) The jelly was boiled too rapidly as setting point was reached, and is therefore full of air bubbles.

There are streaks of white in the jelly

    Scum was stirred in or was not carefully skimmed off.

The jelly sets in the pan before there is time to pot it

    The acid content of the fruit was too high. This often happens with redcurrant jelly. More water should be used with the fruit *or* more sugar with the extract—1¼ lbs of sugar to each pint of juice should be allowed.

The jelly sets if potted in small pots but is watery in larger jars

    Jelly should cool quickly and set well. With large jars the heat is maintained for longer and the set is poor. A jar larger than 1 lb size should never be used unless no others are available.

The jelly will not set, and on storage forms crystals

    There was insufficient pectin and/or acid in the fruit. Reboiling with lemon juice or citric acid often helps.

Jelly is going dark at the top

    This is usually due to age or storage in the light, or in too warm a place. This is most common with apple and light jellies due to enzyme action.

Jelly is thick and syrupy but not set

    The fruit had too high an acid content and insufficient pectin. This can be improved by boiling for 5 mins. with a juice rich in pectin, e.g. juice from cooking apples, red or black currants, or lemon juice.
    The choice of juice depends upon the colour and flavour of the jelly. Jelly thus treated should be used up quickly.

MARMALADE

Marmalade is normally made from citrus fruits, sugar and water. Each part of the fruit is important. The rind gives oil which has a strong flavour, the pith and pips are very high in pectin, and the pulp is rich in acid and contains some pectin and flavour. Sometimes the pith is omitted as it has a bitter flavour.

Selection of fruit

Lemons and bitter oranges are rich in acid, but sweet oranges, grapefruit, and tangerines have much less; therefore it is usual to mix the fruits or add lemon juice.

Bitter oranges are the most popular but are in season only from January to March. The mixture of fruits can vary according to the flavour desired.

Allow 3 lbs fruit
6 pts water
6 lbs sugar
Yield 10 lbs

Method 1

1. Scrub the fruit well and scald it.
2. Peel the fruit and cut into 4 sections.
3. Shred the rind, cutting off the thick pith. Allow for the shreds to swell a little when cooked.
4. Put the rind and any acid necessary plus $\frac{1}{2}$ the water in a pan and simmer until the rind is well softened (about 2 hours).
5. Cut up coarsely the rest of the fruit, including the pith, and put in a pan with the remaining half of the water. Simmer with the lid on for 1–1$\frac{1}{2}$ hours.
6. Strain or sieve the pulp.
7. Mix the strained pulp with the peel.
8. Boil off any excess water until the weight is 4$\frac{1}{2}$ lbs (see p.431).
9. Add the sugar and boil until setting point is reached.
10. Skim and allow to cool a few minutes before potting.

This gives a medium thick marmalade.

Method 2

1. Scrub and scald the fruit.
2. Cut the fruit in half and squeeze out the juice with a lemon squeezer.
3. Shred the peel, removing the excess pith.
4. Put the excess pith and pips into a muslin bag.

5. Put the peel, pulp and water in a pan, add the bag of pips.
6. Simmer for 2 hours.
7. Squeeze out the bag, add the sugar and finish as method 1.

This gives a clearer marmalade.

Method 3

1. Scrub and scald the fruit.
2. Put the whole fruit in a casserole with the water.
3. Cook 3–4 hours in a moderate oven or 2 hours on the top of the stove.
4. Remove the fruit, cut it into shreds.
5. Remove the pips and put them in the water and cook for 15 mins. Strain.
6. Add the shredded fruit to the liquid and boil off any excess water.
7. Add the sugar and continue as Method 1.

This gives a thick marmalade.

Method 4 (Using a pressure cooker)

1. Prepare the fruit as in method 2 or 3.
2. Put the rack in the cooker and add the fruit.
3. Use $\frac{1}{2}$ the amount of water given in the recipe.
4. Put on the stove and keep the vent open until it starts to steam.
5. Close the vent.
6. Bring up to 15 lbs pressure and hold there for 20 mins.
7. Cool at room temperature.
8. Remove the fruit and finish according to the method chosen.
9. Do not finish in a pressure cooker with an in-curve at the top, owing to the difficulty in pouring out.

Maximum amount to make: 5 lb.

Method 5
Jelly Marmalade

1. Use not more than 6 ozs of the outer part of the rind only.
2. Shred very finely.
3. Cut up the rest of the fruit and pith and cook with $\frac{3}{4}$ of the water.
4. Strain through a jelly bag.
5. Cook the rind slowly with $\frac{1}{4}$ of the water.
6. Add the sugar and the rind and water to the strained juice.
7. Finish as for jelly making.

More than 3 lbs fruit may be needed. Usually 4 lbs fruit + 6 lbs sugar = 10 lbs jelly marmalade.

WHAT WENT WRONG—AND WHY

The peel rises in the jar leaving jelly without peel below

The marmalade was potted while too hot.   It should be allowed to cool a few minutes before being put in the jars.

The marmalade does not set

(*a*) There was insufficient boiling with the sugar.

(*b*) There was lack of acid, especially with grapefruit, sweet oranges and tangerine marmalade.   This may be remedied by the addition of lemon juice ($\frac{1}{2}$ pint to each 6 lbs).

The marmalade is too stiff and solid

Insufficient water was used with the fruit.   Citrus fruits require more water than fruits used for jam.

The peel is tough

(*a*) The peel was cut too coarsely.

(*b*) There was insufficient simmering with water before the sugar was added.

The marmalade has a bitter flavour

Too much pith was included, this depends on individual taste.

The marmalade is cloudy and dull

The peel was badly cut up.   This will always occur if peel is minced.

In tangerine marmalade it is very common as the peel tends to be mealy.

MARMALADE RECIPES
(to give 10 lbs yield)
Thick Dark Marmalade

2 lbs Seville oranges	6 lbs sugar
1 lemon	1 oz dark treacle
7 pts water	

Method

Use either 1 or 3.

Average Seville Orange

3 lbs Seville oranges	Juice of 2 lemons
6 pts water	6 lbs sugar

Method
   Use methods 1–4.

Jelly

4 lbs Seville oranges   juice of 4 lemons
9 pts water   6 lbs sugar

Method
   Use method 5.

Tangerine

Tangerines ⎫
2 grapefruit ⎬ Total 5½ lbs   10 pts water
2 lemons   ⎭   5 lbs sugar
½ oz tartaric acid

Method
1. Shred tangerine peel finely, and tie in muslin.
2. Mince the grapefruit, the lemons and the tangerine pulp.
3. Put all pulp, plus tangerine peel, water and acid in a pan.
4. Simmer 30 minutes, remove tangerine peel.
5. Simmer the rest for an additional 1½ hours.
6. Strain the pulp, add the sugar and the rinsed tangerine shreds.
7. Cook 20–30 mins.

Three Fruits

Grapefruit   ⎫
Lemons   ⎬ Total 3 lbs   6 pts water
Sweet oranges⎭   6 lbs sugar

Method
   Use 1 or 3.

Grapefruit

3 grapefruit (approx 2¼ lbs)   6 pts water
6 lemons   (approx ¾ lb)   6 lbs sugar

Method
   Use 1 or 2.

BUTTER, CHEESES AND CURDS

Fruit butters and cheeses are similar in method of preparation; sieved fruit pulp is cooked with sugar until the required thickness is reached. Fruit cheese requires 1 lb sugar to each pint of pulp, and the mixture is cooked until, when a spoon is drawn across the bottom of the pan, a clean line is left.

The cheese is served turned out on a plate and is therefore patted into a mould or jar from which it can be turned out. The cheese should be firm enough to slice. The jar should be smeared inside with glycerine so that the cheese turns out easily. The jars are covered as for jam. Cheeses improve with keeping.

Blackcurrant, Damson, Plum or Quince Cheese

3 lbs fruit picked, washed and cut up if necessary
¼ pt water
Sugar: 1 lb to every pint pulp

Method

1. Cook the fruit with the water very slowly in a closed pan until it is tender.
2. Sieve and measure.
3. Return to a clean pan with 1 lb sugar to each pint of pulp.
4. Bring slowly to the boil so that the sugar is completely dissolved before boiling point is reached.
5. Cook until a spoon drawn across the bottom of the pan leaves a clean line.
6. Put in jars smeared with glycerine, cover while hot.

Apple and Mint or Sage Cheese

Prepare as for other fruit cheeses. Just before the cheese is ready add 4 tbs chopped sage or mint leaves. Cook for 5 mins and pot as above.

Mint and Gooseberry Cheese
(for serving with mutton or veal)

4 lbs green gooseberries   sugar
2 pts water   30 sprigs fresh mint

Method

1. Cook the fruit and water to a pulp and rub through a sieve.
2. Measure the pulp and add 1 lb sugar to each 1 pt pulp.
3. Heat together in a preserving pan with the sprigs of mint tied in muslin.
4. See that all the sugar is dissolved before the mixture boils.
5. Boil for 10 minutes and then begin to test for the setting point.
6. Remove the mint and pot in small jars. Cover whilst hot to help to retain the delicate flavour.

Fruit butters are generally spiced and are of a softer consistency than fruit cheese. They do not keep well unless the jars are sterilised by immersing in boiling water for 5 minutes after potting the butter.

$\frac{1}{2}$–$\frac{3}{4}$ lb sugar is used for each lb pulp and the mixture is cooked with the spices and vinegar if used until thick.

The test for the end of the cooking is that there is no free liquid left and the mixture is thick and creamy.

Spiced Apple or Pear Butter

3 pts fruit pulp $\frac{1}{4}$ pt vinegar
3 teasp ground cinnamon or a mixture of cinnamon and ground cloves
2$\frac{1}{2}$ lbs sugar

Proceed as for cheese.

Fruit curds are a combination of fruit pulp or rind and juice, with sugar, eggs and butter.

Apple or Gooseberry Curd

3 pts pulp (4 lbs fruit + $\frac{1}{3}$ $\frac{1}{2}$ lb butter
   pt water)   2 lbs sugar
6 eggs

Method

1. Put the butter into the top of a double saucepan, melt and add the well beaten eggs and the sugar and the pulp.
2. Cook until the mixture thickens, probably 30 mins.
3. Put in hot tins and seal at once.

Lemon or Orange Curd

3 lemons or 3 oranges + juice $\frac{1}{2}$ lb loaf sugar
   of $\frac{1}{2}$ lemon   4 ozs butter
3 eggs

Method

1. Rub the sugar over the washed fruit to remove the zest.
2. Squeeze the juice from the fruit.
3. Melt the butter in a double saucepan, add the sugar, the juice and the well beaten eggs.
4. Cook until the mixture thickens.
5. Pour into hot dry jars.   Cover as for jam.

PICKLES, CHUTNEYS AND SAUCES

The aim is to preserve the fruits and vegetables by increasing the acidity.   Vinegar is usually added, and spices are used for flavour and their small preservative function.

The water content is reduced:—

(a) by soaking in brine; this substitutes salt solution for water in the vegetable;
(b) by heating to dry out some of the water.

Sufficient vinegar must be added to prevent the development of organisms which cause decay.

Classification

1. Sweet and sour pickles; vegetables etc. whole or in pieces in vinegar. They may be either crisp or soft.
2. Chutneys: these are smooth and jam-like, and should have no pieces except dried fruit or mustard seed.
3. Sauces: These are sieved and may result in

   (a) a thick cream consistency
   (b) a thin liquid with a sediment to shake up.

4. Mustard pickles: whole or pieces of vegetables in a thickened mustard sauce.

Sweet Pickles

These are generally made from fruit, but vegetables may also be used. Cook for a little while to reduce the water content without breaking down the fruit, instead of brining. This can be done either on the top of the stove or in the oven. Cook in sweet vinegar. Strain off the vinegar and reduce the liquid to the original amount of vinegar. Use 4 lbs fruit or vegetables to 2 lbs sugar and 1 pint vinegar.

Sour Pickles

These are usually made of raw vegetables, except beetroot which is cooked before use. Prepare the vegetables as for cooking and divide or slice into pieces of a convenient size.

Soak for 24 hours in brine made from 1 lb salt and 1 gallon water. Put a plate on the top of the vegetables to keep them down.

After 24 hours drain. Rinse quickly to remove any excess salt, and drain well again.

Pack into jars.

Cover with spiced vinegar (see p. 449) and with a cover which is vinegar-proof. Pickles should be crisp and well flavoured, and most of them require time to mature before use.

Chutneys

The vegetables and fruit should be a blended pulp. For this reason those that are difficult to soften, such as onion, should be cooked first, as the addition of vinegar will toughen them. The ingredients may be minced or chopped and should then be cooked slowly all together to blend the flavours, and the vinegar added as they soften. The type of spices may be varied according to taste. If a hot chutney is required more cayenne, chillies and ginger can be used. The consistency should be that of jam, and on standing the ingredients should not separate. The keeping quality depends on this rather than on the acidity. Sugar tends to darken the chutney so should be added late in the cooking for light-coloured ones such as tomato.

Sauces and Ketchup

The fruit and/or vegetables are well cooked and then sieved; spices and vinegar are added but the sauce should keep the characteristic flavour of its name.

The consistency should be that of thick cream. In the majority of sauces the liquid should not separate; mushroom ketchup is one of the exceptions.

Tomatoes and mushrooms do not contain sufficient acid to preserve them, so they must be sterilised after bottling and the corks painted with hot wax after cooling.

Mustard Pickles

Brine the vegetables as for sour pickles.

Prepare the sauce and cook, as it has thickening in it.

The vegetables may be cooked in the sauce, in which case they will be soft, or they can be added to the cooked sauce in which case they will remain crisp.

The amount of sweetening varies according to taste.

The consistency should be creamy.

Covers for pickles, chutneys and sauces

These preserves may be put into any shaped jar or bottle but they must be protected by a suitable cover. This cover *must* be vinegar-proof and airtight so that the contents do not evaporate and shrink or grow mould, etc.

If metal covers are used the metal must be protected from the action of acid by special paper or wax.

Paraffin wax is a suitable seal, painted over either cardboard and paper or cardboard and calico. Paper or calico alone will not be sufficient. If bottles are used the corks must be well boiled, and if the preserve has a low acid content they must be waxed before storage.

SWEET PICKLES

Kind	Recipe	Method	Length of Time to Mature	Yield
Damson or Pear	8 lbs fruit 4 lbs sugar (brown for damsons) Rind of lemon ½ oz cloves ½ oz allspice ¼ oz root ginger ¼ oz cinnamon stick 1 qt vinegar	1. Leave the damsons whole. 2. Peel and quarter the pears. 3. Dissolve the sugar in the vinegar and add the spices (tied in a muslin bag). 4. Simmer the fruit in the vinegar until tender. 5. Drain. 6. Pack the fruit neatly in the jars. 7. Reduce the vinegar until it is a thin syrup. 8. Pour over the fruit while *hot*. 9. Tie down and seal at once.	3–6 months	9–10 lbs
Sweet Green Tomato	6 lbs green tomatoes 4 lbs sugar 1 oz salt 1 teaspoonful ground cinnamon 1 pt vinegar 4½ pts water	1. Wash the tomatoes and put in 4 pts boiling water, plus 1 oz salt. 2. Boil for ten minutes, drain and peel. 3. Put vinegar, plus ½ pt water, the sugar, and the spice into a pan, bring to the boil, add the tomatoes and boil for 5 minutes. 4. Put in a basin. 5. Leave for one week. 6. Drain, boil the vinegar for 10 minutes. 7. Add the tomatoes and boil for 5 minutes. 8. Pack in jars, and pour over the hot vinegar. 9. Seal at once.	1 month	9–10 lbs

SOUR PICKLES

Kind	Recipe	Method	Length of Brining using 1 lb salt to 1 gallon water	Length of Time to Mature
Cauliflower	1 cauliflower A few chillies Spiced vinegar	1. Break the head into small pieces. 2. Cover with the brine. 3. Drain well. 4. Pack and cover in the *cold* spiced vinegar.	24 hours	6 weeks–3 months
Cucumber	1 cucumber A few chillies Spiced vinegar	1. Slice the cucumber and put in the brine. 2. Drain well. 3. Pack neatly into jars and decorate with chillies. 4. Cover with *cold* vinegar.	24 hours	1 week Does not keep well for more than six months.
Gherkins	Gherkins Spiced vinegar	1. Place in the brine. 2. Drain and pack in jars. 3. Pour over the *hot* vinegar. 4. Cover and leave for 24 hours in a warm place. 5. Drain off the vinegar, boil up and pour over the gherkins. 6. Leave 24 hours again. 7. Repeat until the gherkins are dark green in colour (probably three times).	3 days	6 weeks
Onions	Small even-sized onions Chillies Spiced vinegar	1. Place unskinned in brine. 2. Peel, put in fresh brine, cover with a plate to keep onions under the liquid. 3. Drain well. 4. Pack into jars. 5. Cover with *cold* spiced vinegar.	12 hours 24–36 hours	3–4 months
Mixed Pickle	Cauliflower French beans Onions Cucumber Spiced vinegar	1. Cut into small pieces. 2. Sprinkle with *dry* salt. 3. Wash and drain well. 4. Pack neatly into jars. 5. Cover with *cold* spiced vinegar.	48 hours	2–3 months

Red Cabbage	1 firm red cabbage Spiced vinegar	1. Clean and shred. 2. Put in a large basin with layers of dry salt. 3. Rinse and drain well. 4. Pack loosely in jars. 5. Cover in the *cold* spiced vinegar.	24 hours in dry salt	1 week Do not keep more than 1–2 months.
Walnuts	Walnuts with shells still soft Spiced vinegar	1. Prick to see that the shell is soft. 2. Put in the brine. 3. Change the brine and soak again. 4. Drain, spread out exposed to the air until they are black (1–2 days). 5. Pack in jars and cover in the *hot* spiced vinegar.	3–4 days 1 week	1–2 months

Spiced Vinegar

1 quart white vinegar
¼ oz cinnamon bark
¼ oz cloves
¼ oz mace
¼ oz whole allspice
A few peppercorns

Method 1.
Allow the spices to steep in the cold vinegar for 1–2 months. Shake the bottle occasionally.
This method produces the best results.

Method 2.
Put the spices and the vinegar into a basin in a pan of hot water. Cover with a plate. Allow the water to boil. Stand on the side of the fire for two hours. Strain and use.

Herb Vinegar

1 quart white vinegar
Tarragon or other herbs

Method
Steep the herbs in the vinegar in a corked bottle for two weeks. Strain.

P

CHUTNEYS

Kind	Recipe	Method	Approximate Length of Cooking	Time to Mature	Yield
Apple	5 lbs apples 1 lb onions 1 teasp ground ginger 1 ,, salt 12 cloves 6 allspice 6 chillies 1 pt vinegar 1½ lbs brown sugar	1. Mince the onion. 2. Peel and mince the apple. 3. Cook the onion in ½ pt water for 20 minutes. 4. Add the apple and the spices (tied in muslin). 5. Simmer until tender. 6. Add the vinegar and sugar. 7. Boil until it has a jam-like consistency. 8. Remove the spices and bottle.	1½ hours	2–6 months	6 lbs
Apple, Date and Raisin	2 lbs apples 1 lb raisins 2 ozs ginger 2 ozs salt 1 lb dates 1 lb brown sugar ¼ oz cayenne pepper 2–3 small onions 1 pt vinegar	1. Mince the onion, apples, dates and stoned raisins. 2. Cook the onion in a little water. 3. Add the fruit and the vinegar and simmer until tender. 4. Add the salt, spices and pepper. 5. Boil until thick. 6. Put into bottles, seal at once.	1½ hours	2–6 months	6 lbs
Date	1 lb dates 1 lb raisins 1 lb onion ¾ lb brown sugar ¼ oz garlic ¼ oz salt 6 chillies 1 pt vinegar	1. Cook the finely chopped garlic in a little water until tender. 2. Add the other ingredients and boil until tender and fairly thick. 3. Bottle and seal at once.	¾ hour	2–3 months	2¼ lbs
Gooseberry	3 lbs gooseberries ½ lb onion	1. Mince the onion and cook in the water until tender.	1 hour	6–9 months	4 lbs

	1 lb sugar ½ pt water ½ oz salt ¼ oz ground ginger ½ teasp cayenne 1 pt vinegar	2. Mince the gooseberries and add to the onion. 3. Simmer until tender. 4. Add the other ingredients, cook until thick and pour into jars.			
Marrow	5 lbs marrow ½ lb onions ½ lb raisins (stoned) ½ lb sultanas ½ lb currants ½ lb brown sugar ½ oz ground ginger 1 oz mustard seed 1 pt vinegar Dry salt for brining	1. Prepare the marrow and cut into small cubes. 2. Put in a bowl with the salt in layers. 3. Stand for 24 hours. 4. Chop the onion and simmer in a little water until tender. 5. Add the spices, sugar, fruit and vinegar. 6. Bring to the boil. 7. Drain and wash the marrow and add to the mixture. 8. Simmer until thick. 9. Bottle at once.	2 hours	2–4 months	6 lbs
Plum	3 lbs plums 1 lb apples 1 lb onions 1 lb raisins (stoned) 1 lb sugar 2 ozs salt 1 teasp cloves 1 ,, cinnamon 1 ,, ground ginger 1 ,, allspice 1 pt vinegar	1. Chop the onions and cook in a little water until tender. 2. Chop the apple, cut the plums into quarters, stone them and chop the raisins finely. 3. Add the apple, plums, raisins, sugar, spice and vinegar. 4. Boil until thick. 5. Bottle and seal at once.	1½ hours	3–6 months	5 lbs
Rhubarb	5 lbs rhubarb 1 lb onions 2 lbs brown sugar ½ oz ground ginger ½ oz salt ½ oz curry powder 1½ pts vinegar	1. Mince the onion and cook in a little water until tender. 2. Add the chopped rhubarb, sugar and spices, cook with half the vinegar until tender. 3. Add the rest of the vinegar. 4. Cook until thick. 5. Bottle and seal at once.	1½ hours	2–3 months	6 lbs

CHUTNEYS *continued*

Kind	Recipe	Method	Approximate Length of Cooking	Time to Mature	Yield
Green Tomato	5 lbs green tomatoes 1 lb onions ½ oz salt ½ oz pickling spice 1 pt vinegar 1 lb brown sugar	1. Mince the onion, cook in a little water until tender. 2. Add the chopped tomatoes, salt and spices (in muslin bag). 3. Simmer until tender. 4. Add the vinegar and sugar. 5. Boil until thick. 6. Remove the bag of spices. 7. Bottle while hot and seal at once.	2 hours	2–3 months	6 lbs
Ripe Tomato	6 lbs tomatoes ¼ lb onion 1 lb sugar 1 oz salt 1 level teaspoonful paprika Pinch cayenne ¾ pt white vinegar	1. Skin and chop the tomatoes and the onion. 2. Simmer the onions in a little water until tender. 3. Add the tomatoes and cook until pulpy. 4. Add half the vinegar and the spices, and reduce by about ¼ of the bulk. 5. Add the rest of the vinegar and sugar. 6. Cook until thick.	1½ hours	1–2 months	5 lbs
Brown Chutney	¼ lb root ginger 2½ ozs garlic 1 oz mustard seed 1 oz chillies 2 lbs brown sugar ½ lb salt ¼ lb onion ½ lb stoned raisins 1 lb sultanas 3 pts malt vinegar 24 apples 6 sliced figs 1 oz citron peel 1 tablespoonful grated horseradish	1. Bruise the ginger and the chillies. 2. Chop the garlic and the onion, and cook in a little water until tender. 3. Chop the raisins, apples, figs and peel. 4. Add the spices and sugar. 5. Mix all together with the cooked onion and garlic. 6. Add the vinegar and cook until tender. 7. When it is thick, bottle in hot jars and seal at once.	1 hour	2–3 months	10 lbs

MUSTARD PICKLES

Kind	Recipe	Method	Length of Time in Salt	Length of Time to Mature	Yield
Piccalilli	6 lbs prepared vegetables— a mixture of marrow, cauliflower, french beans, onions, cucumber ¾ lb salt 1 oz flour ½ oz turmeric 1½ ozs mustard 1½ ozs ground ginger 1 quart vinegar 6 ozs sugar	1. Cut the vegetables into neat pieces. 2. Sprinkle with the salt. Leave. 3. Mix the spices and flour, and blend with a little vinegar. 4. Rinse and drain the vegetables and boil for 20 minutes in the rest of the vinegar and the sugar. 5. Stir in the blended spices etc. 6. Boil for 3 minutes. 7. Pack into jars and seal at once.	24 hours	2–3 months	The number of jars depends upon the size of the pieces of vegetable. Approximately 12 1 lb jars
Beans in Mustard Sauce	2 lbs french beans ¼ oz turmeric ¼ oz mustard 6 ozs sugar ½ oz flour 1 pt spiced vinegar	1. Slice the beans. 2. Put into the brine. 3. Blend the other ingredients and bring to the boil. 4. Rinse and add the beans. 5. Cook for 5 minutes. 6. Bottle at once and seal.	24 hours	1 month	Approximately 4 1 lb jars

SAUCE AND KETCHUP RECIPES

KIND	RECIPE	METHOD	METHOD OF BOTTLING	TIME OF STERILISATION	APPROXIMATE YIELD
Mushroom Ketchup	6 lbs mushrooms 6 ozs salt 2 pints malt vinegar ¼ oz allspice 1 teasp mace 1 teasp ginger 12 cloves ½" stick cinnamon ¼ oz pepper	1. Chop the mushrooms, sprinkle them with salt and leave to stand overnight. 2. Pulp the mushrooms with a vegetable presser, and simmer in a pan with the vinegar and spices. 3. Keep the lid on the pan. 4. Strain through a fine sieve (hair or nylon) and pour at once into warmed bottles.	1. Fill the bottle to 1" from the top. 2. Cork, and tie corks on or screw on caps. 3. Stand in a deep pan of boiling water and simmer. 4. Wax corks when cold.	30 minutes	3 pints
Tomato Sauce	6 lbs ripe tomatoes ½ lb granulated sugar 3 teasp salt 1 level teasp paprika pepper Pinch cayenne pepper 1 pint spiced white vinegar 1 tbs tarragon vinegar	1. Wash, slice and cook the tomatoes slowly until well pulped. 2. Rub through a fine hair or nylon sieve, add the salt and peppers and cook gently until the mixture begins to thicken. 3. Add the vinegars and cook again until thick and creamy. 4. Add the sugar and reduce until it does not separate.	1. Fill the warmed bottles to 1" from the top. 2. Cork and tie corks on firmly or use screw caps. 3. Stand in a deep pan of boiling water and simmer. 4. Wax the corks when cold.	20–30 minutes	2½–3 pints

THE CANNING OF FRUIT AND VEGETABLES

The aim is similar to that of bottling, but the fruit or vegetables and the liquid are sealed in the can before processing.

Type of can

Cans are made in standard sizes and are of special steel which will withstand processing. Plain cans are steel lined with a layer of tin, and are suitable for light coloured fruits such as apples and pears, and all green and yellow fruit.

Fruit lacquered cans have a thin lacquer over the tin and can be distinguished by the " dimple " in the centre of the base and lid. They should be used for all red fruits and tomatoes.

Vegetable lacquered cans have no " dimple ". The lacquer looks like the fruit can but will withstand the additional heat and pressure required for processing. It is sulphur resisting, and the cans are often called S.R. cans. The correct kind of can should be used for each group of fruit or vegetables.

The seam of the can is locked by the " run and fell " type of join, the top of the seam being flattened to allow for the sealing on of the lid. For this reason most cans cannot be cut down for further use.

The canning machine is simple to operate, directions being supplied with each type. The sealing is done in two stages. First the lid is rolled over the flange of the can, and the lid and can are then pressed together to make an airtight seal.

Selection of cans

When the fruit or vegetables are to be canned the correct type of can and lid should be chosen. The cans and lids should be rinsed and drained but not dried, as the thin lacquer may be broken by the friction of a comparatively smooth tea towel.

Selection of fruit and vegetables

Those suitable for bottling are also suitable for canning and the preparation is identical.

Packing

The can should be filled to $\frac{1}{8}''$ of the top, never over the rim to avoid squashing the fruit. Soft fruit should be tapped to " settle " it in the can. With an A2$\frac{1}{2}$ can the average quantity of fruit packed in is 18 ozs. Apple in syrup will weigh less, but " solid-pack " apples will be up to 26 ozs and solid pack tomatoes up to 27 ozs.

Pack the vegetables loosely and avoid over-packing.

Liquid for filling

Syrup is preferable for fruit as it gives a better flavour and the fruit is ready for the table without any further cooking. An average of 8 ozs sugar to 1 pint water should be allowed, using more for acid fruit and less for apples. For strawberries and raspberries colouring may be used.

A brine solution should be used for vegetables, allowing 1 oz salt to 2½ pints water. For peas a little sugar may be added and, if liked, green colouring.

Filling fruit cans with liquid

Have the sugar syrup boiling. Rest the can at an angle on the edge of a tray about ¾" high. Fill the can to the brim so that when it is placed level the liquid is ⅜" from the top of the can.

Put the lid on at once and seal on the machine. The steam drives out the air and this means less strain on the seal and seam of the can during processing. The cans may be marked with a wax pencil to help when labelling. Once sealed, keep on a warm stove until the other cans of that batch are ready. Do not seal too many cans in each batch.

Processing of fruit cans

The fruits are divided into the following groups:

Group I   Apples (in syrup), Apricots, Blackberries, Damsons, Gooseberries, Citrus fruits, Greengages, Loganberries, Plums (firm ripe), Raspberries, Redcurrants, Rhubarb, Strawberries.

Group II   Apples (solid pack), Bilberries, Blackcurrants, Cherries, Peaches, Pears (ripe dessert), Pineapple, Plums (under ripe).

Group III   Tomatoes (in brine).

Group IV   Tomatoes (solid pack).

Put the cans into boiling water so that they are completely immersed, and note the time taken for the water to return to boil. Process each group according to the chart below. Do not attempt to process more cans at one time than will return to the boil in 20 minutes or less.

Time taken for the water to reboil (minutes)	Additional time for cans to be reboiled (minutes)			
	Group I	Group II	Group III	Group IV
0–5	18–15	22–20	35–32	45–42
6–10	15–13	20–18	32–30	42–40
11–15	12–10	17–15	30–27	40–37
16–20	10–8	15–13	27–25	37–35

Solid packs should be canned while still hot after blanching.

Filling of vegetable cans with liquid

Have the brine solution boiling. Rest the can on the edge of a tray. Fill the cans to the brim so that when level the liquid is $\frac{3}{8}''$ from the top. Rest the lid on the can. Have ready a shallow pan of simmering water and as each can is filled set it to stand in the pan. The water should come to 1" from the top of the cans. Leave for 5 minutes. This drives the air out of the cans and is called " exhausting the cans ". It reduces strain on the seams of the can and helps to create a vacuum. Remove the cans, one at a time, and seal immediately.

Processing of vegetable cans

Put the hot cans into the *pressure cooker* with 2" of hot water in it. Put on the lid and allow the cooker to steam for 7–10 minutes. Then close the valve and raise the pressure to 10 lbs. Maintain at this pressure for approximately 5 minutes less than is required for bottling.

Cooling of all cans

When removed from the boiling water they should be plunged immediately into clean cold running water, to prevent over-cooking of the contents. Cool to blood heat. Then remove and dry off.

To test if cooled, roll the cans between the palms of the hands for about $\frac{1}{2}$ minute. If the can is just warm it can be allowed to dry.

When processing, the lids and base of the can are convex and on cooling they return to a concave shape.

Labelling

Use a label that encircles the can and if possible note on it the kind and variety of the contents; also the strength of the syrup or brine and the date of processing.

FREEZING OF FRUIT AND VEGETABLES

The aim is to store the food at a temperature that is too cold for the development of the organisms which cause decay and enzyme activity, and to keep the ice crystals that form during the freezing as small as possible to prevent the rupturing of the tissues.

To do this, food must be kept below 5° F.   To allow for fluctuation of temperature due to the removal and addition of food, the freezer should be kept at 0° F.

The temperature of the food to be frozen should be reduced as rapidly as possible, and reduction should be complete within 24 hours of the food being placed in the freezer.   Therefore it should be placed in the coldest part of the freezer, preferably against the side, for at least 24 hours.

To prevent surface evaporation which causes drying or " freezer burn ", the food must be wrapped in containers which are moisture-proof and vapour-proof.   As much air as possible should be extracted and they must be sealed securely to make them airtight.

Containers for food

1. Plastic boxes are good but expensive and should be sealed with a special " scotch tape ".   They may be used several times.
2. Waxed cartons.   These may be round or rectangular and may be bought in various sizes.   The rectangular boxes pack economically.   As it is difficult to make these boxes airtight it is advisable to put the food into sealed plastic bags inside the carton.
3. Plastic bags:—

    (a) Polythene bags are good, but when frozen stick together and tear easily.   It is necessary to wrap them in brown paper or mutton cloth or put them in a waxed carton.

    (b) Cellulose tissue bags made especially for freezing can be used only once and need the same protective covering as the polythene bags.

    (c) Paper bags lined with polythene or cellulose tissue are very useful for small packages and have the protective covering incorporated with the polythene bag.

It is important to press out all the air from the bags before sealing.

Sealing

1. Polythene or cellulose bags may be sealed by turning down the open end twice and ironing with a warm iron (rayon temperature) or by twisting plastic wire round the opening of the bag. The polythene must be protected with paper while ironing.

2. Plastic boxes or waxed cartons should be sealed with " scotch tape ".

Freezing Fruits

1. Prepare the fruit as for stewing—rinse in cold water if necessary, drain very well.
2. Mix with sugar or cold sugar syrup.
3. Put into suitable containers, leaving room for the syrup to expand, but squeezing out the air before sealing the bags.
4. Mark with a pencil or crayon.
5. Freeze quickly.
6. Thaw slowly in the unopened container.

Freezing Vegetables

1. Prepare fresh vegetables as for cooking.
2. Scald a small quantity at a time in boiling water from 1–6 mins (see chart).
3. Drain and cool in ice cold water.
4. Drain and pack into containers. Squeeze out the air and seal.
5. Freeze quickly.
6. Cook in boiling salt water without previous thawing.

Vegetable	Scalding time (minutes)
Asparagus	thin stems 2, thick stems 4
Broad Beans	3
French or Runner Beans	2–3
Peas	1–2

Success of deep freezing depends on:—

1. Fresh, good quality produce.
2. Quick and thorough preparation.
3. Suitable packing materials to prevent evaporation and to retain the flavour.
4. Rapid freezing.
5. Low temperature, 0° F or less during storage.
6. Careful cooking or thawing.

Using Frozen Fruits

Some fruits, notably pears, apples and peaches, turn brown quickly if exposed to the air during preparation and these will, in the same way, go brown on thawing when taken out of deep freeze. Therefore such fruits must be thawed in the sealed container in which they have been packed. If it is necessary to keep them for more than an hour after thawing is complete, the fruit should be transferred from the sealed container into an airtight preserving jar.

Soft fruits with a high water content, such as strawberries and raspberries, should be served while still slightly frozen. If they are allowed to thaw completely they are inclined to go soft and look unappetising. This is due to the rupturing of the delicate tissue by the ice crystals during freezing and cannot be avoided.

Using Frozen Vegetables

As vegetables are scalded before freezing, they need less time to cook than the fresh vegetable of a like kind, but the time of cooking must be calculated from the moment the water returns to the boil. The frozen mass is put into boiling water and reduces the temperature. The time required for cooking *after the water has returned to the boil* is $\frac{1}{3}$–$\frac{1}{2}$ the normal cooking time. Salt is added in the usual proportions. Mint and sugar should be added to peas to improve the flavour. The vegetables are served in the usual way.

CHAPTER XXVI

SEASONINGS AND FLAVOURINGS

" SEASON to taste " often appears in a recipe, without any further guidance being given, and many inexperienced cooks are left wondering what it means. As every dish is made to be eaten, and much of the enjoyment of eating depends upon the taste of the food, it is well to understand what combination of flavours has been found, by long experience, to be pleasant. This does not prevent a cook from trying out new combinations, indeed most cooks have their special dishes, the exact means of flavouring being a family secret.

Now, seasonings and flavourings are used to bring out the natural flavour of the food and should be used subtly so that they do not mask the natural flavour. They should be cooked in with the food or added before cooking to make sure that the flavours are thoroughly blended. A well-flavoured dish is appetising and therefore digestible.

Condiments and spices should be kept in airtight containers to retain their natural oils and consequently their flavours.

Herbs are best used fresh from the garden, for they give a finer and more intense flavour to soups and stews than do the dried herbs. Fresh herbs give variety of flavour and colour to salads.

Those, however, which will not withstand the winter even if protected should be dried and used in a powdered state for flavouring. They can be stored in airtight tins or dark glass jars or bottles with effective screw lids. Clear jars would let in light which spoils the colour and flavour of the herbs.

To Dry Herbs

These should be gathered when the young plant is just about to flower ; the leaves are then at their best. They should be gathered on a dry day after the dew has gone and before the sun is strong— if possible while the plants are still in the shade. Small-leaved herbs such as thyme, winter savory, and fennel should be tied loosely in small bundles in muslin and hung near the kitchen fire. They should be left for 3–4 days and if tied loosely they will not need any attention until they are dry and crisp, when the leaves are rubbed from the stalks, crushed and sieved.

With large-leaved herbs such as mint and sage the leaves should be stripped from the stalks, and any inferior leaves discarded. The leaves should be tied in muslin and then dipped in boiling water for one minute. The water should then be shaken off and the leaves dried in a cool oven (not more than 130° F) for about an hour, by which time the leaves should be crisp. It is not essential to blanch by dipping in boiling water and many people get better results by omitting this process.

Parsley needs special treatment. After picking over as above the leaves are put in an oven of 400° F for one minute (very carefully timed) and then finished off in a warm place. This retains the colour and flavour.

The crushing, sieving and storing are the same for all herbs. Generally speaking herbs are used in savoury dishes and salads, spices in both savoury and sweet dishes and cake essences in sweet dishes including cakes.

Allspice, also known as Jamaica pepper or pimiento, is used ground to flavour savoury dishes. It should not be confused with Mixed Spice which is similar in colour and aroma and is used in sweet dishes and cakes.

Bouquet Garni is made by tying a bay leaf, a piece of parsley, a small blade of mace, and a few peppercorns in muslin. To vary the flavour replace the mace with a sprig of thyme or the peppercorns with a sprig of marjoram.

This is used to flavour soups and stews and is taken out before serving.

Chives are used to replace onions in salads, omelets, sandwich fillings. An excellent garnish to white soups is obtained if chopped chives are sprinkled on just before serving.

Cinnamon (ground) is used in cakes, puddings and biscuits and as an accompaniment to fresh raspberries and melon.

Essences should always be of the best quality, bought in small quantities so that they do not become stale.

A more subtle flavour is obtained if two or more essences are used, the one giving the desired predominant flavour being used more generously, e.g. almond and vanilla used together, vanilla and rose water, vanilla with coffee or chocolate flavouring.

Fennel should be used with fish or sauces or as a garnish. It is especially good with mackerel.

Horseradish should be served with roast beef or fish dishes or as a flavouring in fillings for sandwiches and savouries.

Garlic must be used very sparingly, a quarter or half a clove being enough to flavour a dish for 4 people. The clove of garlic should be sprinkled with salt, crushed with a knife and then finely chopped. When using with salad the bowl should be rubbed with the crushed clove. It should not be left in the salad.

Lemon Rind should be used grated to flavour cakes and puddings, stuffings and forcemeats.

It may be used as a strip, afterwards removed, to give flavour to milky dishes and some sauces.

An essential garnish to fish, veal, dressed or réchauffé chicken dishes is lemon cut in pieces, slices or " butterflies ".

Mixed Spice A combination of ground cloves, cinnamon and nutmeg. Used for flavouring puddings and cakes.

Nutmeg Used ground in cakes and biscuits, grated on top of milk puddings and custards, also in cauliflower sauce and in stewed rhubarb.

Mustard As an accompaniment to beef, veal and pork dishes. Used to flavour most cheese dishes, the mustard enhances the cheese flavour but should not overwhelm it.

Pepper Peppercorns are used as a flavouring in the milk or stock for sauces, in chutney and pickles.

Cayenne To flavour savouries or any " bonne bouche " requiring a really strong flavour. It is very hot.

Paprika A red ground pepper with a delicate flavour used mainly for garnish on account of its attractive colour. It is not hot to the taste, but helps to draw out other flavours without in any way masking them. It is particularly useful in stews and may be used lavishly; a dessertspoonful added to a stew for 4 people will improve an otherwise ordinary dish. Care should be taken to taste carefully to avoid overdoing it.

Green or Red Peppers or Pimientoes are used as a vegetable (see p. 180) or sliced thinly after removing seeds and pith.

Salads may be flavoured with one or more of the following herbs chopped finely: summer and winter savory, sweet marjoram, lovage (a cross between celery and parsley in flavour), variety of mints, thyme, balm, tarragon. Decorate and flavour at the same time by adding to the salad nasturtium petals, rose petals or borage flowers.

Omelets may be flavoured with chopped garlic, chives or other green herbs.

Recipes for Using Herbs
Herb Butters

For serving with grilled meat and fish, as a savoury or sandwich filling, as a garnish for hors d'œuvres. ½ oz butter is creamed with ½ teasp lemon juice, 1 teasp of finely chopped herbs, either keeping to one variety or mixing two or more together. The most usual herbs to select from are: parsley, mint, fennel, chervil, winter savory, chives, thyme or sage. The last two should be sparingly used.

Allow to set hard before using.

Herb Cheese

4 ozs grated cheese   3 tbs sherry
2 tbs thick cream   salt and pepper
2 tbs of mixed herbs (parsley, sage, thyme, tarragon, chives, chervil, and winter savory).

Method

1. Put all the ingredients into a double saucepan and stir over a gentle heat until the mixture is pale green in colour and of a creamy consistency.
2. Pot in small hot jars—cover as for jam.

This is an excellent sandwich spread and is delicious on fingers of hot toast as a savoury.

Hot Horseradish Sauce

1 heaped tablespoonful of grated horseradish
½ pt of good white sauce
enough tomato juice to give a good colour

Serve with meat or fish entrées or vegetarian dishes.

Mint Jelly

(to serve with mutton in winter instead of redcurrant jelly or onion sauce)

1 pt of apple juice (made from green apples and mint stalks) *or*
1 pt of white currant juice
juice of 1 lemon
1 lb sugar
6 sprigs of mint (preferably apple mint)

Method

1. Bring the juice to boiling point and boil until the flavour of mint is pronounced.
2. Remove the mint, add the sugar and boil till it sets.
3. Just before potting add some finely chopped mint and, if necessary, a few spots of green vegetable colouring.
4. Pot in small jars so that opened jars do not lie about for many days. This jelly does not keep its flavour for long after being opened.

Redcurrant Jelly Special for serving with meat

This recipe gives a firm, sharp-flavoured jelly which is perfect for serving with meat. The fruit must be ripe and juicy and the yield is small. This recipe yields about 3 lbs of jelly.

6 lbs redcurrants
Sugar: 1¼ lbs to each pint of juice
Rinse the preserving pan in cold water and leave damp.
Put in the cleaned fruit and heat gently until the currants are soft. This will take about 45 minutes and care must be taken to prevent burning.
The fruit may be put in a covered basin in the oven (temperature 300° F approximately). It will take about an hour to heat through and become tender.
Mash the fruit, strain through a scalded jelly-bag or double linen and allow to drain for about 25 minutes.
Measure the juice, add 1¼ lbs sugar to every pint of juice and bring to the boil. Stir carefully.
Boil for 1 minute at a rapid roll.
Skim quickly and pot at once in small hot jars.
This jelly sets rapidly, so quick handling is necessary.
Cover with waxed circles at once.

Rowan Jelly

3 lbs berries which have just turned red
2 pts water
sugar: 1 lb to every pint of juice measured after straining

Method

1. Wash and pick over the berries.
2. Simmer till tender (40 minutes) and the water is red.   Strain.
3. Measure the juice, return to the clean pan and add the required sugar.
4. Bring slowly to the boil and when the sugar is dissolved, boil rapidly for 10 minutes or until the setting point is reached.
5. Skin and pot in small jars.
6. Cover and tie down whilst hot.

Herb Vinegars

Well-flavoured vinegar makes a great deal of difference in the production of well-flavoured sauces and savouries.
Herb vinegars are made by gathering the herbs just before they flower, usually in late June or July, and soaking them in vinegar. The leaves, which must be dry when picked, are stripped off the

stalks, washed and put into a bottle. Four ounces of herb leaves are used to 1 quart of best wine vinegar. The bottle is then corked and allowed to stand for 2 weeks. The vinegar is then strained off, rebottled and well corked.

Tarragon, chervil, basil or elderflowers, or a mixture of these, can be used. See also p. 449.

CHAPTER XXVII

QUICK-METHOD FOODS

CAKE MIXES

ORIGINALLY the formulas for " quick mix " or " easy-mix " or " one-bowl " cakes were worked out for commercial use, but they can now be bought packaged in a variety of flavours and types. The mixes are particularly well adapted for use with an electric mixer, but in small quantities are excellent made by hand.

The method requires a higher ratio of sugar and liquid than in the standard recipes. They produce a mixture of good volume rather more open grained than a standard cake and frequently they become stale quickly.

The fat used in a cake mix generally has an emulsifier added. If the mix is made at home a vegetable shortening or a lard which contains a percentage of hydrogenated lard or vegetable oil as well as an emulsifier should be used. Pure lard is not suitable for a quick mix.

Home Made Cake Mix

A. 2 lbs soft flour   4 tbs baking powder
   2½ lbs fine sugar   1 teasp salt
   1 lb vegetable shortening

Method

1. Sift the dry ingredients three times.
2. Cut the fat with a pastry blender until a fine crumbly mixture is produced.
3. Store in a covered jar at room temperature.

B. 12 ozs prepared mix   6 fluid ozs milk
   2 eggs   1 teasp flavouring

Method

1. Use the ingredients at room temperature.
2. Measure the mix into a bowl.
3. Add the flavouring to the milk. Pour half into the mixture and beat for 1½ mins at a low speed on a mixer.

4. Scrape down the sides of the bowl and add the remainder to the milk and the eggs.
5. Mix again at a medium speed for 2 minutes.
6. Pour into two 8 inch prepared tins and bake at 350° F for 20–25 mins.

C. ½ lb soft flour   4 fluid ozs cooking oil
1 teasp salt   2 eggs or 5 egg yolks
3 teasp baking powder   1 teasp vanilla essence or
½ lb sugar   2 teasp grated lemon rind
8 fluid ozs milk

Method

1. Sieve the dry ingredients into a bowl.
2. Add the oil (*not olive oil*) and ½ the milk. Stir well and beat for 2 minutes.
3. Add the remainder of the milk, the eggs and the flavouring.
4. Beat for 2 minutes. The batter will be smooth and thin.
5. Pour into two 8 inch sandwich tins or one 9 × 5 oblong tin. The tins should not be greased.

Bake the sandwich cakes at 350° F for 30 mins and the oblong cake at 325° F for about an hour.

D. A " white cake " is made like recipe " C " using 5 egg whites instead of 2 whole eggs. It should be cooked in 8 inch sandwich tins or a 10 inch sponge cake tin with a centre tube. Temperature 350° F. Time 30–40 minutes.

When a cake mix is bought ready prepared, additional ingredients will be needed, and the instructions on the packet should be followed exactly. This is very important indeed as deviations from the maker's instructions (such as using milk where the recipe says water) will spoil the result. Exact measurements, correct size of tin and accurate oven temperature and time of cooking must be observed.

The use of White Shortenings for quick methods

White Shortenings, other than lard, are made from tropical seeds and nuts. The oils are hardened by hydrogenation which is the forcing of hydrogen through the oil in the presence of nickel which acts as a catalyst. The process also improves the plasticity of the product. So that this shortening can be easily dispersed in a mixture, air is introduced into the hydrogenated oil and the resulting shortening is quickly creamed and easily handled.

The vegetable shortenings are 100% fat and therefore less fat is needed than when butter or lard is used. There is very little flavour in White Shortenings, and while this can be an advantage when frying, it is a disadvantage for such things as omelets, shortbread and sauces with a delicate flavour.

Care must be taken when using these fats for deep frying, as they smoke at 375° F which is a higher temperature than is generally required. A thermometer should be used to ensure correct frying temperature.

Fork Mix Pastry

8 ozs flour	1 teasp salt
4 ozs white shortening	2 tbs water

Method

1. Sieve the flour and salt.
2. Add the shortening and water.
3. Mix with a fork till a dough is formed.
4. Use as for Short Crust pastry.

Water Whip Pastry

8 ozs flour	3½ ozs shortening
1 teasp salt	2½ tbs *boiling* water

Method

1. Mix the fat and boiling water with 1 tbs flour until a paste is formed.
2. Add the remainder of the flour.
3. Use as Short Crust pastry.

Sandwich Cake using White Shortening

4 ozs flour	4 ozs castor sugar
½ teasp salt	2 eggs
3 ozs white shortening	2½ teasp baking powder

Method

1. Sieve the dry ingredients into a bowl.
2. Add the eggs, water and fat (all in one piece).
3. Beat for one minute with a wooden spoon.
4. Bake as for a Victoria Sandwich, i.e. divide between two 7-inch sandwich tins and cook at 350° F for 25–30 mins.

PASTRY

No Roll Pastry

A. 6 ozs flour   2 tbs cold milk
   1 teasp salt   1½ teasp sugar
   8 tbs vegetable or corn oil

Method

1. Sieve the dry ingredients.
2. Mix the oil and milk with a fork.
3. Pour on to the flour and mix with the fork until a paste is formed.
4. Press into a tin to line, working the mixture over the base and up the sides of the tin.
5. Finish the edge by fluting. Prick the base.
6. Bake for 12–15 mins at 425° F.

Easy Mix Flaky Pastry

B. 8 ozs flour   8 tbs oil
    1 teasp salt   5 tbs ice cold water

Method

1. Sieve the flour and salt.
2. Whip the oil and water together with a fork.
3. Pour over the dry ingredients and mix to a soft dough.
4. Work into a ball and divide into two.
5. Flatten each half into a round and roll each between layers of waxed paper until the circle of pastry measures about 11 inches. This gives the thickness required for baking.

   If the table top or pastry board is slightly damp, the waxed paper will not slip during the rolling.
6. Peel off the top paper and, using the edges of the under paper to hold, turn the paste into a pie tin or plate.
7. Press and shape. Prick over base.
8. Bake at 475° F for 12–15 mins.

SOUP MIXES

There are many manufactured dehydrated soups which contain mainly uncooked ingredients, and often have a fresh flavour which makes them a desirable dish quickly and easily prepared. The discovery of monosodium glutamate was important, as it is a product which has the property of restoring to food the piquancy lost in dehydration. It is supposed not to add any flavour of its own, but many people claim they detect a particular saltiness.

These soups are obtainable in a wide variety of flavours and are packed in heat-sealed envelopes which are moisture, vapour and heat proof. They keep fresh for about 12 months. To prepare them it is necessary only to add the required amount of water or milk, and cook for the time specified on the packet.

The flavour can be varied by the addition of stock instead of water, garnishes of various kinds or fresh cream where suitable.

Bouillon cubes are an improvement on the " meat cube " which has been available for many years. They are made by heating to dryness, in a vacuum oven, a mixture of meat extract, fat, herbs and spices and seasoning paste. This mixture is then broken into granules and compressed into cubes. Beef and chicken meat is used instead of meat extract in the better quality cubes. These form an excellent stock when dissolved in water.

A little of the soup powder can be used as a flavouring in home made soups and sauces. For instance, a little mushroom soup powder makes a good substitute for mushrooms in a stew, and some onion soup can be used in place of onions in flavouring sauces.

Good sauces can be made by using a packaged soup with half the stated quantity of liquid and following the directions in other respects.

The addition of some cream or evaporated milk improves the sauce as does the addition of chosen herbs during the cooking.

Some soup mixes which have pieces of vegetable in them, e.g. onion, can be sieved to make a smooth sauce.

Sauce from Canned Soups

The best results are obtained from the condensed soups as these can be diluted to the consistency needed for sauce. Ordinary tinned soups make pouring sauces but are too thin for coating food.

The following are suggestions for using condensed soup for sauce.

Celery Sauce. Heat a tin of soup with a bouillon cube crumbled in it. Sieve if a purée sauce is wanted. Add cream from the milk and season.

Mushroom Sauce. Heat condensed cream of mushroom soup, add cream if liked and season with nutmeg.

Onion Sauce. Heat the soup, sieve if a " soubise " is wanted, otherwise check for seasoning. This soup is often salty when in the condensed form. If so flavour with a little sugar and evaporated milk or cream.

Tomato Sauce. Heat the condensed soup with a sprig of marjoram and a bouillon cube. Remove the marjoram and check the flavour, using lemon juice and sugar as required.

CHAPTER XXVIII

PRESSURE COOKING

DURING the past ten years pressure cooking has become very general owing to the saving of cooking time and the greater simplicity of the modern cooker.

Choice of Cooker

There are several varieties on the market today and each has points in its favour.

A. *Saucepan Type*

As the name suggests, this one is like a saucepan with a lid that is secured into position by a twist so that, by the interlocking of a flange on the pan and lid, the latter is firmly held down. The airtight seal of the lid is obtained by a rubber washer or gasket fitting inside the edge of the lid.

B. *Casserole Type*

These cookers have no long saucepan handle but a small grip on each side of the pan. The lid fits inside the cooker with a bar holding it from falling in. The opening of the cooker and the lid are both oval in shape. The lid is slipped inside and given a half turn to secure it. A spring holds the lid tightly against the flange of the cooker. Again the airtight seal is obtained by a rubber or papier mâché washer fitted into the top edge of the lid so that it lies between the cooker and lid when in position.

C. *Heavy Cast Iron Type*

These are very strong but difficult to move owing to their weight. Some work like the casserole type with a lid that is fitted inside. Others have a lid which hinges on and is screwed down with a clamp-like fitting.

Principles under which Pressure Cookers work

Whichever type is chosen the principle upon which it works is the same. The cooker must have some water in it to be converted into steam. Once the lid has been secured no air or steam should be able to escape round the joint; in this way pressure can be built up in the cooker. The greater the pressure the higher is the temperature at which water boils—i.e. is converted into steam.

At normal atmospheric pressure (approximately 14 lbs per square inch) water boils at 212° F. When an additional pressure of 5 lbs per square inch is exerted the boiling temperature goes up to 228° F.

With 10 lbs per square inch additional pressure the boiling temperature is approximately 240° F.

With 15 lbs per square inch additional pressure the boiling temperature is approximately 250° F.

These are boiling temperatures of water pressurised by steam. The temperatures at which water boils when pressurised by air are rather less.

The ability of air under pressure to raise the boiling point of water is less than that of steam at the same pressure, due to a difference in molecular velocity. Hence it is most important that all air should be driven out of the cooker before starting to build up the pressure. When the water boils the steam will push the air out of the "vent". The cooker should be exhausted of air by steaming for a few minutes before building up the pressure. At first steam will be emitted in small jets but gradually a steady stream will be coming out of the vent. This will take about 5 minutes. The vent should then be closed and the pressure built up rapidly.

The control of the pressure varies with different cookers.

A. *Weight Control*

The weight is in proportion to the size of the vent hole. Excess steam will lift the weight, causing a hiss. The control of pressure is gained by :—

(1) using different weights
(2) marks indicated on the button which is pushed up under pressure.

B. *Spring Control*

The vent is closed by turning down a metal flap which is operated by a spring. When 15 lb pressure is reached the cooker hisses. 5 and 10 lb pressure cannot be obtained with this means of pressure control.

C. *Dial Gauge*

This may be the only means of controlling the pressure or may be operated with one of the above methods. The hand on the dial indicates the pressure in the cooker. The dial is controlled by a spring.

Q

Wherever the pressure is controlled or indicated by a spring, it may prove inaccurate after a time, owing to the spring becoming slack under constant strain. If the cooker seems to be very quick in reaching pressure—i.e. the point at which hissing is produced— or if the food is not fully cooked when pressure has been exerted for the normal cooking time, a new spring or control should be fitted. Often the slackness of the spring of the dial may be detected if the hand does not return to zero when the cooker has cooled. The spare parts can be obtained from the manufacturers through the shop from which the cooker was bought.

Safety Devices on Pressure Cookers

Most cookers have a safety plug as well as the whistle or hiss apparatus, which indicates that pressure has been obtained. It is important that the cooker should whistle softly or hiss during the entire cooking time if there is no dial as otherwise full pressure is not being maintained.

Should the pressure in the cooker continue to build up beyond 15 lbs per square inch there is *no danger* of the lid blowing off or the cooker bursting as the second safety device will come into operation and release the pressure.

This second safety release or over-pressure plug is either of rubber or fusible metal. When the pressure increases over 15 lbs the rubber plug is pushed out or the soft metal melts and the steam is released. This excess pressure should never build up if the heat is reduced when cooking pressure is obtained. If the vent is not kept clean and is blocked the cooking pressure may not be indicated by the whistle or hiss and excess pressure may build up. It is very important that the vent is kept clean and is checked after every use.

General Instructions for the Use of Pressure Cookers

1. Put in the required amount of water. For vegetables $\frac{1}{4}-\frac{1}{2}$ pint. For other foods see the cooking chart.
2. Place the rack at the bottom if required and put the cooker to heat.
3. Place the food in the cooker. Never overfill. The cooker should never be filled more than $\frac{2}{3}$ full.
4. Fit the lid on the cooker and secure firmly.
5. Keep the cooker over a high heat until a steady stream of steam comes from the vent. This will take at least 5 minutes.
6. Close the vent by moving the metal flap or place the weight control in position.
7. Continue to heat rapidly until the cooker hisses or whistles, or the indicator shows that pressure has been obtained.

8. Reduce the heat and maintain the pressure for the required length of time. *Timing starts at this point.*
9. If the cooker needs to be cooled rapidly, stand in a bowl of cold water or under a running tap. Do not let the water run over the over-pressure plug.
10. When the temperature has gone down, *carefully* remove weight control or open pressure flap. If there is any sound of hissing, continue cooling before removing it.
11. Remove the lid of the cooker with the lid coming towards you so that it acts as a protection against a sudden spurt of steam. *Never* remove the lid until the pressure is down to normal and the vent is *open*.

To Clean the Cooker

1. The weight control should stand in a safe place to cool. It should never be washed.
2. Wipe the lid as soon as it has been removed. See that the rubber washer or gasket is quite clean. If there is a tendency for the cooker to leak round the lid after some use, remove the washer and reverse it. New washers or gaskets may be obtained very easily.
3. Clean the vent opening with a bottle brush or pipe cleaner if necessary. Always check the cleanliness of the vent.
4. Clean the cooker like any saucepan. Dry it thoroughly.
5. Place the weight control (if any) inside the cooker with the rack.
6. Place the lid *upside down* on the cooker. Never place the lid in the cooking position as this will wear the gasket and prevent circulation of air.

CHART OF COOKING TIMES

Food	Amount of Water (Pints)	Special Instructions	Time Under Pressure (15 lbs) (Minutes)
SOUPS			
Carrot	2		4
Cauliflower	2		3
Celery	2		10
Lentil	3	Never fill the cooker more	20
Oxtail	2	than ½ full.	30
Pea (dried)	2½	Cool rapidly.	30
Potato	2		5
Scotch Broth	2		20
Tomato	2		3
Vegetable (mixed)	2½		5
FISH			
Cod steaks	½		4
Fillets of Plaice or Sole	½		2–3 according to thickness.
Whole Plaice and Sole	½	Wrap the fish in grease-proof paper or vegetable parchment.	3–4
Herrings	½	Cool rapidly.	4–5
Mackerel	½		5–6
Kippers	½		2–3
Smoked Haddock	½		5–6
Salmon steaks	½		6–8
POT ROAST			
Beef	½	Brown in hot fat in open	10 per lb.
Mutton	½	cooker before adding the	10–12 ,,
Veal	½	water.	10 ,,
Pork	½	Cool rapidly.	15 ,,
STEWS			
Beef	or more { ½	Use the rack in the cooker.	15
Irish	if ½	Cool rapidly.	15–20
Fricassée of Veal	liked { ½		20
CHOPS			
Mutton	¼	Brown in hot fat before	4–5
Veal	¼	adding the water—cool	5
Pork	¼	rapidly. Grill for ½ min.	6
STEAK AND KIDNEY PUDDING	2	Stand the basin on the rack. Steam for 15 mins. with the vent open. Cool at room temperature.	30
OXTAIL	1½	Do not thicken until after cooking. Cool rapidly.	45

CHART OF COOKING TIMES *continued*

Food	Amount of Water (Pints)	Special Instructions	Time Under Pressure (15 lbs) (Minutes)
Chicken (Young)	½	Cook on the rack. Brown in a hot oven after cooking.	12
Boiling Fowl	1	Cook on the rack.	20–30
Rabbit	½–1	Prepare as for ordinary cooking.	15–20
Hare	¾–1	Thicken after cooking.	30–40
Heart	¾		30
Ox Tongue	1½	Blanch first. Stand on rack. Cool at room temperature.	15 to the lb.
Vegetables (Fresh)			
Artichokes (Jerusalem)	¼		6–8
Asparagus	¼		2
Beans—Broad	¼		3–4
French	¼		2–3
Runner	¼		3–4
Beetroot	½		10–16
Broccoli	¼	Cook vegetables on the	2–3
Brussels Sprouts	¼	rack. Have water boil-	2–4
Cabbage, shredded	¼	ing. Bring to pressure	2
Carrots	¼	very quickly and cool	3–5
Cauliflower	¼	rapidly.	3–5
Celery	¼		4–5
Leeks	¼		3–5
Marrow	¼		2
Onions	¼		3–6
Parsnips	¼		3–5
Peas	¼		1–2
Potatoes—new	¼		6–8
old	¼		4–6
Swedes	¼		4–6
(Dried)			
Beans—butter	2 per lb	The water should just	20
Haricot	2 ,,	cover them.	15–20
Lentils	1½–2 ,,	Bring to pressure slowly.	10–15
Peas—whole	2 ,,	Cool for 15 minutes at	15
split	2 ,,	room temperature. Never fill cooker more than ½ full.	10–15
Fruit (Dried)			
Apples	1	Soak for 1 hour in meas-	3–5
Apricots	1	ured water, then cook in	5
Figs	1	the water in which they	10–15
Peaches	1	were soaked.	5
Pears	1	Cook on a rack.	3–5
Prunes	1	Cool rapidly.	5–8

CHAPTER XXIX

THE SERVICE OF WINE

ANY good meal is made better by wine; wine well chosen to complement the food and the company will bring out the best in both, and people who care about their food and their friends will not want to entertain without it.

These elementary notes are meant to encourage people who know little about wine to experiment with it; for full knowledge can only come from drinking. Any good wine merchant will be pleased to advise you, and it is worth taking his expert advice till you have built up your own store of experience; do not be afraid he will press you to buy only expensive wines. There is a good deal of snobbery about the choice of wine, and a lot of nonsense is talked about its service; you can safely ignore both.

Types of Wine

Wine is simply fermented grape juice.

It can be still, like port or sherry or claret; slightly sparkling, what the French call *pétillant*, like many Loire or Rhenish wines; or foaming, *spumante* in Italian, like champagne. Again, it can be " red "—any colour from pink through pale scarlet to purple—like claret or port; or " white ", like hock or champagne, ranging in colour from pale straw to golden yellow or even brown. Rosé wines, palish pink, count as red; madeiras, marsalas, and dark sherries, in shades of brown, count as white. Most red wines are made from black grapes, and most white ones from white; though champagne is made from black.

All wines have alcohol in them; the amount varies with type and age. Plain table wines, those drunk during a meal, have two or three times as much alcohol in them as plain draught beer; though rather less alcohol than there is in cider. Sherry is a little more alcoholic than cider, and port more so still; but sherry and port are both " fortified "—that is, strengthened with brandy—while they are being matured. Their maturing may extend over years; champagne also requires frequent attention before it is put on sale—hence its high price. Most table wines are more simply treated; the rarest are cherished and bottled where they are gathered—hence the *cachet* of " château-bottled " wines. Of course the quality of any wine varies widely from one vintage year to another, according to the amount of sun and rain the vines have had. Once you have discovered your favourite kinds of wine, it is worth asking your wine merchant which their best recent years are.

A good way of starting to discover your favourites is to take wine by the glass in restaurants. You will be offered nothing startlingly good, but will give your palate a start.

Choice of Wine

There are few rules that matter about what can and what cannot be drunk with what.

Only two wines can abide tobacco smoke: sherry and madeira. If you offer your guests vintage port, they should not insult you and it by smoking with it.

The familiar tag, " don't mix your drinks ", means " don't mix drinks made from one thing with drinks made from another ": gin and table or dessert wines do not go well together. Beer, made from malt and hops, goes with whisky or vodka, made from malt, better than wine goes with either. Whisky and vodka have five or six times as much alcohol in them as most table wines. If you want a strong drink to follow wine, take brandy, or any of the other scores of grape-based liqueurs; but if your meal has been well enough composed, with food and wine and companions that hit it off exactly, strong drink afterwards will be more a luxury than a necessity.

If you serve only one wine with the meal, choose it to fit the main course. Conventionally white wines are supposed to be served with fish, cold poultry, and white meat, and red ones with red meat, hot poultry, and game; but there is no reason why you should not drink red wine with cold chicken or white with hot, if you enjoy it. Be guided by what you like; but remember that the delicate flavour of most fish dishes is swamped by most red or sparkling wines.

Until you have confidence in your own judgement, these suggestions may help:

with soup or hors d'œuvres, drink dry or medium sherry or dry madeira;

with fish, including oysters and other shellfish, with salads and with cold birds drink a dry white wine such as hock or Moselle, or Chablis or a heavier white Burgundy;

with hot entrées, roast poultry or game, and hot joints drink claret, or for the stronger flavoured dishes a red Burgundy.

Apéritifs

Gin, whisky, vodka, and cocktails based on them will only make you uncomfortable if you drink any of them before wine. There are plenty of wine apéritifs; such as dry madeira or marsala or, best known of all, sherry.   There are dozens of kinds of sherry, ranging from a very dry, keen-tasting almost colourless sharp wine to a liquid reminiscent of molten black treacle.   All true sherries come from south-western Spain, though many passable imitations are made elsewhere.   They are classified as: dry; medium dry (fino, or the less fortified Manzanilla);   medium (amontillado);   and sweet (oloroso or amoroso).   Sweet sherries are more suitable after a meal than before.

Sherries are served neat, and cold—not chilled.   As an alternative to sherry, either French or Italian vermouth or a mixture of the two makes a pleasant drink;   Italian is darker, less dry, and less bitter. Vermouths are served very cold;   a sliver of lemon rind can be added to Italian, and so can soda water.   Dubonnet, a sweet fortified red wine flavoured with quinine, can be drunk neat or with lemon rind or ice or both.

The best of apéritifs is a glass of champagne, served chilled; and the same wine can be served right on through the meal—if your pocket allows, and your guests do not find the fizziness distressing.

Table Wines

These are known by the districts they come from; the most famous of them carry also the name of their vineyard or château of origin.

The most popular table wines, red and white, sweet and dry, come from the Gironde estuary near Bordeaux.   Red Bordeaux, known as claret, comes from several communes of the Médoc—Pauillac, which includes the three celebrated châteaux of Lafite, Latour, and Mouton-Rothschild;   St Julien, Margaux, Cantenac, and others— or from the neighbouring district of St Emilion.   White Bordeaux wines, dry Graves or the sweeter Barsac or Sauternes, are less plenti-ful, but abundantly varied also;   one of the Sauternes châteaux Yquem, is world-famous.

Burgundies are richer and fuller-flavoured than the wines of Bordeaux, though similar in colour.   Beaune, Pommard, Volnay, Corton are familiar names among the reds;   Chablis, Montrachet, Pouilly among the whites.   Mâcon and Beaujolais are lighter in texture than the other red Burgundies, as well as easier in price. Further down the Rhone, Hermitage and Châteauneuf-du-Pape are two famous full-flavoured wines suitable for drinking with Provençal food.

Loire wines such as Muscadet and Vouvray are most of them light, fresh, slightly sparkling, and white;   many are good with fish, but they do not all travel well.

Rhenish wines, grown in the Palatinate and known as hocks and

Moselles, are almost all light dry white wines; some of the best white wines ever grown have come from here. But you need care and knowledge, or well-informed advice, when you buy them; following the names of Liebfraumilch, Niersteiner and Johannisberger will carry you some way, but not far.

Not all table wines come from France or Germany. Italian Chianti, red or white, Yugoslav white Riesling, light rough Spanish wines of the Burgundy type, and several other kinds are now readily available in England, but their rather lower prices reflect their lack of the delicate flavour of claret or hock or the invigorating sparkle of champagne.

Dessert Wines

These are rich strong sweet wines served at the end of a meal.

Port, the best of all, comes only from the upper Douro valley in Portugal (if it comes from elsewhere, it has by law to be called " port type ", not " port "). Vintage port has to be of the finest quality, and may take as long as 25 years to mature; while it matures it collects sediment (this is called " throwing a crust "), which it is important to disturb as little as possible. All the grapes of a vintage port are of the same year. Tawny port, a blend of several good but not superb years, is matured in cask and can be drunk soon after bottling; unlike vintage port, it does not improve in the bottle. Ruby port is a sweetish blend of less good years, bottled early.

Port is rather more a man's than a woman's drink. At a dinner for both men and women, you may prefer to serve madeira, or marsala, or a rich brown sherry such as Bristol Milk or Cream; or a Sauternes. Very good clarets can also be drunk enjoyably with dessert.

Preparing Wine for the Table

Keep your wine as still as you can till you need it, preferably at a fairly cool even temperature. Remember to serve apéritif wines cool or chilled; white table wines chilled; and all other wines at the temperature of the room you drink them in. The simplest way of bringing wines to room temperature is to move them into the room some hours before the meal.

No wine except champagne is harmed, and most wines are improved, by being decanted; vintage port should always be decanted. Whether you decant or not, open each bottle carefully and slowly. Insert a corkscrew firmly in the centre of the cork, and twist gently till the tip of the screw just shows at the cork's base; then draw the cork out by slow and steady pulling—if necessary, putting the bottle on the floor first, and holding it steady with your feet while you pull. Remember to wipe the neck of the bottle, inside and out, with a clean cloth before you do anything else. Wine should be poured steadily from bottle to decanter; over a napkin, or against a light, so that any crust can be noticed and left in the bottle instead of being decanted. Well over an inch of vintage port may have to be left in the bottom of the bottle, and some vintage clarets also carry sediment; most other wines are almost free of it.

Red table wines should be opened, and if you choose decanted, an hour or so before they are drunk; contact with the air improves the flavour. White table wines or vermouths should be chilled by half an hour in the refrigerator just before they are drunk; or if you have a good cool cellar, leave your white wine there till you need it. These wines should feel cool on the tongue.

Glasses should be plain and clear, so that the wine shows in its true colour; like decanters, they must be scrupulously clean and dry and well polished. Coloured glasses will hide turbidity in wine; heavily cut glasses look impressive, but reduce rather than enhance appreciation of what is inside them. A thin glass enables the drinker's hand to warm a red wine; a stem keeps the hand's warmth away from a white one. A plain thin sizeable tulip-shaped glass will serve all purposes—sizeable, so that there is room for the wine's bouquet to rise in the glass and be enjoyed by the drinker. But traditionally sherry is served in long narrow glasses, port in short squat ones, and brandy in large bowl-shaped balloons.

Serving the Wine

You can expect to get from a bottle:

     of table wine, 6 glasses (5 of hock); allow $\frac{1}{4}$–$\frac{1}{2}$ bottle for each person;

     of sherry or port, 12–13 glasses;

     of brandy, about 30 tots, each of $\frac{1}{6}$ gill (for other liqueurs, serve $\frac{1}{8}$ gill to each glass).

Serve from the drinker's right, where the glasses stand. Pour a few drops into the host's glass first, as wine waiters do in a restaurant, and let him sip it, to make sure the bottle is not spoiled, before his guests drink. Always circulate bottles and decanters to the left—clockwise.

Do not fill wine-glasses more than two-thirds full, or you rob the drinker of the pleasure of the bouquet. Pour steadily and without splashing; a napkin wrapped round the bottle will catch drips.

Lastly, remember to eat as well as drinking. Alcohol in any quantity on empty stomachs defeats its purpose, the bringing of a feeling of well-being and kindliness.

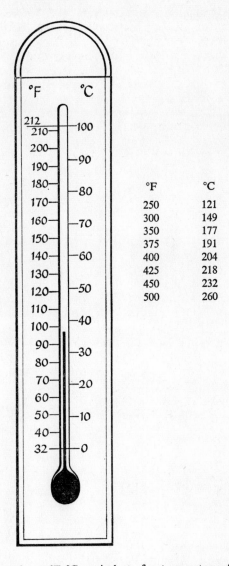

°F	°C
250	121
300	149
350	177
375	191
400	204
425	218
450	232
500	260

The thermometer above shows °F–°C equivalents for temperatures from freezing to boiling, and conversions of some higher temperatures used in cooking are given in the table at the side. A simple formula for converting °F to °C is to subtract 32 and multiply by 5/9.

INDEX

Allspice 462
Almond
  cake 344, 345, 352
  paste icing 381
  pudding 255, 258
  ring biscuits 374
  rock 304
  sandwich filling 421
  slice biscuits 371
  soup 51
  stuffings 412
Anchovy
  butter 37
  cream 37
  for hors d'œuvres 36
  sauce 60
Angels on horseback 39
Appetisers 33
Apple
  amber 271
  apricot flan 267
  baked 279
  balls 264
  and blackberry jam 434
  and blackberry jelly 437
  butter 444
  charlotte 278
  cheese 443
  and chocolate sandwich filling
    422
  chutney 450
  curd 444
  and date and raisin chutney 450
  dumplings 264
  flan 265
  jelly 437
  pie 262
  and prune stuffing 413
  pudding 260
  sago 279
  salads 186, 188
  sauce 70
  tart 270
  tart, spiced 270
  water 407
Apricot
  cream 297–8
  flan 267
  ice 315
  mousse 305
  stuffings 412–13

Arrowroot
  glaze 266
  mould 287
  pudding 248
Artichokes
  globe 173
  Jerusalem, cooking 173
  Jerusalem, preparing 168
  soup 51
Asparagus
  boiled 173
  omelet 209
  preparing 170
Aspic
  jelly 292
  mayonnaise 67
  mould 137
Aubergines 179
Au gratin 26
Avocado pear 33

Bacon
  baked 137
  boiled 136
  and egg tart 228
  fried 191
  grilled 107
  joints 135
  sauce 229
Bain Marie 26
Baking—Chapter XX, 319
  blind 266
  general information 319
  (for bread, buns, cakes, scones, see
    under separate headings)
Baking powder, 321
Banana
  cream pie 267
  custard flan 267
  fool 284
  fried 154
  mousse 305
  and nut salad 186
Barding 26, 158
Barley
  pudding 246
  water 407
Basting 26
Batters—Chapter XV, 212
  baked pudding 213
  basic recipes 212

Batters—Chapter XV (*continued*)
  black cap pudding 213
  flour and milk 192
  fritter 192
  fruit 213
  general information 212
  pancakes 213–14
  savoury pudding 213
  toad-in-the-hole 213
  whole egg 192
  Yorkshire pudding 214
Beans
  broad 169, 173
  dried 169, 173
  french 169, 173
  haricot 167
  pickled 453
  runner 169, 173
  soup 51
Béchamel 26, 60
Beef
  appearance of 100
  boiled 111
  braised 110
  cuts of 101, 104
  fillets 127
  fillets duchesse 128
  fillets madeleine 128
  fillets pompadour 128
  fillets, Russian 129
  goulash 123
  minced 116
  mock game 125
  olives 124
  pressed 141
  roast 104–7
  roll 140
  shin of 138
  steak, grilled 107–9
  steak, fried 191
  steak and kidney pie 132
  steak and kidney pudding 132
  stew, general 114
  stewed in wine 122
  (and see Stews)
  tea 407
  tournedos 127
  Vienna steaks 129
Beetroot
  baked 173
  boiled 173
  in hors d'œuvres 35
  preparing 168
  roast 172
Beignets 26
Biscuits 368–377
  Almond ring 374
  almond slice 371
  bourbon 374
  brandy snap 376
  cheese 390

Biscuits (*continued*)
  chocolate 371
  cinnamon 371
  coconut 372
  coffee cream 374
  date torte 370
  easter 374
  flapjack 376
  florentines 376
  ginger nuts 376
  Grantham gingerbread 374
  Grasmere gingerbread 372
  napoleon 372
  nutty balls 370
  oatcakes 377
  oatmeal 372
  orange cream 375
  parkin 377
  priory 375
  rice 373, 377
  shortbread 373, 375
  Shrewsbury 375
  spice 373
  sponge fingers 377
  Viennese 375
Bisques 48
Blackberry
  pie 262
  pudding 260
  and apple jam 434
  and apple jelly 437
Blackcock see chapter on Game
Blackcurrant cheese 443
  jam 434
  jelly 437
Blanch, to 26
Blend, to 27
Blued sugar 383
Bottling 425
Bouquet garni 27, 462
Brain
  cakes 134
  sauce 60
Braise, to 27, 110
Brandy
  butter 65
  junket 286
  snaps 376
Brawn 138
Breadcrumbs, to fry 158
Breadmaking
  bara brith 330
  basic methods 324
  bridge rolls 326
  brown bread 325
  cake 360
  Christmas spice bread 331
  currant bread 329
  date 360
  dinner rolls 325
  malt loaf 332

Breadmaking (*continued*)
  orange 332
  Sally Lunn 326
  Vienna 326
  wholemeal 325
Bream see chapter on Fish
Brisket 141
Broccoli 173
  and bacon sauce 229
Broths
  basic method 48
  (and see Soups)
Brussels sprouts 174
Buck rarebit 43
Buns
  bara brith 330
  basic recipe 328
  Bath 329
  Chelsea 329
  currant 329
  hot cross 329
  princess 333
  Swiss 329
  Yorkshire tea-cakes 329
Butter
  anchovy 37
  apple 444
  brandy 65
  to clarify 417
  cream icing 381
  devilled 65
  green 37
  maître d'hôtel 65
  melted 65
  parsley 38

Cabbage 168, 174
  red 177, 181
  red, pickled 449
  sour 181
Cake-making—Chapter XXI, 341
  creamed mixtures 348
  melted fat mixtures 356
  quick mixes 467
  rubbed-in mixtures 341
Cakes
  almond 344, 345, 352
  Banbury puffs 272
  basic recipe, creamed 351
  basic recipe, large 345
  basic recipe, small 343
  basic recipe, sponges 365
  Battenberg 366
  buns see Buns
  cherry 344, 352
  cake bread 360
  chocolate 344, 345, 352
  Christmas 352
  Coburg 359
  coconut 311, 344, 345, 352
  coffee 344, 345, 353

Cakes (*continued*)
  cornflour 353
  countess 345
  cream cheese 311
  cream horns 273
  cream puffs 378
  currant 346, 353
  date 346
  date bread 360
  date and walnut 346
  Dundee 353
  Eccles 272
  éclairs 378–80
  Genoa 353
  Genoese pastry 365–6
  ginger 344, 353
  gingerbread 358–61
  ground rice 353
  housekeeper 346
  Japanese 311
  layer 364
  lemon 344, 346, 353
  lemon jumbles 344
  luncheon 346
  madeira 353
  malt loaf 332
  meringues 307
  mille-feuilles 274
  mocha 364
  mushroom 311
  nut meringues 311
  nutty balls 370
  orange 344, 346, 353
  parkin 358, 360
  pineapple 353
  plum 353
  queen 354
  raspberry 344
  rock 344
  sandwich 354, 364
  sandwich, quickly made 469
  seed 344, 354
  simnel 354
  soul 333
  spice 344
  sponge 361
  sponge fingers 364
  sultana 346, 354
  swiss roll 364
  tennis 354
  vanilla slices 274
  victoria sandwich 354
  vinegar 346
  walnut 346, 354
  Welsh 338
Canapés 27, 37
Canning 455–7
Cantaloupe melon 33
Capsicums 180
Caramel 27
Carbohydrates 21

Carrots
  and apple salad 186
  cooking 174
  in hors d'œuvres 35
  preparing 168
Casserole 27
Cassolette 27
Cauliflower
  boiled 174
  fried 171, 174
  pickled 448
  preparing 168
  in salads 183
Caviare 33
Cayenne 463
Celeriac
  cooking 174
  preparing 168
Celery
  cooking 175
  in hors d'œuvres 35
  preparing 169
  soup 51
Charlotte 28, 278, 285, 297
Chaudfroid 28, 154
Cheese
  aigrettes 39, 194–5
  biscuits 390
  cottage 37
  eggs 230
  flan 230
  general information 228
  macaroni 235
  and macaroni croquettes 219
  Marmite 38
  omelet 209
  pastry 390
  potatoes 230
  pudding 231
  sauce 61
  scones 336
  soufflé 231
  spreads 37, 419–20
  straws 40
  and tomato pasties 242
Chelsea buns 329
Cherry
  cake 344, 352
  pie 262
  pudding 258
  tart 264, 270
Chestnut
  croquettes 232
  forcemeat 413
  soup 51
Chicken
  in aspic 137, 154
  barbecue sauce 68
  boiled 150
  broth 49
  casserole 152

Chicken (continued)
  chaudfroid 154
  choosing 145
  cream 411
  drawing 146
  fricassée 151
  and ham croquettes 219
  hors d'œuvres 36
  liver pâté 141
  Marengo 152
  Maryland 153
  trussing 147, 150
  roast 147
  roast, accompaniments for, 149
  to stuff 147
Chicory 169, 175
Chillies 180
Chives 183, 462
Chocolate
  biscuits 371
  cake 344, 345, 352
  cornflour pudding 248
  cream 298
  éclairs 380
  ice 315
  junket 286
  mould 287
  mousse 306–7
  pudding 255, 258
  queen of puddings 205
  rice pudding 246
  sauce 73
  semolina pudding 247
  soufflé (cold) 303
  soufflé (hot) 277
  swiss roll 364
Christmas
  cake 352
  pudding 252–3
  spice bread 331
Chutney
  apple 450
  apple, date and raisin 450
  basic method 445
  brown 452
  date 450
  gooseberry 450
  green tomato 452
  marrow 451
  plum 451
  rhubarb 451
  ripe tomato 452
Cinnamon 462
  biscuits 371
Coatings 192–3
Coconut
  biscuits 372
  cake 344, 345, 352
  pudding 255, 258
  pyramids 311
Cocottes 28

Coffee
cake 344, 345, 353
cream 298
cream biscuits 374
éclairs 380
ice 315
junket 286
making 415
mould 287
mousse 305
pudding 255, 258
soufflé 277, 303
Cod—see chapter on Fish
Cold meat
curry 220
mould 222
recipes 126–8
reheated—see Chapter XVI
Compôte 28
Consommés, basic method 55
(and see Soups)
Cooking temperatures x
Cooking terms 26
Cornflour
cake 353
chocolate pudding 248
mould 287
Corn fritters 153
Cornish pasties 232
Cornish treacle tart 271
Corn on the cob 175
Coupe glacée 318
Crab, to buy 20, 93
dressed 93
Crabapple jelly 437
Crayfish 34
Cream
anchovy 37
cheese cakes 312
cheese spread 37, 420
horns 273
mock 382
puffs 378, 380
salad dressing 184
soups 53
Cream, to 28
Creams (sweets) see Puddings
Cress 168
Croquettes 28, 218–19
Croûte 28
Croûtons 28
Cucumber 175
in hors d'œuvres 35
pickled 448
salad 186
Currant
bread 329
buns 329
cake 346, 353
jam 434
jelly 437, 465

Currant (continued)
pie 262
pudding 255, 258, 260
Curry
accompaniments to 244
cold meat 220
egg 220
fish 220
fresh meat 131
sauce 65
vegetable 220
Custard
baked 203, 206
banana flan 267
caramel 204
confectioner's 382
creams 298
cup 203, 206
fish or tripe 411
mould 287
pouring 203, 206
puddings 204
sauce 70
savoury 56
steamed 203, 207
tart 268
trifles 298, 300, 301
Cutlets (réchauffé) 218

Damson
cheese 443
jam 434
pickle 447
pie 262
pudding 260
Danish pastry 330
Dariole 29
Date
bread 360
cake 346
chutney 450
crunch 256
pudding 251, 255
torte 370
and walnut cake 346
Delaware filling 262
Devilling 29
Doughnuts 194–5, 331
Dried peas 169, 179
Dripping 416–17
Duck
braised 156
choosing 145
Normandy 156
roast 149
wild 157–8, 162
Dumplings
apple 264
suet 113
tomato 243
yeast 326

Dutch flummery 290

Eclairs
  basic method 378
  chocolate 380
  coffee 380
  savoury 380
Egg
  and bacon tart 228
  baked (en cocotte) 229
  batter 192
  boiled 202
  and breadcrumb coating 193
  cheese 230
  coddled 202
  cookery—Chapter XIV, 199
  croquettes 219
  curried 220
  flip 408
  foundation sauces 68
  fried 202
  general information 199
  in hors d'œuvres 36
  jelly 290
  nog 408
  omelets see Omelets
  poached 203
  preserving 201
  sandwich filling 420
  sauce 61
  scotch 239
  scrambled 203
  separating 199
  storing 201
  stuffed 240
  whisking 200
Egg-plant 179
Endive
  cooking 175
  preparing 168
Energy foods 22
Entrées 29, 126–137
Enzymes 167
Espagnole 29, 63
Essences 462
Eve's pudding 255, 259

Farce 29
Fat
  to clarify 417
  to render 416
Fennel 462
  sauce 61
Fish—Chapter VIII, 77
  baked 81
  buying 77
  cakes 191, 221
  cleaning 78
  cream 411
  croquettes 219

Fish—Chapter VIII (*continued*)
  curried 220
  custard 411
  filleting 78
  fillets with smoked haddock 88
  flan 87
  fried 83, 191, 195
  au gratin 86
  grilled 84
  maître d'hôtel 87
  meunière 86
  muscat 88
  niçoise 89
  oily 77
  oysters 34, 97
  pie 224
  to poach 80
  portugaise 89
  quantities to buy 20
  rouennaise 90
  salad 92
  to scale 78
  scalloped 224
  shell 74, 93
  skinning 79
  soufflé 90
  steamed 80, 197
  stock 46
  stuffed 81
  tartare 91
  timbale 91
  veronique 92
  white 77
Flans
  apple apricot 267
  baking blind 266
  banana custard 267
  cheese 230
  fillings for 266
  fish 87
  fruit 265
  rings, to line 265
Flapjacks 376
Flavourings 183; Chapter XXVI, 461
Fleurons 29
Flour
  batter 192
  general information 319
  seasoned 192
  test for oven heat 340
Foie gras 34
Foods, types of 21
Forcemeats, Chapter XXIV, 412
  almond 412
  almond, apricot and rice 412
  apple and prune 413
  apricot 413
  chestnut 413
  for hare 160
  pickled walnut 414
  sage and onion 414

Forcemeats (*continued*)
  sausage 414
  for tomatoes or peppers 414
  veal 415
Freezing 313, 458
Fricassées 29, 120, 220
Fritter batter 192
Fritters
  cauliflower 174
  meat 195
Fruit
  batter 213
  bottling 425
  butters, cheeses and curds 442–4
  canning 455
  charlotte 285
  coupe 318
  creams 297–8
  crumble 256
  flans 265
  fools 284
  freezing 458
  gingerbread 359
  ices 315
  mousses 305
  pies 262
  puddings 255
  quantities to buy 20
  salad 285
  stewed 283
  tarts, 270, 408
Frying—Chapter XII, 190

Galantine 29
  of veal 139
Game 157–166
  accompaniments for 162
  choosing 158
  hanging 158
  in hors d'œuvres 36
  mock 125
  pie 165
  preparing 158
  salmi of 164
  seasons for 157
  stock 46
  vol-au-vent 144
Gammon 107
Garlic 462
Garnish 29
Gâteau 30
Genoese pastry 365
Gherkins 183
  pickled 448
  sandwich filling 420
Ginger
  cake 344, 353
  ice 315
  nuts 376
  pudding 251, 258
  sandwich filling 422

Gingerbread
  basic recipe 358
  fruit 359
  Grantham 374
  Grasmere 372
  plain 358
  rich 358
  spice 359
  thick 359
  with nuts 359
Glaze, to make 45
Glazing 30
Golden buck 41
Goose
  choosing 145
  roast 149
Gooseberry
  chutney 450
  cream 297–8
  curd 444
  flan 265
  fool 284
  jam 434
  jelly 437
  and mint cheese 443
  pie 262
  pudding 260
  tart 270
Goulash 123
Grapefruit 34
  marmalade 442
Gravy 106
Green butter 37
Green tomato
  chutney 452
  pickle 447
Greengage
  jam 434
  pie 262
  pudding 260
Grilling 107
Ground rice
  cake 353
  pudding 248
  pudding with egg 248
Grouse see chapter on Game
Guinea fowl see chapter on Game

Haddock see chapter on Fish
  smoked 88
Hake see chapter on Fish
Halibut see chapter on Fish
  mayonnaise 92
Ham
  baked 136
  boiled 136
  croûtes 41
  fried 191
  grilled 107
  joints 135
  omelet 209

Ham (*continued*)
  smoked 36
Hare
  jugged 160
  roast 159
  season for 157
Haricot mutton 116
Hash 220
Heart, roast 134
Herbs 461
  butter 463
  cheese 464
  vinegar 449, 465
Herrings
  to bone 79
  to clean 78
  fried 84, 191
  grilled 84
  roes on toast 41
  soused 84
High Tea Dishes—Chapter XVII, 226
Hors d'œuvres—Chapter V, 33
  anchovy 36
  anchovy butter 37
  anchovy cream 37
  avocado pear 33
  canapés 37
  cantaloupe melon 33
  caviare 33
  chicken 36
  crayfish 34
  cream cheese 37
  dressed 36
  egg 36
  foie gras 34
  grapefruit 34
  green butter 37
  green pea purée 38
  Marmite cheese 38
  olives 34
  oysters 34
  parsley butter 38, 65
  patties 36
  pineapple 34
  prawn paste 38
  salad varieties 35
  sardines 36
  sausages 36
  shellfish 36
  shrimp paste 38
  smoked salmon 34
Horseradish 462
  sauce 73, 464
Hotpot 117
  vegetable 243
Hough, potted 138

Ices
  chocolate 315
  coffee 315
  fruit 315

Ices (*continued*)
  fruit coupe 318
  general information 312
  ginger 315
  neapolitan 315
  peach melba 316
  pudding 316
  omelette soufflée en surprise 317
  sorbets 318
  vanilla 315
  water 318
Icings
  almond paste 381
  American frosting 383
  butter 381
  glacé 382
  royal 383
  transparent 384
Invalid cookery—Chapter XXIII, 404
Invalid fruit tart 408
Irish stew 118

Jam
  basic methods 431
  blackberry and apple 434
  blackcurrant 434
  damson 434
  gooseberry 434
  greengage 434
  layer pudding 262
  loganberry 434
  plum 434
  raspberry 434
  rhubarb 434
  sauce 72
  strawberry 434
  tart 264, 270
Jelly (preserve)
  apple 437
  basic method 435
  blackberry and apple 437
  blackcurrant 437
  crabapple 437
  gooseberry 437
  loganberry 437
  marmalade 440
  mint 464
  raspberry 437
  redcurrant 437, 465
  rowan 465
Jelly (table)
  aspic 292
  cleared 291
  Dutch flummery 290
  egg 290
  lemon 292
  milk 290
  orange 290
  tomato 243, 290
  uncleared 288
  wine 292

Jerusalem artichoke 168, 173
Junkets 286

Kale 168
Kedgeree 30, 233
Ketchup 446
  mushroom 454
  tomato 454
Kidney
  grilled 107–9
  omelet 209
  sauté 134
  soup 52
  stew 119
Kitchen equipment—Chapter I
Knead, to 30
Kromeskies 30, 222

Lamb
  appearance of 100
  braised 110
  chops, fried 191
  chops, grilled 107–9
  cutlets 107–9, 127
  cuts of 102, 104
  roast 105–7
Langoustines 96
Lard, to 30, 110
Lasagne 233–4
Leeks
  cooking 175
  preparing 169
Legumes 169
Lemon
  cake 344, 346, 353
  curd 444
  jelly 292
  jumbles 344
  junket 286
  meringue pie 269
  pudding 251, 255, 258
  sago 247
  sauce 72
  semolina 247
  soufflé 277
  soufflé, Canadian 280
Lemonade 409
Lentils
  cooking 175
  preparing 169
  soup 51
Lettuce 168
Liaison 30
Liver
  farced 131
  fried 191
  grilled 107–9
  with herbs 135
  soup 52
Lobster
  to buy 20, 94

Lobster (*continued*)
  claws in aspic 137
  Newburg 95
  to prepare 94
  rouennaise 90
  salad 95
Loganberry
  flan 265
  jam 434
  jelly 437
  mousse 305

Macaroni 233–4
  cheese 235
  croquettes 219
  pudding 246
Macédoine 30
Mackerel see chapter on Fish
  frying 191
Madras filling 421
Maître d'hôtel
  butter 65
  fish 84
  sauce 61
Malt loaf 332
Marinade 30, 67
Marmalade
  basic methods 439
  grapefruit 442
  jelly 440, 442
  orange 441
  pudding 251
  sauce 72
  tangerine 442
  tart 264
  thick dark 441
  three fruits 442
Marmite cheese 38
Marrow
  baked 175
  chutney 451
  jam 434
  preparing 169
  soup 51
  steamed 175
  stuffed 242
Mayonnaise
  aspic 69
  salmon 91
  sauce 68–9
Meal planning 21
Measures—Chapter II, 17
Meat—Chapter IX, 100
  accompaniments for 104
  barbecue sauce 67
  boiled 111
  braised 110
  cakes 191, 221
  choosing 100
  cold see Cold Meat
  croquettes 219

Meat (*continued*)
  curry 131
  cuts of 100
  entrées 126–137
  fried 109, 191, 195
  glaze 45
  grilled 107–9
  minced 116, 221, 223
  pickling 142
  pot-roasting 105
  quantities to buy 20
  roast 104–7
  steamed 197
  stewed 114–26
  thermometer 105
  and vegetable pudding 132
  (see also under Beef, Mutton etc.)
Melba toast 409
Meringues 307
  Meringue-based recipes 311
Merluche fumée (haddock) 88
Milk
  jelly 290
  puddings see Puddings
Mince 116, 221
  and potato casserole 223
Mince pies 281
Mincemeat 280
Mint
  and apple cheese 443
  and gooseberry cheese 443
  jelly 464
  sauce 74
Mirepoix 31, 110
Mixed spice 463
Mock crab 42
Mock cream 382
Mock game 125
Moulded sweets see Puddings
Mousse 31, and see Puddings
Mushrooms
  baked 175
  dried 176
  fried 176
  grilled 176
  ketchup 454
  omelet 209
  and scallops 98
  stewed 176
  stuffed 176, 240
  vol-au-vents and patties 130
Mustard
  and cress 168–9
  pickles 446, 453
  sauce 61
Mutton
  appearance of 100
  boiled 111
  braised 110
  broth 49
  chops, fried 191

Mutton (*continued*)
  chops, grilled 107–9
  cutlets 107–9, 127
  cutlets milanaise 129
  cutlets réforme 130
  cutlets Soubise 130
  cutlets, tomato 130
  cuts of 102, 104
  haricot 116
  roast 105–7
  stew 114

Noodles 233–4
Nut
  cutlets 236
  gingerbread 359
  meringues 311
  salads, 186, 188
  sandwich fillings 421–2
Nutmeg 463
Nutty balls 370

Oatcakes 377
Oatmeal
  biscuits 372
  scones 336
Olives 34
Omelets 208–11
  asparagus 209
  cheese 209
  fines herbes 209
  french 209
  ham 209
  kidney 209
  mushroom 209
  pan, care of 207
  plain, basic method 208
  puffed 210
  Spanish 209
  soufflé 211
  soufflé en surprise 317
  sweet, basic method 210
  tomato 209
Onions
  baked 170
  boiled 176
  braised 176
  fried 171, 176
  pickled 448
  preparing 169
  roast 172
  sauce 61
  stuffed 176, 241
Orange
  bread 332
  cake 344, 346, 353
  cream 297–8
  cream biscuits 375
  curd 444
  jelly 290
  junket 286

Orange (*continued*)
  marmalade 441
  mould 287
  pudding 255, 258, 282
  salad 187
  salad for duck 183
  sauce 72
  soufflé 277
Orangeade 409
Oven temperatures x
Ox heart 134
Ox-tail
  soup 52
  stew 119
Ox Tongue 113
Oysters 97
  angels on horseback 39
  for hors d'œuvres 34
  patties 144

Panada 31, 59
Pancakes 213
Paprika 463
Parboiling 31
Parkin 358, 360
  biscuits 377
Parsley
  butter 38, 65
  dried 462
  fried 84
  sauce 61
Parsnips 168, 176
Partridge see chapter on Game
Pastas 233–4
Pastry—Chapter XXII, 38
  cheese 390
  choux 378
  Danish 330
  general information 385
  flaky 394
  flans 265–9
  hot water crust 400
  puff 397
  puff pastry patties 142, 273
  quick mixes 469–70
  rough puff 392
  short 387
  short, rich 389
  suet 385
  vol-au-vents 32, 142, 144
  (see also under cakes, pies, puddings, tarts)
Pasty
  Cornish 232
  tomato, cheese and onion 242
Pâté
  of pork 140
  of chicken livers 141
Patties 36, 142, 144, 273
Peach
  ice 315

Peach (*continued*)
  melba 316
  mousse 305
Pear
  butter 444
  ice 315
  pickled 447
  trifle 300
Peas
  dried, cooking 179
  dried, preparing 169
  fresh, cooking 176
  fresh, preparing 169
  in hors d'œuvres 35
  purée 38
  soup 51
Pectin 432
Peppers 180, 414, 463
Pheasant, roast 158
Piccalilli 453
Pickles
  beans in mustard sauce 453
  cauliflower 448
  chutneys see Chutney
  cucumber 448
  damson 447
  gherkins 448
  green tomato 447
  meat 142
  mixed 448
  mustard 446, 453
  onions 448
  pear 447
  piccalilli 453
  red cabbage 449
  sour, basic method 445
  sweet, basic method 445
  walnuts 449
Pie dish, to line 271
Pies
  banana cream 267
  beefsteak and kidney 132
  fruit 262
  game 165
  making 262
  mince 281
  pork 133
  rabbit 133
  raising 401
  veal and ham 133
Pigeon,
  braised 164
  casserole 163
  roast 162
Pimientos 179
Pineapple
  cake 353
  cream 297
  and cream cheese salad 187
  hors d'œuvre 34
  mousse 305

Pineapple (*continued*)
pudding 282
and raisin pudding 258
sandwich filling 422
Plaice
baked and stuffed 82
cleaning 78
filleting 78
skinning 79
Plover see chapter on Game
Plum
cake 353
cheese 443
chutney 451
jam 434
pie 262
pudding 251, 260
tart 270
Poaching 31
Pork
appearance of 100
boiled 111
brawn 138
chops, fried 191
chops, grilled 107–9
cuts of 103, 104
pâté 141
pie 133
roast 105–7
stewed 114
Porridge 417
Potatoes
baked 170, 177
boiled 177
casserole 223
cheese 230
chips 171, 177, 194–5
creamed 177
croquettes 219
duchess 179
fried 171–2, 177
in hors d'œuvres 35
mashed 172, 177
preparing 168
roast 172, 177
salad 187
scones 336
soup 51
Potted hough 138
Poultry—Chapter X, 145
accompaniments for 149
boiled 150
drawing 146
fricassée 220
general information 145
hanging 146
roast 147–9
trussing 147
Prawn paste 38
Prawns
in aspic 137, 292

Prawns (*continued*)
curried 96
Dublin Bay 95–6
for hors d'œuvres 36
quantities to buy 20
Preservation—Chapter XXV, 424
bottling fruit 425
bottling vegetables 429
butter, cheeses and curds 442
canning 455
chutneys 445, 450
freezing 458
jams 431
jellies 435
ketchups 446, 454
marmalades 439
pickles 444–9, 453
sugar syrup 426
Pressure cookery—Chapter XXVII, 472
Princess bun 333
Proteins 21
Prune sandwich filling 423
Ptarmigan see chapter on Game
Puddings (savoury)
beefsteak and kidney 132
cheese 231
meat and vegetable 132
savoury batter 213
Yorkshire 214
Puddings (sweets) Chapters XVIII (245) and XIX (283
Batter mixtures
baked batter 213
basic recipe 212
black cap 213
fruit in batter 213
pancakes 213–14
Creams
Bavarian 296
"burnt" 299
caramel rice 299
charlotte russe 297
chocolate 298
coffee 298
custard 298
fruit 297
fruit custard 298
general rules 295
honeycomb mould 296
rum 297
trifle Eugénie 298
vanilla 298
velvet 297
Creamed mixtures
almond 258
basic recipes 257
Beresford 258
canary 258
castle 258
cherry 258

Puddings (sweets)—*Creamed mixtures*
  (contd.)
  chocolate 258
  coconut 258
  coffee 258
  currant 258
  Eve's 259
  general information 257
  ginger 258
  lemon 258
  orange 258
  patriotic 259
  pineapple and raisin 258
  Prince Albert 259
  sultana 258
  upside down 259
Custards and custard puddings
  baked custard 203, 206
  bread and butter pudding 204
  cabinet 204
  cup custard 203, 206
  caramel custard 204
  custard creams 298
  custard mould 287
  custard tart 268
  general information 206
  queen of puddings—plain 205
  queen of puddings—variations 205
  steamed custard 203, 207
  trifles 298, 300, 301
  Viennoise pudding 205
Fruits and fruit mixtures
  apple charlotte 278
  apple sago 279
  baked apples 279
  fruit charlotte, cold 285
  fruit fools 284
  fruit salad 285
  fruit, stewed 283
  orange (mandarin) 282
  pineapple 282
Iced puddings see Ices
Jellies
  cleared 291
  Dutch flummery 290
  egg 290
  lemon 292
  milk 290
  orange 290
  to turn out 289
  uncleared 288
  wine 292
Junkets
  basic recipe 286
  brandy 286
  chocolate 286
  coffee 286
  lemon 286
  orange 286
  rum 286
  vanilla 286

Puddings (sweets) (*continued*)
  Milk Puddings
  arrowroot 248
  barley 246
  caramel rice 299
  chocolate cornflour 248
  chocolate rice 246
  chocolate semolina 247
  cornflour 248
  general information 245
  ground rice—basic 248
  ground rice with egg 248
  lemon sago 247
  lemon semolina 247
  macaroni 246
  rice—basic 246
  rice with egg 246
  sago—basic 247
  sago with egg 247
  semolina—basic 247
  semolina with egg 247
  tapioca 246
Moulded sweets
  arrowroot 287
  chocolate 287
  coffee 287
  cornflour 287
  custard 287
  ground rice 287
  orange 287
  rice 288
  semolina 287
Mousses
  basic recipe—gelatine 306
  basic recipe—plain 306
  basic recipe—rich 305
  chocolate 306–7
  chocolate without cream 307
  coffee 305
  fruit 305
  vanilla 306
with Pastry
  apple amber 271
  apple balls 264
  Bakewell pudding 267
  Bakewell tart 267
  banana cream pie 267
  butterscotch tart 268
  custard tart 268
  Delaware pudding 262
  Felixstowe tart 268
  flan, apricot apple 268
  flan, banana6 custard 267
  flans, general 265
  fruit pies 262
  fruit puddings 260
  fruit tarts 264
  general information 260
  layer pudding 261
  lemon meringue pie 269
  plate tarts 264, 270

Puddings (sweets)—*with Pastry*
(contd.)
  Russian pudding 269
  Scotch tart 274
  spiced apple tart 270
  treacle pudding 261
  treacle tart 264, 270
  treacle tart, Cornish 271
  Welsh cheese cakes 269
  West Riding pudding 269
Rubbed-in mixtures 254
  almond 255
  basic recipe 254
  chocolate 255
  coconut 255
  coffee 255
  currant 255
  date 255
  date crunch 256
  date and walnut 255
  Eve's 255
  fruit 255
  fruit crumble 256
  lemon 255
  orange 255
Soufflés—cold
  basic recipe 302
  chocolate 303
  coffee 303
  milanaise 303
  praliné 303
Soufflés—hot
  basic recipe 276
  Canadian lemon 280
  chocolate 277
  coffee 277
  general information 275
  lemon 277
  orange 277
  vanilla 277
Suet puddings
  basic recipe 250
  baroness 251
  Christmas 252–3
  date 251
  fig 251
  general information 249
  ginger 251
  lemon 251
  marmalade 251
  plum 251
  raisin 251
  Rothesay 252
  Snowdon 252
  suet pastry 385
  syrup 252
  treacle 252
Unclassified
  Austrian cheese cake 279
  mincemeat 280
  strawberry gâteau 300

Puddings (sweets)—*Unclassified*
(contd.)
  trifle 301
  trifle, pear 300
Pulses 169
Pumpkin
  cooking 177
  pie 262
  preparing 169
Purées
  basic method 50
  definition 31
  green pea 38
  sauce 68
  (and see soups)

Quails see chapter on Game
Quantities to buy 20
Queen of puddings 205
Quiche lorraine 237
Quick-method foods Chapter XXVII,
467
Quince cheese 443

Rabbit
  blanquette 121
  broth 49
  casserole 118
  fricassée 120, 220
  pie 133
  ragoût 124
Radishes 182
Ragoût 31
Raising agents 320
Rarebit 43
Raspberry
  cake 344
  cream 297–8
  fool 284
  ice 315
  jam 434
  jelly 437
  mousse 305
  pie 262
  tart 270
Raspings 31, 417
Ratatouille 237
Ravioli 233–4
Réchauffés—Chapter XVI, 216
Red cabbage 177, 181
  pickled 449
Red currant jelly 437, 465
Reheating see Réchauffés
Rhubarb
  chutney 451
  jam 434
  pie 262
  pudding 260
  tart 270
Rice
  biscuits 373, 377

Rice (*continued*)
  boiled 418
  caramel 299
  kedgeree 217
  mould 287
  pudding 246
  pudding, chocolate 246
  pudding with egg 246
Risotto 238
Rissoles 31, 223
Roes on toast 41
Rothesay pudding 252
Roux 32
  foundation sauces 58
Rowan jelly 465
Rum
  baba 333
  cream 297
  junket 286

Sage and onion stuffing 414
Sage and apple cheese 443
Sago pudding 247
  egg 247
  lemon 247
Salad dressings
  boiled 184
  cream 184
  french 185
  mayonnaise 68
  plain 185
  summer cream 185
  sweet 185
  vinaigrette 186
Salads
  banana and nut 186
  carrot and apple 186
  cucumber 186
  fish 92
  for hors d'œuvres 35
  general information 181
  lobster 95
  orange 183, 187
  pimiento 180
  pineapple and cream cheese 187
  potato 187
  red apple and nut 188
  Russian 188
  tomato 35, 189
  winter 189
Sally Lunn 326
Salmon
  baked 82
  mayonnaise 91
  poached 82
  sandwich filling 421
  smoked 34
Salsify 168, 177
Sandwich fillings 419–23
Sandwich tins, to line 350
Sardines 36, 420

Sauces—Chapter VII, 58
  American 63
  anchovy 60
  apple 70
  bacon 229
  barbecue 67–8
  basic methods 58
  Béchamel 60, 154
  bigarade 64
  bolognese 234
  brain 60
  brandy butter 65
  bread 71
  brown 59, 155
  butter foundation 65
  butterscotch 73
  canned soups for 470
  caper 60
  cardinol 60, 155
  charcutiere 63
  chaudfroid 154–5
  cheese 61
  chocolate 73
  Cumberland 66
  curry 66
  custard 70
  demi-glace 59
  devilled butter 65
  egg 61
  egg foundation 68
  espagnole 63
  fennel 61
  green 155
  hard 65
  hollandaise 62, 68
  horseradish 73
  Italian 64
  jam 72
  ketchups 446
  lemon 72
  maître d'hôtel 61, 65
  marmalade 72
  mayonnaise 68
  mayonnaise, aspic 69
  melted butter 65
  milanese 235
  mint 73
  mornay 62
  mousseline 70
  mushroom ketchup 454
  mustard 61
  onion 61
  orange 72
  parsley 61
  piquante 63
  poivrade 64
  purée 70
  réforme 64
  roux foundation 58
  rum butter 65
  simple (without fat) 58

Sauces (*continued*)
  Soubise 61
  syrup 72
  tartare 62, 69
  terracotta 155
  tomato 71
  tomato ketchup 454
  tomato, for pasta 235
  uncooked 73
  velouté 61
  verte 69
Sausage
  egg and tomato pie 238
  for hors d'œuvres 36
  forcemeat 414
  fried 191
  grilled 107–9
  rolls 238
Sauté 32
Savarin 32, 334
Savouries 38–43
  angels on horseback 39
  buck rarebit 43
  cheese aigrettes 39
  cheese straws 40
  golden buck 41
  ham croûtes 41
  herring roes on toast 41
  mock crab toasts 42
  scotch woodcock 42
  welsh rarebit 42
Savoy 174
Scallops
  fried 97
  and mushrooms 98
Scones 335
  afternoon tea 336
  basic recipe 336
  brown 336
  cheese 336
  dropped 337
  girdle 338
  oatmeal 336
  potato 336
  treacle 336
Scotch eggs 239
Scotch woodcock 42
Seakale
  cooking 177
  preparing 168
Sea pie 118
Seasonings—Chapter XXVI, 461
Semolina pudding 247
  chocolate 247
  egg 247
  lemon 247
  mould 287
Shallots 169
Sheep's head 134
  broth 49
Sheep's heart 134

Shellfish 77, 93–9
  for hors d'œuvres 36
  for vol-au-vents and patties 142
  (and see names of shellfish)
Shepherd's pie 224
Shopping—Chapter III, 19
Shortbread 373, 375
  biscuits 375
Shortening, white 469
Shrimp paste 38
Shrimps
  in aspic 137, 292
  to buy 20, 99
  creole 99
  hors d'œuvres 36
Simmer, to 32
Sippets 32
Snipe see chapter on Game
Soda bread 337
Sole
  baked and stuffed 82
  cleaning 78
  Colbert 85
  filleting 78
  skinning 79
Sorbets 318
Soufflés 32
  basic methods 275
  Canadian lemon 280
  cheese 231
  chocolate 277
  coffee 277
  cold 302
  fish 90
  hot 275
  lemon 277
  orange 277
  vanilla 277
Soups—Chapter VI, 44
  almond 51
  artichoke 51
  bean 51
  broths, basic recipe 48
  canned, uses for 471
  celery 51
  chestnut 51
  chicken broth 49
  consommé à la brunoise 56
  consommé à l'italienne 56
  consommé à la jardinière 56
  consommé à la julienne 56
  consommé à la royale 56
  consommés, basic recipe 55
  cream soups, basic recipe 53
  hollandaise 54
  kidney 52
  lentil 51
  liver 52
  marrow 51
  mixes 470
  mutton broth 49

Soups (*continued*)
  ox-tail 52
  pea 51
  potage à la bonne femme 54
  potage à la royale 54
  potato 51
  purées, basic recipe 50
  rabbit broth 49
  scotch broth 49
  sheep's head broth 49
  tomato 51
  veal broth 49
  vegetable broth 49
  Vichyssoise 55
Spaghetti 233–4
Spinach 169, 178
Sponges 361
Sprats, fried 191
Spring greens 174
Starchy foods 22
Steaming—Chapter XIII, 197
Stewed fruit 283
Stews 114
  beef in wine 122
  blanquettes 121
  brown 115, 121
  fresh meat mince 116
  fricassées 120
  goulash 123
  haricot mutton 116
  hotpot 117
  Irish 118
  kidney 119
  ox-tail 119
  rabbit casserole 118
  ragoûts 124
  richer type 120
  sea pie 118
  simple type 115
  white 120
Stocks—Chapter VI, 44
  brown 46
  fish 46
  game 46
  general information 44
  vegetable 47
  white 46
Strawberry
  cream 297–8
  gâteau 300
  ice 315
  jam 434
  mousse 305
Stuffing see Forcemeat
Suet
  dumplings 113
  pastry 385
  puddings see Puddings
Supper dishes—Chapter XVII, 226
Swedes
  cooking 178

Swedes (*continued*)
  preparing 168
Sweetbreads
  Italian 131
  stewed 409
Sweets see Puddings
Syrup
  pudding 252, 261
  sauces 72
  for stewed fruit 283
  sugar 426
  tart 264, 270

Tammy 32
Tarts
  covering 270
  decorating 265
  plate 264
  pastry for 264
  (for varieties, see Puddings made
    with Pastry)
Tepid 32
Toad-in-the-hole 213
Tomatoes
  baked 178
  and cheese pasties 242
  chutney 452
  dumplings 243
  fried 178
  grilled 178
  in hors d'œuvres 35
  jelly 243, 290
  Madras filling 421
  omelet 209
  pickled (green) 447
  salad 35, 183, 189
  sauce 71, 235, 454
  soup 51
  steamed 178
  stuffed 241, 414
Tournedos 32, 127
Treacle
  pudding 252, 261
  scones 336
  tart 264
  tart, Cornish 271
Trifle 301
  Eugénie 298
  pear 300
Tripe
  in custard 411
  stewed 409
Trout see chapter on Fish
Turkey
  choosing 145
  roast 148
  roast, accompaniments 149
Turnips 168, 178

Utensils—Chapter 1

Vanilla
  cream 298
  ice 315
  junket 286
  mousse 306
  slices 274
  soufflé 277
Veal
  appearance of 100
  blanquette 121
  braised 110
  broth 49
  cream 411
  cuts of 104
  escalope Talleyrand 130
  fillets 127
  forcemeat 415
  fricassée 120
  galantine 139
  and ham pie 133
  olives 124
  ragoût 124
  roast 105-7
  stewed 114
Vegetable marrow see Marrow
Vegetables—Chapter XI, 167
  baking 170
  boiling 170
  bottling 429
  broth 49
  buying and storing 168
  canning 455
  curry 220
  freezing 458
  frying 171
  hotpot 243
  pickling 445
  preparing 168
  quantities to buy 20
  roasting 172
  stock 47
  vitamins in 167
  (see also Salads and under name of
    vegetables)
Vegetarian cooking 227
Venison 157, 161
Vermicelli 233
Vichyssoise 55
Victoria Sandwich 354
Viennoise pudding 205
Vinaigrette dressing 186
Vinegar
  cake 346
  herb 449
  spiced 449
Vitamins 22, 167
Vol-au-vent 32, 142, 144

Walnut
  cake 346, 354
  and date cake 346
  pickled 449
  pickled, stuffing 414
  sandwich filling 421
Water-cress 168
Water ices 318
Welsh cakes 338
Welsh rarebit 42
Weights and measures—Chapter II, 17
West Riding pudding 269
"What Went Wrong"
  breadmaking 326
  cakes, creamed 354
  cakes, melted fat 360
  cakes, rubbed-in 346
  frying 195
  gingerbreads 361
  jam 433
  jelly 438
  marmalade 441
  meringues 312
  moulded sweets 301
  pastry, cheese 391
  pastry, choux 380
  pastry, flaky 396
  pastry, hot water crust 403
  pastry, puff 399
  pastry, rich short 391
  pastry, rough puff 396
  pastry, short 391
  pastry, suet 387
  puddings, creamed 259
  puddings, milk 249
  puddings, rubbed-in 257
  puddings, suet 253
  sauces 73
  scones 338
  soufflés, cold 304
  soufflés, hot 277
  soups 56
  sponges 367
  yeast mixtures 326
Whiting see chapter on Fish
Widgeon see chapter on Game
Wild duck see chapter on Game
Wine Chapter XXX, 478
Wine jelly 292
Woodcock see chapter on Game

Yeast
  dumplings 326
  general information 321
  plain mixtures 322
  richer mixtures 327
Zest 32

We have a wide-ranging list of books on housecraft, cookery, needlework, embroidery, arts and crafts, etc. If you would like to know more about them, please send a postcard for our free catalogue, mentioning which subjects specially interest you.

MILLS & BOON LIMITED
17–19 Foley Street
London W1A 1DR